Bazaar and State in Iran

The Tehran Bazaar has always been central to the Iranian economy and, indeed, to the Iranian urban experience. Arang Keshavarzian's fascinating book compares the economics and politics of the marketplace under the Pahlavis, who sought to undermine it in the drive for modernization, and under the subsequent revolutionary regime, which came to power with a mandate to preserve the bazaar as an "Islamic" institution. The outcomes of their respective policies were completely at odds with their intentions. Despite the Shah's hostile approach, the bazaar flourished under his rule and maintained its organizational autonomy to such an extent that it played an integral role in the Islamic revolution. Conversely, the Islamic Republic implemented policies that unwittingly transformed the ways in which the bazaar operated, thus undermining its capacity for political mobilization. Arang Keshavarzian's book affords unusual insights into the politics, economics, and society of Iran across four decades.

ARANG KESHAVARZIAN Middle East and Islamic Studies Department, New York University.

D1059658

Cambridge Middle East Studies 25

Editorial Board
Charles Tripp (general editor)
Julia A. Clancy-Smith   Israel Gershoni   Roger Owen
Yezid Sayigh   Judith E. Tucker

Cambridge Middle East Studies has been established to publish books on the modern Middle East and North Africa. The aim of the series is to provide new and original interpretations of aspects of Middle Eastern societies and their histories. To achieve disciplinary diversity, books will be solicited from authors writing in a wide range of fields, including history, sociology, anthropology, political science, and political economy. The emphasis will be on producing books offering an original approach along theoretical and empirical lines. The series is intended for students and academics, but the more accessible and wide-ranging studies will also appeal to the interested general reader.

A list of books in the series can be found after the index.

Bazaar and State in Iran

The Politics of the Tehran Marketplace

Arang Keshavarzian

Middle East and Islamic Studies Department
New York University

CAMBRIDGE
UNIVERSITY PRESS

CAMBRIDGE UNIVERSITY PRESS
Cambridge, New York, Melbourne, Madrid, Cape Town, Singapore, São Paulo, Delhi

Cambridge University Press
The Edinburgh Building, Cambridge CB2 8RU, UK

Published in the United States of America by Cambridge University Press, New York

www.cambridge.org
Information on this title: www.cambridge.org/9780521103305

First published 2007
This digitally printed version (with corrections) 2008

A catalogue record for this publication is available from the British Library

ISBN 978-0-521-86618-7 hardback
ISBN 978-0-521-10330-5 paperback

For Fahimeh Azadi and Ali Keshavarzian, my parents

Contents

Maps

Figures

Acknowledgments

' "Doctor,' the bazaar is kind of a university," mentioned a *bazaari* as he explained the ins and outs of his trade. "Well then, I am the student and you are the professors," I responded. I would like to express my deep gratitude to my *"bazaari* professors," who taught me through sharing their experiences, fears, doubts, criticisms, memories, and aspirations. Since I pledged that our conversations would remain confidential, I cannot mention them by name. Many were hospitable, forthright, and over time trusting. This project would have been impossible without their knowledgeable participation and extraordinary patience.

Equally critical was the support and guidance of my dissertation committee, "my university professors." Nancy Bermeo's encouragement, forbearance, and insightful comments during all stages of my graduate studies have been invaluable. Like so many graduate students at Princeton's Department of Politics, I am thankful to have had such a motivating and respectful advisor. Atul Kohli and Ira Katznelson helped me reevaluate and refine my thoughts at various stages of the project, always in ways that challenged me to reflect on the principal concerns of the project and fundamental analytical issues of studying politics.

I would like to acknowledge the critical support of several others who helped shape my research and analysis and have read parts or all of various versions of this manuscript. These include Ervand Abrahamian, Ahmad Ashraf, Asef Bayat, Keith Donoghue, Ellis Goldberg, Erik Kuhonta, Charles Kurzman, Evan Lieberman, Mazyar Lotfalian, Tamir Moustafa, Vahid Nowshirvani, Misagh Parsa, Setrag Manoukian, Naghmeh Sohrabi, and Deborah Yashar. I want to thank Homa Hoodfar, in particular, for her intellectual support and the generous way that she and Anthony Hilton made me feel welcome in Montreal. Two anonymous reviewers provided perceptive comments and suggestions, which I have tried to address and incorporate.

I am grateful to many individuals who helped in gathering information and sources and shared with me their insights into Iranian politics and society. Azam Khatam and Kaveh Ehsani have shared with me their immense knowledge and original research on Iran. Hadi Semati, Bijan Afsar-Keshmiri, and Siavash Moridi kindly advised me and provided valuable input while I was in Iran. I wish to thank Nazanin Shahrokni for her energetic help with many facets of the research, including gathering some critical data. I would like to thank Siamak Namazi for sharing with me his knowledge and information about Iran's economy. The librarians at the Faculty of Social Science, Fine Arts, and Law and Political Science at Tehran University, Shahid Beheshti University, the Iranian Carpet Company, the Public Relations office at the State Tea Organization, and other research institutes all proved very helpful. Fariba Adelkhah, Mohammad Reza Ashouri, Reza Azari, Abbas Bolurfrushan, Mohammad Eskandari, Ramin Karimian, Ali Reza Karimi-Shiraznia, Mohammad Maljoo, Mohammad Masinaei, Mohammad Moeini, Jim Muir, Jahanbakhsh Nouraei, Soad Pira, Fatameh Pira, Ali Rezaei, Ahmad Tabesh, and Kian Tajbaksh all generously helped me negotiate the difficulties of field research and provided essential insights for developing the project. At Princeton University's Firestone Library, Ms. Azar Ashraf professionally and cheerfully guided me through the library's resources. Katayon Kholdi-Haghighi provided diligent research assistance and made preparing the manuscript surprisingly enjoyable. Dominc Parviz Brookshaw fielded and addressed questions regarding transliteration with much patience and humor. I am deeply grateful to Michael Braun, Adrian Dumitru, and Heather Fussell for their research and editing assistance. Various stages of this project were generously supported by the Social Science Research Council's International Predissertation Fellowship Program and the Funds Québecois des recherche sur la société et la culture. My colleagues at the Department of Political Science at Concordia University provided a stimulating environment to revise my manuscript, and the university granted research support. I thank Marigold Acland, Isabelle Dambricourt, John Fine, and Viji Muralidhar for their expert guidance and support in preparing this book for publication.

I have been fortunate to share the travails, and even joys, of being a graduate student with Adam Becker, Sven Vahsen, and Yuen-Gen Liang. I believe this book is better thanks to their intellectual generosity and their friendship. I have profited from conversations with Narges Erami, or what she may call "bazaar speech." She has kindly shared with me her unique knowledge of Qom, its bazaar, and the carpet producers; I look forward to reading her work.

Laleh Khorramian has drawn maps, listened to and indulged my idiosyncrasies, and waited for me to return from libraries and research trips, but she did all of this (and much more) with exceeding care and love. Her companionship and her art have shaped how I see the world and are an inspiration. I trust that by the time she reads these words, she is fully recovered and making plans to travel around the world, as well as dancing as often as possible. I hope I will have many opportunities in the future to express my appreciation and love for her.

I was too young to grasp the distinction between objectives and outcomes from the events surrounding the 1979 Revolution, which I believe are so essential for making sense of Iran and politics more generally; instead my understanding of this matter was initially shaped by football of the early 1980s. In 1982, I abruptly learned that to focus on an outcome (a final between Italy and Germany) would distract me from the complete story, which can be far more profound. The glorious French and Brazilian teams of the World Cup have remained for me a spectacular example of how football can and should be played, but also a lesson that I will overlook much if I direct my attention too narrowly on score lines and results. Thankfully, at this same time I also realized that my dreams of vanquishing Red Devils and overturning Boring, Boring Arsenal are realizable possibilities. By watching the mesmerizing teams of Liverpool and Tottenham Hotspurs I discovered that one's dreams sometimes can recoup trophies and be enshrined as outcomes.

Ghazal Keshavarzian has been a patient and understanding editor, a supportive and concerned commentator, dear friend, and generous sister. My family and relatives scattered across the world helped me to conduct research and opened their homes to me. Hengameh and Afsaneh Keshavarzian, Kaveh and Sara Nili, Baharak and Yasaman Zarbafian, and Majid Zarbafian and Kamran Nili made stays in Iran joyful and unforgettable. My four grandparents – Ani and Maman Ashi, and Baba and Madar – have all been influential, powerful, and loving in their own unique ways; I am very thankful to have talked to them about many of the issues in this book (even if neither I nor they always realized that was what was taking place). While encouraging me to be inquisitive and to follow my interests, Fahimeh Azadi and Ali Keshavarzian have been adoring parents. This book is dedicated to my parents as a small token of my sincere respect and immense love for them.

Note on transliteration

Transliterations of Persian words follow a modified version of the transliteration system used by the *International Journal of Middle East Studies*. For simplicity no diacritical marks are used except for the ayn ('), and in order to render words as they are pronounced in Persian, short vowels follow Persian rather than Arabic pronunciation (e.g. "e" instead of "i" and "o" instead of "u"). Common names and terms, such as Khomeini, Koran, and Shiite, follow their established English spellings.

Map of Iran

Source: This map was adapted from a map courtesy of the General Libraries, The university of Texas at Austin.

1   The puzzle of the Tehran Bazaar under the Pahlavi monarchy and the Islamic Republic

We have a saying, "There is one Iran and one Tehran and only one Sara-ye Amin (Amin Caravanserai),"[1] meaning that anything that happens in Iran can be captured right here in the Tehran Bazaar.

Fabric wholesaler in the Amin Caravanserai, Tehran Bazaar

A year after his fall from power, Mohammad Reza Pahlavi, the last Shah of Iran, recalled, "I could not stop building supermarkets. I wanted a modern country. Moving against the bazaars was typical of the political and social risks I had to take in my drive for modernization."[2] Meanwhile, three years after the establishment of the Islamic Republic, Ayatollah Ruhollah Khomeini stressed that "We [the Islamic Republic] must preserve the bazaar with all our might; in return the bazaar must preserve the government."[3] Given this drastic change in the state's outlook toward the bazaar, it is not surprising that the Tehran Bazaar had radically different experiences under these regimes. What is startling, however, is that the transformation is not as we would expect – the Bazaar survived and remained autonomous under the modernizing Pahlavi regime (in fact so much so that it was one of the leading actors in the Revolution), while it was radically restructured and weakened under the unabashedly "traditionalist" Islamic Republic.

By comparing how the last Shah of Iran sought to "move against the bazaar" and how the founder of the Islamic Republic "preserve[d] the bazaar," it will be the burden of this book to depict these outcomes and to examine why they followed these counterintuitive trajectories. The Pahlavi regime's policies during the 1960s and 1970s did not dismantle the Tehran Bazaar's economic institutions; the modernization scheme formed an autonomous setting for members of the Bazaar, or *bazaaris*, to regulate their economic lives and prosper. Conversely, while many individual merchants may have prospered, the Islamic Republic's policies radically

---

[1] The Amin Sara is one of the main caravanserais in the Tehran Bazaar.

[2] Mohammad Reza Pahlavi, *Answer to History* (New York: Stein and Day, 1980), p. 156.

[3] *Asnaf* no. 22 (Ordibehesht 1373 [May 1992]), 47. This statement was made in 1982.

altered relations within the Bazaar, altered its institutions (i.e. laws and policies), and reduced its capacity to mobilize against the state. The irony is that while the overthrow of the monarchy was in large part a response to the exclusionary and clientilistic practices that alienated groups such as the Bazaar (along with the working class, the middle class, the clergy, and the urban poor), large segments of the very same social classes that it professed to champion are currently discontent and politically dislocated.

This is why today if you talk to *bazaari*s, you hear statements such as the one made by Hajj Akbar, a carpet wholesaler in the Tehran Bazaar. When I told him that I had come to Iran to analyze the Tehran Bazaar, Hajj Akbar, probably in his sixties and not one to mince words, responded, "You mean this Bazaar? This Bazaar doesn't need any analysis. It doesn't even exist any more; it's dead!" During the course of my research I discovered that when *bazaari*s mention that the Bazaar has "died" or "changed" or "is not like the past," they are referring to its restructuring and political marginalization.

Transformation and change are essential both to politics and to the study of politics. Political activists and normative thinkers have ima-gined and acted on their impulse to better the world around them by transforming the minds of the people who inhabit it and the rules that govern it. Within the social sciences, change forces observers to critically appraise the relationships between various factors comprising complex societies and polities in order to identify the forces behind this trans-formation. Once change is detected, observers are invited to question how and why it transpired. Scholars must move beyond labeling and categorizing objects in order to contemplate what leads to abrupt reconfigurations or gradual evolutions away from particular constella-tions and social forms. Consequently, the reconfiguration of Iran's state and the refiguring of the Bazaar, as sensed by Hajj Akbar, are the wellspring of this book. Thus, I ask: How and why has the Tehran Bazaar had such disparate and counterintuitive experiences under these two regimes? More precisely, why was the Pahlavi monarchy, a regime that was openly hostile toward bazaars as a group and an institution, unable to restructure the Bazaar? Conversely, why was it that since the establishment of the Islamic Republic, a regime that came to power with the support of *bazaari*s and with the specific mandate to preserve "indigenous and Islamic" institutions, state policies have unwittingly reconfigured the organization of the Bazaar's value chains (i.e. com-mercial networks tying together import–exporters, wholesalers, and retailers) and their position in the political economy? And finally, what political impact did these transformations have on the Bazaar's capacity to make claims against the state? Since Tehran's central marketplace is an economically powerful and potentially politically potent group, the experience of this social microcosm under these two regimes reflects the larger dynamics of state–society relations and forces of social change and continuity over the past four decades.

To foreshadow the arguments of the book, I contend that the two regimes, varying in terms of their development policies and their normative agendas, led to different incorporation strategies, which reshaped the institutional setting and physical location of the networks that constitute the organization of the Tehran Bazaar and engender its commonly noted capacity to mobilize. In the case of the Pahlavi monarchy, the regime followed high modernism that tended to downgrade the state's incorporation of the Bazaar.[4] This approach fostered the Bazaar's autonomy and a concentration of commercial value chains within the physical confines of the marketplace. Under the Islamic Republic's populist transformative agenda, the state was caught within a complex matrix of objectives and agendas, which resulted in the incorporation of *bazaari*s as individuals and the cooptation, regulation, and reterritorialization of commercial value chains physically dispersed beyond the Bazaar. In the former case relations in the Bazaar constituted a series of cooperative hierarchies (long-term, multifaceted, and crosscutting ties) fostering a great sense of group solidarity despite differences in economic power, social status, and political proclivities. In the latter period this mode of coordinating actions and distributing resources and authority, or what I term "form of governance," was transformed into coercive hierarchies (more short-term, single-faceted, and fragmented vertical relations) with a diminished sense of collective solidarity. Finally, this shift from cooperative to coercive hierarchies limited the Tehran Bazaar's capacity to mobilize against the state and explains its relative quietism since the Revolution. This study reminds us that state policies and institutions shape social cleavages, empower and constrain political organizations, and restructure socioeconomic relations; however, they often do so in indirect and unforeseen ways. In fact, these outcomes may go so far as to undermine the political agendas of those rulers and policymakers who initiated these programs in the first place.

---

[4] By "state incorporation," I am referring to the Colliers' concept of the legal and bureaucratic mobilization and control of a social group (in their case labor, and in mine the bazaar) with the goal of repressing and depoliticizing that group. Ruth Barins Collier and David Collier, *Shaping the Political Arena: Critical Junctures, Labor Movement, and Regime Dynamics in Latin America* (Princeton: Princeton University Press, 1991). On political incorporation of economic elites see David Waldner, *State Building and Late Development* (Ithaca: Cornell University Press, 1999).

Continuity, revolution, and state–society relations

The Pahlavi monarchy and the Islamic Republic differ on many fronts: foreign policy, social agendas, ideological sources to legitimate their rule, and state relations with the religious establishment, to name just the most obvious. However, they share important similarities in method of rule, socioeconomic trends, and position in the world economy. In the words of one scholar:

[L]ike the Shah the ruling Muslim fundamentalists are trying to preserve their dictatorial regime by resorting to the suppression, imprisonment, and execution of their political opponents and are quite prepared to rule by terror. Just as the Shah tried to foster the idea that loyalty to the monarchy and national patriotism were the same, Khumayni has been adamant about the view that loyalty to the Velayat-i-Fagih and Islam are identical. Any opposition to Khumayni as the Fagih (just jurist) or his regime is regarded as anti-Islamic in the same way that opposition to the Shah used to be treated by the old regime as unpatriotic and treasonous. The state-owned propaganda networks have been used by the Islamic regime to develop and sustain the "cult of personality" and charismatic leadership around Khumayni in much the same way as was done for the Shah under the monarchy. Dictatorship, either in the form of the Shah's patrimonial system or Khumayni's government of theologians, when combined with oil wealth, is most likely to create and perpetuate the system of dependent capitalism which possesses all the evils and very few of the alleged benefits of a competitive market economy.[5]

Furthermore, both regimes have highly transformative programs. The Shah was an arch-proponent of developmental planning, what David Harvey refers to as "high modernism."[6] He set out to transform Iran into a "modern" industrial power by implementing a stylized and linear developmental model of Western industrialization and social modernization. In part as a response to what many viewed as the blind imitation and idealization of the Western model by the *ancien régime*, the Islamic Republic has sought to establish an independent and economically self-sufficient society – a society, moreover, that abides by the principles and laws of Islam. This Islamic model, however, was strongly aligned with a populism that combined the radical language of anti-imperialism and egalitarianism borrowed from secular and religious Leftism.[7] These two projects have radically different objectives, yet they

---

[5] M. H. Pesaran, "The System of Dependent Capitalism in Pre- and Post-Revolutionary Iran," *International Journal of Middle East Studies* 14 (1982), 518–19.

[6] David Harvey, *The Conditions of Post-Modernity: An Enquiry into the Origin of Social Change* (Oxford: Basil Blackwell, 1989).

[7] Ervand Abrahamian, *Khomeinism: Essays on the Islamic Republic* (London: I. B. Tauris & Co., 1993); and Val Moghadam, "Islamic Populism, Class and Gender in

share the belief that the state is a force that can, and indeed should, engineer a new society – a "modern" and "Islamic" society respectively. As referred to in the quote above, the two regimes also share the quality of being oil exporters, which bestows on both the imperial and the revolutionary state a high level of autonomy from social forces. With oil revenues flowing directly to the state, this factor allowed these regimes to remain financially independent from domestic social groups.[8] Therefore, the Tehran Bazaar, as one of the foremost economic institutions in Iran, was susceptible to the transformative demands of these state agendas.

In addition, as in most developing countries, in the past half-century, Iran's demographic and socioeconomic variables have gone through dramatic changes. The level of urbanization and rates of literacy have increased and the relative share of the agricultural sector and the pervasiveness of ascribed identities (e.g. tribal, kinship, and ethnic identities) have waned. Yet these changes began in the first half of the twentieth century and have generally exhibited the same fundamental trends and pace during the past seventy years. Representing various indicators of urbanization, literacy, industrialization, and modern banking and education, Figures 1.1, 1.2, 1.3, 1.4, and 1.5 show that these trends began decades before the 1970s and that there is no dramatic escalation or shift in these indexes after 1979. Thus, the socioeconomic transformations in and of themselves cannot explain changes in the structure of the Bazaar across these two regimes or the particular timing of this rupture after the Islamic Revolution.

Therefore, this project investigates the transformative agendas of states by focusing on the variations between the Pahlavi monarchy and the Islamic Republic and their relationship to a particular physical space, economic form, and social class – the Tehran Bazaar. The analysis, therefore, will move back and forth between the caravanserais of the Bazaar and the ministries of the government, to emphasize the interaction between state and Bazaar. And, in a larger sense, I shed light on state–society relations under the two regimes.

Marketplaces are important institutions in Middle Eastern and North African societies for a number of reasons. Bazaars and *suq*s are an economic focal point where both retail and wholesale commerce takes place and large sums of credit circulate among members of the private

Postrevolutionary Iran," in *A Century of Revolution: Social Movements in Iran*, ed. John Foran (Minneapolis: University of Minnesota Press, 1994).

[8] Hootan Shambayati, "The Rentier State, Interest Groups, and the Paradox of Autonomy: State and Business in Turkey and Iran," *Comparative Politics* 26 (April 1994), 307–31.

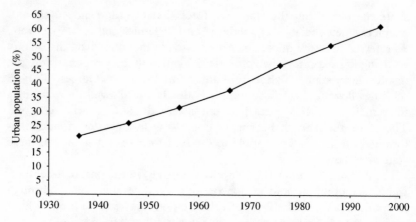

Figure 1.1 Urbanization: percentage of total population living in urban areas, 1936–1996
Sources: Julian Bharier, *Economic Development in Iran 1900–1970* (London: Oxford University Press, 1971), p. 27; Statistical Centre of Iran, *Iran Statistical Year Book* (various years).

sector. Large and internationally oriented marketplaces, like Tehran's central bazaar, house many import–export trade houses. Also, as states in the region have rolled back their distributive and redistributive roles, private and informal sectors have played increasingly important roles in providing jobs and credit and distributing goods and services.

In the case of the Tehran Bazaar, despite the Shah's hostility, it played a very significant and central role in Iran's prerevolutionary economy. At the time of the Revolution it was estimated that the Bazaar controlled two-thirds of national domestic wholesale trade, at least 30 percent of all imports, and an even larger portion of consumer goods.[9] In terms of credit, in 1963 the bazaars in Iran loaned as much as all the commercial banks put together,[10] while in 1975 the Tehran Bazaar was believed to control 20 percent of the official market volume, or $3 billion in foreign exchange and $2.1 billion in loans outstanding.[11] Also, sources suggest that there were 20,000–30,000 commercial units and 40,000–50,000

[9] Robert Graham, *Iran: The Illusion of Power*, rev. edn. (New York: St. Martins Press, 1980), p. 221.
[10] Richard Elliot Benedick, *Industrial Finance in Iran: A Study of Financial Practice in an Underdeveloped Economy* (Boston: Division of Research, Graduate School of Business Administration, Harvard University, 1964), p. 52.
[11] Alan D. Urbach and Jürgen Pumpluen, "Currency Trading in the Bazaar: Iran's Amazing Parallel Market," *Euromoney* (June 1978), 116.

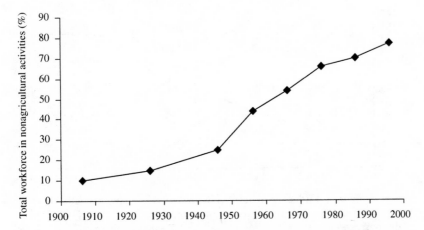

Figure 1.2 Industrialization: percentage of total workforce active in nonagricultural sectors, 1906–1996
Sources: Julian Bharier, *Economic Development in Iran 1900–1970* (London: Oxford University Press, 1971), pp. 34–5; Statistical Centre of Iran, *Iran Statistical Year Books* (various years).

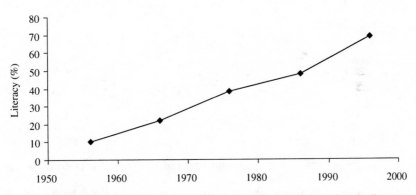

Figure 1.3 Literacy: percentage of total population that is literate, 1956–1996
Source: Statistical Centre of Iran, *Iran Statistical Year Book* (various years).

employees within the Bazaar and the immediately surrounding streets during the 1970s.[12] The Tehran Bazaar functioned as the national commercial emporium for the import of almost all consumer goods and

---

[12] *Asar* nos. 2, 3, 4 (1359 [1980]), 22 and 25; and Misagh Parsa, *Social Origins of the Iranian Revolution* (New Brunswick, NJ: Rutgers University Press, 1989), p. 92.

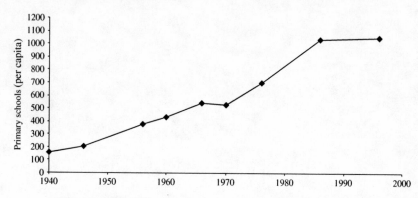

Figure 1.4 Education: number of primary schools per capita, 1940–1996
Source: Statistical Centre of Iran, *Iran Statistical Year Book* (various years).

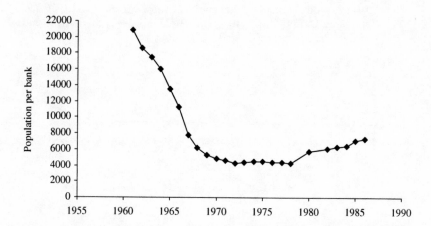

Figure 1.5 Commercial and financial development: population per bank, 1961–1986
Source: Statistical Centre of Iran, *Iran Statistical Year Book* (various years).

many intermediary goods into Iran, as well as the export of many non-oil goods (e.g. hand-woven carpets, dried fruits and nuts, and some textiles). Thus, wholesalers in the provinces, retailers in Tehran, private manufacturers, and many others relied on the Bazaar for inventories and credit. The Tehran Bazaar, possibly unlike the provincial bazaars, prospered during the oil boom of the 1970s.[13] One indicator of the Bazaar's wealth and the value of its property is "key money" (*sarqofli*). Key money is the market-determined sum of money paid by an incoming renter of a space. The amount depends on the location, size of the property, and wares sold, but it is also a measure of the commercial potential of the property. All the *bazaari*s I talked to agreed with Martin Seger's finding that during the late Pahlavi era the value of key money increased greatly in the Bazaar (surpassing the rate of inflation) and reached several hundred thousand dollars for spaces as small as ten square meters.[14]

Yet bazaars are not simply economic institutions; they are a fundamental part of the urban morphology. The older bazaars are also typically located in the heart of the city, and often neighbor government offices, courts, major religious institutions, and traditional social gathering places such as coffee shops and public baths. The hustle and bustle and central location of bazaar areas make them a major public forum, attracting diverse people who in the process of conducting their personal affairs exchange and overhear information, rumor, and opinions about economic conditions, family affairs, and political disputes. In certain contexts this socioeconomic mélange was a base for political organization and mobilization. The political dimension of bazaars is particularly important in the Iranian context, where *bazaari*s have consistently played an active and central role in major political episodes, including the struggle for constitutionalism (1905–11), Mosaddeq's movement to nationalize the oil industry and strengthen democratic rule (1953), the protests against the Shah's "White Revolution" (1963), and the overthrow of the monarchy and establishment of the Islamic Republic (1978–9).

Given the multiple dimensions and prominent position of bazaars in the region, it is unfortunate that they have not received scholarly attention. Clifford Geertz introduces his study of Sefrou's bazaar by pointing out:

What the mandarin bureaucracy was for classical China and the caste system for classical India – the part most evocative of the whole – the bazaar was for the more pragmatic societies of the classical Middle East. Yet ... there is only a handful of extended analyses ... seriously concerned to characterize the bazaar as a cultural form, a social institution, and an economic type.[15]

---

[13] Parsa, *Social Origins of the Iranian Revolution*, p. 101.

[14] Martin Seger, *Teheran: Eine Stadtgeographische Studie* (New York: Springer-Verlag Wien, 1978), pp. 164–5.

[15] Clifford Geertz, "Suq: The Bazaar Economy in Sefrou," in *Meaning and Order in Moroccan Society*, ed. Clifford Geertz, Hildred Geertz, and Lawrence Rosen (Cambridge: Cambridge University Press, 1979), p. 123. European travelogues on Iran and the Middle East often discuss bazaars as essential components of Middle Eastern society. For example, "To see Persia without knowing its bazaars is seeing it like a small boy watching a

Almost three decades since his remarks, Geertz's dismay at the lack of research on Middle Eastern bazaars continues to resonate.[16]

Furthermore, despite the universal acceptance that bazaars are fundamental socioeconomic and political loci in Iranian society, intensive empirical research on bazaars has been very limited since the Revolution. Thus, scholars have tended to assume that the organization of the bazaars, their relationship to other social groups, and their political efficacy have remained unchanged. Two important analyses of postrevolutionary politics, however, speculate that the bazaars have undergone important transformations. Ahmad Ashraf's history of bazaars includes a suggestive paragraph: "On the whole ... the bazaaris have been threatened by such unprecedented radical governmental measures as nationalization of foreign trade and elimination of brokerage junction through the development of cooperative societies."[17] Meanwhile, in his political history of the first decade of the Islamic Republic, Shaul Bakhash points out: "In the bazaar, the old merchant families were edged out by the new men with connections to the clerics in the government."[18] In the chapters that follow, I extend Ashraf's and Bakhash's astute, but unelaborated, observations to show that state policies have not simply threatened the Tehran Bazaar or changed its composition, but have radically restructured its internal organization and its relationship to the state and economy – a restructuring, moreover, that has consequences for the political efficacy of the Bazaar.

Studying transformative states

This initial observations take us away from the alleys and shops where the Bazaar's bargaining and trade takes place and moves us to the political architecture where policies are formulated and conceptions of development and social transformation are enacted. That is, to understand the organization of the Bazaar we must consider the policies of the state.

The state was recovered from relative analytical obscurity by political scientists and sociologists in the 1980s.[19] Positioning themselves in

---

circus through a hole in the tent." Fred Richard, *A Persian Journey* (London: Jonathan Cape, 1931), p. 39.

[16] A recent exception is Annika Rabbo's *A Shop of One's Own: Independence and Reputation among Traders in Aleppo* (London: I. B. Tauris Press, 2004).

[17] Ahmad Ashraf, "Bazaar-Mosque Alliance: The Social Basis of Revolts and Revolutions," *International Journal of Politics, Culture, and Society* 1 (Summer 1988), 564.

[18] Shaul Bakhash, *The Reign of the Ayatollahs: Iran and the Islamic Revolution* (New York: Basic Books, 1990), p. 290.

[19] Atul Kohli, "State, Society, and Development," and Margaret Levi, "The State of the Study of the State," in *Political Science: The State of the Discipline*, ed. Ira Katznelson and Helen V. Milner (New York: W. W. Norton and Co., 2002).

opposition to pluralism, structural-functionalism, and modernization theory, which tended to see social and economic processes as the mechanistic engine for change, both macrostructural and rational choice scholars turned their attention to the state as an autonomous force and critical factor in withstanding revolutions,[20] fostering economic growth by reducing transaction costs,[21] and influencing a whole host of policy options and outcomes.[22] The object of study for this literature was the state's interests and institutions, with scholars considering both causes and consequences of variations of these factors.

These early works, however, had serious shortcomings in that they tended to conceptualize the state as an overly unitary, coherent, and omnipresent structure or actor. More recently a group of scholars have advocated important modifications to the state-centered approach of the 1980s. Scholars have increasingly cautioned against exaggerating the state's autonomy from society and its capacity to restructure society. Instead they have advocated greater attention to the dialogical process in which state and social forces shape one another. In turn, state effectiveness is based on particular state–society relations, with more effective states tapping into social resources and institutions. For example, the volume edited by Migdal, Kohli, and Shue offers a more modest and nuanced perspective on the role of the state in development. They critique the more dogmatic state-centered approaches, proposing a shift in focus from "the state" to the "state-in-society frame of reference."[23] First, they posit that variation in state effectiveness is a function of the scope and type of ties it enjoys with society. Second, they call upon scholars to disaggregate the state and view it more as a diffuse set of institutions with permeable boundaries. Also, the form and capacity of social forces are dictated by empirical conditions. Finally, these scholars claim that the relationship between state and society is not zero-sum.

---

[20] Theda Skocpol, *States and Social Revolutions* (Cambridge: Cambridge University Press, 1979).

[21] Robert H. Bates, *Markets and States in Tropical Africa: The Political Basis of Agricultural Policies* (Berkeley: University of California Press, 1981); Margaret Levi, *Of Rule and Revenue* (Berkeley: University of California Press, 1988); Douglass C. North, *Structure and Change in Economic History* (New York: Norton, 1981); and Douglass C. North, *Institutions, Institutional Change and Economic Performance* (Cambridge: Cambridge University Press, 1990).

[22] Peter B. Evans, Dietrich Rueschemeyer, and Theda Skocpol, eds., *Bringing the State Back In* (Cambridge: Cambridge University Press, 1985).

[23] Joel Migdal, Atul Kohli, and Vivienne Shue, eds., *State Power and Social Forces: Domination and Transformation in the Third World* (Cambridge: Cambridge University Press, 1994).

This "state-in-society frame" is part of an emerging trend in social science scholarship seeking to explain variation in policy choices, success, and origins as a product of the form of engagement and mode of interaction between state and society. Peter Evans devised the concept of "embedded autonomy," for instance, to explore the variation in ability of states to industrialize and develop comparative advantage.[24] For Evans "embedded autonomy" captures the institutional configuration enjoyed by coherent autonomous states and their enabling network of ties with knowledge- and resource-rich groups in society, a coupling which is necessary for successful development. Like Evans, Theda Skocpol has expanded and refined her earlier state structuralist perspective to what she more recently has called a "polity-centered" approach.[25] While analyzing the development of welfare policies in the post-Civil War United States, she argues that the origins of state policy choices are contingent upon the "fit" between politicized social groups and the organization of states. In all these frameworks state–society boundaries are neither fixed nor clearly demarcated, but are formations of multiple, often competing, institutions.

My approach follows the outlook of recent works on state–society relations by claiming that the transformation of the Tehran Bazaar is a product of specific state policies and the manner in which they interact with the existing social order. I make this argument by incorporating two critical addenda. (1) Not only do we need to disaggregate the state, but we must also analyze state transformative projects as circumscribed, incomplete, and nonomnipresent master plans. (2) Political scientists must not treat the internal governance of groups as a black box, as something that happens automatically or is static. If the state's authority is incomplete or partially effective – what is referred to as the state "fail[ing] to penetrate"[26] or the state being "disengaged"[27] – then the contours of social order should not be treated as a given, but are determined through a process of negotiation between existing social institutions and state institutions.

---

[24] Peter Evans, *Embedded Autonomy: States and Industrial Transformation* (Princeton: Princeton University Press, 1995).

[25] Theda Skocpol, *Protecting Soldiers and Mothers: The Political Origins of Social Policy in the United States* (Cambridge: Harvard University Press, 1992).

[26] Joel Migdal, "The State in Society: An Approach to Struggles for Domination," in *State Power and Social Forces*, ed. Joel Migdal, Atul Kohli, and Vivienne Shue (Cambridge: Cambridge University Press, 1994).

[27] Michael Bratton, "Peasant-State Relations in Postcolonial Africa: Patterns of Engagement and Disengagement," in *State Power and Social Forces*, ed. Joel Migdal, Atul Kohli, and Vivienne Shue (Cambridge: Cambridge University Press, 1994).

What is beyond the state's vision?

State efficacy can be tempered by revenue and legitimacy constraints, historical legacies, relations between central and local authorities, and disjunctions between institutions and organizations, parties, and social groups. Yet, most political scientists still assume that states' transformative projects are all-encompassing. For instance, Migdal proposes that transformative states seek to "dominate in every corner of society."[28] However, it is apparent that states are selective in their engagements and often leave many realms of social life to their own devices, however limited or elaborate.[29]

Why do states, even highly authoritarian ones, have difficulty in devising complete domination over all dimensions of society? In *System Effects*, Robert Jervis helps us address this question in a more general manner.[30] He argues that political complexity and indeterminacy has its roots in its systemic nature. We cannot understand systems (e.g. the ecosystem, the international state system, a social system, or a system of production) by examining the attributes and goals of individual elements of that system (e.g. species, states, individuals, or classes). This is because many effects are delayed, indirect, and unintended, relations between units of a system are determined by third parties, and decisions and actions are based on multiple agendas. Therefore, Jervis concludes that regulating the entire system is particularly difficult, and this is especially true of highly complex and aggregate systems such as "political systems." More directly related to the nature of the state, James Scott's work on the failures of development projects considers the incompleteness of state reach and vision. A state's capacity to implement its schemes is restricted by what Scott calls "tunnel vision."[31] Modern nation-states, argues Scott, focus on limited segments of an intricate and multifarious reality. They simplify societies in order to make the world more "legible" and to fine-tune their administrative methods, focusing on specific sectors, locations, and factors of production. These simplifications are like maps. "That is, they are designed to summarize precisely those aspects of a complex world that are of immediate interest to the mapmaker and to

[28] Joel Migdal, *State in Society: Studying How States and Societies Transform and Constitute One Another* (Cambridge: Cambridge University Press, 2001), p. 114.

[29] Deborah J. Yashar, *Contesting Citizenship in Latin America: The Rise of Indigenous and the Postliberal Challenge* (Cambridge: Cambridge University Press, 2005).

[30] Robert Jervis, *System Effects: Complexity in Political and Social Life* (Princeton: Princeton University Press, 1999).

[31] James Scott, *Seeing Like a State: How Certain Schemes to Improve the Human Condition Have Failed* (New Haven: Yale University Press, 1998).

ignore the rest."[32] Scott is interested in what is of "immediate interest" to the state *cum* mapmaker – their projects for a better society, and their failures. In addition, this portrayal is useful because it reminds us that even the grandest state projects necessarily disregard some elements of social life. What states ignore is just as important as the focus of their con-centration; what is ignored is likely subsequently to haunt the planners.[33] Just as Hausmann's plans for Paris did not envision the vibrancy of Bell-ville, the Brazilian government may have planned and built Brasilia, but the unplanned "Free City" escaped its vision and has a larger population than the planned city.

Framing the issue of state transformative projects in terms of scope directs us to important new questions for the study of state–bazaar relations in Iran and for understanding the consequences of state poli-cies. What was the state's developmental program during the respective periods? What were the institutional instruments established to imple-ment these visions? And finally, what place did the Bazaar have in these programs and what were the direct and indirect consequences of these policies for the Bazaar?

What generates governance when a group is beyond the state's vision?

Scholars focusing on state–society nexuses argue that power is dis-tributed and operates beyond state institutions. Migdal states: "My emphasis will be on process – the ongoing struggles among shifting coalitions over the rules for daily behavior. These processes determine how *societies and states create and maintain distinct ways of structuring day-to-day life* . . . ."[34] The bulk of Migdal's collection of essays carefully delineate the limits of the state's transformative powers and illustrate how social forces pattern state actions. The question of how quotidian life is organized and how exactly societies might structure day-to-day life in the absence of the state, however, is left unaddressed. Contrary to Hobbesian outlooks, it is assumed that without the state, social order spontaneously occurs. Questions about social order and governance are deemed relevant only when the state is involved. In this sense the approach continues to be state-centric, and politics remains the exclu-sive domain of the state.

Area studies experts, especially those who have conducted field work on marginal groups, have continually shown that the state–society

---

[32] Ibid., p. 87. Emphasis added.

[33] The increasing interest in informal sectors is an explicit acknowledgment of social worlds outside the complete purview of states.

[34] Migdal, *State in Society*, p. 11. Emphasis added.

dynamic is not a simple choice of whether to engage or disengage, resist or acquiesce, dominate or be dominated, transform or fail to transform. Rather, contingencies, strategic interactions, and incomplete or inaccurate information often lead to struggles and unintended consequences surpassing planned goals being the main cause of outcomes. Those who are economically marginal, ethnic and religious minorities, women, and those who are on the legal margins have developed multiple repertoires to pattern state–society relations, and to negotiate their social position and political plight. The individual and collective techniques include manipulation, avoidance, defensive movements, and daily encroachment.[35] As such, politics takes on an "expanded form to signify the interactions that shape ideas, behaviors, constraints, and opportunities – the realm of power relationships on all levels, and not only the actions of governments or political parties."[36]

Social groups confront state initiatives with a set of associations, resources, and repertoires of action that complicate, and even subvert, institutional designs. Thus, before understanding the dynamics of state–society relations we must decipher the prevailing structures of given groups and societies. The Bazaar's practices and ongoing relations are just as pertinent as the state's policies and institutions. Therefore, our investigation must ask: What is the Bazaar? How are transactions conducted, contracts enforced, and credit distributed? Given that the Bazaar was on the margins of the Shah's plans and was cut off from direct state patronage, why did the Bazaar survive and even prosper? And how was it governed, given that the state did not see it and *bazaari*s ignored state institutions (e.g. the Chamber of Commerce and the Chamber of Guilds) designed to represent them and control commercial activities? Conversely, since the Bazaar entered the vision of the state under the Islamic Republic, how has the state influenced it? How has it transformed the Bazaar's self-governance and the way *bazaari*s have related to one another?

[35] Since the 1970s this has been the bread and butter of most "area studies" work in the social sciences, a rich literature has developed discussing subaltern resistance within hegemony and under colonialism. In the context of the Middle East see Asef Bayat, *Street Politics: Poor People's Movements in Iran* (New York: Columbia University Press, 1997); Guilain Denoeux, *Urban Unrest in the Middle East: A Comparative Study of Informal Networks in Egypt, Iran, and Lebanon* (Albany: State University of New York Press, 1993); and Diane Singerman, *Avenues of Participation: Family, Politics, and Networks in Urban Quarters in Cairo* (Princeton: Princeton University Press, 1995).

[36] Arlene Elowe MacLeod, "The New Veiling and Urban Crisis: Symbolic Politics in Cairo," in *Population, Poverty, and Politics in Middle East Cities*, ed. Michael Bonine (Gainesville: University Press of Florida, 1997), p. 305.

Variation in forms of governance

The discussion brings us to the question of how to specify the exact meaning of "the social order of the Bazaar," "transforming the Bazaar," or "changing the economic structure of the Bazaar" – that is, the central dependent variable of this project. As I argue in Chapter 2, the Bazaar is best conceptualized as a series of socially embedded networks within a bounded space that is the mechanism for the exchange of specific commodities. This approach treats markets as constellations of economic relations and roles and not mere aggregations of isolated and interchangeable transactions. It also contends that actions in the Bazaar are the results of relationships among multiple individuals who may or may not share a common set of cultural attributes or structural positions. Thus, the bazaar's structure is an articulation of ongoing, patterned relations within the group, rather than the product of static attributes and attitudes of entities or macrosocial structures.[37] These networks aggregate actions of individuals, who have specific roles and statuses that emerge in relation to others in the group. These roles and relationships connote duties, expectations, obligations, and powers. Therefore, as capillaries that distribute power and situate individuals, networks comprise a form of governance. By the "form of the governance of the Tehran Bazaar," I mean the pattern of ongoing interactions and distribution of authority and resources throughout the commercial networks that comprise the Bazaar. The form can be defined along a continuum between communal and hierarchical relations.[38]

A group is said to have "communal governance" when it is characterized by long-term relations and multiplex interactions, and when the ties within that group are crosscutting. Long-term, stable relations exist when actors relate to one another repeatedly over time and believe that their interactions will persist. In the language of game theory, play is iterated and is not one-shot.[39] Continuity in relations provides opportunities to assess the actions of others in order to reward good behavior and punish uncooperative behavior. This potential for sanctioning also helps even up power relations because subordinates are given an opportunity to admonish, if not punish, their superiors by resisting or exiting in the

---

[37] For a discussion of the distinction between structures as relations and structures as attributes see David Knoke, *Political Networks: The Structural Perspective* (Cambridge: Cambridge University Press, 1990).

[38] My typology is adopted from and parallels Michael Taylor, "Good Government: On Hierarchy, Social Capital, and the Limitations of Rational Choice Theory," *Journal of Political Philosophy* 4 (1996), 1–28.

[39] Note that in Prisoners' Dilemma games a high probability for future interactions is a necessary (not sufficient) condition for cooperative play.

future. Durable relations are especially important since in economies where independent appraisal of past performance is lacking, actors know that uncooperative behavior today will have costs in the long run. Long-term relations also reduce uncertainty about the preferences of others, and the accumulation of precedents helps diminish bargaining costs associated with transactions.

Multiplex relations consist of interactions along multiple social dimensions (commercial, social, political, religious, familial, neighborly, etc.), as opposed to purely economic interactions. From an instrumentalist perspective, so long as the overall account is in balance, individuals involved in multiplex relationships can overlook imbalances in particular areas. And with a more structuralist bent, as actors interact on more dimensions, preferences and beliefs become more similar, certainty about preferences and the meaning of signals increases, and bargaining costs are reduced by increased opportunities to make trade-offs on other fronts. Finally, as relations endure, they are more likely to take on a multiplex nature.

Third, crosscutting ties facilitate exchange of information about potential trade partners within the group. They are the relations that bridge networks or connect members of the same level in a given group. Gossiping allows for public shaming and champion making. Someone who cheats can be betrayed to the community, while a reputation for honesty can be identified and reenforced. Thus, crosscutting ties help reduce monitoring and enforcement costs in situations where third-party appraisal and records are absent (e.g. consumer reports, law merchants, better business bureaus). Taken together, all these characteristics allow groups to forge a sense of solidarity and corporate identity.

At the other end of the spectrum, relations resemble *hierarchical* governance characterized by one-way and top-down channels of communication, with specific actions dictated, designated, and adjudicated by a single legitimate authority. At the absolute limit – pure hierarchies – these ties have a one-shot and coercive nature, with actions based on command rather than deliberation, and between identity-less agents in the hierarchy; in these acute cases it is difficult to talk of "relationships" or "networks" since actors interact based on roles. In less extreme cases, which I term "coercive hierarchies," members of a group interact over time, but interactions are sporadic and take place without expectations and commitments for future interactions. A single superior heads these networks with the vast majority of ties flowing to and from that one actor or office. In this form of governance, crosscutting and multifaceted relations are muted, with relations in groups limited to economic matters and fewer relations cutting across the various networks. "[I]n the coercive approach," argues Taylor, hierarchical superiors treat subordinates as individuals, as social isolates, proceeding as if they were unconnected with one another (and by doing so may in fact *make* them less connected); they make no use of (and so do not try to create or foster) any capacities the governed might have to regulate their own behavior, capacities they are endowed with in virtue of such local community or social networks or organizations as may already exist among them – or, in brief, in virtue of such *social capital* as they posses."[40]

Consequently, subordinates have little opportunity or capacity to negotiate relations with superiors. In terms of Hirschman's triad, coercive hierarchies allow only for "exit" or "loyalty," with "voice" being inaudible.[41]

In between the communal relations and coercive hierarchies lie more *cooperative hierarchies* that tap into communal structures. Long-term and two-way channels of communication delegate responsibility to subordinates, making interactions more responsive and encouraging a sense of vertical community. Like communal relations, cooperative hierarchies allow individuals to develop multiplex and crosscutting relations. Trust and reciprocity emerge, and crosscutting relations integrate actors positioned in different hierarchical networks. Superiors are able to tap into embedded local networks, work groups, resources, knowledge, and channels of communication, while subordinates have some capacity for "voice." Taylor writes:

Because relations between superiors and subordinates in hierarchy of this second kind are characterized by long-term repeated interaction, cooperation, reciprocity, and trust, we might say that there is *vertical social capital* within the hierarchy. ... governance of this type also makes use of and fosters *horizontal social capital* (working through and with local communities, networks and organizations).[42]

Finally, cooperative hierarchies exhibit greater group coherence since potentially isolated clusters of actors are connected through ties that bridge structural divides.

Taylor develops this typology and conceptualization of community in order to explain why certain groups are able to produce social order without third-party mechanisms, while others are not. His intellectual enterprise is one of comparative statics, rather than tracing change within a group. This book's objective is to understand transformation from one form of governance to another, and the empirical analysis begins by first

---

[40] Taylor, "Good Government," 3.
[41] Albert Hirschman, *Exit, Voice, and Loyalty* (Cambridge, MA: Harvard University Press, 1970).
[42] Taylor, "Good Government," 4.

demonstrating that since the establishment of the Islamic Republic, the Tehran Bazaar has moved from more cooperative hierarchies to a form of governance that is dominated by coercive hierarchies.[43]

The argument

Why has this transformation occurred and what political consequences has it had? As illustrated in Figure 1.6, I argue that the developmental programs of the state embodying the change in the transformative visions of the two regimes manifest themselves in (1) the institutional setting and (2) the location of Tehran Bazaar's networks by providing opportunities and restrictions on commercial relationships and the form of governance within the marketplace. While background changes in socioeconomic variables (e.g. demographic changes, patterns of urbanization, increased literacy, and improved national transportation and communication) cannot be bracketed out of the study, it is argued that these factors are relatively constant before and over the period of the study and thus unable to account for the variation in the Bazaar's form of governance.

First, the institutional setting of networks refers to the policies and legal parameters (e.g. import–export rules, subsidies, urban planning projects, and government agencies and companies) that shape ties by creating and empowering actors and enabling and constraining actions. These myriad institutions are born out of the grand developmental agendas, or what I term "transformative programs of states," and therefore can be thought of as the "congealed tastes" of rulers.[44] These specific policies, in turn, dictate how economic networks must be constructed in order to access resources and maneuver around government-imposed limits. Networks may tie businesses and economic agents to state institutions, they may employ localized norms and practices to escape state institutions, or they may tap into state resources and divert them for alternative ends. In all of these cases, a dynamic tension

---

[43] I see parallels between my research question and Waterbury's comments that variations exist in patron–client relations. He writes, "[E]xchanges [between patrons and clients], like the relationship itself, may be diffuse, multiplex, involving deference, physical support, gifts, labour in return for the paternalistic involvement of the patron in all aspects of the client's life; or they may be single-purpose, specific and quasi-contractual." John Waterbury, "An Attempt to Put Patrons and Clients in Their Place," in *Patrons and Clients in Mediterranean Societies,* ed. Ernest Gellner and John Waterbury (London: Gerald Duckworth and Co., 1977), p. 332.

[44] Institutions as "congealed tastes" is Riker's term. William H. Riker, "Implications from Disequilibrium of Majority Rule for the Study of Institutions," *American Political Science Review* 74 (June 1980), 445.

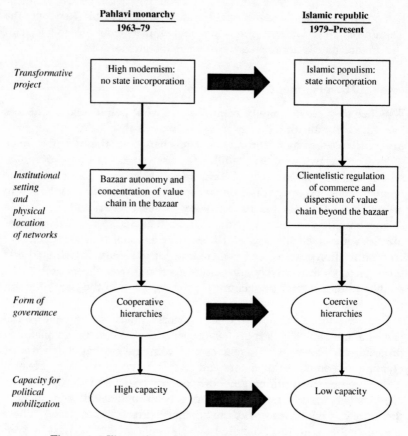

Figure 1.6 Illustration of the argument

develops between state institutions and existing norms and informal practices, the resolution of which sets the parameters for networks that are intended to avoid, acquiesce in, or abuse state regulation. I will demonstrate that the Pahlavi regime's high modernist transformative project resulted in the bazaars being ignored by the state and that there was little attempt by the state to incorporate the Bazaar or directly engage the institutions that reproduced its economic and political autonomy and power for it was assumed it would simply pass away with modernization. Conversely, while the Islamic Republic did not set out to decommission the Bazaar's prevailing practices and institutions, its package of populist macroeconomic and nationalist trade policies resulted in state incorporation of *bazaari*s via cooptation and clientelism. The *bazaari*s' responses, though shaped by the various state institutions, combined multiple strategies to forge new networks and consequently a new form of governance for the Bazaar.

Second, I examine how social relations are often situated in specific locations, reproducing identities, situating relations, and engendering loyalties. For instance, *bazaari* ties are reproduced by and within the confines of the central marketplace – in its stores, alleyways, warehouses, coffee shops, restaurants, and mosques. By the locations of networks, I mean the physical spheres and spatial dimensions where interactions take place and how ties transcend and are situated in relation to specific locales. The physical locale(s) influence(s) the breadth, scope, and frequency of interactions, transfiguring objective space into relational space.[45] The location and scope of networks are crucial to the study of the Tehran Bazaar because while some commercial networks are concentrated at certain times in the physical space of the covered central marketplace (e.g. the prerevolutionary Bazaar), others stretch well beyond the Tehran Bazaar, reaching distant provinces and countries (e.g. the postrevolutionary Bazaar). I argue that as networks expand in terms of scope, as they did through the 1980s and 1990s, the internal structure of those networks will adjust. The network ties connecting a series of wholesalers and retailers in the close quarters of the china and glassware bazaar are more likely to be employed on a regular basis, to take on a multifaceted nature, and to be face-to-face than the postrevolutionary network ties stretching from retailers in Tehran to importers across the Persian Gulf in Dubai. Nevertheless, physical proximity is not sufficient to produce *active* networks. Many groups share a location and even a common social structural position (e.g. the urban poor, ethnic minorities, and suburban housewives), but this helps establish only a minimum condition of group identity formation and consciousness.[46] To move from being a *passive* network to being an *active* one, *physical* space must become a *social* space through activities, rituals, and interdependencies wherein individuals identify themselves as part of a group and as distinct from others. The comparison between the pre- and postrevolutionary Bazaar demonstrates how ongoing, multifaceted, and crosscutting ties facilitate this transfiguration.

---

[45] On the impact of space on socioeconomic configurations and political action see Ira Katznelson, *Marxism and the City* (Oxford: Clarendon Press, 1992); Paul Krugman, "Space: The Final Frontier," *Journal of Economic Perspectives* 12 (Spring 1998), 161–74; Saskia Sassen, *The Global City: New York, London, and Tokyo* (Princeton: Princeton University Press, 2001); and William H. Sewell, "Space in Contentious Politics," in *Silence and Voice in the Study of Contentious Politics*, ed. Ronald R. Aminzade et al. (Cambridge: Cambridge University Press, 2001).

[46] Bayat, *Street Politics*, pp. 15–19.

In addition, I examine the hand-woven carpet, tea, and china and glassware sectors[47] within the Tehran Bazaar to illustrate that the process was mediated by the qualities of commodities traded (standardized versus nonstandardized commodities) and the specific state institutions that pertained to each sector. While most discussions of bazaars treat them as a uniform whole, my research revealed that important differences exist across the many sectors making up the greater Tehran Bazaar. With this in mind, I conducted in-depth research on the hand-woven carpet, tea, and china and glassware sectors to investigate different institutional settings and the consequences of these for the process of commercial exchange in the Bazaar. Through cross-sectoral analysis I evaluate alternative hypotheses for the generation of cooperative hierarchies and coercive hierarchies, and also trace the process underlying my network-based argument. In particular, I show that network ties in the Bazaar are conditioned by whether the commodity traded is a standardized and substitutable good or not.[48] In cases where information regarding the quality or quantity of a good is scarce or limited to sellers (e.g. carpets and tea) there will be a tendency toward more embedded ties among producers, wholesalers, retailers, and consumers in order to gain access to trustworthy information. In certain cases, institutions (e.g. state agencies grading tea quality or trade associations ensuring sellers' qualifications) may help address quality evaluation, but informal institutions often remain essential means for reducing these transaction costs. On the other hand, substitutable commodities that have clearly defined quantities and known qualities are more amenable to hierarchical forms of governance. Finally, the analysis of the tea and hand-woven carpet sectors also demonstrates that the survival of these markets in the Tehran Bazaar is not related to the amount of state regulation of commerce, but to the particular type of state policies and the responses of *bazaaris*.

The analysis concludes by examining the political import of this change in governance by linking the discussion of forms of governance to social

---

[47] In Persian, "bazaar" refers to the city's marketplace as a whole (e.g. the Tehran Bazaar, Isfahan Bazaar, and Tabriz Bazaar), and is also used for the individual trades that make up the bazaar. Therefore you can speak of the carpet bazaar, coppersmith bazaar, or jewelry bazaar. To prevent confusion, I use "sector" to refer to individual crafts and trades within the greater bazaar area.

[48] Frank Fanselow, "The Bazaar Economy or How Bizarre Is the Bazaar Really?" *Man* 25 (June 1990), 250–65. On the issue of information and markets more generally see George A. Akerlof, "The Market for 'Lemons': Quality Uncertainty and the Market Mechanism," *Quarterly Journal of Economics* 84 (August 1970), pp. 488–500; and G. J. Stiglitz, "The Economics of Information and Knowledge," in *The Economics of Information and Knowledge*, ed. D. M. Lamberton (Harmondsworth: Penguin, 1971).

mobilization and asking why the Bazaar was better able to mobilize against the state prior to the establishment of the Islamic Republic. I demonstrate that the form of governance, and not ideological factors or the bazaar–mosque coalition or purely individual interests and grievances, better accounts for this shift from high to low mobilization capacity. The Tehran Bazaar's particular prerevolutionary forms of governance – namely, cooperative hierarchies – were the critical factor facilitating its mobilization and participation in contentious politics because these networks were effective means to coordinate actions, disseminate information, mobilize funds, and bring the disparate strata within and beyond the Bazaar together. When the Pahlavi regime stepped in to directly restructure the Bazaar in 1976, these functions were politicized and directed resources toward mass politics. However, the shifting institutional setting and location of networks that transformed the Bazaar structure after the Islamic Revolution also inhibited its potency. Thus, despite evidence that members of the Tehran Bazaar have been dissatisfied with the Islamic Republic's economic policies and have recently supported the political reform movement, they have not been able to translate their dissatisfaction into mobilization against the state. The more fragmented and less socially embedded networks that emerged in the 1980s and 1990s have limited the Bazaar's cohesiveness and capacity for collective action. In short, the study proposes that macrostructural changes (i.e. the state's developmental approach and regime institutions) influence microlevel quotidian politics by altering network structures, which in turn shape the political capabilities of social groups. The analysis of the Bazaar's declining capacity to mobilize against the state is a powerful means to indirectly infer and evaluate arguments regarding the socioeconomy of the Bazaar. The extension of the network approach to the Bazaar from the field of economic organization to political mobilization, in addition, demonstrates its analytical scope.

Networks as causal mechanisms

Even this summary of the book's main arguments illustrates that the concept of embedded networks is the integral unit of analysis and the underlying mechanism that grounds various aspects of my argument. Those working with the New Economic Sociology paradigm have developed theories of embedded networks arguing that economic action is situated within regular sets of interactions that generate specific opportunities and constraints on action[49] (see Chapter 2 for a more

---

[49] Richard Swedberg and Mark Granovetter, eds., *The Sociology of Economic Life* (Boulder: Westview Press, 1992).

complete discussion of this literature). Networks are the means by which actors develop reputations, negotiate prices, evaluate information, resolve conflicts, and mobilize assets in all economies, but especially in settings where information is sparse or asymmetric. Traders disseminate and receive information about quality, price, and past performance to and from members of the community through embedded networks, and not via isolated bilateral exchange partners involved in strategic interactions or normative notions of moral obligations and injustices. Thus, in this account, embedded networks are relational mechanisms, or the unobservable devices that connect causal variables to outcomes.

I treat the Tehran Bazaar as a series of networks, rather than as a cultural form, class, informal economy, or product of informational scarcity. The Bazaar's embedded networks are the devices that relate actors to one another and in doing so are the means by which forms of governance operate. I focus on "networks as a form of governance, as social glue that binds individuals together into a coherent system."[50] The persistence of forms of governance and their characteristics such as group solidarity or disunity are the result of, and not the cause for, the regeneration of ongoing ties.[51] As Mark Granovetter has argued, "networks of social relations penetrate irregularly and in different degrees,"[52] and thus we must pay attention to variations and the evolution of these systems. The empirical discussion focuses on the internal mechanism in this regenerative process and the external factors in their disjuncture.

To make my argument more fine-grained, and hopefully more compelling, I investigate the influence of structural and state forces by endogenizing their impact on the Bazaar at the level of networks. Thus, state and society-wide shifts are related to microlevel outcomes via changes in the dimensions of networks (location and institutional setting of networks). Finally, forms of governance, as conglomerations of networks, affect the capacity of *bazaari*s to acquire a sense of solidarity in the face of internal differences and the Bazaar to mobilize resources and coordinate actions in order to transform grievances into political mobilization.

[50] Walter W. Powell and Laurel Smith-Doerr, "Networks and Economic Life," in *The Handbook of Economic Sociology*, ed. Neil J. Smelser and Richard Swedberg (Princeton: Princeton University Press, 1994), p. 369.

[51] Podolyn and Page also use "form of governance" to differentiate network forms. See Joel M. Podolyn and Karen L. Page, "Network Forms of Organization," *Annual Review of Sociology* 24 (1998), 57–76. Also, see Powell and Smith-Doerr, "Networks and Economic Life," pp. 369–70.

[52] Mark Granovetter, "Economic Action and Social Structure: The Problem of Embeddedness," *American Journal of Sociology* 91(November 1985), 491.

Case design and method

The argument outlined above rests on empirical research primarily conducted during two separate stays in Tehran, one from June 1999 to August 1999 and the other from September 2000 to July 2001, as well as several shorter subsequent visits. While the general research puzzle, the case study, and time period were selected beforehand, the nature of my topic precluded precise deductive theorizing; the arguments laid out here are products of inductive analysis of the data collected.

Why the Tehran Bazaar?

The Tehran Bazaar is primarily a wholesale and import–export market-place. In comparison with provincial and local bazaars, the Tehran marketplace is involved in large-scale commerce, putting it more immediately in contact with government agencies and making it directly susceptible to changes in trade policies. The capital's Bazaar, rather than its smaller provincial counterparts, captures better the transformative powers of the central government's influence. Finally, for at least four decades the Tehran Bazaar has consisted of at least 20,000 traders, service workers, and employees from diverse ethnic, religious, and class backgrounds. Thus, unlike village settings that enjoy the advantages of small size and often cultural homogeneity, the bazaar in Tehran is a highly complex case where one can investigate the creation, reproduction, and demise of community, collective action, and informal institutions under less restrictive parameters. Social scientists have studied the conditions for the persistence and success of self-government, communalism, and collective action in rural and homogeneous settings,[53] but attempts have not been made to extend these issues to more complex sites, such as economies in large metropolitan settings.

Second, even though Tehran's Bazaar does not enjoy the majestic architectural quality of Istanbul's or Isfahan's grand bazaars, or the historical legacy of its counterparts in Cairo or Aleppo, by virtue of its numerous private trading companies distributing imported goods throughout the country and consolidating goods for export, it boasts an economic centrality unparalleled by other marketplaces in the region. The Tehran marketplace combines import–export, wholesale, and retail

---

[53] Elinor Ostrom, *Governing the Commons* (Cambridge: Cambridge University Press, 1990); Robert C. Ellickson, *Order without Law: How Neighbors Settle Disputes* (Cambridge: Harvard University Press, 1991); Jean Ensminger, *Making a Market: The Institutional Transformation of an African Society* (Cambridge, MA: Cambridge University Press, 1992).

operations with large money-lending networks that provide credit to members of the Tehran Bazaar, as well as private firms in the manufacturing, construction, and service sectors located all over Iran.

Nevertheless, the Tehran Bazaar has not been commonly studied. Empirical research focusing on bazaars is typically conducted by anthropologists, geographers, and historians. Only rarely have sociologists and political scientists studied Middle Eastern central marketplaces.[54] Given anthropologists' and geographers' empirical focus on studying more primitive and unadulterated native worlds, most studies of Iranian bazaars have been conducted on bazaars in more provincial and older cities, like the ones found in Kashan, Yazd, or Shiraz. Historians have paid less attention to the Tehran Bazaar, since it only acquired its primacy after World War I. One of the main motivations for my selecting the Tehran Bazaar is that despite its significant and central position in Iran's economy we have hardly begun to understand it.

Temporality: synchronic and diachronic analysis

Time is bifurcated in Iran. There is a "before" (*qablan*) and a "now" (*alan* or *hala*), with the future (*ayandeh*) being obscured by unpredictable machinations. A bewildering array of topics, including the price of goods, stature of the religious establishment, population of cities, level of air pollution, and quality of pastries, are commonly analyzed by comparisons between "before" and "now."[55] Popular commentaries propose that changes are products of ideological, geopolitical, sociocultural, and macroeconomic forces, with many of my interlocutors contradicting C. Wright Mills's adage that "men do not usually define the troubles they endure in terms of historical change and institutional contradiction."[56] Like many societies, older generations treat the "before" as a golden age and lament its permanent loss, while younger Iranians, who often doubt the perfection of the past, seek to transform the present and prefer to compare the current situation with ideals (and only rarely Iran's neighbors). The difference in Iran is that the transformation

---

[54] A notable recent exception is Singerman, *Avenues of Participation.*

[55] For an example from the Bazaar context see *Asnaf* no. 22 (Ordibehest 1373 [May 1994]), 38–40. *Asnaf,* the official magazine of the Association of Guild Affairs, concluded that the economy has not worsened when one accounts for issues of equality and dependence on external actors. It labeled the welfare of the Pahlavi era as "artificial welfare" (*refah-e masnu'i*) and "false welfare" (*refah-e kazebi*). Also, *Asnaf*'s interviews with members of various trade associations all begin with a question about the problems and situation prior to the Revolution and after the Revolution.

[56] C. Wright Mills, *The Sociological Imagination* (London: Oxford University Press, 1959), p. 3.

between these two eras is marked by a well-defined dislocation – the Islamic Revolution.

Researchers, nonetheless, have not followed this periodization in their analyses of Iran. In its place, much ink has been spilt to debate the causes of the Shah's downfall, the political forces involved in bringing to power the Islamic Republic, or the consequences of policies since 1979. Comparison does enter these works, but it does so in order to evaluate the Iranian Revolution in light of the experiences of other revolutionary episodes, typically the French, Russian, and Nicaraguan cases.[57] On the other hand, we have few comparisons of Iranian society before and after the revolutionary juncture.[58] Social scientists in Iran have probably shied away from this topic because of its political implications and their colleagues outside Iran tend to eschew this approach because of inconsistent and incomplete time series data, difficulties in conducting field research in Iran, and generational and political divisions among Iran experts. By temporally segmenting the historiography of modern Iran, scholars have subsumed questions about process and rupture, or continuity and change.[59]

I have designed the project to isolate and interpret particular events, processes, and suppositions about the Bazaar and its interactions with the state by investigating the impact of the Revolution on the Bazaar. I have specifically framed my case study around historical comparisons, believing that revolutionary upheavals are fruitful episodes for social scientific study since they serve as "natural" experiments wherein state–society relations are radically altered.[60]

[57] Misagh Parsa, *States, Ideologies, and Social Revolutions: A Comparative Analysis of Iran, Nicaragua, and the Philippines* (Cambridge: Cambridge University Press, 2000); Farideh Farhi, *States and Urban-Based Revolutions: Iran and Nicaragua* (Chicago: University of Illinois Press, 1990); and Said Amir Arjomand, *The Turban for the Crown: The Islamic Revolution in Iran* (New York: Oxford University Press, 1988).

[58] Exceptions include Asef Bayat's study of the plight of Iran's urban poor, Ziba Mir-Hosseini's study of family courts, and Hooshang Amirahmadi's study of the macroeconomy. Bayat, *Street Politics*; Ziba Mir-Hosseini, *Marriage on Trial: A Study of Islamic Family Law* (London: I.B. Taurus, 1993); and Hooshang Amirahmadi, *Revolution and Economic Transition: The Iranian Experience* (Albany: State University of New York, 1990).

[59] It should be noted that continuity is emphasized by Marxist and more specifically world systems, approaches. Also, scholars in Iran, as well as reformist politicians, tend to understand the persistence of authoritarianism, economic stagnation, and limited civil society as a product of strong historical tendencies. Conversely, the official discourse of the Islamic Republic accentuates discontinuities, while maintaining that shortcomings (e.g. economic decline) are repercussions of the old order. Following the exact same logic, but with different ends, monarchists interpret the two eras as completely discontinuous.

[60] On strategies of periodization see Evan S. Lieberman, "Causal Influence in Historical Institutional Analysis: A Specification of Periodization Strategies," *Comparative Political Studies* 34 (November 2001), 1011–35.

To understand historical trajectories we have two general and complementary methods of study: one that is synchronic and is a comparison at different historical moments, and another that is diachronic and traces processes through time. In the first instance, a case (e.g. a state, cultural practice, or economic form) is evaluated at two separate points in time in order to identify and explain the structural changes. This temporal comparison is in fact a synchronic analysis in the guise of a diachronic approach, with each time period being treated as an isolated and distinct case. (You may think of this as treating the case at $t1$ and $t2$ as distinct observations representing variations in the dependent variable.) This approach is not particularly useful in addressing questions about process, dialectical relations, and sequence of events and may even lead to teleological and over determined accounts. However, it is an expedient means to engage in case study comparison for it holds many variables, such as cultural factors or position in the world economy, reasonably constant. This case design lends itself to macrolevel research where the dependent variable is analyzed in the context of transformations in policies, institutions, and relations, resulting in a description that measures the overall variation and shift in parameters.

The diachronic method analyzes the interaction between variables through a defined time frame (from $t1$ to $t2$). Here the processes and mechanisms that engendered the transformation in the dependent variable are the units of analysis. Rather than structural forces, the diachronic approach identifies sequences of events, intermediary variables mediating structural shifts, and bargaining between groups as critical factors. By stressing hermeneutics, this approach may introduce a large number of factors and contingences alongside a causal argument. Yet, diachronic perspectives are critical for comparing and differentiating causal chains that lead to the same outcome and often demonstrate the multiplicity of paths to a single outcome. Also, tracing these processes will remind us that our worlds consist of continuities as well as discontinuities.

By consciously applying these two approaches to study change, one can shift back and forth between the trees and the forest. The synchronic approach is privileged in Chapters 3 and 4, in which I compare the form of network governance of the Tehran Bazaar and the transformation of the state in the two general eras (1963–79 and 1979–2000). In Chapters 5 and 6 the three selected sectors within the Tehran Bazaar and the variations in the Bazaar's capacity to mobilize, are analyzed by taking a more diachronic approach to evaluate alternative frameworks by investigating the sequence of events.

Finally, I have chosen a time frame (1963–2000) in order to hold several key variables constant. First, the historiography is in agreement

that Iran's modern rentier state was established in 1963 when the price
and production of crude oil steadily began to increase and constitute the
bulk of the state's budget.[61] The petro-dollar economy, with all its
virtues and shortcomings, began to develop in 1963 and has persisted
uninterrupted until today. In terms of political rule, 1963 is also a
useful starting point. Owing to foreign interference, democratic and
separatist movements, and the inexperience of the young Mohammad
Reza Shah, the period from 1941 to 1963 was marked with political
instability and uncertainty. It was only after 1963 that the central state
reestablished its supremacy and the monarchy's autocratic rule was
fully imposed through strict control over the press, parliament, and
political parties.

Data collection

As already mentioned, secondary sources on the Tehran Bazaar, and
Iranian bazaars in general, are sparse, not comprehensive, and not
directly related to my research questions. Thus, in order to make valid
descriptive and causal inferences, I needed reliable and accurate indicators of key variables. No such data are readily available, and as a
result, it was necessary to generate my own data and take into account
interpretive matters. The methodological goal during my field research
was to tap into a wide variety of primary sources, especially ones that
could capture the workings of the Bazaar. I used various forms of
interviews, participant observation, and primary and secondary documents, including surveying newspapers and dissertations and theses
written in Iranian and U.S. universities. Appendix 1 provides a fuller
treatment of various aspects of the field research.

This book follows a thematic rather than a chronological format. The
next chapter presents a brief historical background, a typology of the
literature on bazaars and markets more generally, and outlines my
approach to bazaars that views them as embedded networks. Chapter 3
details the variation in the form of governance between the Pahlavi
monarchy and the Islamic Republic by describing the commercial,
financial, religious, and social bases of these networks and the mechanisms
that reproduce them. It pays particular attention to how the Bazaar's

---

[61] Homa Katouzian describes the post-1963 era the "Petrolic Despotism." Homa
Katouzian, *The Political Economy of Modern Iran 1926–1979* (New York: New York
University Press, 1981). For similar periodization see Ervand Abrahamian, *Iran:
Between Two Revolutions* (Princeton: Princeton University Press, 1982), p. 426.

cooperative hierarchies, unlike coercive hierarchies, generated a reputation system able to appraise reputations, sanction behavior, and inculcate cooperative norms and a sense of solidarity. Chapter 4 explains why this shift occurred, arguing that the particular transformative programs of the two regimes generated different forms of governance in the Bazaar by altering the institutional and physical setting of networks. Chapter 5 traces the dynamics in the structural change in the hand-woven carpet sector, tea sector, and the china and glassware sector. These narratives show that the sectors, although all moving from cooperative to coercive hierarchies, followed different trajectories because of contingencies related to the particular nature of the commodities traded and the institutional patterns negotiated by the state and *bazaari*s, rather than mere presence or absence of the state in the economy. Chapter 6 considers how the Bazaar's structure relates to its capacity to mobilize against the state. It presents a summary of the literature that focuses on Islam and the clergy as the explanatory factor for the Bazaar's vigilance against state encroachment, and through a re-reading of the historical record shows that this prevailing view cannot account for various dimensions of *bazaari* mobilization. I return to my discussion about cooperative and coercive hierarchies to posit that the transformation in the form of governance accounts for both high levels of mobilizing capacity during the Pahlavi era and lower levels under the current regime. I conclude by drawing out the broader implications of the analysis for the study of state–society relations, and Iranian politics in general.

Appendix: Methods of Data Collection and Evaluation

This appendix makes the research process more transparent for the reader and forces me to self-consciously reflect on how information for this project was collected and evaluated. Specifically, data were gleaned from several different types of interviews, participant observation, and various primary and secondary texts. The bulk of this research took place during fifteen months of field research including stays in Tehran in the summer of 1999 and from August 2000 to August 2001, when I also made short visits to Dubai, UAE, and Hamburg, Germany, to conduct interviews with Iranian merchants.

Interviewing

My main method was in-depth interviewing of *bazaari*s using closed and open-ended questions. The interviewing process was not a simple affair. Public opinion polling and surveying are not well-established practices in Iran, where authoritarian governments from the shahs to the mullahs have tended to abuse such information to the detriment of the people – or at least that is how it is perceived. Gathering information about *bazaaris* is especially difficult since, as part of today's limited private sector, they are often avoiding taxes and involved in strictly illegal activities. Strolling into a shop and declaring myself a researcher was not the best method of soliciting information, let alone engendering trust and cooperation, from the cautious *bazaaris*.

I gained access to *bazaaris* through what is known as the "snowball sampling method." In contexts where members of a community know each other and entry into the group is difficult (e.g. local elites, insular minorities, drug addicts in a neighborhood), access is gained by identifying a few members to refer you to further members, who in turn direct you to other members, and so forth. This entails using a few initial contacts to generate further interviews via referrals and thus create entry points into the community. Through previous contacts I established six independent entrées into the Bazaar. In turn, as I met these *bazaaris*, explained my project and earned a level of trust, I asked them to introduce me to other members of the Bazaar. The snowballing system was quite effective since references and interpersonal relations are a critical means of gaining access to information and earning trust. In this manner, I was directed through networks of relatives and commercial partners. A simple mention that I was so-and-so's friend would usually solicit cooperation. On some occasions my interviewees would call on my behalf to arrange for an appointment, write a letter of introduction, or personally take me to their colleagues. Over time and by following the leads established by the initial contacts, I was brought into contact with a large number and relatively disparate group of *bazaaris*.

To reassure interviewees that evidence was not going to be used against them, all names of interviewees are strictly confidential.[62] Moreover, I typically did not tape record interviews. In cases when I felt that it would not alter the content of the interview, I requested permission to tape the interview. Most interviews were conducted with me simply jotting down important phrases, dates, and names during the

---

[62] Although all interviews were entirely confidential, *bazaaris* were generally wary of discussing their personal finances and specifics of their business practices. Thus, I did not solicit information about their income, assets, and specific investments. On several occasions *bazaaris* made references to land and real estate they owned, but I never sought to systematically gather financial information. Also, sensitive political topics (allegiances to particular parties or political personalities, views on the legitimacy of the Islamic Republic, or specifics of their political activity during the Revolution) were pursued only after a rapport was established or if the information was volunteered.

session. Then, after the interview was completed I would write down the discussion in detail.[63]

It should be noted that although I used interviews with individual *bazaaris*, the unit of my analysis is not the individual. Rather it is the Bazaar (or sectors) at different points in time. Thus, unlike most survey research or projects based on interviews, the data collected from these interviews were not used to understand and explain variation at the individual level, but rather the sets of relationships, practices, and institutions that constitute the Bazaar. Nonetheless, it is still important to pause here and identify the drawbacks of this type of snowball sampling. Ideally the snowball method will lead to interviewing all members of a group. In the context of the Tehran Bazaar, a large differentiated society, this is not feasible and interviews were only a sample. Second, since my initial contacts (or sample) were not random, and the subsequent references were most definitely not random, this introduces the problem of selection bias at the level of sources,[64] wherein members of the Bazaar are not interviewed randomly (if I were to conduct regression analysis I would have to be concerned with the potential for creating autocorrelation between observations and error terms between the observations that are greater than zero). Thus, in order to guard against selection bias in sources, I used multiple and independent initial entrées. More important though, the overall bias involved in the interview pool was mitigated by the use of different interviewing techniques and other methods to check facts. As a general rule, I have followed the journalist's rule of securing an absolute minimum of two independent and credible (preferably primary) sources for each fact. At face value this seems like a modest bar for fact checking, but it proved to be a high enough bar to weed out much information.

Three types of interviews were conducted within the Bazaar:

Structured interviews were arranged in advance and typically took place in the Bazaar. The interviews consisted of preplanned questions that solicited basic information about the interviewees' business and work history as well as a series of more open-ended questions about their views of the state's role in the economy, the changes in the Bazaar structure, and policy prescriptions. Interviews ran from thirty minutes to

---

[63] I attempted to write up my notes immediately after the interviews were finished; however, this was not always possible and often the interviews and discussions were recorded only later. Thus, quotes in the manuscript are not always exact and should not be treated as verbatim.

[64] Ian S. Lustick, "History, Historiography, and Political Science: Multiple Historical Records and the Problem of Selection Bias," *American Political Science Review* 90 (1996), 605–18.

an hour and a half, and at the end of each interview I sought referrals for additional interviews.

Follow-up semi-structured interviews were conducted in almost all cases. These interviews, which were often not prearranged, were by far the most fruitful encounters and provided the bulk of the qualitative material. They consisted of (1) thanking the interviewee for their initial cooperation, (2) verifying information gathered in the initial meeting, (3) fact checking information from other sources, (4) gathering oral histories from older *bazaaris*, and (5) soliciting more information in areas that the interviewee felt were important and where I believed they had special knowledge. These informal interviews occasionally took place in front of other *bazaaris* who would also participate. The presence of other people (apprentices, customers, colleagues, relatives, or my friends) added a new dynamic, introducing new topics or different presentations of issues. This allowed me to evaluate information and identify sensitive topics. The length of these follow-up interviews ranged from fifteen minutes to several hours and ideally entailed several meetings. Fortunately for me (but unfortunately for my interviewees), business was hardly brisk during my fieldwork stay, and merchants had time to discuss matters.[65]

Random interviews were conducted in order to offset the potential for sample bias involved in the snowballing method. These consisted of spontaneous discussions with members of the Bazaar. I would briefly explain who I was and my research and then sought to ask questions from the structured interviews. The quality of response was highly variable and interviews ran from a couple of minutes to half an hour. If the interviewee was busy, but seemed genuinely interested in participating, I would arrange for a meeting at a future date.

At times, I will refer to statements made by *bazaaris* in a preliminary survey. This is because initially I designed a pilot survey and planned to distribute it during interviews. The questions were derived and tested during a research trip in the summer of 1999. Thirty-two surveys were completed. However, this method was highly unsuccessful since (1) most *bazaaris* were wary of the written method and (2) they viewed this as too time consuming. On a number of occasions I was told that they would answer all my questions and more, if I put away "that paper." Consequently, the survey was abandoned and the questions were subsumed into the various interviews.

Interviews with non-bazaaris involved shopkeepers and wholesalers outside the Bazaar area to gain a wider perspective on economic issues,

---

[65] Over time I was able to identify the best days (Saturdays) and times in the day (early afternoon) to conduct interviews.

uncover how the Bazaar was viewed by other commercial actors, and check information from interviews in the Bazaar. Also, included in this category are the interviews I conduct during a one-week trip to Dubai in May 2001. There I met a number of Iranian businessmen who operated import–export businesses between Iran and the UAE, some of whom had been based in the Tehran Bazaar. In December 2000, I spent one week in southern Iran and visited two of the three free trade zones (Qeshm and Kish) and several ports (Bandar Abbas, Bandar Lengeh, and Bandar Charak). I interviewed merchants and locals involved in legal and quasi-legal trade between the free trade zones and Iran. Next, I spent a week in the Hamburg free port, where a large concentration of hand-woven carpet trade houses is located. I conducted a dozen interviews with carpet merchants who had experience in the Tehran Bazaar or worked with relatives and partners there. Finally, to hear the views of government officials and associations related to commerce, I interviewed several officials who are, or were, members of the Chamber of Commerce, Ministry of Commerce, Association of Guild Affairs, Organization of Planning and Budget, Central Bank, Tea Organization, trade associations, and Islamic associations in the Bazaar.

Participant Observation

Another component of my data collection was participant observation, or direct and prolonged observation. My particular variant of participant observation can be described as passive participant observation. I did not fully participate in the lives of *bazaari*s, in the sense that I did not live with a *bazaari* family during my research trip, nor did I work inside the Bazaar, nor am I a "native" *bazaari*. Nevertheless, during my time in Tehran, I spent three to five days a week in the Bazaar. A large portion of this time involved gleaning information indirectly by "soaking and poking." I spent hours in the Bazaar consciously observing and conversing with *bazaari*s about all types of issues, many of which did not directly pertain to my research questions.

My participant observation took several forms. While I was in the Bazaar's stores and offices, I observed how *bazaari*s interacted with colleagues (competitors, suppliers, and buyers), customers, apprentices, friends that I brought to the Bazaar, and me. These interactions were useful because they allowed for open and interactive discussions. Having lunches with *bazaari*s, either at restaurants or in their offices, proved to be a friendly and more relaxed forum for conversations about various issues not always raised in the structured interviews. To remind me of the importance of meals, one *bazaari* mentioned, "we [*bazaari*s] are of the stomach as well as of the bazaar." In addition, commuting with *bazaaris* to the Bazaar both in the express bazaar buses (*autobus-e vizhe*) and the shared cabs was an important way to engage with *bazaaris*. Since I traveled to and from the Bazaar at peak travel hours, the buses and shared cabs were full of *bazaaris* (the Bazaar is in the restricted traffic zone and many *bazaaris* do not drive to work; rather they either take public transportation or cabs to the Bazaar).[66] In Iran, public transport often is transformed into a public space for anonymous venting – men and women use it as a forum to complain about the economy, discuss the day's headlines, or simply share the latest news about the price of the dollar or a kilo of chicken. The cabs and buses to and from the Bazaar were no different and on several occasions my cab rides turned into discussions with businessmen about Iran's political economy. My note taking, newspaper reading,[67] or perusing of material on the Bazaar at times fueled the conversation. On two occasions, I conducted interviews on the express bus after *bazaaris* noticed that I was reading material that they found interesting or noticed that I was busily jotting down notes. Finally, on a few occasions, I participated in extra-bazaar activities with *bazaaris* in their homes and at social gatherings. For instance, I went to the Tehran Bazaar for the religious gatherings commemorating the martyrdom of Imam Hosayn (*tasu'a* and *'ashura*).

Participant observation played an important role in developing and substantiating my arguments. First, participant observation is a useful method of understanding how actions are patterned – that is, the structure of activities. Mitchell Duneier comments that because most life is structured, "this is why investigators ... sometimes can learn about a social world ... despite the fact we occupy social positions quite distinct from the persons we write about."[68] Repeatedly observing the ways in which *bazaaris* relate to different people in various contexts was an excellent means to uncover the organization and relational foundations of the Bazaar.[69]

---

[66] With the opening of the metro and the station at the Bazaar in 2002 this dynamic has changed. When I was in Tehran in 2003 and 2005, I noticed that commute times were dramatically reduced, but the large, crowded, and more public metro and metro stations also seemed to reduce discussion.

[67] I was in Iran during a time when a number of independent and politically critical newspapers were being published. It was quite common for passengers to read newspapers in the shared cabs, discuss the latest topics, and, at times, let one another read the front-page headlines and articles. These newspapers were a useful excuse to start conversations.

[68] Mitchell Duneier, *Sidewalk* (New York: Farrar, Straus, and Giroux, 1999), p. 338.

[69] Richard F. Fenno Jr., "Observation, Context, and Sequence in the Study of Politics," *American Political Science Review* 80 (March 1986), 3–15.

A critical virtue of participant observation is that it allows researchers to learn the frames of reference and expressions of its subjects. Participating in open-ended informal conversations and overhearing discussions between *bazaaris* were important ways for me to learn how to pose my research questions in terms that were more intelligible to my interlocutors. The extended research time allowed me to fine-tune my questions and gave me multiple opportunities to pose the same question to the same person. Similarly, listening to conversations among *bazaaris* and having repeated interactions with the same subjects helped me to grasp what issues and critical episodes were important to *bazaaris*. Also, as I learned the speech pattern and jargon of *bazaaris*, I began to pose my questions in their own terms. Hence, I was viewed as a more legitimate researcher – one who may not be an "insider," but who was informed. For instance, during my first research trip I distinguished the stores in the Bazaar from those in the newer parts of Tehran by referring to the latter as the "new stores" (*maghazeha-ye jadid*). This term confused my interviewees. It was only after spending time in the Bazaar that I learned that the *bazaaris* differentiate these two groups by referring to them as *bazaaris* and *khiyabanis* (the adjectival form of street, or *Khiyaban*). As I began to use the Bazaar's terminology and their expressions, *bazaaris* noted that I was becoming *vared* (literally meaning "entered"), implying that I was becoming knowledgeable.[70] The modicum of legitimacy that this "knowledge" afforded me more informative and in-depth discussions.

Third, participant observation is a useful means to confirm that actions are compatible with the statements of interviewees. For instance, one *bazaari* mentioned to me that he did not buy goods from smugglers. Then one day as I passed his store I noticed that he was accepting a delivery from one of these dealers. When I asked him what had led him to purchase these goods, he acknowledged that he sometimes turned to these sources to replenish his inventory. Finally, my conversations with *bazaaris* during those months were an opportunity for me to solicit critiques of my ideas and have them engage with my hypotheses. Many of the ideas in this book were presented in their nascent form to *bazaaris* and evolved after our conversations about them.

I have relied heavily on participant observation, referred to a number of anthropological studies of bazaars and marketplaces, and used interpretive methods to conceptualize and identify group boundaries.

---

[70] On a couple of occasions, trying to become *vared* was problematic because subjects wondered why I cared so much about the Bazaar. I was asked whether this information was being collected for the tax collectors or the CIA.

But this work differs significantly from more orthodox ethnographies. Unlike most ethnographies, culture (as symbolic structures or meta-narratives that give meaning to actions) and subjectivities are not the focus of this study. Although changes in norms and expectations play a role in demonstrating the shift from cooperative to coercive hierarchies, my main concern is with how goods and services are traded, how state–bazaar relations are patterned, and how members of the Bazaar are able to mobilize to make claims against the state.

Also, the purpose is not "to give a voice to the native"; this may be a consequence, but it is not an objective as is often the case in ethnographies. Moreover, because ethnographies are based on the narratives of people, they tend to highlight contingencies of particular lives. Actors describe events in their lives as peculiar to their life stories. In his study of book and magazine vendors in New York's West Village, Duneier describes how subjects tend to see themselves as if "they are authors of their lives."[71] He cautions against reproducing the overly agency-driven narratives, and he himself judiciously weaves and highlights structural-level transformations into the personal narratives. To balance this tendency toward isolating events and characters, I have related specifics of life stories to broader patterns of change, such as regime change, urbanization, and demographic shifts. At the same time an overly determined view of structural change is problematic, because we must have evidence of how large-scale structural forces are determinative in actual lives. Participant observation and interviewing identify concrete ramifications of these meta-level adjustments. The combination of different structural forces, resistance to them, and methods of negotiating new terrains trigger unplanned results. I make a concerted effort to place the internal operation of the Bazaar in the larger political economy by what I term a double embedding of actions – embedding–actions in networks and embedding networks in political economies.

Primary and secondary texts

As a complement to these primary sources, I devoted a portion of my research time to comprehensively reviewing the secondary sources (primarily in English and Persian) and reading pre- and postrevolutionary daily newspapers and popular and academic journals. Among this type of textual analysis, *Asnaf* (Guilds), the internal publication of the Society of Guild Affairs of Distributors and Service Sectors of Tehran, provided valuable insights into internal debates and views during the 1990s. These secondary sources and historical accounts were

---

[71] Duneier, *Sidewalk*.

critical for verifying and contextualizing the oral histories that *bazaari*s told me. In addition, I consulted relevant interviews from the Iran Oral History Project at Harvard University. This unique collection focuses on elites and political history, yet it shed light on certain issues regarding the Pahlavi regime's approach to development and its relations with commercial associations. To construct the analysis of the Bazaar before the Revolution and check facts from my interviews, I turned to two unpublished ethnographic dissertations from the early 1970s. Gustav Thaiss, an anthropologist who conducted field research in 1967–9, studies the religious practices and symbolism in the Tehran Bazaar.[72] Howard Rotblat spent 1968–70 in Iran conducting research on the Qazvin Bazaar to investigate the changes and continuities in this provincial bazaar (Qazvin is 100 km from Tehran).[73] Despite the differences between my research questions and those of Thaiss and Rotblat, these two works contain rich glimpses into the prerevolutionary socioeconomic structure of bazaars, which I have extensively used in my description of the 1963–79 phase and have juxtaposed with my findings thirty years after their field research.[74] While in Iran, I also browsed the archives of dissertations and theses at Tehran University.[75] These dissertations were used both for factual information and as historical sources to gain insights into how the Bazaar has been depicted in the past few decades. These theses varied in focus and quality; however, as a collection they were quite informative. Gathering information from government sources proved difficult because public sources are scarce and often only general overviews of topics based on aggregate data. Nonetheless, several researchers in government-affiliated institutes kindly shared their research and provided important information. Finally, a number of official publications of trade and guild associations were reviewed.

---

[72] Gustav Thaiss, "Religious Symbolism and Social Change: The Drama Husain," Ph.D. dissertation, Washington University (1973).

[73] Howard J. Rotblat, "Stability and Change in an Iranian Provincial Bazaar," Ph.D. dissertation, University of Chicago (1972).

[74] Narges Erami, a Ph.D. candidate in the Department of Anthropology at Columbia University who is conducting research on the carpet producers in the Qom Bazaar, has kindly discussed her research findings with me in order to check and compare our findings on the contemporary situation in Iranian bazaars.

[75] I consulted theses from the Faculty of Social Sciences and the Faculty of Fine Arts at Tehran University and Shahid Beheshti University (National University). Notably, I was not able to find a single thesis on bazaars at Tehran University's Faculty of Law and Political Science.

2   Conceptualizing the bazaar

A complete victory of society will always produce some sort of "communistic fiction," whose outstanding political characteristic is that it is indeed ruled by an "invisible hand," namely by nobody.[1]

Hannah Arendt

Hajj Ahmad is a gruff middle-aged man with an appearance befitting a stereotypical *bazaari* – portly with an unshaven full visage, pudgy hands emblazoned with bulky carnelian rings, and a well-worn set of prayer beads constantly in motion. His head and eyebrow gestures were expressive, and his measured words betrayed his Azeri roots. I met him at an early stage in my research on the Tehran Bazaar during the summer of 1999. A carpet seller who dabbled both in production and export, he was quite willing to share his experiences and opinions. Over several cups of tea and cigarettes, he patiently and quite enthusiastically answered my questions about the carpet trade, all the while keeping a watchful eye on the happenings in the caravanserai. Since he was from a long line of carpet dealers centered in the Tehran and the Tabriz bazaars, I turned our conversation to the practices and life in the Tehran Bazaar. Immediately, however, our roles as interviewer and interviewee were reversed. Hajj Ahmad matter-of-factly asked, "What do you mean by the Bazaar?" I quickly responded by explaining that I meant this marketplace and not the broader abstract notion of the market.[2] Still unsatisfied he said that he understood that, and asked me whether I was referring to the building, the people in the Bazaar, the practices, or something else. Hajj Ahmad was well aware that the Bazaar is simultaneously innocuous and elusive. This chapter is an attempt to demystify the notion of bazaar and locate its guiding characteristics – a series of attributes that take us beyond "communistic fictions" and

---

[1] Hannah Arendt, *The Human Condition* (Chicago: University of Chicago Press, 1958), pp. 44–5.
[2] Like "market" in English, "bazaar" in Persian refers to both the physical place where exchange takes place and the abstract and metaphysical notion of "the market."

"invisible hands," and identify concrete relations as the producers of economic exchange and communal sensibilities.

"Bazaar" is a loaded and dense term. It and its adjectival form, *bazaari*, carry many layers of meaning in Persian and in English. It is a concept that can be used to depict a place, an economy, a way of life, and a class, and even to embody Iran, the Middle East, or the Islamic world. This multiplicity of roles and dimensions make bazaars a subject of architectural, anthropological, economic, sociological, historical, and political studies that either directly analyze bazaars or use them as an integral part of their representation of Middle Eastern societies. Moreover, it is one of those epithets, not unlike "rural" or "provincial," which conjures up ideals and stereotypes that embody both the pristine and the pejorative. For some, the bazaar and its inhabitants hark back to a pure and moral life, while others depict it as a bastion of mindless traditionalism and vulgar mercantilism. Moreover, western travelogues and popular culture envelop the bazaar's traditionalism with exoticism and otherness.

While the bazaar has taken on contradictory meanings and enjoys an important place in analyses of modern Iranian politics and economics, it does not always receive critical reflection. In many major works it continues to be undefined. Scholars, journalists, as well as the Iranian public take it as a matter of fact that the bazaar exists like it always has as a "meaningful entity."[3] When we speak of "the bazaar" it is assumed that we all know where and what it is. Thus, it simply escapes definition or conceptualization. For instance, Fariba Adelkhah, in her otherwise nuanced and revisionist work, does not define the bazaar or *bazaari*, terms that frequently appear in her anthropological study of post-revolutionary urban society.[4] Gustav Thaiss in his studies of religion in the Tehran Bazaar also leaves the bazaar undefined.[5] Howard Rotblat's thorough description and analysis of the Qazvin Bazaar also does not clearly specify what constitutes a bazaar. At various stages he equates it with a "marketing system," all types of commerce, and "traditional forms of organization."[6] Even non-Iran specialists writing for a general audience sometimes leave the bazaar undefined. In her

[3] "Meaningful entity" is a term used by Keddie to describe the Bazaar. Nikki R. Keddie, *Roots of Revolution: An Interpretive History of Modern Iran* (New Haven: Yale University Press, 1981), p. 268.

[4] Fariba Adelkhah, *Being Modern in Iran*, trans. Jonathan Derrick (New York: Columbia University Press, 2000).

[5] Gustav Thaiss, "Religious Symbolism and Social Change: The Drama Husain," Ph.D. dissertation, Washington University (1973).

[6] Howard J. Rotblat, "Stability and Change in an Iranian Provincial Bazaar," Ph.D. dissertation, University of Chicago (1972).

analysis of the Iranian Revolution, Theda Skocpol focuses on the bazaar as "the basis of political resistance," but vaguely describes it as a "socioeconomic world."[7] The vast majority of our knowledge about bazaars exists in two forms – assertions that take on mythic proportions or broad abstract statements placing bazaars within general theoretical approaches.

This chapter presents a brief overview of how bazaars have been conceptualized. While I will pay particular attention to the literature that focuses on Iranian bazaars, I will also integrate works on other bazaars and urban marketplaces in the Middle East and North Africa. Unfortunately, this literature does not constitute a clearly defined historiographic debate with conscious analytical jousting, yet some discernible strains exist. I begin with a very brief historical sketch of the Tehran Bazaar and then turn to summarizing the literature on bazaars using a four fold typology of conceptualizations – the bazaar as traditional, as a class, as informal networks, and as a product of informational scarcity. These four perspectives are not mutually exclusive and many scholars meld together aspects of more than one approach. This chapter shows that the existing perspectives on bazaars are limited in that they cannot fully account for change over time or variation within bazaars, and in many cases tend to be descriptive accounts labeling rather than analyzing phenomena. Finally, politics and the state enter the discussion only when the bazaar mobilizes against the state. Before and after these events, state policies and institutions are conspicuous by their absence.

I conclude by recasting the bazaar within the general debate over markets and economies. This conceptualization of the bazaar recalls the new economic sociology literature that posits embedded networks, rather than individuals, as the building blocks of economies. Thus, I define the bazaar as a bounded space containing a series of socially embedded networks that are the mechanisms for the exchange of specific commodities. This conceptualization builds on and integrates the insights of this diverse empirical literature, engages debates on economies, and relates the transformation of the Tehran Bazaar to questions about regime change and state–society relations.

A brief history of the Tehran Bazaar

By the end of the twentieth century Tehran became so sprawling and so central to Iran's political and economic life that it is hard to imagine it as

---

[7] Theda Skocpol, "Rentier State and Shi'a Islam in the Iranian Revolution," *Theory and Society* 11 (May 1982), pp. 271–2.

the modest town at the crossroads of the Silk Road and Indian highway; but that is what it was for much of its history. Tehran was still a sleepy town even in 1800, when the Qajar dynasty proclaimed it their seat of their government. Despite its newfound status as the capital, for most of the nineteenth century, Tehran played second fiddle to the more populous, economically prosperous, and politically vibrant Tabriz and Isfahan. Up through the 1870s, Tehran consisted of five compact quarters; there were three residential districts ('Awdlajan, Chaleh Maydan, and Sangelaj), the Arg or the royal citadel, and the Bazaar or the commercial quarter. The Tehran Bazaar, like most Middle Eastern marketplaces, was adjacent to the royal and administrative head-quarters, representing a fusion of palace and marketplace. Gradually, Tehran's status as the capital began to bring rewards, and Tehranis, including members of its Bazaar, benefited from increased security, capital accumulation, and an internationally recognized political standing. The city expanded in terms of population and size, and government investments in the Bazaar area helped improve and increase the number of caravanserais and shops.[8]

Then, in the first third of the twentieth century, political events transformed Iran into a centralized national state with Tehran as the seat of power. Clerics, *bazaaris*, and western-oriented intellectuals worked together to champion the Constitutional Revolution (1905–11) that sought to limit the powers of the monarchy and introduced the concept of consultative politics by establishing a parliament. After two decades of internal turmoil and imperialistic forays by the British and Russians, the first Pahlavi monarch, Reza Shah (1925–41), took control of the monarchy. The rather obscure military officer, whose coup and eventual crowning received positive reenforcement, if not outright support, from the British government, rolled back many of the gains achieved by the constitutionalists and established a centralizing state, with Tehran as the indisputable political and economic center of an Iran with increasingly defined borders. Reza Shah's military rapidly set out to impose the

---

[8] Histories of Tehran include H. Bahrambeygui, *Tehran: An Urban Analysis* (Tehran: Sahab Books Institute, 1977); Shahriyar Adle and Bernard Hourcarde, eds., *Tehran Paytakht-e Devist Saleh* (Tehran: Sazman-e Moshavereh-ye Fanni va Mohandesi-ye Shahr-e Tehran and Anjoman-e Iranshenasi-ye Faranseh, 1375 [1996]); and Naser Takmil-Homayun, *Tarikh-e Ejtema'i va Farhangi-ye Tehran*, vol. 3 (Tehran: Daftar-e Pazhuheshha-ye Farhangi, 1379 [2000]). For an account of the Tehran Bazaar in the latter half of the nineteenth century see Mansoureh Ettehadieh (Nezam-Mafi), "Baft-e Ejtema'i-Eqtesadi-ye Bazar-e Tehran va Mahalleh-ye Bazar, dar Nimeh-ye Dovvom-ye Qarn-e 13 h.q.," in *Inja Tehran Ast: Majmu'eh Maqalat Darbareh-ye Tehran 1269–1344 h. q.*, ed. Mansoureh Ettehadieh (Nezam-Mafi) (Tehran: Nashr-e Tarikh-e Iran, 1377 [1998]).

central government's authority by settling tribes, quelling separatist movements, and silencing oppositional groups and figures, such as republicans, clerics, communists, and Qajar-affiliated landlords. Simultaneously, Tehran ushered in national conscription, a taxation system, a state-controlled legal system, and state regulation of commercial and economic activities. The concentration of resources and facilities in Tehran and the creation of state monopoly firms in the 1930s, along with the relative decline of other economic centers (notably Isfahan, Tabriz, and Kashan), helped attract and concentrate commercial and industrial capital in Tehran.[9] The Bazaar that dated back to the seventeenth century was the logical magnet for economic activities.[10]

The Tehran Bazaar was, and continues to be, a dense collection of narrow arteries that make up an area exceeding one square kilometer and consisting of several kilometers of passageways. It is located in the exact same location as the Bazaar of the Qajar era. Since the 1930s, when Tehran's moat was filled and street planning based on a grid system was developed, the Bazaar has been clearly demarcated by the street system that borders it – 15th of Khordad Street (Buzarjomehri Street[11]) on the north, Mawlavi Street on the south, Khayyam on the west, and Mostafa Khomeini Street (Sirus Street) on the east (Map 2.1). Tehran's bazaar is immense, and in 1978 it was said to be the largest covered shopping area in the world.[12]

The Tehran Bazaar is in fact an amalgamation of tens of smaller bazaars, passageways, and caravanserais built between the mid-nineteenth century and the current era. Each sub-bazaar is typically named for the commodity that was historically produced and/or sold there (e.g. the Shoemakers' Bazaar, the Coppersmiths' Bazaar, or the Kebab sellers' Bazaar), the ethnicity, regional background, or religion of the *bazaari*s (e.g. the Kuwaitis' Bazaar, the Armenians' Caravanserai, the Zoroastrians' Bazaar, the Isfahanis' Bazaar), or the owner or benefactor of the building (e.g. Hajeb al-Dawleh Timcheh financed by Hajj Ali Khan Hajeb al-Dawleh [E'temad al-Saltaneh] or Amir Sara built by Mirza Taqi Khan Amir Kabir).

---

[9] Vahid Nowshirvani, *Encyclopaedia Iranica*, s.v. "Commerce in the Pahlavi and Post-Pahlavi Periods," p. 88.

[10] See Hajj Ladjevardi's memoir for an account of the expansion of economic activities in Tehran in the first half of the twentieth century and how many merchant families moved to Tehran. Manuchehr Farhang, *Zendegi-ye Hajj Sayyed Mahmud Lajevardi* (Lincoln Center, MA: Tahereh Foundation, 1990 [1974]).

[11] Prerevolutionary street names are in parentheses.

[12] Alan D. Urbach and Jürgen Pumpluen, "Currency Trading in the Bazaar: Iran's Amazing Parallel Market," *Euromoney* (June 1978), 115.

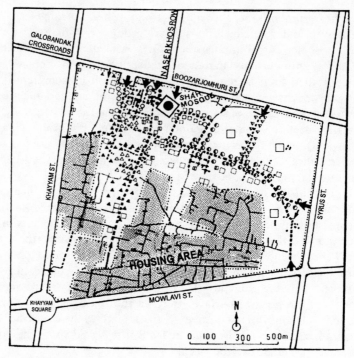

- ● JEWELLERS
- ▲ CARPETS
- ▲ CLOTH
- ○ SHOES & LEATHER
- ▣ PAPER & STATIONERY
- ▽ HOUSEHOLD UTENSILS
- ▼ IRON-METAL WORK
- ◀ MISCELLANEOUS
- ▥ COMMERCIAL OFFICES
- ▢ SERVICE STORAGE AREAS
- ▢ MANUFACTURING AREAS
- ⋯⋯BAZAAR BOUNDARY
- ▪▪▪COVERED BAZAAR
- ◀ ACCESS

Map 2.1 Tehran Bazaar circa 1970
Source: Martin Seger, *Teheran: Eine Stadtgeographische Studie* (New York: Springer-Verlag Wien, 1978), p. 98.

Each trade product sold or produced is localized in a particular sub-section of the Bazaar. The jewelers are housed in the Goldsmiths' Bazaar in the tributaries near the mouth of the Grand Bazaar, the cloth sellers are clustered in and around expansive Amir Sara, and those selling stationery supplies are in Bayn al-Haramayn Bazaar (sometimes

known as the Tinsmiths' Bazaar). Sometimes related trades were situated near each other. For example, the Shroud Sellers' Bazaar used to
be adjacent to the Gravestone Engravers' Bazaar. Today the Hajeb
al-Dawleh Timcheh brings together all goods related to kitchenware –
china and glassware, cookware, cutlery, thermoses, and electric kitchen
appliances.

While the Bazaar is spatially fixed, its contents have been fluid over
time. In many cases entire trades have moved within, as well as out of,
the Bazaar.[13] For instance, today you will be hard pressed to find a
shoemaker or seller in the Shoemakers' Bazaar.[14] The Ironmongers'
Bazaar has now become a center for the sale of dried fruits and nuts.
The booksellers, publishers, and binders also have left the Bazaar area.
After first relocating to the vicinity of the Bazaar, Iran's main booksellers
and publishers have moved more recently to the area surrounding
Tehran University,[15] and over time the booksellers' old place in the
Bazaar, the Bayn al-Haramayn Bazaar, came to be dominated by stationery suppliers. Markets, in general, have become more segmented.
This segmentation had the important social and political consequence of
bringing together less heterogeneous groups. Whereas during the first
half of the century the bookselling sector brought literary figures, publishers, book retailers, leather sellers, and printers together, today these
groups do not interact in one socioeconomic sphere. Finally, Martin
Seger's in-depth geographic study of the Tehran Bazaar from the 1970s
found that in general the Tehran Bazaar became a purveyor of more
expensive goods as rents and key money increased.[16]

As some of the names of these markets attest, the Bazaar was a site for
production and commerce. The decline in artisanal and small-call
manufacturing began with the emergence of industrial manufacturing and
urbanization in the 1930s and its escalation in the post-World War II
era. Many occupations, including metal smithing, shoe production,

---

[13] On the morphological shifts in the twentieth century see Martin Seger, *Teheran: Eine
Stadtgeographische Studie* (New York: Springer-Verlag Wien, 1978). There have been
important shifts in the neighborhoods adjacent to the Bazaar. For an account of how the
'Awdlajan neighborhood went from being a Jewish quarter in the 1950s, to a district
housing immigrants from northern Iran in the 1970s, and more recently to one that
houses Iraqi Shiites who fled during the war see 'Abdolreza Rahmani-Fazeli and
Mohammad-Reza Hafezniya, "Barresi-ye Tahavvolat-e Ekolozhiki va Zendegi dar
Bakhsh-e Markazi-ye Shahr-e Tehran," *Faslnameh-ye Tahqiqat-e Joghrafiyaii* 2 (Bahar
1367 [Spring 1988]), 58–76.

[14] However, the shoemakers' trade association continues to conduct its 'Ashura meetings
in the segment of the Bazaar called the Shoemakers' Bazaar.

[15] Sayyed Abolqasem Anjavi-Shirazi, "Hadis-e Ketab va Ketabforushi az Bazar-e Bayn
al-Haramayn ta ruberu-ye Daneshgah," *Adineh* 18 (20 Aban 1366 [1987]), 52–6.

[16] Seger, *Teheran*.

and publishing, progressively left the tight quarters of the central Bazaar and began to move away from the city center to where property values were less, transportation of heavy and bulky materials was less costly, and space was available for mass production of goods and large machinery. At first workshops moved from the central alleys (*qaysariyyeh*s and *dalan*s) and took over the residential areas in the southern and eastern regions of the Bazaar. However, throughout the 1970s and 1980s those workshops and the remaining residences were converted into warehouses, commercial offices, and retail shops. In a few cases, the state has stepped in to relocate trades in order to reduce pollution, but many of these shifts followed urban and market forces.

The history of a plot of land in the eastern section of the Bazaar illustrates these transformations. A paper wholesaler remembered that a shopping center (*pasazh*[17]), which he owned, was originally his family home. He was born during World War II in a house in the northeastern section of the Bazaar. In the 1950s, when his family left the house, small workshops and warehouses dominated the area, and then in the 1970s owners converted these units into commercial spaces. Through the 1970s as the traffic worsened and industrial regions in Tehran's western satellite cities and in the south expanded, many of the manufacturing activities left the central bazaar area and their buildings were taken over by commercial activities, predominantly international trade, wholesale, and brokerage, rather than retail. Today, the plot of land that used to be the paper wholesaler's family home is now a four-story commercial complex housing some forty small shops and offices.

To sum up, despite the morphological transformations within the Tehran Bazaar over the past century, the spatial continuity of the Bazaar has helped maintain continuity with the past. Trades and levels of economic activities have responded to changing socioeconomic forces and political initiatives, yet the Bazaar's boundaries have remained constant and have been reinforced by the grid system built around it.

Four conceptions of the bazaar

The bazaar as traditional type

The most prevalent depiction of the Iranian bazaar privileges general-ized cultural factors. This long-standing literature views the bazaar as

[17] *Pasazh*, from the French *passage*, is a contemporary term to describe shopping centers inside and outside the Bazaar. Ostensibly they are newer versions of *saras*. Outside of the Bazaar, *pasazh* can refer to larger mall-like shopping centers catering to wealthier Tehranis.

constituting a holistic way of life encompassing economic forms, political sensibilities, social relations, and ideological persuasions all of which fall under the rubric "traditional." This approach highlights the multifaceted nature of marketplaces and forces us to see the Tehran Bazaar as more than a purely economic sector.

Modernization theory, which dominated the social sciences in the United States during the post-World War II era, has influenced much of this literature.[18] In its most theoretically pure form, modernization theory was championed as a general theory of social change – social change being evidenced by changes in the social system as a result of changing values. The approach begins with the assumption that social systems, including political systems, are holistic, bounded, self-sufficient, and persisting units. Like biological and mechanical systems, social systems receive inputs (functions to be fulfilled) and produce outputs via structures, which in turn may feedback into the system. Hence, when inputs "modernize," the configuration of structures must adapt and integrate demands in order for the system to persist.

Modernization theorists view change as an organic procession from traditionalism to modernity. Traditionalism signifies values and cultural factors, including strong kinship ties, "simple" exchange, indirect forms of governance, and nonconsensual authority relations. Modernity, on the other hand, is conceived of as a set of values and personality traits, such as mobility, individuality, and entrepreneurial spirit, necessary for the modernization of society. This in turn translates into an evolutionary process marked by increasing economic growth, social complexity, differentiation in structures, and expanding demand and capacities of structures. Explicit in this formalization of change is the model of western experience as the universal model for change, both analytically and normatively. Lerner, for example, calls on Middle Easterners to study the western historical sequence to understand the steps and path to be taken.[19] It should be noted that the view of western development is uncontentious, unilinear, and not varying across the West. Therefore,

[18] Daniel Lerner, *The Passing of Traditional Society: Modernizing the Middle East* (Glencoe, IL: The Free Press, 1958); Gabriel A. Almond and James S. Coleman, eds., *The Politics of Developing Areas* (Princeton: Princeton University Press, 1960); Neil Smelser, "Mechanisms of Change and Adjustment to Change," in *Political Development and Social Change*, ed. Jason L. Finkle and Richard W. Gable (New York: John Wiley and Sons, 1966); and David Easton, "An Approach to the Analysis of Political System," *World Politics* 9 (April 1957), 383–400.

[19] Lerner, *The Passing of Traditional Society*, p. 46. Gabriel Almond writes, "The political scientist who wishes to study political modernization in the non-Western areas will have to master the model of the modern, which in turn can only be derived from the most careful empirical and formal analysis of the functions of the modern Western politics." Almond and Coleman eds., *The Politics of Developing Areas*, p. 64.

this account, like orthodox Marxism, is a convergence theory, with the end-point being the modern West.

Until recently, the majority of the scholarship on Iran followed the modernization theory approach. For Iran specialists, modernization theory is more a language and a descriptive schema than a systematic analytical tool, yet it is clearly the basic reference to understand socio-economic and political change. The proposition of these works is that Iran is transitioning from traditional to modern forms.

From within this framework the bazaar fits neatly into the category of traditional culture. The exact characteristics of the sources for this traditionalism are not delineated, but it is clear that authors working in this paradigm are implying that the bazaar is united by a generalized set of principles, shared set of norms, and outlook. One of the leading historians of modern Iran, Nikki Keddie, applies the traditional–modern duality to the Iranian case and situates the bazaar squarely in the traditional realm. By *bazaaris* she means

> not only those who had shops in the bazaar but also those who carried on retail and export trade and manufacture of *a traditional rather than a modern type*. Bazaaris are not a class in the Marxist sense, as they have different relations to the means of production; ... nonetheless the expression "bazaaris" has meaning in its involvement with petty trade, production, and banking of a largely *traditional or only slightly modernized nature*, as well as centering on the *bazaar areas and traditional Islamic culture*.[20]

Therefore, the bazaar takes meaning through its traditional type and nature, and is defined neither spatially nor by objective positions in a class system. In Keddie's conceptualization and other writings in this vein, it is unclear which structural or systemic factors define, produce, and regenerate the *bazaari* identity, activity, and culture. In lieu of analyzing the mechanisms behind this traditionalism, her analysis continues by aligning modernity with the West and juxtaposes the bazaar to it: "Most of them [*bazaaris*] are united in their resistance to dependence on the West and the spread of Western ways. Although Western goods are widely sold in the bazaars, the growth of supermarkets, department stores, large banks, and goods like machine-made carpeting that compete with Persian rugs added to Western control of Iran's economy and reduced the role of the bazaar."[21] This suggests that the cultural attributes of the bazaar are related to its position in the world economy. The relationships between these structures, however, are not stipulated and would necessarily have to be highly complex for a number of reasons

---

[20] Keddie, *Roots of Revolution*, p. 244, emphasis added.   [21] Ibid.

(e.g. the multitude of sectors within the bazaar relate to the world economy differently, *bazaaris* generally profited from the expansion of commerce in the 1960s and 1970s, and many members of the bazaar have had close ties with members of the so-called westernized sectors.)

Ahmad Ashraf, another prominent scholar of modern Iran, blends Weberian notions of patrimonialism and Marxist theory of asiatic modes of production to chart a historical trajectory for Iran that is distinct from the western capitalist path. Within his historical structural approach, Ashraf pays particular attention to the bazaar. For Ashraf "the bazaar has served as the cradle of the traditional urban culture in Iran, and has maintained and reproduced its cultural elements in the face of modernization and development."[22] Again such questions as which cultural elements make up this traditionalism and which mechanisms reproduce it are not explicitly addressed.

A possible mechanism underlying this analysis is Ashraf's proposition that the bazaar's character is shaped by its alliance with the mosque. For instance, in his comprehensive article in the *Encyclopaedia Iranica*, the bazaars' functions are listed: "The *bāzār* in the Islamic Iranian city has been (1) a central marketplace and craft center located in the old quarters of the town; (2) a primary arena, along with the mosque, for extrafamilial sociability; and (3) a sociocultural milieu of a traditional urban life style. The *bāzār* in contemporary Iran has performed two more roles of great significance; (4) a socioeconomic and power base of the Shi'ite religious establishment; and (5) a bastion of political protest movements."[23] Ashraf and many other scholars stress the close kinship and economic ties between the bazaar and Shiite clergy as well as the close physical proximity between the bazaar and seminaries and mosques (see Chapter 6). Hence, Ashraf concludes that the *bazaaris* and clergy "share certain similarities in their life-style and world view."[24] An American anthropologist who studied the Tehran Bazaar in the 1960s and 1970s states the religion-centered view more boldly:

The bazaar is a total social phenomenon and a corporate entity, and this corporateness is seen in religious terms. In fact, Islam ... is so comprehensive in the bazaar that it is explicit in almost all the idioms of social action. The formal religion, Islam, is the ideology of the bazaar community in an extreme way. With its high preponderance of individual "subsistence" operators, the bazaar community

---

[22] Ahmad Ashraf, "Bazaar and Mosque in Iran's Revolution," *MERIP Reports* 113 (March–April 1983), 16. Later in the same article he writes, "Most of the *bazaari* elements have maintained their traditional cultural mode of behavior and outlook."

[23] Ahmad Ashraf, *Encyclopdia Iranica, s.v.* "Bāzār: Socioeconomic and Political Role of the Bāzār," p. 30.

[24] Ibid., p. 31.

constitutes a proletariat under the leadership of the religious class, and provides the core of moral support for its more reactionary elements.[25]

Although the conclusion that the bazaar and religious belief and institutions are wedded will be discussed at length in Chapter 6, it is important to note that these views have not been systematically studied or substantiated, and the one-dimensional view of the bazaar as religious has recently been questioned.

One may think that the bazaar-as-tradition view is due to the macro-historical nature of these studies; however, the excellent field research by anthropologists and geographers often returns to this duality when they step out of their hermeneutics. For instance, in a unique and insightful study of Yazd's commercial units, Michael Bonine proposes, "If this title [i.e. *hajji*, or someone who has gone on a pilgrimage to Mecca] may be used as an outward sign of religiosity (as well as wealth), it appears that in Yazd, due to the similar percentages of *hajji*s, the same value systems operate on the avenue as in the bazaar. Hence, it may be incorrect to consider the bazaar as the derelict, traditional commercial area and the avenues as the progressive, modern zone."[26] Yet, Bonine concludes the essay by writing, "The avenues represent an extension of the bazaar system. Although there is less specialization and even some Western-type stores, a similar linear arrangement of small stalls, shop-keeper characteristics, and many other traditional facets characterize the commercial zones of the avenues. In many respects, the avenues are as traditional as the bazaar is modern."[27] While Bonine's empirical insights question the binary opposition of modern and traditional in comparing the bazaar and the street, his conclusions unfortunately frame his findings in this dichotomous manner. Similarly, Rotblat frames his analysis of the Qazvin Bazaar in the tradition of Parsonian systems analysis. However, once you go beyond the introductory chapter, the rich empirical analysis presents a far more complex scenario, with agency and relational factors being critical principles at work in his analysis of Qazvin's commercial sector, rather than the parsimonious equilibrating social systems assumed by modernization theory.[28]

---

[25] Brian Spooner, "Religion and Society Today: An Anthropological Perspective," in *Iran Faces the Seventies*, ed. Ehsan Yar-Shater (New York: Praeger Publishers, 1971), p. 171. Also see, Gustav Thaiss, "The Bazaar as a Case Study of Religion and Social Change," in *Iran Faces the Seventies*, ed. Ehsan Yar-Shater (New York: Praeger Publishers, 1971).

[26] Michael E. Bonine, "Shops and Shopkeepers: Dynamics of an Iranian Provincial Bazaar," in *Modern Iran*, ed. M. E. Bonine and Nikki R. Keddie (Albany: State University of New York Press, 1981), p. 249.

[27] Ibid., p. 258.

[28] Rotblat, "Stability and Change in an Iranian Provincial Bazaar." For example, in his excellent sociological study of the Qazvin Bazaar (a provincial bazaar 140 kilometers

This perspective allows these scholars to understand what they believe to be the persistence of attitudes and structures in the bazaar by definition; traditional implies inertia and a static nature. Rotblat's argument is quite typical of modernization theories: "[T]he persistence of traditional forms of organization in these marketplaces suggests that existing institutional patterns within the bazaars themselves also inhibit their adaptability to ongoing economic change and contribute to their present stagnation."[29] Tradition is a force that insinuates itself into the souls of individuals, altering the way they act. This mechanistic image has obvious pitfalls since culture is not a constant, but an ongoing process, continuously constructed and reproduced by interactions with its community, shaping it as much as being shaped by it.

The shortcomings of modernization theory in general, and the traditional–modern dichotomy in particular, are now well documented and I do not want to repeat them here.[30] Instead, I will briefly discuss how these shortcomings are reflected in the conceptualization of the bazaar as traditional. As the quotes above illustrate, the conceptualization of the bazaar as a bastion of traditional culture over-explains continuities and under-explains discontinuities in the bazaar. It is unclear why the bazaar's nature is tied to a structure encompassing economic, political, and social forms that are melded together in ways that render it impervious to international, national, and even city-level changes. Hence, in more crude works, this orientation has fostered a methodology that cites descriptions of the bazaar in the sixteenth century alongside those from the twentieth century without asking how and why this stasis has prevailed, assuming that it has. This approach is based on a circular argument: the bazaar is described as traditional, and the traditional is static; therefore the bazaar is unchanging. Second, changes in practices and organizations, such as those that I will identify, are left unexplored. The bazaar is tacitly juxtaposed to an ideal "modern

---

west of Tehran) he shows that in the 1960s there existed complex systems of credit and bookkeeping that allowed for the expansion and refinement of market activity. He also pays special attention to the specialized roles and differences between occupations and sectors within the Bazaar and points out how the Qazvin Bazaar differs from bazaars in other parts of Iran. Finally, he demonstrates how the Qazvin Bazaar was profoundly altered by external institutional changes.

[29] Howard J. Rotblat, "Social Organization and Development in an Iranian Provincial Bazaar," *Economic and Cultural Change* 23 (1975), 293.

[30] Empirical and theoretical critiques are presented by Brian Barry, *Sociologist, Economists & Democracy* (Chicago: University of Chicago Press, 1970); Reinhard Bendix, *Nation-Building and Citizenship: Studies of Our Changing Social Order* (Berkeley: University of California Press, 1977); Samuel P. Huntington, *Political Order in Changing Societies* (New Haven: Yale University Press, 1968); Leonard Binder et al., *Crises and Sequences in Political Development* (Princeton: Princeton University Press, 1971).

economy," liberal politics, and "rational society,"[31] with markets in industrial societies assumed to consist of rational, impersonal, and discrete transactions. Narrowly defined maximization of self-interest is said to be the sole motive and the mechanism that allows for markets to clear. This view of western markets has been largely undermined by empirical studies on industrial organization (see below). Finally, the bazaar-as-tradition perspective uniformly presents the bazaar as untouched by state policies, agencies, and agendas. The only moment when the state enters these accounts is when bazaars react negatively to it. In a sense, these authors reproduce the *bazaaris*' claim and desire to be independent and free of state interference. They simply accept that the bazaar is an entity that is impenetrable by state policies just as it is impermeable to socioeconomic changes.

A note on cultural representations of the bazaar

The representation of the bazaar and *bazaari*s in Iranian society would make for a fascinating literary and historical study. Here, I would like to simply touch upon the dominant strains of how bazaars are perceived in nonacademic texts and argue that they share the premises of what I have called the bazaars-as-tradition perspective. The popular views found in both western and Iranian accounts also treat the bazaar as a holistic way of life that fosters a unique set of symbolic structures, cultural traits, and ethics.

Whether in Iran or beyond its borders, the popular view of the bazaar presented in literary, journalistic, and cinematic treatments begins by relating the bazaar to the past. For instance, the bazaar is said to be "like an untouched relic" and it has remained the same "since time immemorial."[32] Not only are its buildings old, but it has "antique ways."[33] For western observers this timelessness represents the essential qualities of Iran, and the entire orient. Typical in this regard, a *New York Times* reporter writes: "If a single place captures the indefinable essence of life in the east, it's the bazaar – a seething irresistible warren of merchandise-laden stalls in twisting, unnamed lanes," and *bazaari* commerce and "mentality" is a fundamental component of Iranian life: "in olden time Persia had two national sports: polo and bargaining."[34] This view makes it into policymaking discussions too. In a cable sent in August 1979 from the U.S. chargé d'affaires to Secretary of State Cyrus Vance,

---

[31] Jennifer Alexander and Paul Alexander, "What's a Fair Price? Price-Settings and Trading Partnerships in Javanese Markets," *Man* 26 (September 1991), 493–512.
[32] *New York Times*, November 7, 1961.
[33] *Wall Street Journal*, November 30, 1978.
[34] *New York Times*, November 18, 1973.

the bazaar is used to evoke the "Persian psyche." The embassy official writes that in order to guard against "a pervasive unease about the nature of the world," Iranians develop a "bazaar mentality so common among Persians, a mindset that often ignores longer term interests in favor of immediately obtainable advantages and countenances practices that are regarded as unethical by other norms."[35]

But this essentialist reading and rendering of the bazaar is not limited to the occident. Many Persian-language magazine and newspaper articles on bazaars view them as abstract physical structures and speak of their historic architecture and centrality in urban life. Jalal Al-e Ahmad, a renowned essayist and proto-Islamist social critic, wrote a letter to the mayor of Tehran in 1958 complaining that he was destroying the character of Tehran's public spaces and replacing it with blind and second-rate imitations of western styles.[36] In the course of this emotional and scathing attack, Al-e Ahmad writes: "Destroy the arches of the bazaar, so we can use more Japanese sheet metal and Belgian and Russian glass. ... I am surprised that there is no one in this huge municipality that knows that the spirit and authenticity (esalat) of Tehran is the bazaars."[37] An article in the popular Talash magazine tells us that the "bazaar takes you to the past."[38] Meanwhile, a 1972 article published in the Yaghma, an intellectual monthly, first summarizes and quotes extensively from eighteenth- and nineteenth-century European travelogues, and then concludes, "If we take the bazaar from the city, it is as if we take the heart from a chest."[39] Oddly, even the mouthpiece of the Shah's ill-fated single party, the Rastakhiz newspaper, included an article that on the eve of the Revolution stated, "The eastern city without a bazaar is exactly like food without salt."[40]

While the bazaars' buildings are cherished as an emblem of a past, the people making a living in them have a more suspect standing in Iranian society. It is true that bazaaris are sometimes depicted as the symbol of a chivalrous and moral way of life grounded in Islamic ethics and more. But more commonly, the tradition and history of the bazaar is viewed as backwardness and its norms are greed and opportunism, with bazaaris,

---

[35] New York Times, January 27, 1981.
[36] This letter was republishsed in Shalamcheh, an ultra-conservative biweekly that frequently attacked the reformist Tehran mayor, Gholam-Hosayn Karbaschi. Shalamcheh 2, no. 13 (Mordad 1376 [August 1997]), 6–7 and 10.
[37] Ibid., 6.
[38] Shahrokh Dastur-Tabar, "Hojrehha-ye Qadimi, Bozorgtarin Markaz-e Dad va Setad-e Tehran," Talash 75 (Day 2536, 1356 [January 1978]), 57.
[39] Kazem Vadi'i, "Bazar dar Baft-e Novin-e Shahri," Yaghma 25, no. 1 (Farvardin 1351 [April 1972]), 16.
[40] Rastakhiz, 11 Ordibehesht 1357 [May 1, 1978].

like the petit-bourgeoisie and merchants under all skies, often ridiculed and chastised for being miserly, instrumental, gauche, and blindly bound to old ways.

The former image of the upstanding *bazaari*, principally held by some members of the bazaar and championed by some members of the Islamic Republic, begins by characterizing *bazaari*s as moral businessmen. They are always in good financial standing and stand by their word in all their dealings by placing their honor and reputation on the line. Knowing this, one would never think of requesting a signed document: "When a *bazaari* says that he will ship you a good, he will. There is no doubt in it," a *bazaari* said. Their moral order is couched in religious principles of justice and contractual relations. I was reminded by one particularly devout fabric seller that the Prophet Mohammad was a merchant, and I was thus to conclude that there was an inherent bond between Islam and commerce, that traders have a clear and impeccable model for their actions. Thus, Islamists describe the bazaar's economy as "Islamic economics."[41] The bazaar is not simply an architecturally historic site; it is an essential component of the "Islamic city."[42] For some supporters of the Islamic Republic, such as Asadollah Badamchian, the moral and Islamic nature of *bazaari* affairs and its organic relations with the clergy have naturally made the bazaar a force against despotism and for Islamic society and government.[43] In these studies the bazaar and *bazaari*s are typically modified by adjectives such as "Islamic" (*eslami*) and "eastern" (*sharqi*). Thus, not only is "The shopkeeper a friend of God," as the Prophet allegedly proclaimed, but the *bazaari* is a friend to the moral Islamic order.

A contradictory, but arguably more common view of bazaars is captured in the adage, "The bazaar is the sanctuary of the devil, and the *bazaari*s are the devil's army." For several decades now *bazaari*, as noun or adjective, has had a pejorative meaning in wider Iranian society. The disparaging of the *bazaari* begins with his physical appearance. In movies, newspaper caricatures, and literary descriptions, the *bazaari* is represented as a middle-aged, overweight, and physically unattractive man with "meaty and hairy hands."[44] He is unshaven, unkept, and wearing the same simple old clothes every day, and we are to infer that

---

[41] *Entekhab*, 13 Day 1379 [January 2, 2001].

[42] Abbas Moghaddam, "Bazaar – the Achievement of the Islamic Civilization: A Short History of the Tehran Bazaar," *Newsletter of Chamber of Commerce Industries & Mines of the Islamic Republic of Iran* (February 1994), 99–101.

[43] Speech given at the conference "The Bazaar in the Culture and Civilization of the World of Islam," Tabriz University, Tabriz, Iran, 28 September–1 October 1993.

[44] Sadeq Hedayat, *Hajji Aqa* (n.p.: Entesharat-e Javidan, 1356 [1977]), p. 16.

physical appearance is meaningless to him, with the pursuit of wealth an end in and of itself or a way to satisfy his greed and gluttony. Since he is old-fashioned and religious, he is often bearded and fingering prayer beads. He is shown calculating large sums of money on an abacus or pencil and paper, rather than a calculator or a computer. These large sums, moreover, are viewed as windfall profits derived from usury, for the *bazaari* is known to be unscrupulous, conniving, and materialistic. In Sadeq Hedayat's satirical *Hajji Aqa*, the main character is a rather despicable import–exporter.[45] Combining all the negative character-istics of a stereotypical merchant, Hajji Aqa is shown to be self-inter-ested, an opportunist, and miserly. Despite being extremely wealthy and enjoying baths and massages, for instance, he reduces his visits to the public bath when the price is increased.[46] In another section, we are told that he buys cotton and doubles the price without even seeing it.[47]

The general depiction of *bazaari*s as greedy and materialistic is pre-sent in Iranian cinema too. Amir Naderi's classic *Tangsir* depicts *bazaari* moneylenders as uncompromising and manipulative men who oppress the tragic hero.[48] Postrevolutionary films, which are imbued with a heavy dose of anticapitalism and condemnation of the wealthy, often present *bazaari*s as villains. In *Marriage of the Blessed*, Mohsen Makh-malbaf's surrealistic ode to veterans of the Iran–Iraq war, the tragically deranged veteran derides a *bazaari* for his passive support "behind the war front."[49] In one of the climactic scenes, the veteran taunts and mocks the *bazaari*, who has handsomely profited from the speculative war economy, by chanting "Forbidden (*haram*) bread is delicious!" This scene represents another popular criticism – that *bazaari*s' reli-giosity is only a façade, a public act to conceal immoral and un-Islamic acts. "*Bazaari*s are full of tricks and even in matters of faith they have ulterior and self-serving motives" may best sum up this accusation.

*Bazaari*s themselves reiterate these contradictory stereotypes. In my conversations some *bazaari*s lauded the "real" *bazaari* (often of the past) as being honest and principled in matters of business and charity, and protective in social matters. I was told that the true *bazaari* has a chivalrous ethic (*ma'refat*) and is socially aware so that he "sees beyond his own pocket." This *bazaari* is aware that trade, whether it is exporting carpets or selling teacups, is part of the national project to

[45] Ibid.   [46] Ibid., 44.
[47] Ibid., p. 50. For similar characterizations also see Anjavi-Shirazi, "Hadis-e Ketab va Ketabforushi az Bazar-e Bayn al-Haramayn ta ruberu-ye Daneshgah," 53.
[48] Amir Naderi, *Tangsir* (1973).
[49] Mohsen Makhmalbaf, *Marriage of the Blessed* (Farabi Cinema Foundation, 1989).

represent Iran in the best light in the world arena, all the while creating jobs for fellow citizens. Other *bazaaris* were more wary and cognizant of the negative connotations associated with the ways of the bazaar. For instance, several asked not to be called *bazaaris*; they preferred to be referred to as merchants (*bazarganan*), traders (*kaseb*), or businessmen (*biznesman*). This was particularly true among younger *bazaaris*. When one young tea trader in the Tehran Bazaar proclaimed that he was not a *bazaari* and was a businessman, his uncle chuckled and turned to me and said, "He is embarrassed to be called a *bazaari*, but that is what he is! He shouldn't be ashamed." Turning back to his nephew he added, "Don't worry, you'll get older, and you won't care what people think. You'll accept that you are a *bazaari*." Among carpet wholesalers in Hamburg, many of whom come from *bazaari* backgrounds, to say that someone's "behavior is *bazaari*" implies that he pays his debts late and that he tries to nickel and dime you.

Tradition is thus interpreted in inconsistent, even schizophrenic, ways in these common characterizations of the bazaar and the *bazaari* – authenticity, morality, miserliness, backwardness, and so forth. What unites this collection of images is that they all treat the bazaar as a holistic social sphere emerging out of a particular psychology or culture that works at the collective and individual levels. These views locate the bazaar in the traits and tastes of the individual and simultaneously deny any agency by homogenizing and reifying all those who are classified as *bazaaris*.

The Bazaar as a class

While Marxist concepts and terminology are often used by Iranian analysts, much work actually goes to show that Iran's conditions and development do not fit Marxist theory.[50] It generally does not trace shifts in modes of production or relate superstructural changes to the economic foundation. Instead, this Marxist-inspired literature is defined by its use of class as a unit of analysis, the privileging of economic variables, and the relating of modern Iranian history to world capitalist developments. When it comes to the bazaar, these scholars stress its economic role and class facets. Historically, the bazaar's incorporation

---

[50] For Instance, Bijan Jazani emphatically writes, "a bourgeoisie failed to develop in Iran as it did in Europe during the Middle Ages." Bijan Jazani, *Capitalism and Revolution in Iran: Selected Writings of Bizan Jazani* (London: Zed Press, 1980), p. 1. For a review and critique of Marxist studies of Iranian history, see Abbas Vali, *Pre-Capitalist Iran: A Theoretical History* (London: I.B. Tauris & Co., 1993).

of production and commercial activity, however, has made it difficult to relate class directly to modes of production, so works blend social and cultural forces to mediate the empirical complexities.[51]

Authors who are more dogmatic in their Marxist analysis, such as Bijan Jazani, describe the bazaar as a somewhat unified entity that is characterized by petit bourgeoisie tendencies; or in moments influenced by dependency theory, bazaaris are classified as the national bourgeoisie.[52] Hossein Bashiryeh's study of state–society relations during the twentieth century traces the various revolutionary movements within the context of the emerging world capitalist system and changing class alliances.[53] In this account, the bazaar's petty bourgeoisie standing is modified by various adjectives, such as "traditional" (p. 5), "national" (p. 11), and "Islamic" (p. 13). Hence, while these authors stress the economic and class dynamics of the bazaar, they inevitably turn to social and cultural aspects that are not included in or derived from economic forces.

Another characteristic of the bazaar-as-class framework is that it views the Iranian petit bourgeoisie as underdeveloped since Iran's capitalist system does not coincide with the western-based Marxist model of society. Sadeq Zibakalam has recently commented, "In short, it should be said that in Iran the bourgeoisie and *the capitalist strata have not developed.* In Pakistan and Turkey and other societies where the party system has taken shape, independent economic strata and layers came into being beforehand. In Iran this layer was never created ... ." But he is quick to add, "The only important and independent sector [in Iranian society] was the bazaar. That is why you see the bazaar playing an important role in political matters during the constitutional movement and the Pahlavi era."[54] Zibakalam attributes political activism to the bazaar, but his preceding statements imply that the bazaar acquires independence and political clout *despite* not constituting a real bourgeoisie. The reader is left wondering what mechanism enabled this class to play such a role in politics.

James Bill's *The Politics of Iran* is one of the few works that exclusively studies Iranian politics from a class and group perspective. His 1972 volume studies modernization in terms of class relations and the rise of

---

[51] Crossick and Haupt discuss how the trading class poses difficulties for most social theories, Marxist and Weberian alike. Geoffrey Crossick and Heinz-Gerhard Haupt, *The Petite Bourgeoisie in Europe 1780–1914* (London: Routledge, 1995).

[52] Jazani, *Capitalism and Revolution in Iran*, p. 36; and Mohammad 'Atiqpur, *Naqsh-e Bazar va Bazariha dar Enqelab-e Iran*, (Tehran: Kayhan, 1358 [1979]).

[53] Hossein Bashiriyeh, *The State and Revolution in Iran 1962–1982* (New York: St. Martin Press, 1984).

[54] Amir Nakha'i, "Tahazzob va Sakhtar-e Eqtesadi," *Jame'eh-ye Salem* 7 (Esfand 1376 [March 1998]), 29, emphasis added.

the professional-bureaucratic intelligentsia. Although the bazaar plays only a minor role in his analysis, he refers to the bazaar as the "symbol and center of activity" of the bourgeois middle class.[55] His class analysis is informed by modernization theory and he adds, "In contrast to Europe where important segments of the bourgeoisie became an early part of the ruling class, in traditional Iran few members of the bourgeoisie ever moved into upper-class ranks. In terms of power position, the bourgeoisie middle class has stood approximately between the bureaucratic and cleric middle class."[56] Bill places the bazaar in the middle of Iran's highly stratified class system, but beyond that he does not elaborate how its class position and inter class relations changed during the course of the twentieth century.

Ervand Abrahamian's meticulous study *Iran between Two Revolutions* begins by positing that politics is the interaction between political organizations and social forces. In turn, social forces are classes, but class as conceived by E. P. Thompson's historically specified conception of class.[57] Thus, Abrahamian traces shifts in the class structure across twentieth-century Iranian history, while focusing on how classes relate to one another and not only to the modes of production. Within this larger story the bazaar is a prime component of the social forces participating in social movements and placing constraints on the state. Abrahamian classifies the "bazaar community" during the post-1963 era as part of the propertied middle class, while in other sections it is referred to as part of the "traditional forces" or the "traditional middle class."[58] "Numbering nearly one million families this class [the propertied middle class] contained three closely knit groups," writes Abrahamian. "The first, which constituted the core of the class, was the bazaar community with almost half a million merchants, shopkeepers, traders, and workshop owners. The second was formed of fairly well-to-do urban entrepreneurs with investments *outside the bazaars*. ... The third group was made up of an estimated 90,000 clergymen. ... Although the second and third groups *were not bazaaris in the literal sense* of the term, strong family and financial ties linked them to the first group."[59] Thus, the bazaar exists as an economic class, but one that is more related to status and wealth than to the ownership of specific assets.

---

[55] James A. Bill, *The Politics of Iran: Group, Class and Modernization*, (Columbus, OH: Charles E. Merrill, 1972), p. 12.
[56] Ibid.
[57] Abrahamian, however, does not incorporate Thompson's moral economy approach into his analysis. Ervand Abrahamian, *Iran Between Two Revolutions* (Princeton: Princeton University Press, 1982).
[58] Ibid., p. 421.
[59] Ibid., pp. 432–4.

One important insight of Abrahamian's approach is the spatial attribute of the bazaar. Implicitly, Abrahamian's narrative posits a spatial component that unites *bazaari*s as a group and differentiates them from others. This is, at least, how I think we should interpret his statement that the urban entrepreneurs are "outside the bazaars" and that *bazaari*s have a literal meaning.

A more recent set of studies by Misagh Parsa also conceptualize the bazaar principally in class terms.[60] Parsa's important research investigates the causes of the Islamic Revolution through a resource mobilization model, and probably more than any other author, Parsa views *bazaari*s as the critical actors in the overthrow of the Pahlavi regime. Parsa broadly defines the members of the bazaar as capitalists or "traditional entrepreneurs." Since Parsa's concern is social mobilization, he is interested in why bazaars enjoy a high propensity for collective action. His response is that bazaars enjoy both abundant financial resources (stemming from their class position) and, not unlike Abrahamian, "social solidarity" emerging out of spatial concentration.

In short, the bazaar-as-class perspective reminds us that the bazaar first and foremost is an economic unit and as such plays a role in Iran's politics. However, much of this literature has not explained how the bazaar's class identity emerges and is reproduced. When scholars have addressed these issues, as in the case of Abrahamian and Parsa, their largely astute emphasis on space as a critical characteristic in defining the bazaars takes away the spotlight from their asset-based understanding of bazaars. More generally, Abrahamian's refinements of strictly economistic notions of class are an acknowledgment that classes are shaped by forces other than production. But because he includes such factors as "common interactions with the mode of administration" and "common attitudes towards economic, social, and political modernization" in his definition, the concept of class becomes so vague as to dull its analytical power.[61] Finally, as Sami Zubaida has pointed out, class analysis treats social solidarities as the "givens to the political sphere. Political institutions and processes themselves play little part in the constitution of political forces."[62] Thus, this line of analysis leaves us little space to ponder the reciprocal relationship between state

---

[60] Misagh Parsa, *Social Origins of the Iranian Revolution* (New Brunswick, NJ: Rutgers University Press, 1989). Misagh Parsa, "Entrepreneurs and Democratization: Iran and Philippines," *Comparative Studies in Society and History* 37 (October 1995); and Misagh Parsa, *States, Ideologies, and Social Revolutions: A Comparative Analysis of Iran, Nicaragua, and the Philippines* (Cambridge: Cambridge University Press, 2000).

[61] Abrahamian, *Iran between Two Revolutions*, p. 5.

[62] Sami Zubaida, *Islam, the People, and the State* (London: Routledge, 1989), p. 87.

institutions and the Bazaar's organization and its apparent solidarity –
factors that this study suggests are crucial.

The Bazaar as informal economy

The informal-economy perspective has recently emerged in studies of
urban marketplaces in the developing world. The central tenet of this
literature is that in the developing world the "self-organized" sector that
escapes the purview of state supervision is an untapped engine for
economic growth and already includes a substantial portion of enterprises, nonagricultural labor, the urban credit market, and the value-
added produced. Thus, orthodox evaluations of these economies are
unable to account for the unregistered productive and distributive
activities of the informal sector. Introduced in the late 1960s and early
1970s to study the urban poor in Africa, the hypotheses of the informal
economic literature have quickly been adopted by such organizations as
the World Bank and the International Monetary Fund to bolster their
neoliberal call for deregulation.

Since the mid-1980s an growing group of scholars working on the
Middle East have begun to use this concept to understand the urban
economies of the region.[63] For example, Diane Singerman claims that
the informal networks of central Cairo help "their members to penetrate
all levels of society, the economy, and the state."[64] Singerman is
interested in how the urban poor escape heavy-handed government
intervention and maneuver within Egypt's gargantuan bureaucracy.
Using ethnographic methods, she recounts how the urban poor tap into
informal networks to achieve individual needs and aggregate interests,
the latter role rendering them political. These "extrasystemic" networks, she argues, distribute goods and services based on shared values
or "familial ethos." Cairo's urban informal networks are described as a
cooperative and ameliorating force achieving common objectives based
on normative commitments and mutual reciprocity.

Guilain Denoeux is another political scientist who uses the concept of
informal networks to study Middle East urban issues.[65] He relates different types of networks to analyze urban social movements in Egypt,

---

[63] Nicolas S. Hopkins, ed., "Informal Economy in Egypt," *Cairo Papers in Social Science*
14(4) (Winter 1991).
[64] Diane Singerman, *Avenues of Participation: Family, Politics, and Networks in Urban
Quarters in Cairo* (Princeton: Princeton University Press, 1995), p. 173.
[65] Guilain Denoeux, *Urban Unrest in the Middle East: A Comparative Study of Informal
Networks in Egypt, Iran, and Lebanon* (Albany: State University of New York Press,
1993).

Lebanon, and Iran, including the bazaar. Denoeux identifies four basic types of networks – clientelist, occupational, religious, and residential – all of which are informal in that they lack written laws and regulations. His comparisons show that networks may play both stabilizing and destabilizing roles in the modernizing process and illustrate the complexities of modernization, with socioeconomic change eroding some networks, strengthening others, and leading to the emergence of others. Thus, he concludes that the traditional–modern dichotomy is analytically inadequate.

Among Denoeux's cases are the Iranian bazaar's "occupational networks." Not unlike the discussion in Chapter 3, for Denoeux the main unifying element of the bazaar is the series of occupational and social networks that helped shape a collective identity and preserve their unity. During the 1960s and 1970s, these ties were mechanisms that related the *bazaaris* to one another, allied them to the clergy, and mobilized them against the Pahlavi regime. Denoeux studies the prerevolutionary bazaar structure to show how it remained resilient and adaptable despite the socioeconomic changes of the post-World War II era.

These important recent works try to identify mechanisms that facilitate collective action by members of the urban economy against the state. They are able to see these areas as more than historical artifacts and instead study how they face modern concerns by resorting to local and everyday means of mobilization, self-help, and reciprocity. *Bazaaris*, thus, become agents who engage, and even challenge, the social structure and political system. The bazaar becomes a series of fluid, independent, and crosscutting networks based on communal settings and necessities for survival. This makes an important contribution to the study of urban economies in that it introduces networks and ties, rather than generalized cultural and group psychology, as the force that unifies marketplaces and allows them to engage in collective action.

The informal networks approach, however, like the traditional-modern dichotomy, freezes interactions into two distinct spheres, namely formal and informal.[66] By narrowly defining the bazaar's activities as informal, many situations that exist in larger, more central marketplaces like Tehran's bazaar will simply not fit this analysis. For

---

[66] Keith Hart, one of the pioneers of the informal economy approach, has re-evaluated his claims: "Everywhere, the commanding heights of the informal economy lie close to the centers of power and reach down to the petty enterprises which first caught my attention." Keith Hart, "Market and State after the Cold War: The Informal Economy Reconsidered," in *Contesting Markets: Analyses of Ideology, Discourse and Practice*, ed. Roy Dilley (Edinburgh: Edinburgh University Press, 1992), p. 219.

instance, if a member of the Bazaar does not have a license, but pays taxes and even resorts to his trade association for tax arbitration, as is a common occurrence in the Tehran Bazaar, is he operating in the informal or formal sector?[67] While this approach might work for the marginalized urban poor, it is too rigid a strait-jacket to analyze the vast Tehran Bazaar that includes institutionalized and legal relations with state agencies. More recently, scholars have attempted to go beyond definitional debates and quantitative analysis to analyze the relationship between the "formal" and the "informal" sector and to investigate the determinants of informality.[68] As we will see in the two subsequent chapters, bazaar communities are useful spheres to reexamine and break down the informal–formal dichotomy as they highlight how informal–formal boundaries are permeable and negotiable.

The Bazaar economy as a product of informational scarcity

Mottahedeh's life story of a seminary student in prerevolutionary Iran includes a wonderful passage about the young seminarian's mother visiting the Qom Bazaar:

To enter the bazaar was to enter a world of slow formalities and quick wit. It was a world of old, even ancestral, loyalties. In general it was loyalty that directed his mother's steps. Whether it was in the small lane of the jewelers or the spacious barrel-vaulted central avenue of the cloth dealers, *his mother always went to the same merchant in any section, a reliable friend of the family.* She did not just march up to *the "reliable friend"* and ask for what she wanted. She always walked around a bit so that the merchant should know that she gave her custom with some thought. *But no woman could really have made up her mind what to buy just by examining the entrances to the shops.*[69]

The necessity of reliable friends, the repetitive nature of transactions, and the difficulty of selecting commodities in certain markets became an analytical question for a number of economists in the late 1960s. George Akerlof, Joseph Stiglitz, and others reappraised neoclassical models of markets by relaxing assumptions about information, and in so doing showed that models of pure competition are seriously undermined by situations and commodities that inhibit full and symmetrical knowledge

---

[67] *Asnaf* no. 92 (Bahman 1379 [February 2001]), 20–1.

[68] M. Castells, A. Portes, and L. Benton, eds., *The Informal Economy: Studies in Advanced and Less Developed Countries* (Baltimore: The Johns Hopkins Press, 1989); Ragui Assad, "Formal and Informal Institutions in the Labor Market, with Application to the Construction Sector in Egypt," *World Development* 21 (June 1993), 925–39.

[69] Roy Mottahedeh, *The Mantle of the Prophet: Religion and Politics in Iran* (New York: Pantheon Books, 1985), p. 33, emphasis added.

between exchange partners.[70] Thus, practices and formal rules must be developed to alleviate market imperfections and nonefficient outcomes related to transaction costs. Often these institutions are sociocultural constructs, as in the case of the seminarian's mother described by Mottahedeh. Reliable friends provide and signal information about the buyer, seller, or commodity (e.g. reputation, quality, and credit-worthiness).[71]

Clifford Geertz was quick to employ this research paradigm's analytical results in his own studies of Moroccan and Indonesian rural markets.[72] His work has inspired many economic anthropologists to examine the structure of marketplaces in the developing world as products of informational scarcity.

Geertz begins with an observation:

[I]n the bazaar information is generally poor, scarce, maldistributed, inefficiently communicated, and intensely valued. ... The level of ignorance about everything from product quality and going prices to market possibilities and production costs is very high, and a great deal of the way in which the bazaar is organized and functions (and within it, the ways its various sorts of participants behave) can be interpreted as either an attempt to reduce such ignorance for someone, increase it for someone, or defend someone against it.[73]

In order to avert informational insecurity and price-signal noise, bazaars exhibit localization of trade, intensive rather than extensive price bargaining, fragmentation of transactions, low levels of capitalization, and stable "clientship." Geertz contends that this "coherent form" that develops from information scarcity is what differentiates "the bazaar economy" from the industrial economy. Finally, Geertz emphasizes the continuity in the bazaar's culture despite institutional and economic changes.[74]

Frank Fanselow presents his theory of the bazaar as a foil to what he sees as Geertz's exotifying presentation of the bazaar. Nonetheless his

---

[70] George A. Akerlof, "The Market for 'Lemons': Quality Uncertainty and the Market Mechanism," *Quarterly Journal of Economics* 84 (August 1970), 488–500; and G.J. Stiglitz, "The Economics of Information and Knowledge," in *The Economics of Information and Knowledge*, ed. D.M. Lamberton (Harmondsworth, England: Penguin, 1971).

[71] Assad, "Formal and Informal Institutions in the Labor Market," 931.

[72] Clifford Geertz, "Suq: The Bazaar Economy in Sefrou," in *Meaning and Order in Moroccan Society*, ed. Clifford Geertz, Hildred Geertz, and Lawrence Rosen (Cambridge: Cambridge University Press, 1979); and Clifford Geertz, "The Bazaar Economy: Information and Search in Peasant Marketing," *American Economic Review* 68 (May 1978), 28–32.

[73] Geertz, "Suq: The Bazaar Economy in Sefrou," pp. 124–5.

[74] Ibid., p. 139.

approach also rests on the informational deficiencies in the bazaar setting.[75] He stresses the features of goods sold in the bazaar, rather than the structure of society, as the main source of the bazaar's institutional form. Fanselow, an economic anthropologist working on agricultural marketplaces in South Asia, contends that the commodities traded in the bazaar are largely nonsubstitutable; that is, they are not standardized in terms of quality. "The standardization of product quality and quantity is a condition for product substitutability, which balances the information asymmetry between buyer and seller and thereby becomes a precondition for the efficient functioning of the price mechanism. If quality and quantity are standardized, the seller cannot, as in the bazaar, adjust them to price by adulterating and short-measuring, but must instead adjust price to quality and quantity."[76] In the southern Indian bazaar that Fanselow studies, goods, buyers, and sellers in the bazaar economy develop strategies and customs to mitigate the perils of uncertain product quality and quantity. He claims that this is markedly different from what we find in western settings where governments, entrepreneurs, and producers ensure quality by establishing trademarks, government quality checks, and exclusionary trade associations that reduce information scarcity and asymmetry between buyers and sellers by signaling the seller's reputation, establishing consistency in quality of goods, and standardizing weights and measures. In the bazaar, information problems related to goods prevail, leading to bargaining over quality and quantity, sellers enjoying competitive advantage over buyers, and reduced price competition.

The informational approach to bazaars is an important breakthrough in marrying cutting-edge economic theories to the cultural study of bazaars. The bazaar's peculiarities are less bizarre, whilst its norms and practices are treated as more than epiphenomenal aberrations. The bazaar-as-information-scarcity approach provides a convincing rationale for what modernization theory labels "traditional" and "backward". Unfortunately, political scientists and Iran specialists have not engaged with these theories.

While Geertz and Fanselow use their approaches to distinguish the bazaar economy from economies with less informational dearth, they are less concerned with comparing across bazaars or studying variations and changes within a marketplace. Since these anthropological studies are limited to rural settings, they disregard the standardized goods

---

[75] Frank Fanselow, "The Bazaar Economy or How Bizarre Is the Bazaar Really?" *Man* 25 (June 1990), 250–65.
[76] Ibid., 252.

(e.g. Pyrex dishes, packaged Lipton tea, Maxell cassette tapes) found in contemporary Middle Eastern bazaars. Also, these studies are based on peddlers, peasants, and village shopkeepers, who, unlike *bazaari*s in the Tehran Bazaar, are not engaged in long-distance, large, and institutionally complex transactions. Tehran's prominent role in Iran's import–export business introduces new actors to the bazaar economy – government ministers, national wholesalers, and producers. Thus, I extend these analyses to the Tehran Bazaar by studying how members of the bazaar and government officials have sought to mitigate informational scarcities in certain sectors (carpets and tea), while relative standardization in other sectors (e.g. china and glassware) has fostered different organizational dynamics (Chapter 5).

The Tehran Bazaar as an embedded network

In order to grapple with the bazaar as a changing entity that has been politically active and part of a highly politicized oil economy, I turn to the diverse literature on markets and economies with debates over the logic of economic action, the origins of institutions, and the historical development of self-regulating markets. Instead of juxtaposing the bazaar with ideal types (i.e. the modern, the capitalist bourgeois, the formal, and markets with complete information) and conceptualizing the bazaar in negative terms, I propose that the bazaar economy can be studied in an analytical framework used to study all markets. In the remainder of this chapter, I will develop a conceptual framework from a modified economic sociology perspective that allows one to be true to the complexities of the Tehran Bazaar, address broad theoretical issues about operations of markets, study the internal politics of bazaars, and analyze the Bazaar within the specific political-economic conditions and institutions of the Pahlavi and Islamic Republic regimes.

Beyond market and moral economy

The manner in which economies operate, change over time, and interact with social and political settings has been among the central questions in the social sciences. Historically, there are two distinct approaches to the logic of economic actions; one is based on a universalizing set of postulates privileging individual utility maximization and the other begins by situating economic action as inextricably bound to the historical and moral context. I will refer to the former as the utilitarian approach and the latter as the contextualist approach.

The utilitarian tradition that is the basis for neoclassical economics and rational choice theory assumes that all actors are rational and self-interested. Actors determine the cost–benefit ratio of all possible actions and choose the actions most consistent with their fixed individual preferences. Markets are the aggregation of the interaction between sets of isolated and interchangeable actors seeking to maximize their utility. The utilitarian approach to economic action disavows the influence of structures and social relations on the economy. Classical and neoclassical economics view actors as price-takers, and thus the identities, social relations, and histories of trading partners are irrelevant.[77] While this deductive approach has been applied to industrial settings, many economic anthropologists have argued that even peasant and pre-industrial societies satisfy the neoclassical assumptions about rational actors with well-defined preferences, facing scarcity and acting as if they comprehended the trade-offs involved in decision making (trade-offs between economic and noneconomic goals such as status or leisure).

Since the 1960s economists have begun to incorporate notions that complicate the standard model of competitive markets and place exchange partners' decision making within a nontransparent context of exchange. As mentioned above, research and subsequent theories show that imperfect information, asymmetric information, and various other factors that lead to high transaction costs hinder the smooth operation of the price mechanism. Therefore, from the utilitarian perspective, "the puzzle" becomes why daily economic life operates seemingly smoothly and is not fraught with disorder and distrust. Although these new institutional economists complicate the pristine neoclassical world by incorporating institutions (e.g. laws, regulatory agencies, and firms), the origins and functions of institutions are explained from the same neoclassical principles (self-interest by rational atomized individuals) and the drive for efficiency, or what Oliver Williamson calls "economizing on transaction costs." This general approach has influenced political scientists working on issues as diverse as peasant communities,[78] economic development,[79] taxation,[80] and the impediments to privatization.[81]

---

[77] Albert O. Hirschman, "Rival Interpretations of Market Society: Civilizing, Destructive, or Feeble?" *Journal of Economic Literature* 20 (December 1982), 1463–84.

[78] Samuel L. Popkin, *The Rational Peasant: The Political Economy of Rural Society in Vietnam* (Berkeley: University of California Press, 1979).

[79] Robert H. Bates, *Markets and States in Tropical Africa: The Political Basis of Agricultural Policies* (Berkeley: University of California Press, 1981).

[80] Margaret Levi, *Of Rule and Revenue* (Berkeley: University of California Press, 1988).

[81] John Waterbury, *Exposed to Innumerable Delusions: Public Enterprise and State Power in Egypt, India, Mexico, and Turkey* (New York: Cambridge University Press, 1993).

Meanwhile, for several decades, scholars in anthropology, political science, and history have been adamant that the utilitarian approach misinterprets economic action because it assumes away the contextual and ethical components that are integral to human relations. Karl Polanyi's impassioned work on the rise of and subsequent backlash against the "the price-making market" champions a research agenda scrutinizing the assumptions of market society and formalist applications of neoclassical economics to primitive societies.[82] Thus scholars working in various fields seek to uncover the substance of industrial and preindustrial economies. These contextualists argue that trade and economic activities in nonmarket societies cannot be explained by profit maximization or more generally means–end rationality. James Scott, for instance, argues that peasant economies are based on subsistence and fear of shortages that translate into particular definitions of exploitation and economic justice (e.g. "the norm of reciprocity" and "the right to subsistence"), rather than individual and objective cost–benefit analysis.[83] Polanyi argues that economies in early societies were ruled by principles of reciprocity and redistribution. Thus, demand and supply, which is derived from rational calculations based on self-interest, do not set prices; rather it is tradition, political authority, or conceptions of fairness that do.[84] It is only with the advent of the self-regulating market in England during the nineteenth century that a new logic emerged which disembedded the economy from society, commodifying land and labor; and this is exactly what is presupposed in economic theory. Hence, the contextualist approaches argue that modernization leads to a decline in the embeddedness of the economy.

It is against both of these approaches that New Economic Sociology emerged in the mid-1980s. A group of economic sociologists consciously developed a theoretical framework that challenged both approaches at once and sought to move descriptions of economies away from generalizing statements. In his seminal work, Mark Granovetter shows how both utilitarian and contextualist approaches to economic behavior are based on similar functionalist conceptions of action and argues for situating all social actions in ongoing relations.[85] Granovetter

---

[82] Karl Polanyi, *The Great Transformation* (Boston: Beacon Press, 1957); Karl Polanyi, Conrad M. Arensberg, and Harry W. Pearson, *Trade and Market in the Early Empires* (Glencoe, IL: Free Press, 1957); and Marshall Sahlins, *Stone Age Economics* (Chicago: Aladine-Atherton, 1972).

[83] James Scott, *The Moral Economy of the Peasant* (New Haven: Yale University Press, 1976).

[84] Sahlins provides evidence supporting this thesis.

[85] Mark Granovetter, "Economic Action and Social Structure: The Problem of Embeddedness," *American Journal of Sociology* 91 (November 1985), 481–510.

argues that neoclassical economists and contextualists, or what he calls formalists and substantivists respectively, conceptualize economic action by resorting to arguments about human nature, rather than structures and relations. The neoclassical economic approach has an undersocialized conception of humans (*homo economicus*) enjoying a fundamental character that is independent of social interactions and membership and roles in communities. Contextualists and those working in the moral economy school, on the other hand, present an atomized story of human nature that sees devotion to community and internalized and generalized norms, instead of motive and gain, as the force behind individual action. Granovetter contends,

Both [conceptions] have in common a conception of action and decision carried out by atomized actors. In the undersocialized account, atomization results from narrow utilitarian pursuit of self-interest; in the oversocialized one, from the fact that behavior patterns have been internalized and ongoing social relations thus have only peripheral effects on behavior. That the internalized rules of behavior are social in origin does not differentiate this argument decisively from a utilitarian one, in which the source of utility functions is left open, leaving room for behavior guided entirely by consensually determined norms and values – as in the oversocialized view.[86]

Hence, Granovetter considers these approaches to be resorting to overly mechanistic views of behavior; while *homo economicus* automatically arrives at ends that meet its maximands, *homo moralis* arrives at outcomes that meet the dictates of its socialization.[87] Action in both the over- and undersocialized approaches is determined by given attributes and not existing and on-going social relations.[88] The difference between these accounts is the decision rule, not how individuals interact with the economy and develop roles in relation to those around them.

Finally, these accounts seem to ignore the empirical evidence demonstrating that economic behavior in preindustrial as well as advanced industrial societies follows both logics (i.e. strict self-interest and moral universe). Anthropological evidence shows that generalizations about nonmarket societies do not hold and we have cases where

---

[86] Ibid., 485.

[87] Granovetter points out, "Social influence here [in the oversocialized account] is an external force that, like the deist's God, sets things in motion and has no further effects – a force that insinuates itself into the minds and bodies of individuals (as in the movie *Invasion of the Body Snatchers*), altering their way of making decisions. Once we know in just what way an individual has been affected, ongoing social relations and structures are irrelevant" (486). Also see Robert H. Bates, "Contra Contractarianism: Some Reflections on the New Institutionalism," 18 (September 1988), 387–401.

[88] Also see David Knoke, *Political Networks: The Structural Perspective* (Cambridge: Cambridge University Press, 1990).

preindustrial economies operate on principles of profit maximization.[89] Meanwhile, industrial societies are not as uniformly disembedded as both approaches would have us believe – many firms are linked by interlocking directorates, disputes among businesspeople are typically solved informally, and subcontracting leads to long-term relations among firms. Granovetter argues "that the level of embeddedness of economic behavior is lower in nonmarket societies than is claimed by substantivists and development theorists, and it has changed less with 'modernization' than they believe."[90] In other words, Polanyi overstates the extent to which embeddedness applied to historical markets and understates the extent to which it matters in modern markets.

Instead, the New Economic Sociologists argue that an approach to economies that places actors within a web of networks shaping their actions and situating markets in a particular time and place can help us understand behavior that both seems to follow profit maximization and is driven by non-means–end logics. The central tenets of New Economic Sociology are that economic action has noneconomic motives (e.g. quest for approval, status, sociability, and power), the economy is socially situated (i.e. not simply driven by supply and demand), and economic institutions are socially constructed within a history, set of power relations, and configuration of institutions.[91] "Embedded action," Swedberg and Granovetter claim, "is socially situated and cannot be explained by reference to individual motives alone. It is embedded in ongoing networks of personal relationships rather than being carried out by atomized actors. By *network* we mean a regular set of contacts or similar social connections among individuals or groups. An action by a member of a network is *embedded*, because it is expressed in interaction with other people."[92]

This notion of embeddness helps us understand why patterns of social relations are critical to exchange. The embedded approach to economic activity views actions as constrained by ongoing and meaningful social relations.[93] On the one hand, economic actions are simply explainable by identifying preferences and assigning strategic actions. Exchanges do not take place in social and temporal vacuums, and once we begin to

---

[89] Mark Granovetter, "The Nature of Economic Relationships," in *The Sociology of Economic Life*, ed. Richard Swedberg and Mark Granovetter (Boulder: Westview Press, 1992).

[90] Granovetter, "Economic Action and Social Structure," 482.

[91] Ibid.

[92] Richard Swedberg and Mark Granovetter, introduction to *The Sociology of Economic Life*, p. 9.

[93] By meaningful, I mean behavior has a logic beyond utility maximization and can have expressive and experiential attributes.

place greater focus on patterns and contexts that transform isolated buyer–seller dyads into component parts of chains of relations, many of the puzzles introduced by new economic institutionalists become less problematic. Networks are the ecology in which negotiating and discovering prices, appraising and gathering information about reputations, resolving conflicts, and mobilizing assets occur in all economies.

In the subsequent chapters I investigate how the actions of individual *bazaaris* and modes of exchange are fundamentally shaped by various relational forces such as the longevity of relations, the multiplicity of spheres of interaction, and the presence of third parties and entire communities that may be privy to transactions. Neither informal institutions nor moral principles are created by isolated willing individuals. However, neither are they preordained givens embedded into the psyches of individual members of a community or class. These norms, expectations of behavior, and symbolic structures are created by ongoing relations and patterns of interaction that both teach (or invent) traditions and devise means to enforce them. Preferences are as much endogenous to the social process, as they are the independent causal forces giving rise to them. As these practices are normalized and actions are disciplined, group identities are forged. Thus, these ongoing relations create both *bazaaris* and bazaars.

The Bazaar as networks

New Economic Sociology's embedded networks approach to markets is the source of my conceptualization of the Tehran Bazaar. I define bazaars as *bounded spaces containing a series of ongoing and socially embedded networks that are the mechanism for the exchange of specific commodities.*

This definition may seem quite ubiquitous; nonetheless from it one can probe for empirical complexities of the bazaar and delve into broader political-economy issues. First, while this conceptualization is similar to the class approach in that it privileges the economic role of the bazaar, it does not disengage the economic from the social setting. Instead, it seeks to specify the mechanisms that bring together the economic and social factors in a manner that may foster unity, in spite of diversity. Second, this definition incorporates the observation found in the informal economy literature and takes networks as the unit of analysis, yet leaves open the issue of whether these networks are informal, formal, or a combination and creation of the two. Third, this broader definition based on ongoing relations implies that bazaars may vary over time when the form of networks shifts. Finally, following the insights of the informational scarcity paradigm, variations across sectors would be expected when the nature of the "specific commodities" involved in transactions differs.

The first term of the definition – a distinct space – is what provides the bazaar its sense of totality. Most definitions literally begin with spatial discussions. For example, the *Encyclopaedia Iranica* begins its entry on the bazaar with one of the basic meanings of bazaar being "the physical establishments, the shops, characterized by specific morphology and architectural design"[94] and continues with a description of the basic architectural components that comprise the bazaar. And I have discussed how the physical space undergirds the conceptualizations of several scholars. Space, however, has rarely been systematically incorporated into discussions about the bazaar. This is an important oversight since the bazaar's essential meaning comes from its physical characteristics – narrow allies, vaulted ceilings, and historic structure. In most Iranian cities, if you tell someone that you are going to the bazaar the other person will know exactly where you are headed. In fact, in Tehran, the shared taxis that transport passengers from major squares and intersections often have a route to the bazaar. You hear drivers calling out "bazaar, bazaar" from all of Tehran's major squares (Azadi, Shush, Tajrish, Vanak, and Resalat Squares). While this is the case in other major cities in the Middle East (Istanbul, Damascus, and Aleppo), it is most definitely not the case in all urban centers. Despite having a historic district and a contemporary tourist market, Cairo does not have an equivalently well-specified locale. (A Cairen, for example, would not fully understand your destination if you said you were headed to the *suq*. They would simply conclude that you are going shopping.)

In my interviews with members of the Tehran Bazaar and retailers and businessmen in the non-Bazaar areas, the spatial component was the common denominator in the definitions of the Bazaar. From the internal perspective the primary definition of the Bazaar is the physical space. When I asked members of the Bazaar what bazaar or *bazaari* meant to them, they almost uniformly first turned to physical definitions – commenting that it was under the shadow of the Shams al-'Emareh (or the Palace clock tower just north of the Tehran Bazaar) or simply described it as what lies within Mawlavi, Khayyam, 15th of Khordad, and Mostafa Khomeini streets (see Map 2.1). The historical continuity of the space helps reinforce the spatial dimension differentiating the Tehran Bazaar from other commercial units and public spaces. Finally, as illustrated in subsequent chapters, the rooted nature of the market in a place helps establish the necessary foundation for communal allegiance, with its

[94] Bonine, *Encyclopdia Iranica*, s.v. "Bāzār," p. 20.

confined nature fostering long-term and face-to-face interactions among *bazaari*s. To put it more emphatically, if you do not spend enough time in the Bazaar, you cannot become a *bazaari*, and if you do spend enough time in the Bazaar, you very well may become a *bazaari* (as some feared would happen to me). Thus, the Bazaar must be spatially, as well as simply functionally, defined – it is not only a market; it is a market*place*.[95]

Finally, this conceptualization does not prohibit a political reading of the conglomeration of socially embedded networks. Embedded network analysis has shed light on the operation of economies and societies and is a useful tool in considering *bazaari*s as a dynamic group. Nonetheless, politics, state institutions, and policies are typically bracketed out of these formulations.[96] This is in part due to their choice of subjects, namely studies of relatively stateless settings such as peasant and tribal communities in the developing world and private industrial sectors in advanced industrial economies. In the process, these studies have largely ignored vast swaths of economic experience where state policies and actors play a fundamental role in capital accumulation and structuring market opportunities. Most contemporary economies, especially those in the developing world, are heavily regulated by states and contain state-owned enterprises. Actors engage both private citizens and public officials though networks, while state institutions stipulate which actors comprise economic networks. By extending economic sociology to more heavily regulated economies, I hope to show that actors do not merely adopt or establish relations within a network, but that types of relations and forms of networks are dictated to them by the political economy. Politics determines how networks, resources, and formal institutions are interlaced with one another.

Also, the embedded networks approach has remained confined to sociology, with political scientists slow to directly apply its concepts and hypotheses in their empirical studies.[97] This study, however, suggests that this approach not only can be applied to a new setting (an urban economy in the Middle East) and to an explicitly political question (the configuring of state–society relation in revolutionary ties), but also can be developed in directions that will contribute to our understanding of

[95] Daniel Kemmis, *Community and the Politics of Place* (Norman: University of Oklahoma Press, 1990).
[96] Neil Fligstein, "Markets as Politics: A Political-Cultural Approach to Market Institutions," *American Sociological Review* 61(August 1996), 657.
[97] Granovetter's essays are often referenced in discussions about theories of institutions, especially as a critique of rational choice approaches to institutions, and also in some discussions of the importance of networks of social movements. But more extended applications of the of New Economic Sociology are rare.

how institutions matter, how social actors negotiate state policies, how states govern, and why group organization changes over time.

Third, while analyses of inter- and intrafirm organization have critiqued the sharp distinction between market and hierarchy, the implicit differentiation between community and hierarchy remains accepted. By resituating the concerns of scholars interested in governance within social groups[98] in terms of understanding how societies are composed of networks, I propose that community and hierarchy are often fused into forms of governance that shape authority and power relations in various ways – allowing us to differentiate between cooperative and coercive hierarchies. I use the concept of embedded networks as a lens with which to study microlevel politics, with the forms of governance of the Tehran Bazaar being the creation of these patterned relations.

Conclusions

By summarizing the prevailing conceptualizations of the bazaar, I have called attention to the tendency of scholars to treat the bazaar as an undifferentiated, static, and collective entity. Integrating the empirical observations of past research into a framework that allows us to address the central questions of the project – and discussions about markets more generally – proves fruitful. An embedded networks approach encourages us to study norms of behavior, social customs, and economic practices as products of ongoing relationships that are continuously constructed and reproduced by interactions with their community, shaping it as much as being shaped by it. Thus, the Tehran Bazaar's corporate identity or apparent homogeneity is problematized. It is not something that organically springs from shared traditional culture or psychology as suggested by modernization theory. Nor is it a product of a shared position in the mode of production, as assumed by class analysis. Rather the Bazaar's capability to act collectively, maintain institutions, and forge a group identity develops from concrete historical space with particular constellations of relations. Bazaars consist of actors tied to one another in ongoing relations that help reinforce codes of conduct by practice and expectation, not functional utility calculation or socialization. We must now apply and elaborate these formulations and begin to contemplate the impact of state policies on various network parameters.

---

[98] Michael Taylor, *Community, Anarchy and Liberty* (Cambridge: Cambridge University Press, 1982); Michael Taylor, *The Possibility of Cooperation* (Cambridge: Cambridge University Press, 1987); Elinor Ostrom, *Governing the Commons* (Cambridge: Cambridge University Press, 1990); and Robert C. Ellickson, *Order without Law: How Neighbors Settle Disputes* (Cambridge, MA: Harvard University Press, 1991).

3   Bazaar transformations: networks, reputations, and solidarities

Law and order arise out of the very processes they govern. But they are not rigid, nor due to any inertia or permanent mould.

Bronislaw Malinowski[1]

Solidarity has to be constructed out of little pieces, rather than found already waiting, in the form of an ur-langauge which all of us recognize when we hear it.

Richard Rorty[2]

I cannot remember the number of times that *bazaari*s complained to me that they could not trust their exchange partners, but it seemed to me to be the grandest of tropes. Their protests were articulated through a comparison between the past and the present. "The past" was a time when a man's word was as good as gold. It was a time when the maxim that a truly honest *bazaari* "places his mustache as collateral" (or even "places a strand of his mustache as collateral")[3] was a fact of daily life. No contracts or checks were signed. Instead a handshake was exchanged and honor was placed as a security deposit. Then came "the present," when even checks and legal documents are not honored, and the threat of shaming and gossip is not a viable sanction. The refrain was "all the checks bounce." The social scientist in me doubted this nostalgic narrative of a lost golden past and sought some form of independent, if not direct, verification. Even though non-*bazaari*s and the secondary literature reaffirmed these narratives, I was still skeptical. Despite knowing that Iran is not the best place for time series data, I decided to search for

---

[1] Bronislaw Malinowski, *Crime and Custom in Savage Society* (Totowa, NJ: Littlefield, Adams, and Co., 1969), pp. 122–3.

[2] Richard Rorty, *Contingency, Irony, and Solidarity* (Cambridge: Cambridge University Press, 1989), p. 94.

[3] The expression is *sebil gero gozashtan* (or *tar-e sebil gero gozashtan*). The mustache is used as a symbol of integrity, manhood, and reputation. The English expression for "greasing someone's palms" in Persian is to "fatten (grease) someone's mustache" and refers to fattening their lot by paying respect to them.

statistics. Surprisingly the *Annual National Statistics* (*Salnameh-ye Amar-e Keshvar*) included statistics for the number of cases of bounced checks settled in civil courts. I began with the 1965 volume and noted the numbers in each subsequent edition. Indeed, despite some inconsistencies in measurement, there was a distinct and dramatic increase in the national figures. While there was a slight increase in the 1960s and 1970s, the major proliferation came after 1988, when the number quadrupled in a five-year span. Then from 1995 to 1998 the number of cases involving bounced checks almost doubled.[4] And this occured while the punishment for bounced checks was resolutely being enforced. Reportedly, over 17,000 inmates in state prisons are serving time for writing bad checks, the second largest group of prisoners after those imprisoned for drug-related charges.[5] The change was undeniable and dramatic; I could not rebuff the *bazaaris'* juxtaposition of the era of placing mustaches as collateral with that of bounced checks.

Assuming that there were fewer cases of bounced checks in the 1960s and 1970s because people either did not use checks or solved their disputes outside the court of law, the data can be interpreted as showing the rise of state-sanctioned exchange mechanisms and arbitration, and the emergence of a more impersonal society in which face-to-face relations and communal regulation are declining.[6] Therefore, the governance of commerce, or the means, monitoring, and enforcement of exchange, has changed. The Bazaar, as an elaborate set of networks tying merchants, wholesalers, brokers, and retailers, continually produces a political economy. These networks facilitate exchange by identifying potential exchange partners and safeguarding agreements. In the process these embedded actions create expectations and assign reputations to actors who depend upon these networks for products,

---

[4] The annual number of cases settled in court for bad checks was roughly 10,000 in the 1970s, remained at the same level in the 1980s and then began to increase in the late 1980s, reaching over 22,000 in 1991, 41,000 in 1993, and over 400,000 in 1997 and 1998. Supporting this trend, figures for embezzlement, bribery, and forgery show an equivalent increase.

[5] *Islamic Republic News Agency*, November 27, 2001.

[6] There are other interpretations; in particular the increase in bounced checks may be caused by an increase in transactions or improvements in record keeping. While I cannot categorically refute these views, I have certain reasons to prefer the governance interpretation. First, the argument based on an increase in transactions suggests a simultaneous gradual increase in transactions and bounced checks, and thus requires a mechanism to link transactions to breaking agreements; therefore in the last instance the rise in bad checks will have to rest on a governance-type analysis. The interpretation based on the assumption of a more robust bureaucracy may in fact have some truth, but it is unlikely that it would have led to such dramatic and *persistent* increases in the rate of bounced checks. Also, neither of these interpretations is consistent with interviews conducted in Iran.

credit, information, and their status. Thus, contrary to Avner Greif's provocative analysis of Maghribi and Genovese traders, cultural beliefs are not the cause of particular commercial institutions and patterns of relations, but the experience of Tehran's *bazaaris* suggests that networks lead to norms of behavior and coordinate expectations.[7]

The Bazaar is primarily an economic unit and, accordingly, this discussion privileges economic matters. Nevertheless, the empirical evidence supports the theoretical contention posited by embedded approaches to markets, that the realm of economics is not detached from the social order. *I will illustrate how economic, social, and political factors were woven together like the fibers of a rope to create cooperative hierarchies during the latter half of the Pahlavi rule and unraveled to generate disparate coercive hierarchies during the Islamic Republic.*

This chapter is largely descriptive and focuses on the internal patterns of the Bazaar, but it is not meant to be an exhaustive and detailed account of the Tehran Bazaar's functioning or transformation. Rather, I seek to identify the mechanisms that tie the various commercial levels together and demonstrate how this pattern has significantly changed since the Revolution. As opposed to conceptions of the bazaar discussed in the previous chapter, I emphasize the objective heterogeneities of its members.[8] Once we accept economic, ethnic, religious, and political diversities exist in the Bazaar, apparent solidarity becomes something that must be explained and maintained.

Second, in providing a description of the Bazaar, the chapter argues that social order, like tradition, is not an organic phenomenon that flows from primordial attributes or cultural affinities. Governance within groups is inextricably connected to purposive actions within specific configurations of relations and ties. In fact despite the presence of multiplicities of class, status, ethnicity, religiosity, age, and trade in the Tehran Bazaar, during the 1960s and 1970s Tehran's central marketplace was characterized by long-term, multiplex, and crosscutting ties. The demise of the cooperative hierarchies in the 1980s and 1990s

---

[7] Greif refers to the "crystallization" of cultural beliefs without elaborating how and why this occurs. The analysis in this chapter suggests that the structure of relations within groups is the critical factor. Avner Greif, "Cultural Beliefs and the Organization of Society: A Historical and Theoretical Reflection on Collectivist and Individualist Societies," *Journal of Political Economy* 102 (October 1994), 912–50.

[8] Most secondary sources mentioned in Chapter 2 view bazaars as homogeneous entities. For more heterogeneous conceptualizations see the work of Howard Rotblat, which differentiates *bazaaris* on the basis of their economic role and sectors. Howard J. Rotblat, "Stability and Change in an Iranian Provincial Bazaar," Ph.D. dissertation, University of Chicago (1972). Ahmad Ashraf's analysis divide *bazaaris* into merchants (*tojjar*) and guilds (*asnaf*), and Misagh Parsa stresses political differences. See various articles by Ahmad Ashraf and Misagh Parsa listed in bibliography.

reinforces the argument that community is not primordially engrained or established because of efficiency concerns, but is produced through actions and within relations that are subject to change and demise. Although most observers continue to assume that the Bazaar's solidarity has lasted, I will conclude by arguing that although many individual *bazaaris* may continue to prosper, the Bazaar's form of governance has changed and, with it, so have the interpersonal relations that are the bedrock for feelings of solidarity.

The cooperative hierarchies of the prerevolutionary Bazaar

The Bazaar of the late Pahlavi era was very much the quintessential embedded economy described by anthropologists and sociologists. Social, spatial, religious, and familial forces were inseparable from the economic sphere and norms and institutions were mutually enforcing. A religious gathering helped introduce *bazaaris* who might eventually become trading partners, and a neighborhood engagement party was an opportunity for fellow members of a trade to meet and gather the latest news about prices. Meanwhile the price of a good was dependent upon past relations, and credit-worthiness was contingent upon reputation within the community, which was, in turn, based on generosity and charity as much as commercial acumen. Exchange dyads could not be isolated from either interpersonal ties or ties in the rest of the community. Commercial exchange and social ties were grafted onto one another through long-term, multifaceted, and crosscutting relations.

Stable ties and roles within value chains

Reliable and consistent estimates for the number of workers and commercial units in the Tehran Bazaar during the Pahlavi era or today are hard to come by. First, the Bazaar has never been a distinct administrative unit, so government figures are not reported for the Bazaar; instead they are reported at the level of the larger districts (district 5 at the time of the 1966 census and district 12 after the Revolution). Second, it is not easy to estimate the sheer number of employees working out of each retail store or wholesale office. Most employees are family members or informal apprentices, and often several members of the family launch separate operations from a single establishment or various individuals place goods on consignment with *bazaaris*. Also, many workshops and commercial units were unregistered or did not maintain their registration. Given these limitations, estimates vary and are highly imprecise.

The Organization for the Protection of Ancient Remains and the Tehran Municipality conducted a survey a few months after the Revolution and estimated that by the late 1970s the Bazaar contained some 30,000 commercial units in thirty-three sectors with an estimated 50,000 employees.[9] Parsa states that by the time of the Revolution the number of shops and workshops in Tehran's Bazaar area reached 40,000, with half of these located in the covered bazaar, and the remainder in the immediate vicinity.[10] As will be discussed in greater detail in the following chapter, we can be fairly certain that the size of the Tehran Bazaar was steadily increasing in the post-World War II era.

Who composed this value chain in the Pahlavi era? The evidence suggests that there were important inequalities and internal differentiations within the Bazaar. This heterogeneity, however, was managed by repeated exchanges between members of a rather well-defined hierarchy where the level of wealth translated into a specific role and status. An older *bazaari* recalled that "each person knew their own position and the situation (*mawqe'iyyat*) of those around them." The commercial distribution channel tied importers and exporters to various levels of wholesalers, distributors, and retailers through brokers, middlemen, and moneylenders acting as network makers who ensured smooth transactions.[11]

The merchants (*tajer*, pl. *tujjar*) were economically the most powerful group in the Tehran Bazaar. These figures operated family-run trade houses specializing in importing consumer and intermediate goods and exporting agricultural goods and hand-woven carpets.[12] While in the first half of the twentieth century importers dealt in a wide variety of goods ranging from foodstuffs to machinery, by the 1960s importers and exporters were specializing in a more select number of often related commodities. Ideally, they would set up agreements with foreign firms establishing them as that firm's sole Iranian representative, thus creating a monopoly over specific brands of goods.[13]

---

[9] *Asar* no. 2–4 (1359), 22 and 25. It is not clear from the text how commercial units are defined.

[10] Misagh Parsa, *Social Origins of the Iranian Revolution* (New Brunswick, NJ: Rutgers University Press, 1989), p. 92.

[11] The Tehran Bazaar is not restricted to these actors, but they constitute the pillars of the value chain. Other categories within the Bazaar are apprentices, bookkeepers, porters, peddlers, those involved in food services, and customers.

[12] I emphasize importers in this discussion since the majority of merchants in the Bazaar were involved in import businesses, rather than export. The export of hand-woven carpets will be discussed in Chapter 5.

[13] 'Ali-Asghar Sa'idi and Fereydun Shirinkam, *Mawq'iyyat-e Tojjar va Saheban-e Sanaye' dar Iran-e Dawreh-ye Pahlavi: Sarmayehdari-ye Khanevadegi-ye Khandan-e Lajevardi* (Tehran: Gam-e Naw, 1384 [2005]).

Importers in the Bazaar almost universally prospered in the 1960s and 1970s. These importers controlled a large share of consumer and intermediate imports prior to the Revolution. The rise in oil revenue and consumer demand drove up imports of consumer goods from $124 million in 1963, to over $217 million in 1970, to a prerevolutionary peak of $2,700 million in 1977. In relative terms, the ratio of consumer imports to total imports declined in the 1960s since Iran was following import-substitution industrialization; however, as the economy began to overheat and the regime opened the gates to outside markets, the ratio steadily climbed to reach almost a quarter of all imports by the end of the 1970s.

Thanks to their wealth, the merchant class was the most socially mobile *bazaari* group. As Iran's economy began to grow in the post-World War II era and the state established tariffs to protect nascent industries, many of the most prominent merchant families in the Tehran Bazaar, as well as others from larger cities, transferred their assets into industry. Many industrialists came from trading and *bazaari* backgrounds. The most high-profile representative of this phenomenon is Ahmad Khayyami, who was from a *bazaari* family from Mashhad that specialized in exporting dried fruits. He first became a representative for European car companies and later became the owner of Iran's largest automobile production firm. With the patronage of the Shah he also branched out to establish a small chain of department stores.[14] Some of the other well-known examples of *bazaari* merchants who moved from importing operations into manufacturing were the Lajevardi family, the Khosrawshahi family, the Mofarrah family, and Vahhabzadeh. In addition, Vaghefi's study of entrepreneurs shows that the vast majority of fathers of entrepreneurs in the mid-1970s were involved in business (as opposed to being landlords or government officials).[15] The merchants were also one of the first groups to move to the lush northern environs of Tehran and by the 1970s established offices in smarter areas of the new business districts north of the Bazaar. Yet, most maintained their offices in the Bazaar's large vaulted warehouse areas known as *timcheh*s and *saras*, and they maintained relatively close contact with the Bazaar neighborhood.

Although wholesale establishments were a relatively small percentage of all the units in the marketplace, in terms of volume of activity they played the most active role, with their commercial activities reaching

---

[14] Robert Graham, *Iran: The Illusion of Power*, rev. edn. (New York: St. Martin Press, 1980), pp. 47–8.

[15] Mohammad Reza Vaghefi, *Entrepreneurs of Iran: The Role of Business Leaders in the Development of Iran* (Palo Alto, CA: Altoan Press, 1975), pp. 81–3.

across the entire country.[16] As merchants cultivated relations with multinational companies and entered industry, the distribution of imported goods was undertaken by a multilayered wholesale class. National-level wholesalers (*'omdeh-forush*) were based in the Tehran Bazaar and operated with a large volume of goods. Often before the goods arrived in Iran, they would sell them to several intermediary distributors (*bonakdar*) who operated warehousing facilities and had an established and stable network of smaller bulkers and jobbers working at the level of provinces and cities and larger retailers in Tehran's marketplace.[17] They owned offices or stores in the Bazaar, with stores being more like showrooms, and they would typically not sell to retail customers, preferring to sell only in bulk. Wholesalers who were able to corner new markets and accrue capital or credit were able to add importing operations to their wholesaling operations.

The success of wholesalers relied on long-term relations with actors further up and down the value chain in order to purchase and distribute goods. In large part this was achieved through specialization. Despite appearances, wholesalers, like merchants, had a high degree of specialization. For instance, to the casual observer it may have seemed that a series of cloth sellers were all selling the same bolts of fabric. On closer examination, it would be evident that one only carried products from Iranian manufacturers, another specialized in black fabric for *chadors*, and the third specialized in high-end European cloth. The narrow specialization helped reduce competition between wholesalers in that a retailer seeking a particular type of cloth could resort to only a limited number of sources.[18] This also explains why wholesalers would readily refer customers to others if they did not sell the item in question.

After filtering down through the network of importers and various wholesalers, goods would finally make their way to the retail stores that lined the streets of the Bazaar and were involved in direct sales of goods to customers. During the 1960s and 1970s, high rents and decline in the residential population of central Tehran helped drive some retailers out

---

[16] Martin Seger, *Teheran: Eine Stadtgeographische Studie* (New York: Springer-Verlag Wien, 1978), p. 134, and *Asar*, 22.

[17] There is some confusion in terminology when it comes to wholesalers. The terms *'omdeh-forush* and *bonakdar* are sometimes used interchangeably by *bazaaris* and take on slightly different meanings depending on the sector in question. For the sake of consistency and clarity I use *'omdeh-forush* or wholesalers to refer to wholesalers who deal in larger quantities of goods and have more long-term operations and *bonakdar* or distributors to refer to smaller-scale wholesalers who operate at the provincial or city level.

[18] Neil Fligstein, "Markets as Politics: A Political-Cultural Approach to Market Institutions," *American Sociological Review* 61 (August 1996), 659.

of the Bazaar region, yet the boom in consumer demand among all classes and the expansion of affluent and poor residential areas away from the center attracted retailers to establish shops in new shopping districts. While retailing for everyday and large items followed the population flows, retailing for luxury goods and big-ticket items (e.g. jewelry, carpets, cloth, and flatware) that were bought seasonally or for special occasions, such as a bride's dowry, continued to prosper. In addition, the retail stores beyond the immediate Bazaar area were tied to the Bazaar's wholesalers for goods and storage.[19] Also, a limited number of retail shops outside of the historic marketplace were owned by *bazaari* families. Although it depended on their marketing strategies, knowledge, and contacts, retail units in the Bazaar had a narrower selection of goods than retail outlets in the streets or in industrial countries. In general, only a few brands were available and they generally specialized in either imported or domestic goods, or in either high- or low-quality goods – market segmentation was the rule. However, retailers attracted customers because their limited selection was cheaper than that of competitors outside the Bazaar and goods tended always to be in stock, sometimes even after the producers stopped producing them. "We did not have a large variety," explained one old retailer selling kitchen appliances, "but we specialized and made sure that we had a stock always ready for customers. Customers knew that they could come to us [for their needs]." Taken as a whole, Bazaar retailers offered a wider variety of goods than outside the Bazaar.

Brokers (*vaseteh*, *dallal*, or *haqq al-'amal kar*),[20] not to be confused with middlemen, played a fundamental role in ensuring a steady flow of information, credit, and goods through the Tehran Bazaar's networks. A wholesaler illustrated the point by explaining, "A good cannot sell itself. It doesn't have legs to walk out and find itself a buyer. And I am too busy to run around to find buyers, ensure that they are reliable, figure out the price, collect my debts, and gather all the information. That is why we need brokers." Brokers specialized in a particular trade and acted as an intermediary between the various levels in the Bazaar. It is important to note that brokers did not assume ownership of goods; rather ownership went directly from the seller to the buyer, for instance from the wholesaler to the provincial distributor. Their marketing earned them a commission ranging from 5 to 10 percent that depended upon the sector, market conditions, and the volume of the transaction.

---

[19] Kazem Vadi'i, "Bazar dar Baft-e Novin-e Shahri," *Yaghma* 25 (Farvardin 1351 [March-April 1972]), 9–19.

[20] *Vaseteh* and *dallal* have pejorative connotations. Brokers themselves often prefer to call themselves "commissioners" or *haqq al-'amal kars* (agents).

Brokers, therefore, had an interest in maintaining a smoothly operating system that generated a high volume of exchanges.

Brokers first identified buyers and sellers. This can be a critical role in actual markets since search costs can be quite high.[21] Brokers did more than simply match transaction partners; they ensured that these parties were reliable trading partners who would deliver goods and payments at the agreed-upon time and to the agreed-upon specifications. Brokers provided sellers information about the buyer's credit history, past performance, and potential for long-term partnership. A proverb heard in the Bazaar begins, "A good customer is a jewel," yet goes on to caution, "but you have to know the jewel to ensure that it is not a fake."[22] Brokers helped separate the "fakes" from the "real" customers. Also, by quickly locating buyers for sellers they helped reduce warehousing costs. Obviously this cost can be quite substantial in cases where goods were more costly to store (i.e. perishables, items that are larger, and illegal goods). On the other hand, brokers assured buyers that the seller would deliver high-quality goods on time and had the financial and marketing capacity to continue providing that particular good.

Brokers could also play an important role in cases where the quality of a good was highly variable but difficult to ascertain. In this case brokers helped differentiate the market and limit adverse selection by ensuring that low-quality goods were not sold at the same price as high-quality goods.[23] Since brokers had regular working relationships with a wide spectrum of *bazaaris* they tended to have first-hand and idiosyncratic knowledge about levels of indebtedness or marketing strategies. A final and less commonly identified reason that brokers were used in transactions is that brokers created anonymity for buyers and sellers. The screen that brokers provided reduced personalism in exchanges, which may have become bogged down in expectations and interpersonal obligations, and replaced it with exchange that was mediated by a broker ensuring reputations via his own personal ties to and knowledge of the parties. *Bazaaris* mentioned that brokers were at times used so that exchange partners, who may have known each other, could transact without the "interference" of nonmarket factors. This logic demonstrates that *bazaaris* have been quite conscious of the interpersonal nature of markets and the potentially disruptive side to them. Ironically,

[21] Ariel Rubenstein and Asher Wolinsky, "Middlemen," *Quarterly Journal of Economics* 102 (August 1987), 581–94.

[22] Mohammad 'Atiqpur, *Naqsh-e Bazar va Bazariha dar Enqelab-e Iran* (Tehran: Kayhan, 1358 [1979]), p. 90.

[23] Paolo Garella, "Adverse Selection and the Middleman," *Economica* 56 (August 1989), 395–400.

networks and personal relations are used to mimic the "arm's-length" exchange assumed by neoclassical economics.

In addition, the brokers' intermediary position and role of overseers of transactions placed them in an ideal position to track price fluctuations and market conditions. By gauging supply and demand, brokers played an important marketwide function of monitoring price. Even today *bazaari*s cite brokers as the best source for information about prerevolutionary market conditions. Their astute knowledge helped reduce bargaining since buyers and sellers deferred to their price as the final price or the focal point around which they negotiated.[24] The term "expert" (*khebreh*) is often used to describe the most notable brokers.[25] In short, brokers were *network makers*, in the sense that they tied together and reinforced the many links in the value chain by creating the foundation for exchanges.

Economists would expect brokerage to lead to principal–agent problems where sellers and buyers would be concerned that brokers had opportunities to manipulate transactions to increase their commission or favor one party or the other. Principal–agent problems in the real world are mediated by networks of ongoing relations that ensure external monitoring and create incentives for honest behavior. Since brokers were potentially involved in long-term and repeated relations with buyers, sellers, and others in the Bazaar, their actions had repercussions well beyond a specific transaction between a given trading dyad.

In such a context, a reputation for honesty, fairness, and expertise was the most crucial asset for a broker. A broker's "whole life depended on being reputable and trustworthy; without a good name he would be paralyzed," mentioned one broker. This reliance on reputation might help explain why some observers have noted that brokers were the most outwardly religious members of the Bazaar.[26] In the Bazaar, brokers can signal their trustworthiness and principled behavior by espousing religious adherence and consciousness. Of course, simple lip-service would not be enough; over time if religious display was not consonant with practice, a broker's reputation would be discredited. Meanwhile, age and tenure in commerce were important indicators of knowledge,

---

[24] Hochschule der Künste Berlin, Fachbereich 2 Architektur "Bazaar Teheran," *Documentation 1: Probleme der Internationalen Stadtentwicklung* (series title) (West Berlin: Selbstverlag [Hochschule der Künste Berlin, Fachbereich 2 Architektur], February 1979), p. 10.

[25] In one instance I mentioned that a particular *bazaari* was a *vaseteh*, and I was quickly reminded that he was not simply a *vaseteh* but was a *khebreh*.

[26] 'Atiqpur, *Naqsh-e Bazar*, p. 91. This also emerged in several interviews.

another component of reputation. Successful brokers tended to be older and experienced, having many and well-positioned contacts who could vouch for their reputation.[27]

There is also a second type of intermediary whom I will call a middleman. In the Tehran Bazaar they are also referred to as *vaseteh* or *dallal*, but should not be confused with brokers, as in much of the secondary literature. Unlike a broker, a middleman did not necessarily specialize in a particular trade; one day he bought domestic vegetable oil and the next he purchased imported cutlery. Their commercial forays were more often based on speculation and short-term profit maximization. When middlemen were able to combine market analysis and timely purchases they were able to accrue windfall gains. Their position, however, was precarious since they actually purchased these goods and accepted the associated risks.

Middlemen were notorious inside and outside the Bazaar. Outside the Bazaar, the public and government blamed them for hoarding, price fixing, and deception. Inside the Bazaar, they were mocked for their lack of expertise, ethics, and stature. They "disturbed market equilibrium," charging "exorbitant prices," and sullying "the good name of *bazaari*s by introducing poor-quality goods and overcharging customers." When I made the mistake of misidentifying a particular broker as a middleman, I was quickly corrected by him, and his friend who had joined us gave me a stern speech explaining the difference between the two. The middlemen were generally younger, began with little capital, and often had few family contacts in Tehran or within the Bazaar. Some may have worked as apprentices, and others may have had no background in the Bazaar but turned to short-term transactions to augment their income. Those who were successful and acquired a reliable and honest reputation could expand their operations and credit lines. Before the Revolution, the middlemen were marginalized by the regularized flow of goods that passed through the commercial hierarchy. The opportunities for buying low and selling high were limited by high levels of liquidity and consumer goods. At times, middlemen were able to operate, however, by taking advantage of run-away demand for imports, transportation bottlenecks, and economic inefficiencies in domestic production.[28]

Thus, *bazaari*s were enmeshed in a tightly knit value chain based on long-term relations and interconnected networks. Despite their being a large, heterogeneous, and stratified group, the pattern of trade relations

[27] Some brokers were merchants who had become bankrupt and used their experience and knowledge to become a broker. Mina Jabbari, *Hamisheh Bazar* (Tehran: Agah, 1379 [2000]), p. 77.

[28] On bottlenecks and inefficiencies in the prerevolutionary economy, see Graham, *Iran*.

integrated the members of the Bazaar into a corporate unit. These contributing factors were enhanced by the credit system.

Extending credit, relationships, and reputations across the Bazaar

In the Bazaar, especially among distributors, there is a mantra: "You don't get anywhere by selling only for cash." Most transactions were on credit, with loans extended through the value chain and beyond it. The availability of credit has been critical for the ability of bazaaris to take advantage of fluid market conditions. The complex money market was the foundation of the Bazaar's marketing system, and prior to the Revolution was an integrative mechanism simultaneously generating and accessing horizontal dimensions of cooperative hierarchies.[29]

Capital was not scarce in Iran during the late Pahlavi era; however, it was highly politicized.[30] The state distributed the abundant oil revenue as subsidized credit through state-owned commercial and development banks. Retailers in the Bazaar and other small manufacturers did not have access to these funds in part because they were high-risk and costly customers for the banking system.[31] Moreover, throughout much of this period, these loans were ostensibly a resource transfer, for the interest rates were set below the rate of inflation, resulting in a high negative real rate of interest.[32] The subsidized credit was an attractive source to finance operations, and in and of itself entailed a profit. Not surprisingly it opened the door to varied forms of rent-seeking behavior and corruption. Given the authoritarian and arbitrary rule of the Shah's government these loans were politicized; that is, access to these highly desirable loans was not universal. Credit-worthiness was based on political and cultural allegiance to the Pahlavi monarchy and specifically to its modernizing agenda. These hidden transfers of capital were channeled to members of the royal family, high- and low-level government officials, and large industrialists who were involved in grand industrial and construction schemes often tied to western firms

---

[29] Clifford Geertz, *Peddlers and Princes: Social Change and Economic Modernization in Two Indonesian Towns* (Chicago: University of Chicago Press, 1963), and Clifford Geertz, "Suq: The Bazaar Economy in Sefrou," in *Meaning and Order in Moroccan Society*, ed. Clifford Geertz, Hildred Geertz, and Lawrence Rosen (Cambridge: Cambridge University Press, 1979).

[30] See Djavad Salehi-Isfahani, "The Political Economy of the Credit Subsidy in Iran, 1973–1978," *International Journal of Middle East Studies* 21 (1989), 359–79. All information in this section is based on this article.

[31] I thank an anonymous reviewer for bringing this point to my attention.

[32] Salehi-Isfahani's estimates of the proportion of the total credit that was a grant were as high as 0.46 in 1975–6 and 0.66 in 1977–1978. Salehi-Isfahani, "The Political Economy of the Credit Subsidy," 367.

and governments.[33] This capital largely bypassed the vast majority of medium-sized and smaller (typically labor-intensive) manufacturers, who instead either tended to receive these assets once they were recycled through the financial system or turned to their own retained earnings.[34] Those who had nationalist or religious credentials, as most *bazaari*s did, were unable to compete for these highly subsidized loans.

In the shadow of this state-owned financial system and because of its biases, the Tehran Bazaar's internal credit system became an important source of funds for all those who were unable to access the official banking system.[35] The nonofficial system was the primary means to finance commercial activities, real estate investments, and the private consumption of *bazaari*s, as well as new immigrants to the city and many ordinary Iranians. The individual loans dispensed in the Bazaar were modest in comparison with the developmental loans distributed by the state, yet the total sum was significant. In 1963, the bazaars in Iran were estimated to loan as much as all the commercial banks put together.[36] In 1975, the Bazaar was estimate to control 20 percent of the official market volume, or $3 billion in foreign exchange and $2.1 billion in loans outstanding.[37] Since the Tehran Bazaar was the hub for Iran's import–export trade and had access to huge sums of credit, its distribution network and credit line extended well beyond the Bazaar and Tehran to cover all corners of Iran. It is in this sense that "the Tehran Bazaar is the mother of provincial bazaars."[38]

The credit system in the Tehran Bazaar worked on two levels: first goods were purchased on credit, and second moneylenders extended credit. In the first instance, *bazaari*s bought from those higher in the value chain by paying for a portion of the goods and receiving the remainder on credit. Future transactions between partners involved purchases on credit and repayment of part of the balance. Occasionally, short-term arrangements were established when credit was repaid as

---

[33] Consistent with the modernist development ideology, during the 1970s industrial loans were increasingly distributed by the specialized development banks. See Maryam Ghadessi, "An Integrative Approach to Finance in Developing Countries: Case of Iran," unpublished Ph.D. dissertation, University of Utah (1996).

[34] Vaghefi, *Entrepreneurs of Iran*, pp. 106–7. For a more comprehensive and complex picture see Massoud Karshensas, *Oil, State, and Industrialization in Iran* (Cambridge: Cambridge University Press, 1990), chapters 4, 5, and 7.

[35] Ghadessi, "An Integrative Approach to Finance in Developing Countries."

[36] Richard Elliot Benedick, *Industrial Finance in Iran: A Study of Financial Practice in an Underdeveloped Economy* (Boston: Division of Research, Graduate School of Business Administration, Harvard University, 1964), p. 52.

[37] Alan D. Urbach and Jürgen Pumpluen, "Currency Trading in the Bazaar: Iran's Amazing Parallel Market," *Euromoney* (June 1978), 116.

[38] 'Atiqpur, *Naqsh-e Bazar*, p. 62.

soon as goods were sold. More commonly, however, transactions were initiated with the expectation that these credit relationships would be long term and buyer and seller would be involved in repeated transactions wherein credit and debts would be balanced out over time. Thus, interconnected and complex accounting ledgers could be carried over years and even across generations.

The second form of lending involved moneylenders (*sarraf*) who provided credit directly to *bazaar*is. These moneylenders often did not have a fixed abode and their lending was not monitored by state institutions. However, the moneylenders had savings accounts in the banks and used their deposits to gain access to short-term credit that they would loan in the Bazaar at a mark-up.[39] Moneylenders also had access to savings that *bazaar*is and households sought, to lend at higher returns than the commercial banking system. While there were many full-time moneylenders in the Bazaar area (including the area between Tupkhaneh and Ferdawsi squares), merchants and other members of the community who had disposable income would also supplement their commercial activities by distributing credit.

When these transactions were between long-term partners, involved regular exchanges (between wholesalers and grocers), or were for small amounts, they lacked any written documents or government-sanctioned instruments; hence the principle of placing one's honor (mustache) as collateral. At most the lender would make a note in his ledger and seek repayment at an unspecified later date or repayment was accounted for in future exchanges.[40] The transactions were conducted informally and based on referrals. In 1978, two European bankers described the lending process as follows: "[I]n touring the bazaar one may hear fragments of a conversation in the corner of a carpet traders' [*sic*] shop: 'Twenty eight percent! Fifty million rial!' – a handshake and another loan is concluded."[41] The informality in transactions has an efficiency gain in that it allows parties to engage in unspecified agreements where not all contingencies are spelled out in advance.

If transactions involved large, long-term, or long-distance exchanges or were between actors who did not know each other, *bazaar*is resorted to either unsecured promissory notes (*safteh*) or postdated checks. A

---

[39] While bank rates were around 12 percent the Bazaar rate ranged between 20 and 30 percent. H. Bahrambeygui, *Tehran: An Urban Analysis* (Tehran: Sahab Books Institute, 1977), p. 100.

[40] At the time the ledgers did not even include names, but simply referred to "the customer that I do not know their name." See *Asnaf*, no. 88 (Shahrivar 1379 [August–September 2000]), p. 10.

[41] Urbach and Pumpluen, "Currency Trading in the Bazaar," 115.

safteh is an unsecured agreement of payment based upon a form that could be purchased from commercial banks for a nominal duty. Each note was good for a maximum amount; therefore, for large purchases several notes were used. The parties agreed on a discount rate and payment date(s) for the *safteh*, which was signed by the borrower. Customarily, repayment was scheduled for three months, but could be extended after renegotiation. In case of nonpayment, the promissory note could be redeemed from the issuing bank or used to initiate a legal action to have the goods returned. Personal checks, however, gradually entered the Bazaar during the 1960s. In this case, the purchaser wrote the check for the agreed amount and date. Since a sliding scale was used, the buyer and seller would bargain in terms of both price and the due date. (Agreements could also be made where the full amount was paid in installments via a series of postdated checks.) Upon the date, either the debtor would deliver cash or the check-holder could go to the issuing bank branch to cash the check. If a check was written for an amount that could not be redeemed, the person writing the check could be immediately jailed upon complaint by the check-holder.

While credit was typically advanced down the hierarchy (from wealthier merchants to middlemen and shopkeepers), it was not unheard of for retailers to loan wholesalers and brokers small sums of credit. At times loans were dispersed horizontally across sectors and distribution chains. The longevity and interconnected credit are viewed as a marker of close relations in the Bazaar; when a *bazaari* wants to convey his close relation to a colleague, he says that their "accounts are mixed" (*hesabhamun qatieh*).

The credit system was based on the socioeconomic networks in a number of ways. First, the gathering of information on who had disposable cash and who needed credit involved access to the Bazaar's gossip mill, which extended across the marketplace. "Information and its quick dissemination are the essence of a money lender's security," commented two observers who spent time in Iran in the 1970s. "Word spreads so quickly that a merchant turned down independently by two lenders is confronted by a third with this knowledge within the hour."[42]

Once potential credit partners were identified, the interest rate charged was highly sensitive to network factors too. The discount rate was loosely based on market forces (the inflation rate, interest rates charged by banks, and supply and demand for credit) and the reputation of the credit seeker, with the latter force having more weight. Like any credit system, the Bazaar system followed the principle that the more "credit-worthy" the

[42] Ibid.

borrower, the lower the rate, the better the terms of the loan, and the more flexible the dealings. What made the Bazaar system different from a modern banking system was that credit-worthiness was defined more by a person's reputation than by their fixed assets (e.g. real estate, inventories, or machinery). Credit was extended based on the past interactions between the creditor and borrower. If the applicant had shown that they were trustworthy, they would be entitled to lower interest rates and/or more flexible payment schedules. When credit histories and reputations were less promising, the discounted rate would increase. Rates fluctuated during the 1960s and 1970s, but in the worst-case scenarios, rates could easily reach 40 percent per month.

Moneylenders who were unfamiliar with a loan applicant turned to their mutual acquaintances and brokers for a credit history. Less dependable or newer borrowers were obliged to get additional cosignatories as collateral. The better known and more respected the signatories were in the Bazaar, the better the terms of the agreement. If a member of the Bazaar became known for writing bad checks or not paying his debts in a timely manner, he and his signature would be sanctioned by creditors charging higher discount rates on their *safteh*s or checks, shorter terms of repayment, higher prices for goods, and/or a requirment to pay in cash. "Not only prices but men's reputations are set, reset, and continually adjusted in the bazaar as information flows through networks of reliable friends."[43] In the Bazaar's money market, a borrower places his good name by placing his signature as collateral. The reputation of a *bazaari* was critical to his ability to gain access to capital and merchandise; simultaneously, the sound appraisal of risk was essential for the financial survival of creditors. A *bazaari* explained, "If *bazaaris* are able, they won't pay back debts. They keep good accounts so as to continue their trade."[44] Thus, the *safteh* system's net of cross-cutting guarantees was a critical cooperative mechanism to help spread risk, expand commercial relationships and capital, and also build one's standing in the community.

Enforcing credit agreements also involved access to the *bazaaris*' networks. Whereas defaulting on debts and bankruptcies were not unheard of, the key point is that cooperative hierarchies prior to the Revolution were strong and prevalent enough to address these cases and solve disputes without resorting to third parties such as state institutions, which would have been slower and more costly than communal-based

---

[43] Roy Mottahadeh, *The Mantle of the Prophet: Religion and Politics in Iran* (New York: Pantheon Books, 1985), p. 35.
[44] Jabbari, *Hamisheh Bazar*, p. 143.

arbitration. If the *safteh* was not paid by the signatory or any of his cosignatories, the holder of the promissory note could legally take action by initiating a claim in court. But, not unlike modern commercial dealings, the norm was that these disputes were handled within the Bazaar via informal arbitration.[45] If the creditor, debtor, and cosignatory themselves were unable to arrive at an agreement, the dispute was taken to a notable in the Bazaar (*rish-sefid* or *ostokhundar*). These informally appointed guild elders gained this stature in the community because they were deemed experienced, trustworthy, and knowledgeable about both past and present market conditions, and usually had a working knowledge of religious customs, although not necessarily knowledge of religious laws or jurisprudence.[46] Active brokers often played this role because they enjoyed working relationships with many layers of the Bazaar and had molded virtuous reputations. Disputes and renegotiation of agreements were settled through the general practices of the community and in casual get-togethers, instead of via strict rules and in an official manner; a *bazaari* expression is that they "solved their disputes at the opium brazier." According to a carpet exporter who had a long-standing role as an arbitrator, he followed a general principle of selecting a path that was both practical (*'amali*) and would result in an outcome that both would recognize as just (*'adelaneh*). The economic climate, the histories of the parties, and the total debts outstanding were all taken into consideration. Settlements included distributing inventories among creditors on a consignment basis, payment extensions, or intermediaries and family contacts accepting part of the debt burden. Again the Bazaar network offered ways to solve disputes by spreading out responsibilities across different groups, extending time frames for debt repayment, and involving third parties in adjudication and compensation. The arbitrator accepted that this was not always easy, but he claimed that in "in ninety-nine percent of cases, everyone was content and would not have to resort to the court system." The capacity to minimize disputes and deal with them when they arose helped strengthen the Bazaar's networks over time by presenting opportunities to collaborate and solve problems.

Thus, prior to the Revolution, the Bazaar was shut out of patronage channels of the state and forced to turn to the "market" for credit. This suggests a different logic than the one underlying Geertz's account of the Bazaar credit system. Geertz argues that the traders in Indonesian

---

[45] Stewart Macaulay, "Non-Contractual Relations in Business: A Preliminary Study," *American Sociological Review* 28 (February 1963), 55–67.

[46] Rotblat notes that by the 1960s most *bazaaris* did not receive seminary education, did not know Arabic, and were not aware of the Islamic rules governing commercial activity. Rotblat, "Stability and Change in an Iranian Provincial Bazaar," p. 180.

bazaars "often prefer expensive private credit to cheap government credit" as a functional response in order to "stabilize more or less persisting commercial relationships."[47] Geertz's argument, besides being overly consequentialist, also makes the faulty assumption that members of small businesses in developing economies have equal access to credit. Even though credit within the Bazaar was available, in interviews with older *bazaaris* the lack of access to state institutions and resources was often cited as one of their main grievances toward the Pahlavi regime. Credit-worthiness in the official financial system was tied to political credentials, while in the Bazaar financial system it was tied to one's reputation in the Bazaar's social order.

Crosscutting and multiplex social relationships

As the discussion of the credit system illustrates, economic exchange in the Bazaar presupposed social mechanisms that identified exchange partners, monitored behavior, and sanctioned malfeasance. The social spheres within the Bazaar and a whole series of social networks helped underwrite many economic transactions by evaluating reputation, ensuring future interactions, creating opportunities to work together, developing horizontal ties, and expanding interactions to include noncommercial matters. In the next chapter it will be shown that the Bazaar's sense of solidarity was accentuated by external forces that ensured the reproduction of the Bazaar's institutions and demarcated the Bazaar. Here I would like to draw attention to the fact that observers of the Tehran Bazaar during the Pahlavi period often pointed out that "among tradesmen there is a strong sense of 'we' feeling and emotional investment or identification with the bazaar sub-culture."[48] This sense of "we" and "community" emerged out of a steady accretion of interactions that blurred the divide between potentially distinct spheres of life – kinship, friendship, partnership, and commerce. Ethnicities, religious practices, kinship patterns, and everyday interactions helped bring *bazaaris* together in a number of ways, allowing them to develop similar belief systems and create a field in which their identities and attributes could be made public and followers of norms could receive approbation or malfeasance could be censured.

Bazaaris often had close relations throughout the Bazaar, and not just in their sectors nor with economic partners. One important factor that

---

[47] Clifford Geertz, *Peddlers and Princes*, p. 36.
[48] Gustav Thaiss, "Religious Symbolism and Social Change: The Drama Husain," Ph.D. dissertation, Washington University (1973), p. 20.

helped establish ties across the Bazaar was ethnicity. Although the official language of Iran is Persian, there were, and are, significant Turkish (approximately 25 percent), Kurdish (approximately 8–10 percent), and Arabic (approximately 3–5 percent) speaking groups and countless dialects. For decades the Tehran Bazaar has reflected the polyglot nature of Iran. As for religious heterogeneity, over 90 percent of Iranians are Shiite Muslims, with the remainder being Sunni Muslims (7 percent), Christains of various denominations, Jews, Zoroastrians, and Bahais. Commercial activities reflected some of this religious variety, with a small number of Jews active in the cloth and carpet industries and the gold and jewelry markets in the Bazaar. Armenians, Zoroastrians, and Bahais were less common in the Tehran Bazaar, but are represented in the newer commercial sections of Tehran. One merchant described Muslims and Jews as *bazaari* and Armenians and Zoroastrians as *khiyabani*, or "of the street". Moreover, regional backgrounds also helped differentiate *bazaari*s. As the largest city and capital, Tehran attracted people from all regions. In the Bazaar there were important groups with family roots in the Isfahan, Yazd, Khuzestan, and Mashhad regions.

Although identity politics could have become a force to fragment *bazaari*s, it does not seem to have been a particularly divisive force prior to the Revolution, at least in the Tehran Bazaar.[49] The Tehran Bazaar did not exhibit strong ethnolinguistic cleavages, because ethnic or religious groups did not map onto trades and Tehran in the 1960s and 1970s included Iranians of all ethnic and religious backgrounds. Conversely, the presence of members from the same ethnic, religious, or regional groups across a number of sectors fostered connections beyond narrow economic ties and the confines of one's occupation. Individuals would develop relationships across guild boundaries by making acquaintances based on their linguistic, regional, or confessional backgrounds. In particular, religious organizations and places were important arenas that helped unite those from the same background. For instance, many Azeri Turkish speakers would congregate at one of the larger mosques in the Bazaar known as the Azerbaijani Mosque or the "Mosque of the Turks" (officially named Shaykh Abd al-Hosayn Mosque). Another mosque is known as the Mosque of the Gilanis (*masjed-e gilaniha*) and attracts people from Gilan province.

---

[49] The notable exception was the Bahai community that was viewed as heretical and severely ostracized by religious conservatives inside and outside the bazaars. I am unaware of any studies of Behais working in the Tehran Bazaar during the second half of the twentieth century, but it is likely that Bahais worked, and may still work, in a less than open and free manner.

Religious activities, the social dimension cited most often within the Bazaar, were an important part of associational life that created interpersonal relationships among members of the Bazaar network. Religious practices were arenas which brought together *bazaaris* from various backgrounds on a regular basis. As the old public heart of the city, the Bazaar contains numerous mosques and shrines, many of which were built by guilds or prominent merchants for the Bazaar community as a form of beneficence. The prominent mosques in the Bazaar included the Jame' Mosque, the Emam Khomeini Mosque (Shah Mosque), Cheheltan Mosque, and the Textile Sellers' Mosque. Prior to the Revolution, *bazaaris* would go to religious sites for their afternoon prayers, for special Koranic readings, or simply for conversation and reflection. In the process there were opportunities to expand one's spectrum of acquaintances or to deepen existing relations.

In the 1970s a number of accounts of the Tehran Bazaar argued that religious meetings held by the members of the Bazaar were crucial in encouraging socially embedded relations.[50] These gatherings, called *hayat*s, had religious trappings, although they were not exclusively religious. These weekly or biweekly meetings brought together small groups of *bazaaris* to discuss the week's events. These *hayat*s were often sponsored by a merchant from a particular neighborhood and organized by a mosque for the neighborhood. These associations crossed class and guild barriers. They were informal in the sense that there was no structure or dictated agenda. They did have a set time and day of the week and rotated among the homes of members. The religious aspect of these meetings was the customary prayers and readings from the Koran led by a younger cleric who often specialized in giving passionate sermons describing the martyrdom of Shiite heroes. The private setting allowed preachers and participants to manipulate religious symbols and characters in ways that made them analogous to present-day political conditions.

These meetings, however, were much more than lessons in Islamic theology and law or expressions of religiosity: they were a regularized meeting place for members of the Bazaar. The topics of discussion often

---

[50] Gustav Thaiss, "The Bazaar as a Case Study of Religion and Social Change," in *Iran Faces from the Seventies*, ed. Yar-Shater (New York: Praeger Publishers, 1971), pp. 201–3; Gustav Thaiss, "Religious Symbolism and Social Change: The Drama of Husain," in *Scholars, Saints, and Sufis: Muslim Religious Institutions in the Middle East since 1500*, ed. Nikki Keddie (Berkeley: University of California Press, 1972), pp. 352–55; and Michael M. J. Fischer, *Iran: From Religious Dispute to Revolution* (Cambridge: Harvard University Press, 1980). Rotblat notes that religious gatherings and religion play a broader role in Tehran than in the provincial bazaar of Qazvin. Rotblat, "Stability and Change in an Iranian Provincial Bazaar," p. 298.

crossed over into worldly issues and included anything from the week's economic and political news to the need to find a spouse for a son or daughter. During these meetings the members collected funds for merchants in financial trouble; financially supported the building of mosques, religious theaters, seminaries, and hospitals; organized weddings and festivals, and sanctioned *bazaari*s who broke "the rules" by spreading rumors about them.

There were different types of *hayat*. Occupational- or guild-related meetings were composed of members from the same trade. Another type of *hayat* was based on ethnic group and was composed of individuals who did not necessarily share the same occupation, but were from the same region, town, or ethnic group. Third, there were women's weekly meetings for mothers, wives, and daughters of *bazaari*s. Thus, these associations blended neighborly, religious, familial, and economic spheres. Therefore, a single merchant could attend more than one meeting during the course of a week. In turn, *hayat*s presented an opportunity to practice organizational skills and extend the chain of reciprocity. Thaiss perceptively concludes, "It is through the [*heyat*s] that individuals have an opportunity to meet and discuss ... [and] that networks of interpersonal relations are established and extended or links in the network dropped. It is through these interpersonal networks and the participation of the same individuals in several different gatherings during the week that bazaar information, ideas, and rumors are passed on."[51]

Religious practices, although having important expressive and altruistic motivations, also played a pragmatic role in that they signaled trustworthiness. Sprinkling one's speech with religious expressions, including pledging oaths to God or referring to the Koran and Shiite Imams, was meant to signal a *bazaari*'s piety, and through that his honesty. Also, establishing charities, paying religious taxes, and organizing and participating in religious feasts were part of the ethic of the chivalrous man.[52] Charity showed the community (meaning both the Bazaar and neighborhood) that one was generous and not materially oriented. Second, these acts were belived to purify one's wealth in the eyes of God, who rewards almsgiving, and simultaneously to protect one's wealth against the evil eye. Of course, too much public display of charity could raise the curiosity of tax collectors and invite questions about the source of the wealth. *Bazaari*s had to find the critical

---

[51] Thaiss, "The Bazaar as a Case Study of Religion and Social Change," p. 202.

[52] Fariba Adelkhah, *Being Modern in Iran*, trans. Jonathan Derrick (New York: Columbia University Press, 2000), pp. 30–52.

equilibrium for good works so that they received the "benefits" without attracting unwanted attention.

Having stressed the religious dimension of *bazaari* life, one must be careful not to overestimate the centrality or singularity of religion. Like any other religion or ideology and despite the pretences of "true believers" or declarations of Orientalists, Islam has various meanings and expressions and may coexist with other, sometimes contradictory, practices and beliefs. The *bazaaris'* religiosity and the role of Islam are too complex to be gleaned simply from the prevalence of prayer beads and pictures of Imams. Moreover, it is not enough simply to be publicly religious; one's behavior must be consistent with outward religiosity. There is evidence that *bazaaris* carefully distinguish the pseudoreligious (*mazhabi-nama*) from those who truly abide by the norms of Islam for unworldly gain. So, religious practices (praying and paying alms) are not sufficient means to achieve a reputable status in the Bazaar. On the other hand, being a good Muslim is not the only means of exhibiting trustworthiness. "Of course we transact with non-religious people if the person is upstanding. The criteria to initiate an exchange with someone is his know-how not his religion."[53] Howard Rotblat, who conducted extensive research in the Qazvin Bazaar in the late 1960s, succinctly captures my own impressions when he writes, "The existence of religion as a common denominator among the bazaaris is a fact which is taken for granted rather than an active basis for social solidarity."[54]

Family ties are another critical mechanism that brought diverse *bazaari* groups together. Commercial ties were reinforced by family connections and alliances. Over the years, endogamy has resulted in a thick web of familial relations among *bazaaris*.[55] Gustav Thaiss, an anthropologist who conducted research in the Tehran Bazaar in the 1970s, writes, "In the past (and today also to some extent), the bazaar was one large kinship unit, since intermarriage within the bazaar was preferred and practiced."[56] Traditionally arranged marriages were common within trades, but often took place between sons and daughters of *bazaaris* from different occupational backgrounds. This helped foster the growth of family-run trade houses that accumulate and reuse capital and maintain reputation by intermarriage. For example, the genealogy presented in

---

[53] Jabbari, *Hamisheh Bazar*, p. 75. One of the main themes of Jabbari's work is that it is inaccurate to reduce the bazaar to its religious dimension or overemphasize its attachment to the Shiite clergy.

[54] Rotblat, "Stability and Change in an Iranian Provincial Bazaar," p. 182.

[55] The value of marriage of cousins in Iranian society is reflected in the saying, "The engagement of cousins is decided in the heavens."

[56] Thaiss, "The Bazaar as a Case Study of Religion and Social Change," p. 199.

Illustration 3.1 demonstrates that even with only three generations of *bazaari*s we witness many marriages taking place among fellow members of the Bazaar. Moreover, although the kinship ties centered on the china and glassware bazaar, they also stretch across several other sectors in the Bazaar (e.g. dye sellers, tailors, and grocers).

Finally, physical space embedded the Bazaar's networks within a shared social context. The distinct geography and architecture of the Bazaar's buildings gave the Bazaar a tangible quality that composed the identity of *bazaari*s. Space was the common differentiating marker between economic activity within the Bazaar and outside of it. Both within the Bazaar and in Iranian society more generally, a distinct difference was (and is) made between the Bazaar and the *khiyaban*, or street.[57] While modernization theorists point to this difference as a reflection of a distinction between traditional and modern cultures, *bazaari*s have given meaning to these categories by designating the *khiyabani*s as inexperienced, being less reputable and skillful, and being more marginal to commercial activity. Even though these perceptions may have been erroneous, it is important to note that *bazaari*s and *khiyabani*s distinguished one another in terms of location, which reflects and delimits participation in *bazaari* socioeconomic networks.

The physical structure of the marketplace is so important that even the very soil, dirt, and grime of the Bazaar's alleys and buildings are believed to be embodied in a *bazaari*. When I developed a chest cold and had a dry cough during my research, a *bazaari* said it was due to the "dust of the Bazaar," and jokingly added, "Only now are you becoming a *bazaari*." An exchange between Gustav Thaiss and one of his informants some three decades earlier illustrates this point further. "Our type is used to the dirt of the bazaar. They can even get any kind of microbe from our blood. Believe me, if they send my blood to be examined, they will find out I am immune to all the diseases. Why? Because the dust from the carpets has filled up our lungs .... ." When Thaiss asked the informant what he meant by "our type," he responded, "*Bazaari's* type (*tip-i bazaari*)."[58] Thus, *bazaari*s conceived of group identity as being forged from the physical attributes of the *bazaar*.

The intimate work environment of the Bazaar helped generate a unique social milieu wherein people from all walks of life did more than simply pass each other. Narrow alleys specializing in particular goods and open storefronts and offices allow the many passers-by, either customers or

---

[57] This distinction was made in a interview with an old member of the Shoemakers' Syndicate; see interview with Javad Mehran-Gohar (Nateq-'Ali), "Dar vajeb budan va dorost budan-e Sandika, Shakki Nist," *Andisheh-ye Jame'eh* 12 (n.d.), 59–65.

[58] Thaiss, "Religious Symbolism and Social Change: The Drama Husain," pp. 24–5.

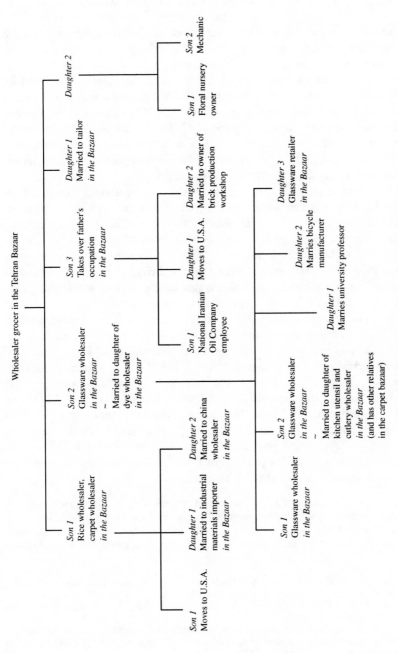

Illustration 3.1 Genealogy of a *bazaari* family

colleagues, to compare goods and prices easily, and to stop by to exchange news and gossip. This public quality allowed everyone to observe the activities of others, whether they were strangers, relatives, neighbors, guild elders, competitors, or trade partners. A shopkeeper could spontaneously go across to a store and chat about the day's news or enquire about the creditworthiness of a potential partner, and all the time keep a watchful eye over his abode. With a quick wave his apprentice could signal to him that he had a phone call or potential sale. The compact morphology allowed "eyes to be upon the streets."[59] Gazes were the Bazaar's market reports and whispers were its ticker-tape. The bazaar's objective spatial dimensions allowed for daily, face-to-face interactions and could spawn authentic friendships as well as economic pacts.

Fostering multifaceted relations was the Tehran Bazaar's textured life that blended various social dimensions within the economic confines. Within and surrounding all Iranian bazaars there were also public baths, restaurants, coffee and teashops, gymnasiums ("houses of strength"), major mosques, seminaries, and shrines. To use a term coined by Jane Jacobs, the Bazaar area was a "mingled city" that had mixed uses – commercial, manufacturing, holy, hygienic, recreational, and culinary. On a daily, or habitual, basis *bazaari*s would eat lunch together, gather in coffee houses, and have meetings at their warehouses and entrance gates to their alleys. Also, many schools were located in the immediate bazaar area (the Marvi school and the Dar al-Fonun being the most notable), and some of these were funded by *bazaari* families. The Tehran Bazaar historically functioned as a holistic sphere with high levels of "social connectivity."[60]

Historically, the Tehran Bazaar included residences in addition to commercial units.[61] Although *bazaari*s who were prospering began to leave the immediate Bazaar area in the 1950s, the old neighborhoods in central Tehran maintained their multiclass nature. Habib Ladjevardi, the son of one of Iran's prominent industrialists who had roots in the Tehran Bazaar, recalls that his family

lived until 1962 in the Amirieh district of central Tehran where his house was across the street from a grocery store, a butcher, and a cobbler, and a bakery. The neighborhood was heterogeneous; the rich and middle-class lived in the same street, frequented the same shops, used the same public baths, and wore cloths of

---

[59] Jane Jacobs, *The Death and Life of Great American Cities* (New York: Random House, 1993 [1961]).

[60] Saskia Sassan, *The Global City: New York, London, and Tokyo* (Princeton: Princeton University Press, 2001).

[61] In the last Qajar census the Bazaar area contained the most homes. Naser Takmil-Homayun, *Tarikh-e Ejtema'i va farhangi-ye Tehran*, vol. 3 (Tehran: Daftar-e Pajuheshha-ye Farhangi, 1379 [2000]), p. 31.

similar quality and style. The proximity of different economic classes, combined with the natural reluctance of members of the merchant class to engage in conspicuous consumption, resulted in a harmonious neighborhood. On Thursday evenings, I remember a local mullah would come to our house, sit in the entrance hall, recite prayers, and then depart. On holy days, there were great religious processions, organized by the local mosque, going through our street.[62]

These group activities within the specific locale of the Bazaar area created a "spatial ecology" that assembled *bazaaris* in ways that exceed what one would expect from a group that contained class, guild, and ethnic divisions.[63] The multiplex and crosscutting relations allowed for a chain of reciprocity to develop in which the balance between gift giving and receiving could be extended over time and across various fields.

In conclusion, the value chain in Tehran's Bazaar during the prerevolutionary era was stable because it consisted of long-term relations between the various levels that fashioned the networks. Nested and evolving credit relations and the regularized exchange between *bazaaris* who specialize in particular lines of work extended relationships over stretches of time. These repeated exchanges, or in Geertz's term "clientelization," introduced reciprocity into the exchange process, while improving the likelihood that promises would be honored.[64] These essentially vertical ties were patterned in a particular type of embeddedness that incorporated communal attributes. Complex webs of credit relations and social activities based on multiple categories of identity and affiliation both built important horizontal bonds that distributed and verified information. The rich social milieu brought the Tehran Bazaar together on a number of overlapping fronts and created an interdependent form that ensured ongoing vertical and horizontal ties, or cooperative hierarchies. *Bazaaris* who had group membership had access to credit, resources, and a potential to accrue a reputation. Meanwhile, participation in the multiplicity of facets of bazaar life instilled in its members norms of cooperation and solidarity. This mutually reinforcing process was the basis for binding obligations, or "conditional cooperation."[65] It was the participation in these

---

[62] Habib Ladjevardi, *Labor Union and Autocracy in Iran* (Syracuse, NY: Syracuse University Press, 1985), p. 236.

[63] William H. Sewell, "Space in Contentious Politics," in *Silence and Voice in the Study of Contentious Politics*, ed. Ronald R. Aminzade et al. (Cambridge: Cambridge University Press, 2001).

[64] Clifford Geertz, "Suq: The Bazaar Economy in Sefrou," in *Meaning and Order in Moroccan Society*, ed. Clifford Clifford Geertz, Hildred Geertz, and Lawrence Rosen (Cambridge: Cambridge University Press, 1979).

[65] Michael Taylor, *The Possibility of Cooperation* (Cambridge: Cambridge University Press, 1987).

polycentric networks that brought diverse *bazaari* groups together to shape the way people thought of themselves and others who were "of the Bazaar." It is these embedded and expansive networks that created a robust sense of solidarity and made the Tehran Bazaar in the pre-revolutionary era a community, despite having a hierarchy.

The coercive hierarchies of the postrevolutionary bazaar

In order to demonstrate to me that the "old ways" were inappropriate for today's Tehran Bazaar, Mehdi, a glassware wholesaler, recounted a story about his friend 'Ali. 'Ali was the eldest son of a prominent and highly respected glass wholesaler in the Hajeb al-Dawleh Timcheh. He helped his father as a child and even worked there while he went to university. In the mid-1970s 'Ali had found employment outside the Bazaar and worked as an engineer. When he lost his job in the economic recession of the early 1980s, he decided to return to the Bazaar and continue his deceased father's wholesaling operation. Mehdi thought highly of 'Ali's "intelligence" and "education" and his "father's good name [reputation]." Yet, when 'Ali sought Mehdi's opinion regarding his return to the Bazaar, Mehdi recalled that he cautioned him by saying that things were different and he must be careful not to view the Bazaar as the same as when he left it. He warned that the market, its people and practices, had all changed. According to Mehdi, 'Ali did not heed his warning. He was "swindled" by suppliers and buyers alike. After only a few years in the Tehran Bazaar, 'Ali left it with heavy debts and a bruised ego.

I heard similar stories from other *bazaari*s. These narratives were both a critique of the present situation and intended to demonstrate that my preconceptions of a systematic hierarchy with well-defined roles and a normative system of checks and balances that protected against guile and dishonesty did not apply "now." If the postrevolutionary Tehran Bazaar was not the same as its prerevolutionary antecedent, what was it?

Change in the Tehran Bazaar's membership

The revolutionary turmoil led to major instability in the composition of the Tehran Bazaar. The plethora of manifestos and slogans of the Revolution included many anticapitalist platforms that threatened the private sector in general, and the larger trade houses in the Bazaar in particular. Newspapers, political declarations, and public rhetoric included descriptions of corrupt capitalist elements as "economic terrorists," "hoarders," "fraudsters" (*kolah-bardar*, literally hat thieves), "pillagers of the national wealth," "oppressors," and the "corrupt of the earth."[66] The climate was at best precarious and at worst hostile toward capital. Prominent importers, especially those who were also active in industry, emigrated to escape the unsympathetic environment. Of those who remained, some faced allegations of cooperating with the Pahlavi regime or having affiliations with an ever increasing list of banned political parties. Those who were unable to demonstrate their revolutionary credentials and allegiance lost their property, were fined and imprisoned, or were executed.[67] All this led to attrition among of the elder and high-profile *bazaaris*.

A select group continued their trading activities under the patronage of state enterprises. A small segment of *bazaaris*, many of whom were brokers, minor wholesalers, and members of the vegetable and fruit bazaar (*mayduni* or *maydani*), had been active in the burgeoning Islamist and pro-Khomeini organizations of the early 1960s (Jam 'iyyat-e Motalefeh-ye Eslami or ICA), the most important of which was the Islamic Coalition Association or Party. Through their *hayat*s and religious schools, ICA developed long-standing social and kinship ties with clerical ideologues of the Islamic Revolution (Ruhollah Khomeini, Mohammad Beheshti, Morteza Motahhari, and Mohyeddin Anvari)[68] and championed an interpretation of Islam that gave authority and responsibility to the clergy and devout Muslims to take action against "illegitimate" rule. Owing to state surveillance the ICA was operated in a secretive, cell-like, and underground manner,[69] and as a result this did not have a broad base of support in society or the Bazaar. Moreover, one of the leading ideologues of the organization disputes the labeling of the ICA as a "*bazaari* party" by differentiating the ICA members from *bazaaris*, by describing them as "cultural figures" (*farhangi*) because they were busy teaching and writing religious works.[70]

---

[66] Khomeini made a reference to these attacks in a 1982 speech to members of the Tehran Bazaar by saying that most *bazaaris* are not these people and *bazaaris* do not act against religious law. Reprinted in *Asnaf* no. 22 (Oribehest 1373 [April–May 1994]), 47.

[67] Abolqasem Lebaschi, interview by Habib Ladjevardi, tape recording no. 3, Paris, France, February 28, 1983, Iranian Oral History Collection, Harvard University. Misagh Parsa claims that over a hundred *bazaaris* were killed or executed after the revolution. Parsa, *Social Origins of the Iranian Revolution*, p. 282. During my interviews many of the *bazaaris* regularly recalled their fear in the first couple of years after the Revolution.

[68] Asadollah Badamchian and 'Ali Banaii, *Hayatha-ye Motalefeh-ye Eslami* (Tehran: Awj, 1362 [1983]); Changiz Pahlavan, "Negahi beh Jam'iyyat-e Hayatha-ye Motalefeh-ye Eslami," *Andisheh-ye Jame'eh* 5 (n.d.), 8–13

[69] Davud Qasempur, ed., *Khaterat-e Mohsen Rafiqdust* (Tehran: Markaz-e Asnad-e Enqelab-e Eslami, 1383 [2004]), 59–65.

[70] *Sharq*, 6 Shahrivar 1384 [August 28, 2005].

During the revolutionary struggle against the monarchy, the Islamist *bazaari*s financed and organized many political rallies and events. After the Islamic Revolution, these groups exhibited loyalty to the Imam and the revolutionary cause by initially disbanding their independent organizations and joining the Islamic Republican Party.[71] They were rewarded handsomely for their vigilance and fidelity with positions in government ministries, the newly formed foundations (*bonyad*s), and the Chamber of Commerce – they became part of the new ruling elite.

Since the economy was dominated by the state, these figures enjoyed ideal positions for direct access to rents via exclusive importing licenses, tax exemptions, subsidized hard currency, and control over procurement boards and industrial establishments. The *bazaari*s who have established patronage channels have used them for personal and exclusive ends, and not as a tool for the benefit of the entire Bazaar.[72] "They had their bread and they weren't going to share it," groaned one wholesaler. He added, "They still haven't. Why should they?" When I checked to see who he meant by "they," I consciously referred to them as "*bazaari*s" in order to solicit a response. I was promptly cut off and told, "They are not *bazaari*, they are *dawlati* (officials of the government)." Another person described them as *ahl-e regime*, literally "of the regime," distinguishing them from those who are *ahl-e bazaar*, or "of the Bazaar." Some of my interviewees would go so far as to deny that these individuals were ever "real *bazaari*s." My interlocutors claimed that prior to the Revolution these figures were mere middlemen (*dallal* and *vaseteh*), thus disparaging them as lesser *bazaari*s. Others mentioned that people like Mohsen Rezaii (a former commander-in-chief of the Revolutionary Guard) and Mohsen Rafiqdust (a former commander-in-chief of the Revolutionary Guard and head of the most powerful *bonyad*, the Foundation for the Disinherited) were from the *maydun*, implicitly denying their affiliation to the higher-status bazaar community.[73]

---

[71] Mas'ud Kuhestani-Nejad, "Mo'arrefi-ye Jam'iyyat-e Motalefeh-ye Eslami," *Gozaresh* 93 (1378 [1999]), 13–21.

[72] Habibollah 'Asgarawladi, the leader of the hardline Islamist faction who was the Minister of Commerce from 1981 to 1983, lost his position after the press accused him of nepotism and sabotage of the distribution system. Ali Rahnema and Farhad Nomani, *The Secular Miracle: Religion, Politics and Economic Policy in Iran* (London: Zed Books, 1990), p. 250.

[73] For comments on Rafiqdust being an "illiterate produce seller," see Mohammad Shanehchi, interview by Habib Ladjevardi, tape recording no. 4, Paris, France, March 4, 1983, Iranian Oral History Collection, Harvard University. On *maydun*is in general and the difference between them and *bazaari*s see Adelkhah, *Being Modern in Iran*, chapter 2.

Those who are outside of the Bazaar causally refer to this state-dependent economic class as the *bazaaris* because some of them at one time worked in the Bazaar, were born to *bazaari* families, were active in the "traditional" commercial activities, or are perceived to have *bazaari* values and sensibilities. However, neither are all *bazaaris* members of this group, nor are all members of the state-affiliated bourgeoisie from *bazaari* backgrounds. More importantly, the Bazaar does not recognize them as such. Rather the location of their occupation (ministries instead of the Bazaar) and access to state power trumps their historical association or genealogy; their clientelist status impedes them from maintaining a dual identity of *bazaari* and *dawlati*. Political scientists studying the developing world have quite rightly argued that patron–client relations blur state–society boundaries and complicate discussions about "the state,"[74] yet the subjective perspective of social groups demonstrates that insiders clearly differentiate between coopted members of the state and those who are not directly incorporated via the patron–client system. This finding is quite consistent with the network approach, for conceptions of group identity and solidarity are byproducts of relationships and interactions, not inherited and unchanging individual markers.

The remaining *bazaaris* faced both real and prospective obstacles. International sanctions, a turbulent political atmosphere, a drop in oil production and revenue, and the Iraqi invasion sent the economy into a tailspin. The Bazaar faced macrolevel restrictions owing to the declining purchasing power of consumers, a sudden and dramatic decline in domestic production, and limited hard currency. From the *bazaaris'* perspective the first few years of the Islamic Republic also brought a highly uncertain future for private business. Owing to pending bankruptcies and under pressure from the secular and Islamic Left, the provisional government nationalized all banks, insurance companies, and large industrial and agricultural enterprises within the first few months of the Islamic Republic.[75] The Constitution, adopted in October 1979, challenged the rights of property owners and created a framework to enhance the role of the state in economic affairs. The Constitution clearly places the bulk of the economy, including foreign

---

[74] Catherine Boone, "States and Ruling Class in Postcolonial Africa: The Enduring Contradictions of Power," in *Social Power and Social Forces: Domination and Transformation in the Third World*, ed. Joel Migdal, Atul Kohli, and Vivienne Shue (Cambridge: Cambridge University Press, 1994).

[75] Ali Rashidi, "De-Privitization Process of the Iranian Economy after the Revolution of 1979," in *The Economy of Islamic Iran: Between State and Market*, ed. Thierry Coville (Tehran: Institut Français de Recherche en Iran, 1994).

trade, banking, and shipping, in the direct hands of the state, while suggesting that the private sector is a mere supplementary appendage. In the following chapter I show that the anti-private-sector constitutional provisions were interpreted and applied in a way that did not in fact result in the abandonment of private property rights, but their sweeping language certainly worried Iran's business community.[76] To heighten tensions, the policy of expanding the state's role and supervision of markets was quickly bolstered by the requisites for developing a war economy.[77]

In response to both real economic contractions and potential future limits on commercial activity, many *bazaaris* judiciously downsized their operations by diverting their capital to profitable activities such as real estate purchases, construction,[78] and the purchase of hand-woven carpets (investments in land proved to be lucrative, but in many cases carpet purchases were unprofitable). These older established *bazaaris*, who had available liquid capital and bought land or warehouses in the 1970s and early 1980s, did benefit from the speculative property market. Yet, their absence from the Bazaar decommissioned its reputation system. An economy based on speculation may be good for individual *bazaaris*, but it is not good for the Bazaar's social fabric.

Finally, as many members left the Tehran Bazaar for lives abroad, activities in other segments of the economy, or positions in government, many new faces entered the Bazaar. The Bazaar was always a locus for those who were unable to find employment, but after the Revolution the numbers of unemployed and those seeking a second income increased dramatically. Throughout the postrevolutionary period, employment in the industrial sector was increasingly scarce and public sector salaries could not keep pace with increasing costs of living. Therefore, many Iranians turned to the Bazaar and the informal sector for employment, moonlighting, and investment. Those who had family members or friends in the Bazaar turned to them for opportunities and referrals. Those who lacked ties to the Bazaar or sought to go into economic activities not represented in the Bazaar joined the ballooning informal sector that both

[76] The threat to private property was heightened when Morteza Motahhari, a leading revolutionary ideologue who favored the market system, was assassinated in May 1979 and when Mehdi Bazargan, the prime minister of the Provisional Government and advocate for liberal economic policies, was ousted from power in November 1979. This last point was mentioned by several *bazaaris* when they discussed the uncertainties during the immediate postrevolutionary period.

[77] Nader Nazemi, "War and State Making in Revolutionary Iran," unpublished Ph.D. dissertation, University of Washington (1993).

[78] Kaveh Ehsani, "Municipal Matters: The Urbanization of Consciousness and Political Change in Tehran," *Middle East Report* 209 (Fall 1999), 22–7.

complemented and supplemented the Bazaar's commercial and service activities. The new "free sector" (*bakhsh-e azad*) included a diverse set of activities, among them the sale of illegal goods (e.g. banned books and alcohol), taking advantage of arbitrage opportunities (e.g. sale of food coupons, subsidized dollars and products), and small-scale and informal markets (e.g. household jobs and petty production in unregistered locales).[79] Extrapolating from official financial accounts, Firouzeh Khalatbari concludes that these activities, which attract all classes and both genders, at the very minimum comprised 25 percent of the official economy in the late 1980s and have increased in subsequent years.[80] The expansion of these parallel markets, the largest portion of which were in the service sector, was part and parcel of the overall trend that saw Iran's economy being diverted from industry to service, in particular trade. The number of commercial units almost doubled from 1976 to 1986,[81] with roughly half of them being unlicensed.[82]

The transfer of scarce resources from manufacturing, and to a lesser extent agriculture, to the service sector and the establishment of parallel markets made the Tehran Bazaar a far larger and disparate commercial economy. The postrevolutionary informal product and service sector obviously competes with the Tehran Bazaar by purveying substitute goods and diverting capital and labor from the Bazaar economy. Many *bazaari*s, however, also depend on the informal economy. For instance, many turn to "the black market" for hard currency or inventories. Those who seek to export or import goods use commercial cards (*kart-e bazargani*) that are sold in "the black market" via classified pages in daily newspapers. The use of government newspapers to advertise the selling of government-issued licenses is indicative of the quasi-informal nature of the underground market, as well as the role of intermediaries and brokerages that are outside of the realm of the Bazaar. The underground economy has forced *bazaari*s to extend their networks well beyond the Bazaar and has introduced a larger and more diverse group of people into the commercial world.

---

[79] Asef Bayat, *Street Politics: Poor People's Movements in Iran* (New York: Columbia University Press, 1997), p. 136.

[80] Firouzeh Khalatbari, "Iran: A Unique Underground Economy," in *The Economy of Islamic Iran: Between State and Market*, ed. Thierry Coville (Tehran: Institut Français de Recherche en Iran, 1994) and Massoud Karshensas and M. Hashem Pesaran, "Exchange Rate Unification, the Role of Markets and Planning in the Iranian Economic Reconstruction," in *The Economy of Islamic Iran: Between State and Market*, ed. Thierry Coville (Tehran: Institut Français de Recherche en Iran, 1994).

[81] Ebrahim Razzaqi, *Ashnaii ba Eqtesad-e Iran* (Tehran: Nashr-e Nay, 1376 [1997]), p. 226.

[82] *Asnaf* no. 90 (Aban 1379 [October–November 2000]), 11.

A shoe seller argued that "trust between people has almost disappeared and the main reason for this is entrance of inexperienced people (*kam-sabeqeh*) and fraudsters (*kolah- bardar*)." The change in actors, in and of itself, had several critical consequences for the form of network governance. The assumption that transactions would lead to future dealings seemed less tenable as membership became more unstable. Exchange dyads were unable to knit together particular transactions into nested commercial relationships comprising past and prospective interactions on multiple fronts. Also, as many of the well-known intermediaries in exchanges left the Bazaar or passed away, the linkages between various layers in the sectors diminished. These factors had dire repercussions for the appraisal of reputation; the key ingredient in ensuring smooth flows of goods was made far more difficult since personal histories in the Bazaar were shallow and not as readily disseminated. Trustworthy new entrants had difficulty in building reputations in order to convince *bazaari*s of their credentials, while dishonest newcomers' fraudulent intensions were disguised by the *bazaari*s' ignorance. New entrants refashioned the system in another way too. A retired merchant commented that the very existence of new and inexperienced entrants destroyed the Bazaar's trusting climate. He argued that these new entrants did not have experience in detecting frauds (i.e. people who would overcharge, not pay for goods, or deliver poor-quality goods) and that this led to an increase in actual fraud, as well as the "the fear of fraud," with the latter being as determental for cooperative hierarchies as the former.

The consequences of fluid commercial relations and smuggling

A simple change in actors, however, should not necessarily have transformed the economic structure of the Bazaar over the long run. Neoclassical economic views of markets, of course, would predict that market operations are independent of actor's identities and relations. *Ceteris paribus*, the factors of production would have generated the same market structures, if not the exact same equilibrium. The moral economy perspective also discounts the relevance of changes in members for the economy. Through modes of cultural and normative learning, the same notions of reciprocity, expectations of behavior, and generalized culture should have re-created "the bazaar economy." The prevailing view within the embedded network approach to markets implicitly posits that the value chain, credit system, and social fabric should have reproduced itself. But while networks have reemerged, cooperative hierarchies with long-term, multiplex, and crosscutting relations have not been restored. In the following chapter I ask why this has not occurred, but in the remainder of this section I sketch the form of network governance that since the 1980s has emerged in the Tehran Bazaar.

The relatively stable hierarchy with defined roles within the Bazaar no longer exists. On numerous occasions my interviewees paused and pondered out loud before they explained to me their ill-defined economic activities. They would begin by saying that they *used to be* wholesalers, but they would add that they now would sell retail if they had the opportunity or necessity. They were simultaneously importers, wholesalers, and often dabblers in speculation. If opportunities offered themselves they would import goods and sell wholesale. However, when stocks ran low and imports were not delivered in a timely manner, they would resort to retail sales and stop-gap measures to replenish inventories. The instability in the flow of products has to some degree hampered specialization after the Revolution, which in turn has helped reduce ongoing commercial relations.[83] Not only did they play multiple and changing positions in the value chain, but *bazaari*s were never quite sure of the roles and scope of activities of their colleagues. On more than one occasion, I was referred to an individual who, I was told, was involved in one level of trade only to discover during the course of the interview that they were in fact involved in different activities.

The value chain begins with importers who are now no longer members of the Tehran Bazaar. Domestic production during the past half century was outside the Bazaar, yet up until the Revolution importers were part of the Bazaar's network. After the Revolution this changed, because the state intervened by becoming the major actor in international trade and by placing substantial restrictions on other products. The president of the Association of Iron sellers of Tehran remarked that "the government has practically taken the market away from the Bazaar in such a way that it is the primary purchaser and wholesaler." He added, "The government is not only not a good wholesaler, but at present is not a good retailer either. Of course it is not that the government itself is a retailer, but the organs under its supervision and dependent on the government and commercial companies connected to the ministries interfere in the commercial sector, to a point that it interferes with the private sector too."[84]

State organs, including trade units within ministries, military organs, religious charities, and foundations (*bonyad*s), have become the primary actors in international trade. These state affiliates have monopolies and access to special licenses, and they benefit from various subsidies and

---

[83] Neil Fligstein, "Markets as Politics," 656–73.
[84] *Hamshahri*, 8 Bahman 1379 (January 27, 2001), 4.

exemptions. Meanwhile, the state has sought to regulate exports in order to prevent capital flight. Exporters had to resort to unofficial channels to export their goods. As one would expect, the licensing process is rife with opportunities for corruption, nepotism, and patronage, with the disparate constellation of state procurement boards, religious trusts, and relatives of senior officials enjoying privileged positions.[85]

Much if not the vast majority, of imported goods sold in the Tehran Bazaar, however, do not arrive directly or by purely legal means.[86] Rather imports are either smuggled into the country or enter through commercial loopholes via special commercial zones (free trade zones or border cooperatives and markets) and are then incrementally brought across the official border. The latter method has been the most common route during the past five years. As described in greater detail in Chapter 4, importers first arrange for goods to be shipped to Dubai. From there, the order is sent to one of Iran's free trade zones in the Persian Gulf (Kish, Qeshm, and Chabahar) and then gradually to the mainland and large cities in central Iran. Since smuggled goods are not taxed and do not pay various duties, they are far cheaper than goods that legally enter the country or are domestically produced. To demonstrate the price differential, *Eqtesad-e Iran* showed that a television set that arrives via the free trade zone would cost only 970,000 rials (roughly $125), which is 24 percent cheaper than a domestically produced equivalent and 38 percent less than a television that is legally imported.[87] A *Wall Street Journal* reporter recounts a conversation with a Pyrex importer in the Bazaar: " 'If it costs me a dollar to get a dish to Dubai, it costs $1.50 by the time it gets here,' the resilient trader says. He laughs, partly because his competitors face the same hurdles. 'I think we just love to make things complicated.' "[88] Almost by definition, it is difficult to calculate the volume of

---

[85] Wolfgang Lautenschlager, "The Effects of an Overvalued Exchange Rate on the Iranian Economy, 1979–84," *International Journal of Middle East Studies* 18 (February 1986), 41–2.

[86] This was deduced from interviews and participant observation. A journalist for the *Wall Street Journal* estimated that two-thirds of all goods sold in the Tehran Bazaar are imported via smuggling networks. *Wall Street Journal*, 7 December 1998. On postrevolutionary policies, smuggling, and "legal smuggling" see the special issue on "Legal Smuggling" in *Eqtesad-e Iran* 360 (Bahman 1380 [January 2002]) and *Barresiha-ye Bazargani* 135 (Aban 1377 [October–November 1998]). For a sociological perspective based on participant observation see Fariba Adelkhah, "Who Is Afraid of Smuggling? We All Are Smugglers, Unless . . . .," Paper presented at the annual meeting of the Middle East Studies Association, Washington DC (November 2002).

[87] "Reqabat-e Na-barabar," *Eqtesad-e Iran* 360 (Bahman 1380 [January–February 2002]), 15. Percentages have been calculated by the author from prices presented in article.

[88] *Wall Street Journal*, February 8, 2001.

smuggled goods, but estimates of smuggled imported goods are around $3 billion dollars per year.[89]

Smuggling networks have particular qualities and consequences for the form of governance within the Bazaar.[90] To begin with, smuggling networks are typically not expected to last for extended periods of time since actors may be arrested, commodities may not reach their destination, and laws may change. The instability of smuggling networks prevents the two sides from making credible commitments. The providers of goods are in a precarious position since they cannot guarantee future shipments. Meanwhile, purchasers, knowing the precarious supply situation, are increasingly attempting to address this uncertainty by considering switching to importers and brands with more certain importing channels or even products. In the process, strict specialization has waned, with experience and experts being replaced by political contacts and the politically connected.

Second, in the context of a closed economy, the norm of face-to-face transactions of the embedded market has given way to the secrecy, if not anonymity, of the black market. Smuggling networks operate clandestinely, and thus hinder the development of crosscutting ties among large groups of people that is critical for the exchange of information and mutual monitoring. By its very definition, smuggling fosters opaque relations that are invisible to those who are not directly involved in the exchanges, whether they are customs officials or other buyers and sellers in the Bazaar. While those participating in illegal activities may be avoiding authorities, they are inadvertently marring transparency among *bazaaris* since they refrain from exchanging information about trading

---

[89] Mehdi Karbasian, the head of Iran's Customs, claimed that only $1.5 to $2 billion worth of goods were smuggled into the country. *Akhbar-e Eqtesadi*, 7 Bahman 1378 (January 27, 2000). Hosayn Nasiri, the Secretary of the Supreme Council of Free Trade Zones, set the figure at $3 billion. "Subsidies and Tariffs Encourage 'Black Economy,'" *Radio Free Europe/Radio Liberty* 3 (September 18, 2000). *Bonyan* estimated contraband imports at $3.5 billion. *Bonyan*, 25 Bahman 1380 (February 14, 2002). *Iran Daily* citing government sources set the figure at between $3 and $5 billion. *Iran Daily*, 28 Febuary 2001. *Eqtesad-e Iran* (Iran's version of *The Economist*) claims that $4 billion worth of goods are smuggled or "legally smuggled" into Iran. "Khosh Khat va Khal," *Eqtesad-e Iran* 360 (Bahman 1380 [January–February 2002]), 11. Finally, the magazine published by the Institute for the Study and Analysis of Commerce, a research center affiliated with the Ministry of Commerce, set the total volume of smuggling at between $2 and $4 million a year. "Sokhan-e Nakhost," *Barresiha-ye Bazargani* 135 (Aban 1377 [October–November 1998]), 2.

[90] Much of the information and analysis in this paragraph comes from my daily observations, eavesdropping, and conversations in the Bazaar. Smuggling has important, often deleterious, consequences for local economies in the border regions of Iran. For a glimpse into this issue see a travelogue of Iran's border region by Mehrangiz Kar, *Nakhlha-ye Sukhteh* (Tehran: Rawshangaran va Motale'at-e Zanan, 1379 [2000]).

partners. Smuggling or illegal networks foster "strong" hierarchical ties among actors directly involved in the transactions, but they do little to foster "weak" and diffuse connections since colleagues no longer share information with others. These exclusivist commercial channels fragment the Tehran Bazaar and impede the development of horizontal and more expansive networks. In many cases, the head of a smuggling network (i.e. the importer) may be unknown to buyers. When I discussed smuggling with a tea wholesaler in the Tehran Bazaar he repeatedly expressed uneasiness that these quasi-legal transactions are conducted over the phone. He said he is never sure who the importers are and where they are. He rhetorically asked, "How can you have any kind of a *relationship* with someone you haven't seen?"[91]

Finally, smuggling relations tend to be top-down and highly unequal. The few state affiliates who enjoy state protection or the off-shore monopolists who dominate the imports are buffered from direct contact with wholesalers and retailers by various levels of middlemen. The coercive nature of smuggling networks is also evident in the form of threats of violence and physical coercion that exist at various levels of the contraband process.

In addition to transnational smuggling, the restrictions on the flow of goods, development of parallel markets, and price distortions generated by subsidies and unequal access to foreign exchange and import licenses generate huge space for arbitrage and speculation (i.e. middleman operations).[92] With heavy-handed use of policies such as exchange rate overvaluation, direct and indirect subsidies, and quotas, market distortions have been endemic, thus making long-term investment and rational decision making close to impossible. The President of the Metal Household Merchandise Trade Association of Tehran said, "Real merchants who abide by the laws cannot work like in the past, and now goods go unsold. Meanwhile, middlemen and unprofessional people sell low-quality goods at special prices and nobody takes responsibility for low-quality or multipriced goods."[93] In such an unstable market structure, wholesalers, brokers, and some retailers view commercial activities with trepidation; while windfalls are available, so are heavy losses. Thus, exchanges are made with little intention or commitment to long-term collaboration. Furthermore, middlemen and brokers have niches in operations connecting Iran's periphery to Tehran. Also, one

[91] Emphasis was in interviewee's speech.
[92] Bernard Hourcade and Farhad Khosrokhavar, "La Bourgeoisie iranienne ou le contrôle de l'apparaeil de speculation," *Revue Tiers Monde* 124 (October–December, 1990), 877–98.
[93] *Asnaf* no. 91 (Azar and Day 1379 [November 2000–January 2001]), 32.

major wholesaler explained his marketing strategy, which diversified his use of middlemen to sell his goods. In place of using a few reliable brokers as he did prior to the Revolution, his trading house works with a larger number of brokers and distributors-cum-middlemen in order not to "put all his eggs in one basket."

The Tehran Bazaar's credit system, which was the backbone of co-operative hierarchies, was radically changed after the Revolution. The wholesale nationalization of the banking system in 1979 and the passing of the Interest-Free Banking Law in 1983 drove the Bazaar's money-lenders underground and sent cash-strapped *bazaari*s to the bureau-cratically mired public banks or more often to the illegal, but accepted, black economy for credit.[94] The newly nationalized banking system, however, channeled most funds to the public sector.[95] Moreover, credit in the Bazaar was restricted on a number of fronts. Immediately after the Revolution, importers faced a dramatic turnaround in the international market. During the prosperous 1960s and 1970s, many of the larger importers had good accounts and enjoyed credit lines with foreign suppliers that extended six-month open letters of credit or kept open accounts. This float was an important factor in ensuring profitability and freed up capital for other business ventures, including their own moneylending. During the economic uncertainties of the early 1980s, foreign suppliers began to ask for confirmed letters of credit, which effectively meant cash.[96] Accordingly, *bazaari* and non-*bazaari* importers demanded cash from their customers. The tight foreign currency market, high rate of inflation, decline in consumer income, and prevalence of fraud (see below) has resulted in a replacement of credit-based transactions with cash and very-short-term credit exchanges.

Moreover, credit exchanges are now conducted almost exclusively using checks. *Bazaari*s and legal experts alike claim that the businessmen have switched from promissory notes to checks in order to gain extra legal protection. In Iran, writing a bad check comes with a penal pun-ishment (*kayfari*) of from six months to two years plus a cash penalty. Nonpayment of a promissory note, on the other hand, is merely subject to civil penalty (*hoquqi*). The threat of a heavy legal sanction is thought to deter potential noncompliance. However, with the use of checks the *safteh* system of referrals and recommendations has been eliminated.

---

[94] *Dawran-e Emruz*, 16 Azar 1379 (December 6, 2000).
[95] World Bank, *Iran: Economy in Transition* (Washington DC: World Bank, 1991).
[96] Daneshjuyan-e Mosalman-e Payraw-e Khat-e Emam, ed., *Asnad-e Laneh-ye Jasusi* vol. 63 (Tehran: Markaz-e Nashr-e Asnad-e Laneh-ye Jasusi, 1366 [1987]), p. 131.

The informal credit system, narrowly defined here as money markets that are not subject to Central Bank supervision, comprises a major portion of the thriving "free sector" that includes but goes well beyond the Bazaar networks and space. In particular, two new money markets were established after the Revolution.[97] The first was a limited partnership contract, known as *mozarebeh*, wherein a financier contributes capital to an agent who invests in trading activities. To be legally binding, profit-and-loss-sharing arrangements must be fixed at the time of the contract. These contracts were initially encouraged by the Islamic Republic to spur investment and economic activity within an Islamic-sanctioned framework. These arrangements quickly mushroomed and became a popular way to put one's capital to use; in the 1980s *mozarebeh* advertisements covered newspaper pages. Within a decade it soon emerged that these schemes were often used as a means to disguise exorbitant interest rates (as high as 50 percent) in an Islamic regime that had outlawed interest. Newspapers began to run exposés uncovering how the limited partnership schemes were being started by everyone from the corner grocer to ministries, were fueling the speculative "middleman economy," and were diverting resources from production to commercial activities.[98] It was argued that *mozarebeh* was used for commerce, especially high-profit smuggling operations, because the receiver of the capital must pay a profit share on a monthly basis. After the media attack and several high-profile cases of fraud, limited partnerships were outlawed.

Interest-free loans, or *qarz al-hasaneh*, are the second credit system in the postrevolutionary era. Unlike limited partnerships, the interest-free loan funds date back to the late Pahlavi rule and have their roots in the Bazaar. In 1961, a group of *bazaari*s in Tehran Bazaar established the Javid Fund and distributed interest-free loans along with a series of charity operations.[99] Prior to the Revolution these funds were located in mosques and had a close connection to clerics and businessmen from the Bazaar. Adelkhah reports that by the time of the Revolution there were roughly 200 such funds, but by 1988 the number reached 3,000, and four years later 4,350 were legally registered and many more were unregistered.[100] Interest-free funds expanded in part because after the

---

[97] Adelkhah, *Being Modern in Iran*, pp. 56–67.

[98] *Kayhan*, 1–7 Aban 1368 October 23–29, 1989.

[99] Jabbari, *Hamisheh Bazar*, pp. 150–3. An obituary of one of the founding members of the Javid Fund, a devoted carpet merchant who opened a branch in one of the caravanserai in the carpet bazaar, states that Javid began in 1966. "Dar Rasa-ye hajji Karim Ansarian," *Qali-ye Iran* 3 (Zemestan 1372 [Winter 1993]), 28.

[100] Adelkhah, *Being Modern in Iran*, 59 and *Entekhab*, 3 Tir 1381 (June 24, 2002). At present, funds that administer interest-free loans may receive licenses from a number

implementation of the interest-free banking system, many Iranians transferred their savings to *qarz al-hasaneh* accounts that gave beneficiaries prizes such as household appliances or travel expenses for pilgrimages to holy sites. Commercial banks quickly copied these marketing strategies and now bonuses and prizes have replaced interest on deposits. The distribution of loans follows the same informal referral system associated with the old bazaar credit system; that is, it is based on reputation and supporting references that can connect applicants to one of the fund's founding members or administrators. *Qarz al-hasaneh* funds are now independent of the Bazaar and the mosques and are spread out across the city and organized and administered by numerous small groups, especially circles of women. Adelkhah writes, "But, in contrast to what had happened before the revolution, this increase [in the number of funds] occurred independently of the mosques, at the heart of the bazaar and the urban neighborhoods."[101]

Thus, these limited partnerships helped finance the expanding "free economy" that has emerged to compete with Tehran's bazaar. The proliferation of informal credit may be a diffusion of the practices of the *bazaaris*, but it has undermined the Bazaar's preeminent role in private distribution of short-term credit in the economy.

In sum, the Tehran Bazaar's economic relationships have been made less long term and integrated owing to the increased prominence of state commercial conglomerates, smuggling networks, and the expansion of the informal economy and parallel money markets. The forces that helped create dependencies and alliances between *bazaaris* over time and across guilds have been replaced by mechanisms that not only do not link *bazaaris* together, but discourage cooperation.

Heterogeneous social networks

If prior to the Revolution social ties solidified economic relations by making them more multifaceted and expansive, since then social relations have become more fragmented and disconnected from the Bazaar's economic life. Rather than interpersonal ties creating a sembalance of homogeneity out of heterogeneity, now interpersonal relations are divisive.

The Bazaar remains ethnically diverse. Many wealthy religious minorities emigrated from Iran after the establishment of the Islamic

of noneconomic state institutions. Recently the Central Bank and the Ministry of Economy and Finance have sought to centralize the licensing and supervision of all financial institutions. Hourcade and Khosrokhavar report that there were 1,300 in 1990 in Iran. Hourcade and Khosrokhavar, "La Bourgeoisie Iranienne," 891.

[101] Adelkhah, *Being Modern in Iran*, p. 59.

Republic, yet a few Jewish merchants continue to work in the Bazaar, particularly in the carpet, stationery, and cloth sectors. There continues to be a large portion of Turkish speakers dominating many sectors. Some *bazaari*s from Tabriz, the largest Turkish-speaking city in Iran, located in Eastern Azerbaijan province, mentioned that several of the wealthier Tabrizis moved to Tehran because anticapitalist sentiments in Tabriz were running high in the early years and, since Tabriz was smaller than Tehran, their wealth was more conspicuous. Kurds are active in the Bazaar as porters and as middlemen linking the Bazaar to the smuggling on the eastern frontier. Arabic-speaking Iranians and immigrants from Iraq and the Persian Gulf have also established niches in the Bazaar, particularly the Marvi Bazaar and Kuwaiti Bazaar. Unlike previous patterns where ethnic and regional minorities entered various sectors, so far these "Arabs" appear to be concentrated in these few bazaars. Notably, the 2 million Afghan refugees living in Iran have not entered the Bazaar's workforce. Despite earning low wages and comprising a large portion of Iran's unskilled labor, Afghan laborers are restricted to construction jobs and some menial labor in warehouses in southeast Tehran (Dawlat-Abad). It seems that they both lack the appropriate social contacts and face hostility in the Bazaar. This goes to show that the network structure has resisted incorporating what most Tehranis continue to view as "outsiders." Thus, it seems that ethnic heterogeneity may play a more divisive role since the Revolution, but this topic needs further research and is experienced differently in locales such as Mashhad, Tabriz, and Bushehr.

Religious organizations experienced somewhat contradictory trends. Existing in almost all guilds, Islamic associations had their roots in the revolutionary era, when they played an important role in organizing anti-Pahlavi rallies, distributing funds and food to striking workers, and disseminating political announcements, newspapers, and tape-recorded speeches. After the Revolution, these associations were quickly dominated by more zealous supporters of the Islamic Republic and advocates of Islamization of society. They organized meetings where leading revolutionary clerics would meet *bazaari*s, and they made public statements criticizing non-Islamic groups and lay Islamic groups, all of whom had support in the Tehran Bazaar. During the war years they were active in donating food, clothes, and vehicles for the war effort and for those fleeing the wartorn areas.

The leader of the Islamic Association of China and Glassware Guild of Tehran admitted, however, that "since the end of the war our activities have diminished and most *bazaari*s do not attend our meetings or contribute to our charity funds." When I asked the old man why this was the case, he lowered his voice and said that *bazaari*s have differences too and since the early years of the Revolution, it was difficult to maintain "that excitement and unity." When I enquired further, he mentioned that the reason for the Islamic Association's success during the 1980s was because "we maintained a *hayati* form and were not *edari*. Unfortunately, many of our organizations have become *edari* and they are no longer interesting to ordinary people." The head of the Islamic Association mentioned that the Ministry of the Construction Crusade (*Jahad-e Sazandegi*), which was a "revolutionary institution" established to improve rural conditions, had become like any other ministry, and "lost its *hayati* characteristics." By using *hayati*, he was referreing to the informal religious meetings that encouraged voluntarism and community-based organization. Meanwhile, *edari*, or "bureaucratic," refers to hierarchical, official, and top-down organizations. The leader of the Islamic Association did not elaborate on who were the leaders of these now *edari* religious organizations, but *bazaari*s explained that they shunned the various Islamic associations because they were headed by staunchly conservative supporters of the Islamic Republic, the very same actors who were now referred to as *dawlati*.

Many noted that religious observance increasingly occurs at the level of the neighborhood and not at the guild or bazaar level. For example, during the holy month of Moharram, many *bazaari*s attend neighborhood-based *hayat* gatherings rather than their guild and bazaar-based events.[102] When I discussed religious matters with *bazaari*s, they commented that over the years the "political abuse" of religion has divided society and many now shy away from public and state-organized religious events. A few *bazaari*s pointed out that they no longer pray in the Bazaar's mosques, but prefer to pray in the back of their store or at home. While it is probably inaccurate to say, as well as difficult to prove, that *bazaari*s are less religious than prior to 1979, religion does not play the critical role of bringing *bazaari*s of all walks of life together and fostering rich interpersonal relations. One possible line of explanation for this could be that since one's public reputation is less vital in business matters, outward display of religiosity is less important. Also, if under the Islamic Republic religious display is increasingly viewed as "political abuse," praying in the mosque or being a Hajji is no longer a marker of trustworthiness. As several *bazaari*s mentioned, "everyone is a *hajji* now." This religious inflation diminishes the symbolic meaning of religion, and thus praying in

---

[102] Research on *hayat*s is limited, but one recent study mentions that while many merchants make up trustees of *hayat*s in central Tehran, none of them participated in these gatherings. "Hayatha-ye Mazhabi Ta'aroz-e Sakhtar va Ravandha-ye Mojud," *Andisheh-ye Jame'eh* 5 (n.d), 29–33.

one's office or attending religious ceremonies outside of the Bazaar has less bearing on one's standing as a reputable merchant. One can also speculate that this interpretive transformation along with high levels of literacy and availability of textual sources may provide an opening for reformist interpretations of Islam within the Bazaar, by which I mean nonconformist and individualistic understandings of religion.

Finally, daily activities and interactions have decreased after the Revolution. Many of the social gathering places, including public baths, traditional gymnasiums, and the large restaurants, have closed down as lifestyles have changed and consumers have found new substitutes or moved away. The famous bazaar coffee shops that were an important gathering place for *bazaari*s are now only a rare sight in the immediate bazaar neighborhood. In early 1979 there were 3,500 coffee houses in Tehran, but by 1990 the total had plummeted to 900.[103] The *bazaari*s' economic and social lives do not overlap as readily.

*Bazaari*s' also seem to be increasingly detached from one another in their social lives. Expecting to hear that *bazaari*s spent their leisure time together at religious gatherings or as part of "circles" (*dawreh*s) that would meet to play cards or go for hikes and vacations, I began asking newer *bazaari*s what they did in the evenings or at weekends and with whom they spent their free time. They responded that much of their limited time goes toward their family, playing sports, and in a few cases pursuing artistic interests – painting and reading poetry, hobbies comparable to other middle-class and upper-middle-class Tehranis. In addition, in and of themselves these responses are not drastically different from what one may have heard in the 1970s. What is different, however, is that these activities were conducted on an individual basis or with neighbors and family members, and not with other members of the Bazaar. One wholesaler mentioned that he would hike in the foothills of the Alborz Mountains a couple times a week. He said that he typically went alone, but on occasion he would go with a high-school friend. Expecting that the high-school friend might be another *bazaari*, I asked what he did. But his friend was an engineer. What makes this story even more poignant is that through other members of the Bazaar, I discovered that this hiker's father headed a group of ten to fifteen men, mostly *bazaari*s, on weekly treks in the mountains. These group events have now been increasingly replaced by individualistic excursions or gatherings of small groups of *bazaari*s who are close friends. Unlike the multitude of weak ties that emerged out of the sociospatial locale of the

---

[103] Ali Al-e Dawud, *Encyclopaedia Iranica*, *s.v.* "Coffeehouse," p. 4.

1960s and 1970s, these strong ties are weak in that they hem actors into limited homogeneous circles.[104]

In addition, as instability in exchange has increased and new actors have entered the Bazaar, social interactions have waned in the Bazaar.[105] While I was interviewing two young, but successful wholesalers, one commented, "You cannot be friends in such a competitive environment. I keep commerce and friendship apart. It is better that way." The other elaborated, "I have heard how our fathers spent a lot of time together and had a circle of *bazaari* friends, but now you can't do that. Our friends are from different backgrounds. Anyway, this is the right way." This second comment suggests a growing differentiation among *bazaari*s. This thirty-year-old *bazaari*, the son of a well-known and wealthy merchant in the Bazaar, went on to say, "I spend my free time with my friends. And my friends are not necessarily involved in commerce. They are friends from school or my neighborhood. We share a culture that does not mix well with many in the Bazaar." His friend referred to the economic disparity between these wealthier "old *bazaari*s" and new lower-class entrants by adding, "We are of a different level than many of these others in the Bazaar; we are from different backgrounds." This stratification in the Bazaar appears to support Joel Podolyn's hypothesis that market uncertainty leads to segmentation in exchange partners, whereby high-status actors avoid affiliation with low-status actors in order not to lose their status and reputation.[106] Other interviewees pointed to this fragmentation in the Tehran Bazaar where "old, reputable traders" shun exchange relations with "younger, postrevolutionary types." I was told on a number of occasions that this tendency was less pronounced in the prerevolutionary bazaar.[107] This uncertainty, which induced fragmentation and segregation, thus works against the development of crosscutting and multifaceted ties, and the development of a far-reaching reputation system. Obviously this is a very different situation from the one described by Ladjevardi, where he remembers being brought up in a heterogeneous yet inclusive

---

[104] Mark S. Granovetter, "The Strength of Weak Ties," *American Journal of Sociology* 78 (May 1973), 1360–80.

[105] Rotblat makes a similar argument about competition and social interaction in the context of the produce market in Qazvin. Rotblat, "Stability and Change in an Iranian Provincial Bazaar," p. 179.

[106] Joel M. Podolyn, "Market Uncertainty and the Social Character of Economic Exchange," *Administrative Science Quarterly* 39 (September 1994), 458–83.

[107] Podolyn also writes, "The more high-status actors restrict their exchanges to others of high status, the wider are the niches that are available to the low-status actors" (Ibid., 458). The carpet sector seems to exhibit some of this tendency since "low-status" upstarts have found niches in exporting *gabbeh*s, henna washed rugs, and the revival of old designs and wools.

neighborhood that included shops and public baths. Today, the Bazaar members have more distinct and separate nonwork lives based on class, neighborhood, and generation. As such the Bazaar is an economic center, but it is no longer a cohesive community that has high degrees of solidarity.

To sum up, unlike the stable and long-term value chains of the pre-revolutionary era, under the Islamic Republic the commercial relations of the Tehran Bazaar are highly unstable, indeterminate, and fragmented. Speculative and transitory trade based on smuggling is predicted on short-term and opaque relations with state agencies, off-shore exporters, and middlemen. The trade networks are based on shorter and narrowly defined agreements, while exchange is conducted with cash or checks, rather than credit relations based on long-term and crosscutting arrangements. Not only have the economic foundations of commerce changed, but they are reflected in a disembedding of exchange relations from social bonds. Like economic relations, social relations are increasingly partitioned into isolated cells lacking the bridging provided by crosscutting social relations and space, or an overarching solidarity. During the 1960s and 1970s, the regular social interactions helped produce weak ties among *bazaari*s. But today, the *bazaari*s' ties are strong ties based on exclusive economic (i.e. smuggling) or social relations (friendships based on neighborhood and social class). As such, relations are less long term, multifaceted, and crosscutting, and the constellation of networks are more like coercive hierarchies than cooperative hierarchies.

Reputation and solidarity

Acquisition and maintenance of reputation

The issue of reputation and trust was the most common theme in my discussions with *bazaari*s. For *bazaari*s the terms "reputation" (*e'tebar* or *khoshnami*, literally "having a good name") and "reputable" (*qabel-e etminan*, literally "worthy of trust") were related to the concepts of "past record," "experience" and "being known". To evaluate someone's reputation you need to know their past (*sabeqeh*) before you can decide whether to deem them trustworthy (*qabel-e e'temad, amin, dorost*). Consequently, a *bazaari* who is reputable is also referred to as one who is "known" (*shenakhteh-shodeh*) or "has a past" (*sabeqeh-dar*). The evaluation of the past is closely related to experience (*tajrobeh*), both the experience, or expertise, of each *bazaari* and their personal expertise with each other. First-hand experience is of course preferred to second-hand information that may cause problems of intersubjectivity. Yet networks may generate a proxy for first-hand experience by publicizing and verifying information about reputation within the community, which relies on them being well connected. Thus, the language of, and cognitive process behind, reputation and trust is inseparable from relational factors, rather than being attributes of individuals.[108] The evidence in this chapter suggests that the cooperative hierarchies that predated the Revolution were better suited to supporting the generation and maintenance of a reputation system than the coercive hierarchies of the postrevolutionary era.

The Tehran Bazaar in the Pahlavi era included a number of methods for differentiating between reputable and disreputable personalities. First, the informal apprenticeship system acted as a means of initiation and disciplining of new *bazaaris* through a gradual process of learning by doing. As apprentices showed their capabilities and gained the trust of their master they were given more responsibilities and taught more of the tricks of the trade. For example, at first apprentices would only stock goods and clean the store, but gradually the master began to guide them in dealing with customers, cashing checks, and making arrangements with suppliers. Through these actions and under the shadow of their master, apprentices would gain experience and demonstrate their trustworthiness to their master and the Bazaar community. All the time they would be learning about the characters of *bazaaris* and norms of the Bazaar.[109]

The master–apprentice relationship was often overlain with actual paternal or kinship ties. Many sons of successful *bazaaris* followed in the footsteps of their fathers and worked alongside them in the Bazaar. Working with one's father was a shrewd way to gain experience and build a reputation via association. Of course, the transfer of reputation across generations can be deleterious as well as beneficial. Thaiss's ethnography reads, "If the reputation of the parents is unsatisfactory, it will be exceedingly difficult for the person to redeem it. A tradesman in the Bazaar nicknamed him 'Haji dozdeh' (a humerous and sarcastic way of indicating that this man had pretensions to piety but in reality was a thief). 'Yes, they will leave this name on him so everyone knows he is dishonest and no one will do business with him. Even now his sons are known as *pesar-i haji dozdeh* (son of haji the thief).' "[110] Although most sons followed in their fathers' footsteps, it was also common that second-generation *bazaaris* would switch lines of work (See Illustration 3.1). Evidence suggests that switching lines of work did not protect from sons association with disreputable fathers. The horizontal

---

[108] Charles Tilly, "Trust and Rule," *Social Theory* 33 (2004), 1–30.

[109] Of course his capacity to flourish was dependent on the munificence of his master. Before the Revolution, however, market conditions (expanding consumerism, urbanization, and commercial areas) favored apprentices by providing them opportunities for establishing their own businesses.

[110] Thaiss, "Religious Symbolism and Social Change," p. 51.

and multiplex relations within the Bazaar created avenues for *bazaaris* to check the past performance of new entrants.

Hence, the structure of the actual marketplace and the relations of exchange partners are the critical requisites to acquire a reputation as trustworthy and learn the standards by which one is to be judged. Instrumentally speaking, it is vital that actors understand what the group deems as good or honorable behavior, while also grasping what is considered reprehensible or unforgivable. In the process one has to learn how to exhibit and signal the appropriate virtues, as well as detect and judge the reputation of potential trading partners. Finally, the learning process includes acquiring knowledge about the sometimes subtle forms of rewarding and penalizing. On-the-job training directly serves to construct group members with these skills, and vibrant communities passively instill these norms through positive and negative inducements and persuasion.

It is not enough simply to learn the criteria for reputability; there must be a means to demonstrate trustworthiness, evaluate actions and actors, and disseminate information. In fact, if a group lacks the mechanism for evaluating reputations and responding to them, there will be no need to invest time and effort to become reputable. The value of acquiring a good reputation is contingent upon a viable arena for evaluating and publicizing reputations, allowing exchange partners to make credible commitments through placing their good name on the line. The necessary conditions for this process include stability in relations. However, simple long-term dyads are not enough to punish disreputable behavior at the level of the group. Reputation, or status, at the group level requires a public arena in which honest (or fraudulent) behavior can be acknowledged and rewarded (or derided). As Portes and Sensenbrenner have noted, the desire to have "good standing" in the group is predominately "utilitarian, except that the actor's behavior is not oriented to a particular other but to the prism of social networks of the entire community."[111] The publicizing process disseminates information throughout the group. As status is gained within the group, those who attain approval have an interest in monitoring and enforcing the criteria by which they achieved their communal status.[112] If the reputation successfully identifies transaction partners who are cooperative

---

[111] Alejandro Portes and Julia Sensenbrenner, "Embeddedness and Immigration: Notes on the Social Determinants of Economic Action," in *The New Institutionalism in Sociology*, ed. Mary C. Brinton and Victor Nee (New York: Russell Sage Foundation, 1998), p. 130.

[112] Victor Nee and Paul Ingram, "Embeddedness and Beyond: Institutions, Exchange, and Social Structure," in *The New Institutionalism in Sociology*, ed. Mary C. Brinton and Victor Nee (New York: Russell Sage Foundation, 1998), p. 28.

and those who are untrustworthy, group members develop trust in the overall system and not simply in their exchange partners.

In the past, reputations were maintained and publicized in the Tehran Bazaar through cooperative hierarchies. Stable clientelist ties were the mode by which reputable *bazaaris* reproduced and enhanced their fame. Meanwhile, as we saw in the discussion of the credit system, cross-cutting and multifaceted relations helped to disseminate information about a wide variety of Bazaar members. In *hayats* and coffeehouses, private knowledge could quickly turn into public/Bazaar knowledge. *Bazaaris* were able to question a myriad actors to gather information about the potential quality of exchange partners. Also, prior to the Revolution, dissemination and evaluation of traders was primarily done by brokers. Brokers had an interest in creating and perpetuating an accurate and timely method of information exchange about the past performance of *bazaaris*. Moreover, the elders had an interest in maintaining the system that brought them their social standing. The preferences of these critical members of the Bazaar were endogenous to the economic process, not prior to it. Thus, all *bazaaris* knew that reputation mattered not only in the context of a particular transaction, but also in the context of the entire group. Commitments were made credible because *bazaaris* were placing their own reputations (mustaches) on the line, and these reputations were the very asset that they needed in the Bazaar.

The Bazaar's instability and fragmentation eviscerated all aspects of the reputation system. The apprenticeship for new entrants is disappearing in many parts of the Bazaar. Many younger *bazaaris* in sectors selling manufacturing goods mentioned that they entered their occupations without any significant time as an apprentice; instead they arrived with capital, and this was enough to set up a business within the coercive hierarchies. Since many commercial activities involve contacts outside the Bazaar (e.g. access to legal and smuggled goods, credit, and hard currency), new entrants are less dependent on "knowing" the Bazaar and its characters. Meanwhile, young apprentices are in a precarious position in the new economy. The cost of shops in the Bazaar and other central commercial areas is extremely high and has made starting up a business in these areas all but impossible. Gradual accumulation of social capital cannot substitute for economic capital.

More significantly, the monitoring and enforcement of reputations is less proficient. The decline in multiplex relations has reduced the opportunities to earn trust, exhibit reputation, and use multilateral sanctioning techniques (shaming and gossiping) at social gatherings and everyday encounters. Second, as the discussion of smuggling networks argued, traders now tend to conceal their identity, let alone their reputation. The decline of brokers has also robbed the Bazaar of an important group of people who acted as the monitors of reputation. Finally, the evaluations of reputation have become far less accurate, because relations have become more short term (i.e. the expectation of future interactions is reduced), new entrants have joined the Bazaar, and relations is more stratified between "old, reputable traders" and "younger, postrevolutionary types."

A discussion with a cloth distributor nicely captures the decline in reputation as a means of enforcing agreements. As I was sitting on the bus from the Bazaar to northern Tehran, I struck up a conversation with the affable middle-aged cloth seller. After some small-talk, the conversation turned to my research interests and his experiences in the Bazaar. To illustrate the travails facing bazaaris, he told me that a retailer in Isfahan (a customer of his for several years) had forfeited the funds that were owed to him. Now the distributor was helpless since he did not have documents or checks to use in a court of law. I asked him why he didn't use intermediaries and shaming as a method to seek reimbursement, or at least to punish him and for his noncompliance. He responded that "these things are no longer any use. Merchants are mobile, they can jump from one wholesaler to another, or from one trade to another." In this context, failing to pay back debts is a public expression that a debtor has renounced his ties to the creditor as well as the Bazaar's reputation system. Poignantly, the cloth seller ended his explanation by noting that people now blame creditors for not getting checks and cash up front. He was well aware that the fluidity of relations and occupations made it difficult to control exchange partners. Moreover, his final comment suggests that bazaaris are modifying their norms and expectations. Handshakes and strands of mustaches are no longer deemed acceptable practices. Reputation as a mode of governing the affairs of the Bazaar has lost its value, and with its decline, past cultural beliefs (held by individuals) are susceptible to network restructuring.

These trends have not escaped the attention of governmental officials. In 1993 the president of the Organization for the Inspection and Supervision of Production and Distribution of Goods and Services at the second conference of the Association of Guild Affairs claimed, "Guilds have been recognized for their reputation (khoshnami) and piety (diyanat), and people look upon the guilds based on their past perspectives and know of merchants the symbol of religiosity and truthfulness (dorostkari)."[113] However, the president continued by implicitly

---

[113] *Asnaf* year 9, special issue (Esfand 1372 [February–March 1993]), 10.

pointing out that this standing is in danger of being sullied: "Therefore, to maintain this past record (sabeqeh), guild organizations must deal with wrongdoers (motekhallef)." The government official perceptively pointed out the connection between past records, reputations, and the capacity to sanction those who violate norms and agreements. However, he did not tell his audience how to do this. Without cooperative hierarchies, the immediate prospects are slim that such assessment and publicizing of reputations will take place.

Reputation is an important mechanism that provides guidance in complex settings with multiplicities of social relations and imperfect information. A person's reputation is the bundle of facts and signals that provide information to others, and is used by them to develop expectations about behavior.[114] Hence, reputation is an asset and needs to be acquired and maintained.[115] It is the vehicle by which symbols and behavior, along with first-and second-hand knowledge of past interactions, coalesce to make the future more predictable. When someone who is reputable can be expected to behave in ways that honor their stipulated commitments as well as the norms of behavior, they are deemed trustworthy. Thus, reputation, trust, and predictability of behavior are closely interrelated qualities of relations. The Tehran Bazaar teaches us that for all these to be maintained, relations must be structured in particular ways that will allow actors to learn the criteria of evaluation, demonstrate their qualifications, and circulate information. All these factors are important for socialization and for monitoring actors, and to enforce agreements and norms. Not all networks can be mechanisms for reputation generation.

Reputation, inequality, and solidarity

Inequality within the Bazaar has always existed. Commentators who make blanket statements about the Bazaar tend to underestimate the dramatic disparities in wealth, educational attainment, access to resources, and means to develop a reputation within the Bazaar. Importers and exporters, even those who have not been aligned with the state, control the flow of credit and commodities in ways that impose price systems upon smaller commercial units. Many of the wealthier bazaaris, moreover, transformed this wealth into more expansive

---

[114] I do not mean to imply that all people have equal opportunity to develop or circulate the same reputation. Economic and social positions surely limit capacity for reputation building in the first place.

[115] Ellis Goldberg, Trade, Reputation, and Child Labor in Twentieth Century Egypt (New York: Palgrave Macmillian, 2004).

economic activities and prestigious social standings. These inequalities existed prior to the Revolution and have persisted today.

Prior to the Revolution, however, the importance of reputation as an asset meant that all *bazaaris*, even the biggest importers, who wanted to continue to trade in the marketplace had to be concerned with the perceptions of those within the community. If word spread that a bazaari did not keep his word or did not abide by the norms of flexibility in transaction, he faced social sanctions that would become economic sanctions. The diffuse relations not only structured cooperative behavior, but were the elixir of the sense of loyalty to the Bazaar and solidarity among its members, through which norms of cooperation and restraint of myopic self-interest developed among the powerful. Alongside this, Islamic principles stressing equity and aiding the poor encourage a culture of charity and modesty. On a daily and multidimensional basis, these forces limited the potential for abuse of power through reneging on promises, imposing prices and contracts that were unfair, or culturally or socially differentiating between classes.

These ameliorating factors that moderated, if not checked, the power of wealthy and high-status *bazaaris* have faded as the requirement to maintain a reputation has waned. The regulatory force of the reputation system is absent. During the late Pahlavi era, an informal ranked hierarchy prevailed wherein as individuals violated norms and did not perform according to expectations, they fell down the hierarchy of reputable actors. Jumping ahead to the present context, the threat of falling down the hierarchy is less credible, since alternative exchange partners in parallel networks exist who do not have information about one's past. Subordinates no longer have the opportunities to use multilateral methods of sanctioning such as community shaming in order to gain leverage against superiors. Now, new *bazaaris* who control large stocks of goods or sums of credit are less likely to abide by norms that encourage leniency in dispute resolutions or modesty in dress. Young wealthy *bazaaris* openly speak of not "being able" to spend time with other *bazaaris* who cannot afford to engage in the same leisure activities. From these transformations we can discern that ethos a *bazaari* has lost its corporate being and normative resonance. *Bazaaris* sell and buy within the Bazaar, but this does not imply the same collective identity, and I am tempted to push the argument further and say collective responsibility.

On a related point, the experience of the Tehran Bazaar during the Pahlavi regime shows that cooperation and a sense of community do not necessarily require absolute or relative equality. While some theorists believe that equality is a basis for creating conditions for community,[116] the evidence from Tehran shows that equality is not a necessary condition for members of a group to establish feelings of solidarity or cooperative relations. Rather the reciprocity and self-help that existed was a product of frequent and multifaceted relations that instilled norms and provided checks on behavior to make actors reputation sensitive. Once the sites and modalities of social structural reproduction changed, so did these norms and a sense of solidarity. Thus, informal institutions of cooperation neither are products of internalized norms nor out of a necessary drive for efficiency, but out of a cognitive process engineered by concrete, yet contingent, relations.

Conclusions

Bazaar outsiders see interpersonal ties and personalism dominating commercial activities in Iran and conclude that the same decades-old networks continue today. However, they do not notice that the form of governance in the Tehran Bazaar is significantly different. While prior to the Revolution, individual exchanges were seen as part of a web of ongoing and multidimensional transactions that helped reduce risk, now transactions are seen as short-term exchanges with little assurance that the actors involved will meet again. The postrevolutionary commercial network is now dependent on agents in the government and black market who enjoy highly unequal and temporary ties. The state-affiliated organs that now control much commercial activity have become unaccountable superiors in a hierarchy that gives subordinates little opportunity to sanction and evaluate the performance of these external monopolistic entities. A retailer selling kitchenware captured the complexity of the problem facing the Bazaar when he commented, "In general there is little trust between people and most only think of themselves instead of each other. The old structure of the Bazaar has been lost. People are less trustworthy (*mawred-e e'temad*) and transactions less frequently follow ethical lines and most resort to legal means that have their own problems. Overall, in the Bazaar, a good economy does not prevail." For him and the majority of *bazaari*s I interviewed "a good economy" was born and nurtured by the forms of its governance.

Governance refers to the manner in which power is exercised. The shift from cooperative to coercive hierarchies is a story about how agreements

---

[116] Elinor Ostrom, *Governing the Commons* (Cambridge: Cambridge University Press, 1990); and Robert C. Ellickson, *Order without Law: How Neighbors Settle Disputes* (Cambridge, MA: Harvard University Press, 1991).

are forged and regulated in the Bazaar, and hence how individual and group power operates. Specifically, the changes in inter- and intra network relations influenced the role of reputation in monitoring, sanctioning, and shaping behavior. Moreover, the forms of network governance offer different capacities for holding superiors accountable and limiting their ability to abuse power differentials. The form of governance also impacts how group members view each other and gives meaning to being members of the group. Thus, the shift from cooperative hierarchies to coercive hierarchies has real consequences for power relations within the Bazaar.

These findings problematize the static and overly mechanistic account of the Iranian bazaar. Misagh Parsa, for example, claims that "the structure of the bazaar tends to generate strong solidarity against external adversaries."[117] However, this chapter shows the mechanisms behind this solidarity by investigating its breakdown as well as its existence. The extent to which *bazaari*s develop ties across hierarchies, the methods for garnering reputation and gathering information, and the potentials for corporate identity reflect the shift from cooperative to coercive hierarchies. If the arguments in this chapter are sound, we would expect these transformations to have consequences for the political potency of the Bazaar. But before contemplating that issue, we next examine why the shift in the internal governance of the Bazaar occurred. The answer to this question takes us out of the confines of the Tehran Bazaar and raises questions about state policies and institutions.

---

[117] Misagh Parsa, "Entrepreneurs and Democratization: Iran and Philippines," *Comparative Studies in Society and History* 37 (October 1995), 812.

4 Networks in the context of transformative agendas

Why have the guilds, which play an influential socio-political role and are ready to cooperate economically with the government, fallen out of favor ... ?

Editor's Note in Asnaf [Guild] magazine[1]

[T]he constitution of political forces relates to various and shifting bases of social solidarities, but crucially, these varieties and shifts often result from changes in political and economic conjuncture, including state structures and policies ... .

Sami Zubaida[2]

Chapter 3 outlined the change in the form of governance in the Tehran Bazaar and demonstrated that the cooperative hierarchies of the prerevolutionary era have given way to coercive hierarchies. In the process of elucidating this transformation it also pointed to the symptoms and immediate causes of this shift – political uncertainty, the increased use of cash, the acute problem of bounced checks, the rise of smuggling activities, the change in composition of bazaar members, and the demise of network producers such as brokers. These proximate causes and effects can be explained by generally accepted economic theories and straightforward political logic. When import monopolies are created and licenses are distributed, one expects rent seeking, corruption, and smuggling; when state institutions are up for grabs, especially in the case of a rentier state, it is unsurprising that competition over their design and the control of organizations that distribute power and wealth will ensue.

What still remain as questions are what underlies the shifts in the Bazaar's governance and what propelled these dynamics to take place specifically in the postrevolutionary era. Why was it that under the anti-bazaar Pahlavi regime the Tehran Bazaar maintained its cooperative hierarchies, which created a sense of community, disciplined group members, and distributed resources without a centralized structure

---

[1] *Asnaf* no. 3 (Day 1373 [December 1994–January 1995]), 7.
[2] Sami Zubaida, *Islam, the People, and the State* (London: Routledge, 1989), p. 87.

capable of making binding decisions? Meanwhile, why under the see-mingly pro-bazaar Islamic Republic did the Tehran Bazaar go through structural changes that made its relations more short term, more single faceted, and less crosscutting, and thus less capable of regulating activities and generating a corporate identity? Presented from the state's perspective, why didn't the Pahlavi regime's policies succeed in undermining the Bazaar's structure, while the Islamic Republic's pro-grams undercut the very group that helped bring it to power? Or, why do many guild members feel that they have "fallen out of favor"?

To address these questions, I focus on the far-reaching processes of change in regime and the transformation of state–bazaar relations during the past half century. It was the state's policies that produced the paradoxical outcome of a stable, prosperous, and politically potent Bazaar under the "modernizing" Pahlavi regime and a changing, declining, and politically ineffectual Bazaar under the "traditional" Islamic Republic. I investigate the impact of each regime's transfor-mative programs and their consequences for the contours of commercial networks.[3] I argue that "the political and economic conjuncture" of the two regimes' different development projects (high modernism and Islamic populism) resulted in the crucial realignment of circumstances that institutionally and spatially dislocated the commercial networks and with them the Bazaar's form of governance.

The Pahlavi regime and the Tehran Bazaar

When comparing the status of the Bazaar in the era immediately prior to the Islamic Revolution and its position since then, most bazaaris stress the relative freedom enjoyed by private capital during the earlier era. Interviewees commented that "back then we had a certain freedom,"

---

[3] Since my main concern is the organization of the Bazaar and its relationship with the state, I will not evaluate the performance of these two regimes in terms of macroeconomic indicators or their ability to meet their objectives, salutary or retrograde. There is a relatively large literature on macroeconomic performance of the two regimes. See Hossein Razavi and Firouz Vakil, *The Political Environment of Economic Planning in Iran, 1971–1983: From Monarchy to Islamic Republic* (Boulder: Westview Press, 1984); Homa Katouzian, *The Political Economy of Modern Iran 1926–1979* (New York: New York University Press, 1981); Fred Halliday, *Iran: Dictatorship and Development* (New York: Penguin Books, 1979); Parvin Alizadeh, ed., *The Economy of Iran: The Dilemmas of an Islamic State* (London: I.B. Tauris, 2000); Hooshang Amirahmadi, *Revolution and Economic Transition: The Iranian Experience* (Albany: State University of New York, 1990); Janhangir Amuzegar, *Iran's Economy under the Islamic Republic* (London: I.B. Tauris, 1993); M.H. Pesaran, "The System of Dependent Capitalism in Pre- and Postrevolutionary Iran," *International Journal of Middle East Studies* 14 (1982), 501–22; and Ebrahim Razzaqi, *Gozideh-ye Eqtesadi-ye Iran* (Tehran: Amir Kabir, 1375 [1996]).

"there existed a space for commercial activity," and "the private sector was meaningful and had room to operate." It is easy to dismiss these statements, as I did when I first heard them, by attributing them to a romantic vision of a bygone golden age. But the consistency of the comments and the variety of *bazaaris* who made these statements (from importers and exporters to retailers, from gold dealers to household appliance sellers, and from supporters of the Islamic Republic to its critics) suggest that there was an underlying set of factors behind these comparative assessments. Moreover, there is evidence that reminiscing about the past is not mere retrospective historicizing. Even immediately after the Revolution, the Bazaar community was aware of the relative increase in barriers to private capital and mercantile activities. In 1980, the *Christian Science Monitor* reported, "Although bazaaris in no way long for a return of the Iranian monarchy, they do concede that 'everything was easier before, in the sense that the Shah supported capitalism and private enterprises.' The bazaaris 'hoped that everything would be better after the departure of the Shah. Instead we have lost our capital and gained nothing,' says one of them."[4] Therefore this chapter begins by investigating the state policies that *bazaaris* believed "supported capitalism and private enterprises," and the Bazaar's position in the policy matrix.

High modernism as a transformative program

Economic policymaking in prerevolutionary Iran revolved around the dual pillars of the state's unwavering belief in the application of a modernist blueprint and the access to rapidly rising oil revenue. The Shah was an arch-proponent of what David Harvey has called "high modernism."[5] Harvey differentiates between the heroic, but disastrous, modernism of the early twentieth century and the post-World War II "universal" or "high modernism" that was trumpeted as it was allied with the centers of capitalist political economy.

The belief "in linear progress, absolute truths, and rational planning of ideal social orders" under standardized conditions of knowledge and production was particularly strong. The modernism that resulted was, as a result, "positivistic, technocentric, and rationalistic" at the same time as it was imposed as the work of an elite avant-garde of planners, artists, architects, critics, and other guardians of high taste. The "modernization" of European economics proceeded apace, while the whole thrust of international politics and trade was justified as bringing

---

[4] *The Christian Science Monitor*, November 18, 1980.
[5] David Harvey, *The Conditions of Post-Modernity: An Enquiry into the Origin of Social Change* (Oxford: Basil Blackwell, 1989).

a benevolent and progressive "modernization process" to a backward Third World.[6]

Not impervious to this trend, the development literature of the 1950s and 1960s was based on a belief that development was a direct product of scientific methods and technical inputs that drive a mechanistic and homogeneous path to modernity. The Shah, building on his father's etatist development project of the 1920s and 1930s, sought to apply these principles to transform Iran into a "modern" industrial power by implementing a stylized and linear developmental model of western industrialization, with modernization flowering out of large-scale and capital-intensive projects – dams, nuclear power plants, and steel mills.[7] In Iran planning, development, and modernization were synonymous with westernization. Leonard Binder captures the resolute and unwavering nature of the Shah's modernization policy when he writes, "Future shock was considered virtuous, the goal of rational modernization, to be pressed forward ruthlessly by means of science, technology, planning and despotic authority. No element of tradition, no personal desire, no aesthetic value, no religious qualm, no philosophical hesitancy was to stand in the way."[8]

The Shah's lofty aspirations and, with hindsight we can say, ill-conceived project of modernity and monarchy were heralded and legitimated by the leading theorists of development, including Samuel Huntington, who viewed the Shah as the epitome of the "modernizing monarch,"[9] and adopted by Iran's political elite, several of whom had studied economics, political science, and sociology at the top universities in the United States.[10]

The Shah's proclivity for the grand symbols of modernity and physical structures was illustrated early on when the government, often via the Industrial and Mining Development Bank of Iran, began to invest in the construction of prestigious projects that they believed were more critical

---

[6] Ibid, p. 35.

[7] Several analysts have described these ends-focused development programs as "pseudo-modernity." Katouzian, *The Political Economy of Modern Iran*; Nikki R. Keddie, *Roots of Revolution: An Interpretive History of Modern Iran* (New Haven: Yale University Press, 1981).

[8] Quoted in Samih K. Farsoun and Mehrdad Mashayekhi, "Introduction," in *Iran: Political Culture in the Islamic Republic*, ed. Samih K. Farsoun and Mehrdad Mashayekhi (London: Routledge, 1992), p. 8.

[9] Samuel Huntington, "The Political Modernization of Traditional Monarchies," *Daedalus* (Summer 1966), 763–88.

[10] On the influence of theories of participation on high-level dignitaries of the Rastakhiz Party see Jerrold D. Green, *Revolution in Iran: The Politics of Countermobilization* (New York: Praeger, 1982), pp. 57–8.

than investing in people. In particular a few select high-profile projects absorbed the vast majority of the capital and with it skilled and semi-skilled labor. In the Fourth Development Plan (1968–72), for instance, half of the credit allocated to industry and mining was directed to build the Isfahan steel mill.[11]

Many rulers and policymakers in the developing world fixated on the technological registers of development and viewed development as a uniform experience that could be modeled on the western trajectory. What made the Iranian case different was that the state enjoyed something that helped fuel this particularly ambitious drive, namely oil revenue. In the 1960s income from oil rose steadily as western demand increased and Iranian production expanded. This resulted in a fivefold increase in oil-related income from 1960 to 1971. Then in 1973 the price of oil more than tripled (from $1.85 to $7.00 per barrel), and by the end of 1974 it exceeded $10 per barrel. In terms of revenue, Iran's earnings rose from $2.4 billion in 1972 to $18.5 billion in 1974. Finally, throughout these two decades oil revenue accounted for well over 40 percent of the government's revenue. The growth of the oil industry allowed the state to provide the capital necessary to draft these grand projects with little requirement to bargain with internal political and social groupings.

This oil revenue has had a number of consequences for planning and development, including allowing the state to compensate inefficient industries.[12] Serious planning had always been difficult given the unpredictability and fluctuations of the international oil market, but in the 1970s the Shah's whims outweighed the Plan and Budget Organization's five-year plans as the template for investment.[13] One method of bypassing the Plan and Budget Organization was to dispense oil revenue directly to ministries and agencies rather than to the budget for development planning.[14] In the wake of the oil boom, the Shah and a few of his close advisors followed a "maximalist approach" to spending the newfound earnings. This modernist vision supported a "big push"

[11] Razavi and Vakil, *The Political Environment of Economic Planning in Iran*, p. 33.
[12] Massoud Karshensas and M. Hashem Pesaran, "Exchange Rate Unification, the Role of Markets and Planning in the Iranian Economic Reconstruction," in *The Economy of Islamic Iran: Between State and Market*, ed. Thierry Coville (Tehran: Institut Français de Recherche en Iran, 1994).
[13] Bahman Abadian, interview by Zia Sedghi, tape recording no. 1, Bethesda, Maryland, July 4, 1985, Iranian Oral History Collection, Harvard University. See Abdol-Madjid Madjidi, interview by Habib Ladjevardi, tape recording no. 4, Paris, France, October 21, 1985, Iranian Oral History Collection, Harvard University, pp. 10–15.
[14] Frances Bostock and Geoffrey Jones, *Planning and Power in Iran: Ebtehaj and Economic Development under the Shah* (London: Frank Cass, 1989).

approach in which the regime invested all funds domestically and immediately, rather than investing in external or internal capital markets.[15] This path was taken despite evidence and warnings that Iran lacked sufficient skilled labor and infrastructural bottlenecks were pervasive. Two members of the Plan and Budget Organization recalled, "As the Shah and his advisors saw it schools could be built, technology could be bought, and the skilled manpower shortage could be overcome, now that the foreign exchange constraint was removed."[16] The petroleum-fueled modernism resulted in the Shah's prediction that within twenty-five years Iran would catch up to, and even surpass, the industrialized economies of the West by ushering in a "Great Civilization" that consisted of industrialization and a reawakening of Iran's ancient heritage.[17]

The replacing of traditional bazaars

One of the grandest of the prerevolutionary programs was the plan to build a 554 hectare commercial, cultural, and diplomatic center in the arid and vacant 'Abbas-abad hills of central Tehran.[18] Named the Shahestan Project, or "land of the kings," the unfinished project was set to consume the entire national budget for urban development for twelve years, and to relocate all ministries, hotels, embassies, and major commercial centers to 'Abbas-abad. "It was to be the Pahlavi equivalent of the Persepolis of the Achaemenian kings of ancient Iran, or the Isfahan of the Safavids."[19] Rather than invest in existing urban communities and renew infrastructures, such as Ray or the Bazaar area, which would have meant addressing property rights issues, negotiating with wealthy constituents, and implicitly acknowledging the viability of the old urban core, the Shah's urban planners directed funds and attention to entirely

---

[15] Many technocrats and economists suggested a gradualist spending schedule that included investing abroad. Part of the problem of this approach was that OECD countries were not receptive to OPEC nations using their windfall earnings derived from sales of oil to buy assets in the West. Razavi and Vakil, *The Political Environment of Economic Planning in Iran*, pp. 73–4.

[16] Ibid., p. 89.

[17] The "Great Civilization" was to occur some time in the 1980s and was cited as the moment when Iranian democracy would be viable. Mohammad Reza Pahlavi, *Beh Su-ye Tamaddon-e Bozorg* (Tehran: Ketabkhaneh-ye Pahlavi, 1356 [1977]).

[18] Bernard Hourcade, "Shahrsazi va Bohran-e Shahri dar 'Ahd-e Mohammad Reza Pahlavi," in *Tehran Paytakht-e Devist Saleh*, ed. 'Adl, Shariyar and Bernard Hourcarde (Tehran: Sazman-e Moshavereh-ye Fanii va Mohandesi-ye Shahr-e Tehran and Anjoman-e Iranshenasi-ye Faranseh, 1375 [1996]).

[19] V. F. Castello, "Tehran," in *Problem of Planning in Third World Cities*, ed. Michael Pacione (New York: St. Martin's Press, 1981), p. 172.

empty stretches of land where modernist schemes could be etched onto on arid *tabula rasa*.

This attitude was in part driven by pure hostility. Mohammad Reza Shah was public and virulent in his disdain for *bazaaris*. He described them as "a fistful of bearded bazaari idiots"[20] and bazaars as a collection of "wormridden shops."[21] The Shah's long-term prime minister, Amir-'Abbas Hovayda, extended this enmity to the entire private sector by routinely referring to the private sector "pejoratively as merchants (*tājir*) and at times simply as 'bastards' and SOBs (*pedarsūkhtiha*)."[22] In a slightly more contemplative mood, the Shah admitted, "Bazaars are a major social and commercial institution throughout the Mideast." Yet he remained steadfast in his opposition, glibly adding, "But it remains my conviction that their time is past. The bazaar consists of a cluster of small shops. There is usually little sunshine or ventilation so that they are basically unhealthy environs. The bazaaris are a fanatic lot, highly resistant to change because their locations afford a lucrative mono-poly."[23] The irony of course is that the Tehran Bazaar had adjusted to the new economic conditions by shifting from manufacturing to commerce and from retail to wholesale.

The Shah's disdain for the Bazaar and all things "backward" had its roots in the modernist developmental ideology that denied the Bazaar's relevance to national and international commerce and predicted its demise. In modernization theory change is seen as an organic procession from traditional to modern. Traditionalism signifies values and cultural factors, including strong kinship ties, "simple" exchange, indirect forms of governance, and nonconsensual authority relations. Modernity, on the other hand, is conceived of as a set of values and personality traits (e.g. mobility, individuality, and entrepreneurial spirit) necessary for the evolutionary process that drives economic growth, social complexity, differentiation in structures, and expanding demand for, and capacities of, these modern structures. Explicit in this formalization of change is the model of western experience as the universal model for change, both analytically and normatively. Lerner, for example, calls on Middle Easterners to study "the western historical sequence" to understand the

---

[20] Mehdi Mozaffari, "Why the Bazar Rebels," *Journal of Peace Research* 28 (November 1991), 383.

[21] Ervand Abrahamian, "Structural Causes of the Iranian Revolution," *Middle East Report* 87 (May 1980), 25.

[22] Vali Nasr, "Politics within the Late-Pahlavi State: The Ministry of Economy and Industrial Policy, 1963–69," *International Journal of Middle East Studies* 32 (February 2000), 109.

[23] Mohammad Reza Pahlavi, *Answer to History* (New York: Stein and Day, 1980), p. 156.

steps and path to be taken – a western developmental path that is depicted as uncontentious and unilinear across western cases.[24]

Starting from this transformative logic, the Pahlavi monarchy implemented an optimistic development agenda that focused on erecting modern functional equivalents for traditional counterparts believed to be antiquated.[25] The regime assumed that banks would replace moneylenders, industry would replace small-scale production, and supermarkets and department stores would replace bazaars by evacuating commercial exchanges from their confines. In his memoirs, published less than two years after his fall from power, the Shah clearly laid out his strategy for dealing with the bazaars. He writes, "I could not stop building supermarkets. I wanted a modern country. Moving against the bazaars was typical of the political and social risks I had to take in my drive to modernization."[26] This impassioned confessional is poignant because it demonstrates how for the Shah "modernization" and "moving against the bazaar" were articulated through the building of parallel structures. The Shah viewed building and supporting alternative commercial enterprises such as large department stores (e.g. Ferdawsi, Iran, Sepah, and Kurosh) and new boulevards lined with boutiques as a direct attack against the bazaars. His contempt for the "unhealthy" and "fanatical" bazaaris did not encourage him to mollify the bazaari class or regulate their activities, nor did he simply level their buildings; rather high modernism was based on the assumption of functional replacement of structures: bazaars could be neglected and would be negated as new "alternatives" were built.[27] Howard Rotblat, a sociologist who conducted a detailed survey of the Qazvin Bazaar in the late 1960s, commented, "The bazaar is not only viewed as a remnant of the past, but

---

[24] Daniel Lerner, *The Passing of Traditional Society: Modernizing the Middle East* (Glencoe, IL: The Free Press, 1958), p. 46. Similarly, Gabriel Almond writes, "The political scientist who wishes to study political modernization in the non-Western areas will have to master the model of the modern, which in turn can only be derived from the most careful empirical and formal analysis of the functions of the modern Western politics." Gabriel A. Almond and James S. Coleman, eds., *The Politics of Developing Areas* (Princeton: Princeton University Press, 1960), p. 64.

[25] For a study of the Pahlavi regime's rural development policy and how it was based on the "objectification of rural society" see Grace E. Goodell, *The Elementary Structures of Political Life: Rural Development in Pahlavi Iran* (New York: Oxford University Press, 1986).

[26] Pahlavi, *Answer to History*, p. 156.

[27] A Master Plan devised by Victor Gruen Associates and Farmanfarmaian Planners and Architects included the building of a highway through the Bazaar, but this project was never implemented. Martin Seger, *Teheran: Eine Stadtgeographische Studie* (New York: Springer-Verlag Wien, 1978), pp. 199–204. Unlike the Tehran Bazaar, Yazd's bazaar was bifurcated by a road, and parts of the Mashhad Bazaar were demolished in the late 1970s.

also as an institution incapable of change, and, therefore, a major impediment to Iran's continued economic development. Because of this, government policy is being directed towards *replacement of the bazaar with modern marketing structures* in hopes of hastening the national economy's growth."[28] Seeing bazaars as a vestige of a bygone era, the state saw no reason to come to terms with their political and economic demands. That is, the state saw no reason to incorporate them into the regime by dominating and institutionalizing state–bazaar relations either through a party that mobilized and represented their particular interests or bureaucratically, as was the case for modernist women.[29]

Thus, under the Shah's rule, multinationals, the state, and state-affiliated capitalists invested in new areas of Tehran, as well as in industries and service sectors that would replace the bazaars' institutions and economic position. Economists in the Central Bank predicted that the Tehran Bazaar "will be reduced to a mere shell, maintained principally as a tourist attraction."[30] As a result, in 1975, when a French consulting firm conducted research for a national spatial plan, it concluded that one of the most urgent and important planning problems facing the country was the excessive capital accumulation in the modern sector of the economy and the neglect of the bazaar region.[31] *Bazaaris*, as members of the disavowed traditional sector, did not have access to the distributive resources, including tax exemptions, bank loans, tax shelters, and paternalistic protection, that the state bestowed upon its clients (the so-called "1,000 families") who were busily investing in protected industrial establishments, often ones that were joint ventures with western firms. This prejudice was not lost on *bazaaris*. "The government has abandoned us because we are bazaari," a bazaari told Thaiss in 1969. "When people want to belittle someone or curse him they say 'Go away bazaari' (*boru bazaari*); yet the economy of this country is based on the bazaar."[32]

The Tehran Bazaar's autonomy

The combination of high modernism's disregard for the Bazaar and the oil wealth afforded a large degree of mutual autonomy between the

---

[28] Howard J. Rotblat, "Stability and Change in an Iranian Provincial Bazaar," Ph.D. dissertation, The University of Chicago (1972), p. 1.

[29] Parvin Paidar, *Women and the Political Process in Twentieth-Century Iran* (Cambridge: Cambridge University Press, 1995), pp. 149–51.

[30] *New York Times*, November 18, 1973.

[31] Bahram Abdollah-Khan-Gorji, "Urban Form Transformations – The Experience of Tehran Before and After the 1979 Islamic Revolution," Ph.D. dissertation, University of Southern California (1997), p. 85.

[32] Gustav Thaiss, "Religious Symbolism and Social Change: The Drama Husain," Ph.D. dissertation, Washington University (1973), p. 25.

state and the Bazaar. This autonomy was two way, giving the state autonomy from the Bazaar and the Bazaar autonomy from the state. "It is right that as a whole the previous regime had many problems. But when it came to material matters, we didn't have anything to do with them, and until right before the revolution they didn't have anything to do with us," summarized a *bazaari*.

From the state's perspective, external rents gave the regime the financial independence to buffer policymaking from interest groups.[33] This state independence from social forces, however, did not lead to a universal disconnect between "the state" and "society." The Pahlavi regime's financial independence, for instance, did not protect leftists, students, landlords, and peasants from coercion, control, and cooptation. Because of political concerns and modernist agendas (e.g. land reform that dislocated the landlords and a sizable portion of the peasantry), the regime confronted those strata that ideologically challenged the state's agenda or impeded industrial growth. The state's monopoly over the use of violence, including the bureaucracy and secret service, was perpetrated against these groups, which were within the scope of the state's transformative agenda.

Unlike labor unions, professional associations, and landlords, who were directly under the state's gaze, *bazaaris* escaped any thorough and sustained monitoring and control by the state until the antiprofiteering campaign prior to the Revolution (see Chapter 6). The state's antipathy and opposition to the Bazaar was not institutionalized in a system of direct and bureaucratic monitoring, controlling, and mobilizing of *bazaari* economic and political activities. The state made only ad hoc and coercive attempts to control the bazaars. These included state intervention in the internal affairs of the Chamber of Commerce and Industries and Mines and Chamber of Guilds and limiting these associations' access to policymaking circles.[34] These associations, along with state-run trade associations, were entirely unresponsive to the demands of both big traders and small retailers, and were used, rather unsuccessfully, to collect taxes

---

[33] Hootan Shambayati, "The Rentier State, Interest Groups, and the Paradox of Autonomy: State and Business in Turkey and Iran," *Comparative Politics* 26 (April 1994), 307–31.

[34] Ahmad Ashraf, "Nezam-e Senfi va Jame'eh-ye Madani," *Iran-nameh* 14 (Winter 1374 [1995]); see Akbar Ladjevardian, interview by Habib Ladjevardi, tape recording no. 1, Houston, Texas, October 11, 1982, Iranian Oral History Collection, Harvard University; Ghassem Ladjevardi, interview by Habib Ladjevardi, tape recording no. 1, Los Angeles, California, January 29, 1983, Iranian Oral History Collection, Harvard University; and Mehdi Motameni, interview by Habib Ladjevardi, tape recordings nos. 1–2, St. Martin, Netherlands, April 30, 1986, Iranian Oral History Collection, Harvard University.

and impose price controls. At the end of the 1960s, a *bazaari* mentioned that the state-established trade associations played a minimal role in structuring the Tehran Bazaar and were a government tool to administer tax collection. "These ettehadieh [trade associations] are new and temporary. If individuals give money, it will stand and if not, they will not exist. For example, if the government says it is not going to tax the asnaf [guilds], they don't need ettehadieh any more because they don't have anything else to do."[35] Thaiss concluded that these trade associations benefited only the commercial groups outside of the Bazaar, "tradesman who have little sense of solidarity or an 'in-group' feeling such as that in the bazaar."[36]

As Thaiss' ethnographic study and the analysis in Chapter 3 demonstrate, the Tehran Bazaar, however, had a very strong "ingroup feeling," and this was enhanced by the state's antagonistic outlook and institutional detachment. The antibazaar sentiment that prevailed among the political and intellectual elite generated a defensive banding together by the *bazaaris*. This can be detected in the two-tier discursive distinction made between *edaris* (literally "of the offices") and *bakhsh-e azad* (the "free-sector") and, second, between the *khiyabanis* (people "of the street") and *bazaaris*.[37] Older *bazaaris* continue to make these distinctions. For instance, while I was drawing the family tree of a merchant, I asked him to identify the occupations of his male kin. The merchant, born in the 1940s, responded by listing the sector and occupation of those who were in the Bazaar, for instance "Uncle so-and-so was involved in the wholesale dye trade." Then he came to a few who were employed by the government bureaucracy and he labeled them as *edari*. Finally, there were a few relatives whose occupations he could not remember, but he recalled that they were members of the "free sector." When I asked him what he included in this category, he commented, "The free sector was anyone who was involved in commerce and industry and *was independent of the government*. But they were not necessarily part of the Bazaar; they can also be *khiyabani* or owners of workshops. At that time these occupations were separate from the [government] offices, so we called one occupation 'free work' (*kar-e azad*) and the other 'office work' (*kar-e edari*)."[38] The *bazaaris*' own classification of the Bazaar in contradistinction to both the bureaucratic offices and the modern street reflected how in the context of the modernist and hostile discourse, their self-identification helped create a communal boundary.

[35] Thaiss, "Religious Symbolism and Social Change," p. 35.
[36] Ibid.
[37] Thais also mentioned the distinction between *bazaari* and *edari*. Ibid., p. 22.
[38] Interestingly, many older non-*bazaari* Iranians also make the distinction between office jobs and occupations in the bazaar.

Like the Dominican neighborhood in New York's Washington Heights, San Francisco's China Town, or Miami's Cuban enclave, in these discriminatory surroundings *bazaari*s came to be viewed by outsiders as a "city within a city," and they developed a reputation for being "secretive" and "traditional" or "clannish."[39] This social marking, meanwhile, fostered a sense of "bounded solidarity." However, discrimination and group identification do not necessarily lead to durable informal institutions, self-help, or a corporate identity. In the Tehran Bazaar's case bounded solidarity was supplemented by the reputation system that circulated resources that in turn accentuated its distinctiveness,[40] and importantly could compete with those available "outside" the group in the realm of the state and bureaucracy. By not incorporating the Bazaar into the state's economic policies or bureaucratically regulating its accumulation of capital, the Pahlavi regime allowed the Bazaar's institutions and ongoing and embedded relations to persist, and more significantly to regenerate themselves in relation to new economic and political situations. Thus, the Tehran Bazaar's social endowments transformed this autonomy into active self-governance. In fact the cooperative hierarchies acted as protection against the rare cases when the state did try to infringe the Bazaar's autonomy. *Bazaari*s mention that the Shah's secret police, or the SAVAK, were generally unable to monitor the Bazaar, since *bazaari*s were quick to identify outside agents and suspicious behavior.[41] A further contributing factor in the viability of the Bazaar's autonomy from the state is that the commercial sector, unlike industry, had a small workforce (often with family employees). Merchants were far less concerned with the state's potential mediating role in solving labor disputes and acting as a regulator of class conflict, a factor that could have encouraged them to seek state support. Under the Shah, the Bazaar was institutionally independent of the state, and on an individual basis and as a collective entity felt little allegiance to the regime.

This line of interpretation also suggests that group segregation and isolation can become a means of protecting the group's common social and political identity, and in the case of the Bazaar, of defining the group's boundaries through the repeated use of their independent

[39] Alejandro Portes and Julia Sensenbrenner, "Embeddedness and Immigration: Notes on the Social Determinants of Embedded Action," in *The New Institutionalism in Sociology*, ed. Mary C. Brinton and Victor Nee (New York: Russell Sage Foundation, 1998).

[40] Zubaida, *Islam, the People, and the State*, p. 75.

[41] Davoud Ghandchi-Tehrani, "Bazaaris and Clergy: Socioeconomic Origins of Radicalism and Revolution in Iran," Ph.D. dissertation, City University of New York (1982), p. 103; and Asadollah Badamchian and 'Ali Banaii, *Hayatha-ye Motalefeh-ye Eslami* (Tehran: Awj, 1362 [1983]), pp. 206–46.

reputation system and cooperative hierarchies. This is not to say tradition guides their lives, but rather modern institutions and economies that disavow the Bazaar as a viable entity engender problems that are solved through historical and communal relations and modes of behavior. These groups are neither integrated into modern society nor fully marginal or essentially unable to be part of it. Thus, they resort to their own repertories and externally unregulated means because the bureaucracy does not meet their needs.

Economic policies and the Bazaar's autonomy

The state's development strategy, combined with its political non-incorporation of the Bazaar, opened a political space for the Tehran Bazaar to prosper and regenerate its internal organization unencumbered by state regulations. The Pahlavi state followed import substitution industrialization (ISI) as a strategy for development that directed resources to the production of consumer durables by placing quantity and price restrictions on competing foreign imports.

As many observers have pointed out, ISI along with its pro-urban economic policies generates and spurs a series of interrelated economic problems, not least inefficient industrial output, depressed agricultural production, and rapid rural to urban migration. Another common consequence of ISI is a shortage of foreign exchange owing to the inability of inefficient industries to export their products and earn the foreign exchange necessary for capital and intermediate imports. However, Iran and other countries with external sources of revenue (oil, remittances, foreign investment, and aid) have been able to alleviate, or more accurately delay, this balance of payments squeeze, which would have forced stringent austerity measures. Thus, limits on imports were never as stringent in the Iranian, Algerian, and Iraqi cases as they were for example in the Turkish or Egyptian cases. Imports of consumer goods and intermediate goods (the prime areas of activity in the Bazaar) rose steadily in the 1960s and went through a fivefold increase from 1973 to 1978 (total imports more than doubled), making them higher than in most middle-income countries.

Several factors merged together to encourage commercial activities, especially imports of consumer goods, under the Shah's regime. First, demand for consumer manufactured goods rose with rising incomes, pro-urban policies that spurred rural–urban migration, a rising population, high levels of liquidity associated with the 1970s oil boom, and the fetishizing of western commodities. A great part of this demand was met through imports of either finished goods or capital goods necessary for the manufacturing sector. Another force shifting labor and capital into the service sector was Dutch Disease, a phenomenon initially detected in the Dutch economy after the large influx of North Sea gas revenue.[42] Economists differ on the exact mechanisms underlying this process, but they agree that government spending of oil revenues induce changes in relative prices, shifting resources out of the production of traded goods (industry and agriculture) into nontraded goods (commerce and services). This process helped channel resources into construction and all levels of commerce, with *bazaaris* profiting from both the expansion of trade and their land speculation. This was all financed through the interlinking credit system within the Bazaar, but with important complementarities in the formal banking system. Informal and formal credit markets were mutually reinforcing since the market was highly segmented, with the formal financial markets focusing on large enterprises and the informal markets focusing on small enterprises.[43] Also, complementarities between the two financial markets emerged since many of the top merchants and moneylenders borrowed funds from major banks and held large deposits in them.[44] Thus, the "national" bourgeoisie, like the "petroleum" or "comprador" bourgeoisie, was dependent on the rentier political economy.[45] Yet, as one analyst at that time noted, the various attempts "to find [an] alternative credit and distribution mechanism to replace the bazaar" were unsuccessful.[46]

The Pahlavi monarchy, in conclusion, neither mobilized the Tehran Bazaar nor sought to control it through patronage or monitoring. Believing that the Bazaar would give way to new commercial and financial institutions, the state's modernist transformative program did not call upon legal instruments to control the activities of the *bazaaris* or to impose a coercive apparatus. The economic policies of the state, although not designed to perpetuate the institutions of bazaars or support their economic activities, created inadvertent opportunities for the commercial community to prosper. Besides providing economic benefit, the state's institutional nonincorporation enabled the continued use of

[42] Alan Richards and John Waterbury, *A Political Economy of the Middle East* (Boulder: Westview Press, 1996), pp. 14–16.

[43] Djavad Salehi-Isfahani, "The Political Economy of the Credit Subsidy in Iran, 1973–1978," *International Journal of Middle East Studies* 21 (1989), 359–379; and Maryam Ghadessi, "An Integrative Approach to Finance in Developing Countries: Case of Iran," Ph.D. dissertation, The University of Utah (1996).

[44] Ghadessi, "An Integrative Approach to Finance," pp. 174–9.

[45] Bernard Hourcade and Farhad Khosrokhavar, "La Bourgeoisie iranienne ou le contrôle de l'apparaeil de speculation," *Revue Tiers Monde* 31 (October-December, 1990), 877–98.

[46] Michael M. J. Fischer, "Persian Society: Transformation and Strain," in *Twentieth Century Iran*, ed. Hossein Amirsadeghi (London: Heinemann, 1977), p. 182.

the Bazaar's reputation system to endogenously regenerate its form of governance. Thus, the exclusion of the Bazaar from the political economy offered an opening for it to reproduce the networks and norms that undergird its cooperative hierarchies.

Spatial centralization and integration of the Bazaar's networks

In the Pahlavi era the Tehran Bazaar's institutional autonomy was reinforced by a physical cohesion and separation. Typically, importers, wholesalers, and retailers all had shops and offices in, or in the immediate area surrounding, the Bazaar. The centralization of commercial networks in the physical setting of the Bazaar was bolstered by the morphology of the Bazaar, which grouped sectors together in particular alleyways. Localization reduced the costs of searching for sellers and facilitated the exchange of information about price, quality, and supply between sellers, buyers, and exchange partners.

This spatial concentration did not preclude shifts in residential patterns. The post-World War II era ushered in a major transformation in the morphology of Tehran. Newer residential areas were built north of the old royal district (*arg*) that was adjacent to the Bazaar and some commercial areas emerged in the embassy quarters. The move was initiated by Reza Shah when he left the Golestan Palace for the Marmar Palace, and was then duplicated in 1966 when Mohammad Reza Shah moved to Niavaran Palace in Shemiran, a northern suburb in the foothills of the Alborz mountains known for its orchards, large plots of land, temperate climate, and spring waters. During the 1956–1966 period, while the population of the whole city increased by 79 percent, the old city area that included the Bazaar and the immediate area surrounding it lost 23.8 percent of its population (the larger city center, which that encompassed the old city, lost 14.9 percent of its residents).[47] The dispersion of the population along class and status lines created a modern city spatially stratified along class, rather than communal, lines. This urban segmentation precipitated Tehran's legendary north–south sociospatial divide, which became the physical manifestation of the dichotomy. At 3,000 meters above sea level, northern Tehran hovers above southern Tehran, which sprawls out into an arid valley (see Map 4.1). Depending on one's theoretical perspective, the dualism city of northern and southern Tehran was representative of the dichotomy

---

[47] H. Bahrambeygui, *Tehran: An Urban Analysis* (Tehran: Sahab Books Institute, 1977), pp. 63–4. The highest population growth was in the southern area, where the population increase in a ten-year period was 300 percent. At the other end of the axis, the population of northern areas increased by 200 percent.

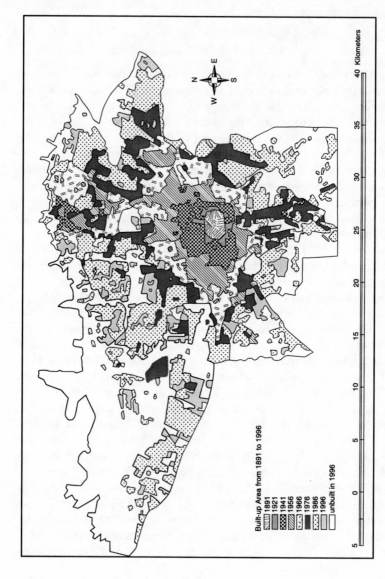

Built-up Area from 1891 to 1996

1891
1921
1941
1956
1966
1976
1986
1996
unbuilt in 1996

Map 4.1 Teheran – evolution of the built-up area between 1891 and 1996

5   0   5   10   15   20   25   30   35   40   Kilometers

between the modern and traditional, western and authentically Iranian
or Islamic, bourgeois and proletarian, or the land of the idol-wor-
shippers and the land of the disinherited. Thus the process of urbanization, complete with the dualistic segmentation that mapped economic
and cultural class relations, was already being etched onto the mountain
slope in the 1960s.

As for members of the Bazaar, there was a strong incentive for
bazaaris to remain in the old city quarters and to preserve their social
attachments and their proximity to their place of work and the institutions
of trade and finance.[48] But even the *bazaaris* began to move away from
the increasingly crowded residential areas near the Bazaar and relocated
their residences to either the northern or the western areas of the city.

Yet commercial life remained concentrated in the old Bazaar quarter.
Upon returning from his undergraduate and graduate school studies in
the United States, Habib Ladjevardi, a member of one of Iran's prominent families of merchants and, independent industrialists commented, "When I returned to Iran in 1967 my parents had moved [from
the Bazaar area] to a new residence in an enclosed compound located at
the foot of the Alborz mountains in Niavaran. ... From 1963 to 1968,
my daily drive from my house in Niavaran to my office on the edge of
the Bazaar was a daily reminder of the great chasm developing between
the northern and southern parts of Tehran – the one pseudo-modern,
the other traditional."[49] Ladjevardi's recollection captures the moment
in time when residential, economic, and cultural patterns were
redrawing the landscape of Tehran, but it also includes an important
reference to his daily drive to his office in the Bazaar area. Despite the
demographic shifts and the development of a "dual city," economic
activities, even by mercantile families that had entered the industrial
sphere, remained located in the Bazaar quarter. "The bazaar was the
pulse of the economy," argued a semi-retired merchant. "Everything
you needed was there. You knew what was going on in the rest of the
city and the country – you had the latest news about the economic
situation in the provinces. The brokers were here. The suppliers, the
buyers, and competitors were all here. Your friends and acquaintances
were here too. There was no need to run around [to other places]."

The Tehran Bazaar, despite being situated in the old city center and
gradually becoming part of "southern Tehran," remained the commercial heart of the capital. Tehran, moreover, was the economic epicenter of

[48] Ibid., p. 48.
[49] Habib Ladjevardi, *Labor Union and Autocracy in Iran* (Syracuse, NY: Syracuse
University Press, 1985), p. 236.

an unevenly growing economy. The bulk of large industrial establishments and about a third of all industrial units were in Tehran. Meanwhile in the mid-1970s, 40 percent of all national investment and 60 percent of all industrial investment was in the capital.[50] According to a survey conducted in 1979, 40 percent of total employment in retail and 60 percent in wholesale activities was in Tehran.[51] Thus, the rapid urbanization in Iran the expansion of infrastructure, and the primacy of Tehran, made the capital an ideal nexus for foreign exporters and local wholesalers to reach the bulk of the Iranian market.

The Bazaar's domination of the wholesale market for consumer goods occurred despite the reorganization of urban space and the emergence of newer commercial areas. In the late Pahlavi era new business districts extended north from the Bazaar along Ferdawsi, Lalehezar, and Sa'di streets and shopping districts around Takht-e Tavus Street, which catered to the upper middle class and ex-patriot communities that lived in Northern Tehran. While these new regions provided new retail areas for consumers, they were dependent on the Bazaar's wholesalers and importers who had access to credit, wholesaling facilities, and networks that ensured large operations.[52] Thus, like the European experience, older enterprises flourished with the urbanization-led capital accumulation, increasing consumerism, monetization of wage labor, and expanding and improving distribution and information systems. Evidence from late-nineteenth-century Europe suggests that locational advantages and established client and supply networks buffered "traditional" retailers and wholesalers from competition with department stores.[53] As in the case of the northeastern industrial region in the United States, which has withstood new migration flows, demographic shifts, and technological changes to maintain its preeminent role as a business and industrial corridor through increasing returns from its location,[54] through the 1970s the

---

[50] On the primacy of Tehran see Ebrahim Razzaqi, *Ashnaii ba Eqtesad-e Iran* (Tehran: Nashr-e Nay, 1376 [1997]), p. 55; Bahram Abdollah-Khan-Gorji, "Urban Form Transformations"; 'Ali Asghar Musavi 'Ebadi, *Shahrdaran-e Tehran az 'Asr-e Naseri ta Dawlat-e Khatami* (Qom: Nashr-e Khorram, 1378 [1999]), p. 105.

[51] Hooshang Amirahmadi and Ali Kiafar, "Tehran: Growth and Contradictions," *Journal of Planning Education and Research* 6 (Spring 1987), 167–77.

[52] Kazem Vadi'i, "Bazar dar Baft-e Novin-e Shahri," *Yaghma* 25 (Farvardeen 1351 [March–April 1972]), 9–19. Ahmad Ashraf, "Bazaar-Mosque Alliance: The Social Basis of Revolts and Revolutions," *International Journal of Politics, Culture, and Society* 1 (Summer 1988), 522.

[53] Geoffrey Crossick and Heiz-Gerhard Haupt, *The Petite Bourgeoisie in Europe 1780–1914* (London: Routledge, 1995).

[54] Paul Krugman, "History and Industry Location: The Case of the Manufacturing Belt," *American Economic Review* 81 (May 1991), 80–3.

Tehran Bazaar maintained its commercial supremacy because of its historical and locational advantages.

Space is not only a physical location; it is also a relational force. The spatial cohesion helped maintain cooperative hierarchies within the Bazaar in a number of ways. The spatial homogeneity created a forum in which the community monitored itself, exchanged information regarding potential partners and clients, spread information about the latest market conditions, and sought advice and arbitration from others in the same field. The narrow alleyways allowed, and continue to allow, gossiping and public shaming of norm violators. One day when I was in a carpet dealer's shop, two merchants who were carrying on a conversation about the availability of a certain type of carpet began to discuss a particular merchant who had reneged on a series of promises. They agreed that the merchant had not been paying his debts to a number of acquaintances. Also, together they counted that he had claimed bankruptcy at least three times. One commented, "Now we have to put aside friendship; we can't keep forgiving him." It was quietly suggested that their mutual acquaintance was an opium addict, and with that the matter was explained.[55] This brief and almost casual encounter permitted these *bazaari*s to verify information and evaluate their own respective situations. The spatial ecology of the Bazaar, which comprised several social layers, enhanced relational depth as much as breadth. Face-to-face interactions also created a potential for extra-commercial relations to develop. In fact, personal interactions almost necessitated exchange of pleasantries and small talk about families, the weather, and politics before turning to business matters. *Bazaari*s were together on a regular basis while they ate meals, drank tea, prayed, or sat around in each other's shops socializing. Potential contentious cleavages along class, guild, and ethnic divisions were also blurred by social interactions that did not completely map onto social segmentation.

In the midst of a recent interview, Fariborz Raiis Dana, an influential Iranian economist and outspoken reformist, mentioned that the Pahlavi "regime didn't have anything to do with the guilds inside the bazaars [and] with the Pahlavi reforms the guild benefited from the cities and the urban middle class expansion."[56] In this section I have supported

---

[55] After one of the carpet dealers left, the other one turned to me and his brother and added that "he had a gambling problem too." Addiction among *bazaari*s is not rare and often is brought up as an explanation for indebtedness. Based on anecdotal evidence, it seems that among *bazaari*s social ills (opium addiction, gambling, and womanizing) are more accepted for older established merchants than newcomers who have not circulated a trustworthy reputation.

[56] *Sobh-e Emruz*, 1 Shahrivar 1378 (August 23, 1999).

and extended this proposition by demonstrating that the Tehran Bazaar's organizational form was strengthened by monarchy, even as it was shunned by high modernism. As the Pahlavi regime left the institutional setting of the Bazaar devoid of its transformative powers, the Bazaar's interconnected value chains and reputation system ensured that the social order was maintained by cooperative hierarchies, and this governance engineered a sense of solidarity.

The Islamic Republic and the Tehran Bazaar

In the past four decades, neither has Iran's dependence on oil waned, nor has its position in the world economy changed significantly. The economy continues to be based on oil exports (over 90 percent of export revenue comes from petroleum products) and the government budget relies on these rents. Moreover, the indexes of modernity have followed comparable trends to earlier decades (see Chapter 1). What has changed since the Revolution, however, is the regime and its approach to the Bazaar. Scholars and popular wisdom have alleged that the Islamic Republic, especially the dominant conservative factions within it, have established a close and mutually beneficial relationship with the *bazaari* class.[57] This argument has two strands. First, analysts argue that there has existed a predilection for bazaar and clergy cooperation ("mosque–bazaar alliance"), and thus surmise that ideological compatibility and familial ties between the clergy and *bazaari*s would naturally continue and develop into a cooperative relationship under a regime headed by segments of the clergy and based on some interpretation of Islamic law. Second, more economically oriented studies argue that the Islamic Republic (at both the national and the municipal level) has implemented pro-mercantile capital policies that are in the interests of the bazaar.[58] Thus, under the Islamic Republic the state approximated a petty bourgeois state.

---

[57] See *inter alia* Wilfried Buchta, *Who Rules Iran? The Structure of Power in the Islamic Republic* (Washington DC: The Washington Institute for Near East Policy and the Konrad Adenauer Stiftung, 2000); Economic Intelligence Unit, *Iran: Country Outlook*, various years; and Mozaffari, "Why the Bazaar Rebels," 377–91.

[58] Wolfgang Lautenschlager, "The Effects of an Overvalued Exchange Rate on the Iranian Economy, 1979–84," *International Journal of Middle East Studies* 18 (February 1986), 31–52; Anoushiravan Ehteshami, *After Khomeini: The Iranian Second Republic* (London: Routledge, 1995), p. 90; Bahram Tehrani, *Pazhuheshi dar Eqtesad-e Iran (1354–1364)*, vol. 2 (Paris: Entesharat-e Khavaran 1986), pp. 384–60; Babak Dorbaygi, "Forushgahha-ye Zanjirehii-ye Refah," *Goft-o-Go* 13 (Fall 1375 [1996]), 19–27; Kaveh Ehsani, "Municipal Matters: The Urbanization of Consciousness and Political Change in Tehran," *Middle East Report* 209 (Fall 1999), 22–7.

This section paints a thoroughly different picture of state–bazaar relations – one that scrutinizes the implicit assumption in these formulations that the Bazaar is a corporate unit that can benefit en masse from patronage or economic policies. I turn to the network approach to demonstrate that the cooperative hierarchies, which were essential in creating the Bazaar's corporate identity, have unraveled under and owing to the policies of the Islamic Republic. Under the new regime the mechanisms that bridged class, status, and sectoral divisions and created a semblance of a corporate *bazaari* body have been increasingly absent. The state incorporation of commercial activities through atomistic patronage and institutional regulations has fragmented the networks, made internal relations more short term, and accentuated the vertical dimensions of interactions instead of horizontal ones. Thus, the Islamic Republic's development projects have not been pro-bazaar, if by that we mean a set of policies that allowed for the persistence of the Bazaar's self-governance and autonomy from the state.

Islamic populism: the pragmatism of a revolutionary regime

During the bitterly cold Tehran winter of 1978–9, Iranians from diverse backgrounds took to the streets as part of the enormous demonstrations that helped topple "the throne and crown." On February 11, 1979, less than a month after the Shah's hurried departure and less than two weeks after the return of Ayatollah Khomeini from exile, Tehran Radio announced the official overthrow of the Pahlavi regime and the end of "2,500 years of monarchy." While some distributed candies and pastries to strangers, other people danced to the sounds of hooting car horns; I imagine that for some it may have seemed that spring had arrived early.

Away from the festive mood in the streets a new state was being established. As with other social revolutions, a new state was fashioned based on the coalition that toppled the *ancien regime*. The 1977–9 coalition encompassed particularly disparate ideologies (including leftists, nationalists, Islamists, and hybrid permutations) and social groups (e.g. university and high-school students, the urban working class, *bazaari*s, the religious establishment, and the salaried middle class). In order to maintain a degree of unity in their pursuit to topple the regime, opposition forces that increasingly orbited around Khomeini developed a rhetoric that was broad and malleable enough to capture the myriad revolutionary logics and aspirations. It included negative statements against monarchy, imperialism, and injustice, and universally appealing slogans for justice, freedom, and independence. Khomeini "managed to be all things to all people. Islamic fundamentalists and westernized intellectuals, bazaar merchants and the urban masses, came to see in his vision of an Islamic state the chance to realize their very disparate aspiration."[59] The success of the eventual rulers of the Islamic Republic was in their ability to devise a message that appealed to a diverse audience, while maintaining their leadership position until they were able to create and seize the institutions of the state. And only then could they systematically turn the coercive instruments of the state against their opponents.[60]

Once in power, the Islamic Republic transformed the existing state organizations and initiated new institutions based on a transformative project to create an Islamic society and economy. The "Islamic" nature of the new regime was not merely wrapped in the turbans worn by many of its leaders, but was an essential objective of the new regime, and one that is clearly stated, if not specified, in the opening to the epic preamble of the Constitution of the Islamic Republic: "The Constitution of the Islamic Republic of Iran advances the cultural, social, political, and economic institutions of Iranian society based on Islamic principles and precepts, which reflects the heartfelt aspiration of the Islamic community [ommat]."[61] The Constitution goes on to specify the interests of government: "In the view of Islam, government does not derive from the interests of a class, nor does it serve the domination of an individual or a group. Rather, it is the crystallization of the political ideal of a people who bear a common faith and common ideology, and have organized themselves in order to initiate the process of intellectual and ideological development towards the final goal (movement towards God)." Khomeini's goal was not only to smash idols, but also to erect state-sponsored paths to the almighty.

On the face of it, the combination of anti-imperialism, Islamic legal principles, and freedom presented the Bazaar community with both opportunities and challenges. The state's intention to "cleanse" the economy of its "comprador" and Pahlavi elements opened up new arenas for ownership and investment. The bazaaris were well positioned to tap into oil revenues and more readily invest in manufacturing and large-scale international trade. Also, most readings of Islam, especially those among the high-ranking clergy, were consistent with the sanctity

---

[59] Shaul Bakhash, *The Reign of the Ayatollahs: Iran and the Islamic Revolution* (New York: Basic Books Inc., 1990), p. 19.

[60] Revolutionaries first attacked monarchists and families allied to the Pahlavi family. Next, the regime used the military and Revolutionary Guard against separatist groups in Kurdistan, Azerbaijan, and Turkmenistan. By 1983 all other opposition groups were outlawed and suppressed, the last of which was the pro-Soviet Tudeh Party.

[61] Constitution of the Islamic Republic of Iran, author's translation.

of private property. In the initial period several key members of the Provisional Government, especially Mehdi Bazargan and others from the Liberation Movement of Iran, which had strong support in the Tehran Bazaar,[62] and the Islamic Republican Party (founded in 1979), such as Mohammad Beheshti and Hosayn-'Ali Montazeri, made public proclamations intended to alleviate the anxiety of a propertied class that was witnessing labor militancy, industrial nationalization, and legal actions against the "corrupt of the earth."[63] On the other hand, the prospects for a pro-capital economic system were made uncertain by other prominent members of the revolutionary coalition (e.g. members of the secular left, as well as Abol-Hasan Bani-Sadr and Mohammad-'Ali Rajaii). This more radical faction spoke of redistribution of wealth and, a sweeping restructuring of the economy (including nationalization and creation of cooperatives), and even singled out members of the private sector who were labeled as antirevolutionaries and economic terrorists.[64]

The "dissonant institutionalization"[65] that is the Constitution of the Islamic Republic reflects this duality. It acknowledges the right to private property and a role for the private sector. Yet on balance it weighs in on the radical side by including a section titled "The economy is a means, not an end" as a general roadmap for the Islamic Republic that is to include "general economic planning," limiting the private sector to "supplementing the economic activities of the state and cooperative sectors," and mentioning the right of the state to confiscate certain properties. The most relevant article is Article 44; it reads:

The economy of the Islamic Republic of Iran consists of three sectors: state, cooperative, and private, and is to be based on systematic and sound planning. The state sector is to include all large-scale and mother industries, foreign trade, major mines, banking, insurance, power generation, dams, and large-scale irrigation networks, radio and television, post, telegraph and telephone services, aviation, shipping, roads, railroads and the like; all these will be publicly owned and at the disposal of the state. The cooperative sector is to include cooperative companies and institutions involved in production and distribution that are established in urban and rural areas in accordance with

---

[62] H. E. Chehabi, *Iranian Politics and Religious Modernism: The Liberation Movement of Iran under the Shah and Khomeini* (Ithaca, NY: Cornell University Press, 1990), pp. 95–7.

[63] In April 1979, Beheshti met with members of the private sector to stress that Islamic economics was compatible with their interests. *Nameh-ye Hafteh:Otaq-e Bazargani va Sanaye' va Ma'aden-e Iran* 1 (19 Khordad 1368 [June 9, 1989]), 5–6.

[64] On the debates among the new elite over economic policies see Bahman Ahmadi-Amuii, *Eqtesad-e Siyasi-ye Jomhuri-e Eslami* (Tehran: Gam-e Naw, 1383 [2004]), especially the interview with 'Ezzatollah Sahabi (pp. 9–59).

[65] Daniel Brumberg, *Reinventing Khomeini: The Struggle for Reform in Iran* (Chicago: University of Chicago Press, 2001).

Islamic precepts. The private sector consists of agriculture, animal husbandry, industry, trade, and services that supplement the economic activities of the state and cooperative sectors. Ownership in these three sectors will be protected by the Islamic Republic as long as they conform to the other articles in this chapter, do not go beyond the bounds of Islamic law, contribute to the economic growth and development of the country's economy, and do not harm society.[66]

The *bazaaris* with whom I spoke readily recalled their shock at the passing of Article 44 and other such provisions[67] that promised wholesale nationalization of the economy. In short, in the early moments of state building, the fate of the Bazaar and private capital in the postrevolutionary political economy was under a shadow.

This duality was arbitrated by the second ingredient of the Islamic Republic's transformative agenda – populism. Khomeini's Islamic model was strongly propelled by mass politics and infused with postcolonial populism influenced by ideologies advocated by secular and religious leftists. Within this discourse, "world exploiters" (read the United States, Britain, and the USSR) were in cahoots with the "Pahlavi lackeys" who had surrendered Iran's assets, impoverishing the nation culturally and economically.[68] Careful not to use the terminology of the left, Khomeini relied on the Koranic terms the "oppressors" (*mostakberin*) and the "oppressed" (*mostaz'afin*) to describe the Manichean battle that he believed resulted in the latter's rightful revolutionary triumph. This discursive maneuver allowed the clerical Islamists to interpret away objective class distinctions as the basis for social conflict, replacing them with notions of virtue and justice. Beyond being the ideological conviction or political proclivity of some members of the revolutionary coalition, in the context of a multiclass revolutionary movement, populism was a strategy that could rally wide support for the new regime.[69] Abrahamian, a leading proponent of this interpretation of the Islamic Republic, argues that "Khomeinism" should not be described as "fundamentalism"; rather its guiding principle is most succinctly, and with greater comparative

---

[66] Author's translation.

[67] Also see Article 45, which outlines a rather liberal and arbitrary definition of public wealth, and Article 49, which stipulates the grounds for confiscation of property.

[68] Hamid Dabashi, *Theology of Discontent: The Ideological Foundations of the Islamic Revolution* (New York: New York University Press, 1993).

[69] Bayat stresses the strategic nature of populism when he argues that the postrevolutionary government used pro-poor rhetoric "because the lower classes were seen as a solid basis for the new regime; second, because lower-class radicalism in the postrevolution forced the clergy to adopt a radical language; and third, because the clergy's emphasis on the oppressed could disarm the left's proletarian discourse after the revolution." Asef Bayat, *Street Politics: Poor People's Movements in Iran* (New York: Columbia University Press, 1997), p. 43.

leverage, captured by "populism." He writes, "Khomeinism, like Latin American populism, was mainly a middle class movement that mobilized the masses with radical sounding rhetoric against the external powers and entrenched power-holding classes, including comprador bourgeoisie. In attacking the establishment, however, it was careful to respect private property and avoid concrete proposals that would undermine the petty bourgeoisie."[70] This populist social contract, therefore, is a compact between the state and the masses, rather than individual citizens, specific factors of production, or social groups as corporate entities.

Khomeini's Islamic populist agenda was to empower the state with the mission to revitalize "the authentic" Islam that would create a self-sufficient, independent society that would answer the woes of the devout and disinherited masses.[71] Wealth and oil earnings were abundant, argued Khomeini, but were not distributed evenly under the Shah's regime, and it was the revolutionary regime's duty to take an active role in abolishing inequality by redirecting expenditures. Nevertheless, the proposal and mode of addressing issues of social justice were not as radical as they may seem; no serious attempt was made to permanently transform property relations in industry or agriculture. Instead, the state took it upon itself to make outlays via charity and patronage. Yet it is doubtful that this development agenda has actually improved the lot of "the oppressed," since "the transfer of wealth was not so much a transfer from the rich to the poor as from the private to the public sector."[72] Both cornerstones of the postrevolutionary economy – the control of vast sums of revenue by the state and the goal of redistributing income to lower echelons of society – have resulted in the state's direct involvement in the production and distribution of goods and services.

Finally, the contingencies of war should not escape our attention. The postrevolutionary fervor for state intervention was stoked by the necessities of the Iran–Iraq war that began in 1980 when Iraq invaded Iran. The bloody eight-year war of attrition required the state to mobilize resources and divert oil earnings for procurement of spare parts and essential consumer goods. An enlarged public apparatus developed as a basis for a war economy and to absorb the increasing numbers of unemployed who had lost their jobs as private investment contracted and people were dislocated from the war zones. 'Ezzatollah Sahabi, who

[70] Ervand Abrahamian, *Khomeinism: Essays on the Islamic Republic* (London: I.B. Tauris & Co., 1993), pp. 37–8.
[71] Ruhollah Khomeini, *Mataleb, Mawzu'at, va Rahnamudha-ye Eqtesadi dar Bayanat-e Hazrat-e Emam Khomeini*, 4 vols. (Tehran, Moasseseh-ye Motale'at va Pazhuheshha-ye Bazargani, 1371 [1992]).
[72] Bakhash, *The Reign of the Ayatollahs*, p. 290.

was a member of the Islamic Revolutionary Council immediately after the Revolution, mentions that the regime engaged in inflationary spending because they feared that the war and the ensuing shortage of goods would lead to disenchantment with the regime and the Revolution.[73] One of the leading economic policymakers of the Islamic Republic, who in the 1990s was a voice for less stringent state intervention, has recently defended the decision for state distribution of goods given the special circumstances of the war.[74] In a detailed study of the impact of the Iran–Iraq war on postrevolutionary state – building, Nazemi concludes, "The various leading figures of the IRP, while disagreeing on a number of issues, nevertheless were unanimous on the necessity of a strengthened state and managed economy during a time of war and state building."[75] The concatenation of Islamic populism and war set the context for the formation of a public-sector-focused economy.

Patronage: the solution to the Islamic Republic's Bazaar dilemma

This transformative program presented the regime with a predicament. How was it to situate the *bazaari* community within this new developmental trajectory that called for statist economic policies? On the one hand, the populist platform of redistribution and championing the popular classes framed the regime's revolutionary agenda, especially amongst the more radical elements of the Islamic Republic. (Re)distribution of oil wealth via state control of the economy was also an expedient method of consolidating the regime's position by limiting independent sources of revenue that could be used by opposition groups. On the other hand, as early as the 1960s Khomeini had identified "the Islamic and traditional" *bazaari*s as a "devout" and "committed" group, which he described in typical populist fashion as a supporter of the "deprived" or by coupling them with "shanty dwellers" and subsuming them within the category of the "oppressed."[76] In the 1960s and 1970s Khomeini was critical of Iran's dependency on western economies that were "bankrupting the bazaar" and converting it into a place for foreign consumer goods.[77] The *bazaari*s' prominent

---

[73] Ahmadi-Amuii, *Eqtesad-e Siyasi-e Jomhuri-e Islami*, p. 40.
[74] Ibid., p. 67.
[75] Nader Nazemi, "War and State Making in Revolutionary Iran," Ph.D. dissertation, University of Washington (1993), pp. 162–3.
[76] For examples see Khomeini, vol. 1, pp. 161–2. "Committed" (*mote'ahhed*) and "devout" (*motedayyen*) are the two favored elements of the discourses used by pro-*bazaari* elements in the Islamic Republic.
[77] Ibid., vol. 1.

position, moreover, was amplified by their ties to the clergy and the well-organized Islamist organizations (i.e. the Islamic Coalition Association [ICA]) that were supported by small circles of *bazaaris*. Thus, it was politically expedient for the Islamic Republic to seek an alliance with the *bazaaris*.

These dual objectives, however, embodied a tension. In the former case, the state was to monopolize the economy. In the latter, it was to ally itself with the private sector – in fact a class that required unfettered access to domestic and international markets and identified itself as the "free sector" mobilizing against both the Qajar and the Pahlavi monarchies in defense of its right to engage in free enterprise. The Islamic Republic negotiated this dilemma by integrating a select few members of the Bazaar into the power structure in order to appease and develop ties with ideological allies, while developing the bureaucratic means and organizations (many of which were headed by ex-*bazaaris*) required to dominate the economy and subordinate the Bazaar in the name of redistribution.[78]

Let me illustrate this dual-track approach. As the Islamic Republic abolished the secular opposition groups, quelled regional independence movements, and began institutionalizing its rule, elite divisions between those favoring state control over the economy and supporters of private property and enterprise repeatedly came to the fore in several policy areas (e.g. land reform, labor reform, and the Islamicizing of banking). These two factions were locked in a rather entrenched stalemate. With the statists controlling the parliament and the free marketers controlling the Guardian Council, these battles were not fully resolved as legislative gridlock and political stonewalling generally resulted in only incremental gains for either side.

Then, in the summer of 1984, a debate over the nationalization of international trade came to the forefront. On the one side were supporters of free-market policies within the Islamic Republican Party, members of industry and commerce, and political actors seeking to undermine the radical and statist coalition headed by Prime Minister Mir-Hosayn Musavi. Meanwhile, the proponents of nationalizing international trade were based in the parliament and rallied around the prime minister. They drafted a parliamentary bill that sought to operationalize Article 44 of the Constitution by placing all international trade under public management. To resolve this political deadlock, the

---

[78] Of course, this simplifies a highly uneven and politically charged battle between various camps. Bakhash, *The Reign of the Ayatollahs*; Bahman Baktiari, *Parliamentary Politics in Revolutionary Iran: The Institutionalization of Factional Politics* (Gainesville: University Press of Florida, 1996).

issue was taken to Khomeini, who pragmatically and judiciously wove together the populist message with his interest in maintaining the support of his followers in the bazaars. "[I]t was the people who established this government and this republic," Ayatollah Khomeini reminded the president, prime minister and cabinet:

[But] not all the people, only the barefooted (*pa-berahneh*, i.e. oppressed) masses. The burden has been on the shoulders of the *bazaaris*, the middle class and the oppressed. That is, the deprived (*mahrumin*) have shouldered the burden of the revolution. If you remember the demonstrations of the people pouring into streets in the era of the former regime and shortly afterwards in the early days of the revolution, ... it was the oppressed who participated in the marches. Therefore, your government is a government of the deprived and it should work for the deprived.[79]

But, in his typical didactic manner, Khomeini paused to underscore *bazaaris*' special place in the economic system:

You should not discard the bazaar. That is, if the bazaar is incapable of doing something, then the government should do that job. But if the bazaar is quite capable of doing something, do not stop it; this is not legally accepted by Islamic Law. The people should not be deprived of their freedom. The government should supervise (*nezarat*). Take for example importing goods from abroad. The people should be left free to import as far as possible. Such goods should be imported by both the people and by the government. But the government should supervise and make sure that goods which are against the interests of the Islamic Republic and Islamic Law are not imported. This is called supervision, meaning that you should not leave them free to saturate the bazaar with luxuries and other such goods which were common in the past. But, if you were to refuse to allow the people to share with you in trade, industry and similar things, you would not succeed.

These statements, which helped impede the rush to nationalize trade, have been interpreted as an example of the Islamic Republic's pro-bazaar or pro-capital position.[80] Although signaling a retreat from the full implementation of Article 44 and surrendering a space for private involvement in international and domestic trade, Khomeini made a subtle and overlooked, yet important, modification. "Obviously, there are some corrupt individuals in the bazaar; there are some self-seeking individuals there. ... However, there are many correct, religious and skilled people in the bazaar, too."[81] As in many other cases, Khomeini

---

[79] Khomeini, vol. 4, p. 17.
[80] *See inter alia* Asghar Schirazi, *The Constitution of Iran: Politics and the State in the Islamic Republic*, trans. John O'Kane (London: I. B. Tauris, 1998), p. 67; and Ehteshami, *After Khomeini*, p. 8.
[81] Khomeini, vol. 4, p. 19.

was emphasizing that policymakers should not treat the bazaars as a homogeneous corporate body or an independent class.[82] Rather, as part of their role as "supervisors," the state officials were to be selective in their relations.

In fact, this was exactly the regime's approach from the outset. Individual *bazaaris*, or those with *bazaari* roots, who were "correct, religious, and skilled" were to be rewarded with government portfolios and protection from property seizures. Many of these figures were part of the clandestine ICA that had been under the tutelage of Khomeini and his students since the 1960s.[83] For instance, Habibollah 'Asgarawladi-Mosalman, who is one of the founding members of the ICA and its long-standing secretary general, has held a number of government posts including head of the Ministry of Commerce (1981–3), the Supreme Leader's Representative at the Imam Relief Fund Committee, and member of the central council of the 15th of Khordad Foundation.[84] His brother, Asadollah 'Asgarawladi-Mosalman, who was a more active trader in the Bazaar, has been a mainstay of the Chamber of Commerce. 'Ali-Naqi Khamushi, an ICA member and an engineer from a *bazaari* family, was a director of the Foundation of the Oppressed and Disabled, and initially Khomeini's representative to Iran's Chamber of Commerce, Industry and Mines. Since then he has been the Chairman of the Chamber of Commerce and has also worked in the Ministry of Commerce. Taqi Khamushi, 'Ali-Naqi's brother, was a member of the board of directors of the Islamic Propaganda Organization and the Islamic Economy Organization. Asadollah Lajevardi, who was assassinated in the Tehran Bazaar in 1998, was the Chief Prosecutor who oversaw the summary executions of political prisoners in 1988. Mohsen Rafiqdust, who as a teenager joined the ICA, became the Commander-in-Chief of the Islamic Revolutionary Guard Corps and later became the head of the most powerful *bonyad*, the Foundation for the Oppressed and Disabled. Meanwhile, Kazem Hajj-Tarkhani, who was a member of the Revolutionary Council and had close ties to the ruling clergy and the actors mentioned above, avoided full-scale expropriation of his assets in cement and carton production and sugar processing. However, probably because of personal disputes with revolutionary figures, 'Ali Hajj-Tarkhani, Kazem's younger brother and owner of Shahd Sugar Company, was on the initial list of fifty industrialists who had their assets

---

[82] Ibid., vol. 2, pp. 43–4 and 56.
[83] See Chapter 3 for references.
[84] 'Asgarawladi is alleged to have helped place ICA members in the Center for Procurement and Distribution of Goods. Ahmadi-Amuii, *Eqtesad-e Siyasi-e Jomhuri-e Islami*, p. 23.

appropriated. This example indicates that personal relations and political ideology, rather than *bazaari* affiliations, are what created the close connection between ICA members and the state.

Thus, the prominent supporters of the Islamic Republic within the Bazaar community were coopted and accommodated into the regime's bureaucracy, giving them direct supervision over state assets, and aligning their individual interests with those of the regime to maintain the political order. The very fact that individual members of the Bazaar have so readily broken ranks with their fellow *bazaaris* and pursued personal advantage demonstrates the precarious and nonessential nature of the Bazaar's solidarity and corporate logic. From the perspective of the state, this mode of patronage and blurring of state–society boundaries was a method of rule and atomistic incorporation of *bazaaris*. The link between state power and patronage is traced by Catherine Boone in her study of postcolonial Senegal. "Patronage relations linked those with direct control over state power to those interested in, or in need of, state resources." She continues, "By infusing these resources into new and existing social hierarchies and organizations, possibilities for gathering and reproducing power in these settings became more contingent on political favor from above."[85] Likewise in postrevolutionary Iran, the state established patron–client relations with members of the Bazaar through the distribution of a wide range of resources and the use of state authority to produce rents for allies.

In the early years of the Islamic Republic, the supporters of economic nationalization and state-led development clashed with those favoring a more laissez-faire approach to the economy. However, these disputes also changed the political economy in ways that made it reasonable to regulate economic activities without undermining the principles of private property and accumulation. In summary, the regime identified and separated the "correct" from the "corrupt" *bazaaris*, the former being revered and the latter reviled. In the process, the ruling class, as a social stratum wielding power, was fashioned through the exercise and reproduction of state power, through the creation and application of institutions, and through the forging of mutual interests. Since the Bazaar's economic position clashed with the populist agenda that called for a distributive policy in favor of the lower and lower-middle class, the *bazaaris* were integrated into the political elite as individuals, not as a corporate entity.[86] Postrevolutionary state–bazaar relations were an

---

[85] Catherine Boone, *Merchant Capital and the Roots of State Power in Senegal 1930–85* (Cambridge: Cambridge University Press, 1992), p. 17.

[86] James Bill writes, "Whenever in doubt, however, he [Khomeini] would go with the attitudes of the lower and lower-middle class masses – even at times to the

articulation of the new Islamic populist transformative project that was inclusionary without being pluralist or corporative.

Repertoires of state incorporation

Islamic populism does not operate only on a discursive plane or through informal clientelistic channels; rather by transcribing this policy of "supervising" the economy into multiple regulatory institutions and creating new organizations, the new political elite transformed Iranian society as it created a new regime. The Islamic Republic's approach toward the *bazaaris* approximates Ruth and David Collier's concept of state incorporation.[87] For the Colliers state incorporation entails the legal and bureaucratic incorporation of a social group in order to control and mobilize it for the regime's ends. In their treatment of state–labor relations in Latin America, they show that unlike cases in which particular parties represented the interests of labor (i.e. party incorporation), in the Brazilian and Chilean cases, the state initiated inclusion through a legal framework and at the administrative level of the state. Analogously, under the Islamic Republic, the state turned to trade policies, foreign currency regulations, and economic organizations to control and subordinate the Bazaar. My treatment of state incorporation, nevertheless, modifies the Colliers' analysis in one respect. While the Islamic Republic developed a wide array of legal and bureaucratic methods to control and regulate the economy as a whole, and as I will argue in Chapter 6 this resulted in the depoliticizing of the Bazaar, it does not necessarily follow that this outcome was engineered by deliberate and conscious actions of the regime to demobilize the *bazaaris*. Lacking explicit statements of such motivations, I interpret the process of incorporation as a means by which the regime situated the *bazaaris* within its transformative project through the creation of clusters of policies that over time and unwittingly reconfigured the Bazaar's internal form of governance.

---

consternation of other important supporters such as the influential merchants and bazaaris." James Bill, "Power and Religion in Revolutionary Iran," *Middle East Journal* 36 (Winter 1982), 43. While I agree with the general tenor of Bill's assessment, as the example above demonstrates, Khomeini was careful to appear as if he was not picking sides and strove to carve a middle ground between the two groups within "the oppressed" (the poor masses and the devout *bazaaris*).

[87] Ruth Barins Collier and David Collier, *Shaping the Political Arena: Critical Junctures, Labor Movement, and Regime Dynamics in Latin America* (Princeton: Princeton University Press, 1991).

Before we investigate exactly how the state incorporated the Bazaar, we must analyze the architecture of the regime itself. Under the Shah, the state was ostensibly a monolithic and centralized entity that placed all decision-making powers in the hands of the monarch. An official in the prerevolutionary Ministry of Commerce writes, "[the Shah's] administrative hierarchy was highly centralized, totally unintegrated, and responsive only to him."[88] Conversely, the postrevolutionary regime, even though it is neither pluralistic nor corporatist in its representation of interests, consists of multiple and competing decision-making and power centers.[89] Not unlike China's communist regime, which has been described as "fragmented authoritarianism,"[90] below the office of the Supreme Leader (Khomeini, 1979–88, and 'Ali Khamenei, 1988–the present), a fragmented and overlapping bureaucratic grid persists, allowing and engendering elite factionalism and competition. This has been a product of constitutional design and is reflected in the clustering of loci of power within both the republican institutions of the regime (the legislature and the presidency) and the unelected "Islamic" institutions (Supreme Leader, Guardian Council, and Expediency Council). This regime structure has resulted in the flourishing of numerous parallel organs, many of which have survived throughout the postrevolutionary era.

These countervailing foci of authority and power have given the political system stability by managing regular elite contestation,[91] but they have also rendered policymaking ineffective. The multiple institutions with overlapping jurisdictions have impaired the state's ability to develop a uniform and coherent regulatory system that can design and implement policies effectively. For instance, an official of the Central Bank, which is authorized to monitor all banking operations, has recently argued that it is unable to control the nation's finances since the

---

[88] Khosrwo Fatemi, "Leadership by Distrust: The Shah's *Modus Operandi*," *Middle East Journal* 36 (Winter 1982), 9. Also see Homa Katouzian, "The Pahlavi Regime in Iran," in *Sultanistic Regimes*, ed. H. E. Chehabi and Juan J. Linz (Baltimore: Johns Hopkins University Press, 1998), pp. 182–205.

[89] Houchang Chehabi has recently described the Islamic Republic as "factionalized authoritarianism." H. E. Chehabi, "The Political Regime of the Islamic Republic of Iran in Comparative Perspective," *Government and Opposition* 36 (Winter 2001), 48–70. On this issue also see Hojjat Mortaji, *Jenahha-ye Siyasi dar Iran-e Emruz* (Tehran: Naqsh va Negar, 1378 [1999]); and Buchta, *Who Rules Iran?*

[90] Kenneth G. Lieberthal, "Introduction: The 'Fragmented Authoritarianism': Model and Its Limitations," in *Bureaucracy, Politics, and Decision Making in Post-Mao China*, ed. Kenneth Lieberthal and David Lampton (Berkeley: University of California Press, 1992).

[91] Arang Keshavarzian, "Contestation without Democracy: Elite Fragmentation in Iran," in *Enduring Authoritarianism: Obstacles to Democratization in the Middle East*, ed. Marsha Pripstein Posusney and Michelle Penner Angrist (Boulder: Lynne Rienner, 2005).

Ministry of Interior and the Security Forces, rather than the Bank, issues licenses to the thousands of interest-free credit associations (*qarz al-hassaneh*) in Iran.[92] The issuing of import licenses meant to restrict imports is another example. A member of the parliament's Economic Committee reported that as many as thirty centers and organs issue import licenses. The parliamentary representative bemoaned the fact that the plurality of licensing authorities has undermined accountability and transparency in the process.[93] Not surprisingly this heterogeneity also hinders value integration and planning. A young technocrat in a development ministry, who by his own admission had idealistically taken the job thinking that he could have an impact on Iran's development trajectory, commented that the multiple institutions, which do not share objectives, information, or responsibilities, often contradict, and even neutralize, each other.[94] Finally, these multiple state affiliates are an important means by which to distribute patronage and encourage cronyism. In the field of domestic trade, for instance, multiple ministries, municipalities, and Islamic associations play a role in supervising, licensing, and representing traders. Under the promise of confidentiality a member of the Association of Guild Affairs bluntly told me, "Nobody knows exactly who is in charge of what. All these ministries, associations, and societies are just ways to provide jobs and 'to lend each other bread.'" Through these multiple and parallel organs a myriad patronage networks have developed, tying clusters of clients to multiple patrons.

Another consequence of the heterogeneous decision-making organs and competing factions in the Islamic Republic is policy volatility. As already mentioned, the Constitution stipulates that international trade should be under the supervision of the public sector, but this has not been fully implemented. Instead, depending on macroeconomic fluctuations and which faction enjoyed the upper hand, governments have contracted or liberalized trade policies. Private capital faced a more restrictive economy during 1980–4, 1987–90, and 1993–7, and a relatively more liberal regime in 1979, 1985–7, 1990–3, and 1997–the present. The numerous shifts in trade, foreign exchange, and tax policies have resulted in truncating the time horizon for economic actors and the transfer of existing assets into quick-return, high-profit services and trades, including speculation in foreign currencies. A survey of economic units found that

[92] *Aftab-e Yazd*, 18 Shahrivar 1381 (September 9, 2002).

[93] *Nawrouz*, 23 Khordad 1381 (June 13, 2002).

[94] This official mentioned that one of the most important achievements of the Khatami government was to merge several of these ministries for, example the Ministry of Industry with the Ministry of Mines and the Ministry of Agriculture with the Ministry of the Crusade for Construction.

three-quarters of managers surveyed believed that frequent changes in laws and regulations were either "very" or "quite important" in hindering production, making this issue the leading factor cited.[95] Addressing the issue of policy volatility, the chairman of the Isfahan Chamber of Commerce, Industries and Mines said, "Experience gained from the last decade shows that certain influential figures have made new decisions each day. They have modified the regulations for imports/exports, investment, taxes and duties to either facilitate or restrict the respective sectors. Without doubt, no one would be willing to make industrial investments under these conditions, unless on exceptional occasions."[96]

The issue of perpetual instability in trade regulations was one of the most consistent themes in my interviews with traders and wholesalers. Distinguishing between market fluctuations and policy and regulatory instability, the *bazaari*s spoke of how changes in laws affect prices, quantities, and the channels through which goods may enter the economy. *Bazaari*s reiterated that they are never sure whether import rules, hard currency laws, and customs regulations announced one month will be in place the next. Changes in customs duties have been among the factors leading to a large quantity of imports being abandoned at ports. A businessman told a newspaper "that constant changes in the customs duties is one of the main reasons why importers abandon their commodities in customs. 'These changes take place in the mid-year, while legally, they can only occur on a yearly basis. It seems the government should take more serious measures to resolve this problem and fix duty rates.'"[97] Importers no longer freely import since licenses might be lifted and state organs may import the same good at lower costs (since they have access to subsidized dollars and do not pay duties). Speculation has replaced long-term investments in reputation, and economic relations have become more temporary.

To manage the volatility successfully one needs information, and here the state, or allies within its penumbra, enjoy a highly privileged position. But these alliances too are riddled with instability and have become short-term assets. Political turmoil, factionalism, and personalism at the level of the bureaucracy all work to make even contacts and informal relationships between *bazaari*s and government officials ephemeral. Cabinet reshuffles and parliamentary turnovers can easily make contacts worthless.

---

[95] Seyed Morteza Afghah, "The Effect of Non-economic Factors in the Process of Production in Iran," in *The Economy of Iran: The Dilemmas of an Islamic State*, ed. Parvin Alizadeh (London: I. B. Tauris, 2000).
[96] *Iran Daily*, December 7, 2000.
[97] *Iran Daily*, February 27, 2001.

From the perspective of the state, moreover, trade rules must remain indeterminate, variable, and even arbitrary in order to maintain patronage and clientelism as a viable political tool of social control. Uniform and consistent laws based on fair access and equal application of laws "preclude the striking of particularistic deals."[98] Instead, policy indeterminacy allows ministers, tax collectors, and bureaucrats to act as beneficent patrons who cultivate dependency relations with clients with pecuniary benefits. Thus, under the Islamic Republic the state was the patron to a newly emerging "private" commercial elite, based on personalism rather than group affiliation. [99]

Methods of incorporation

The incorporation of commerce operated at three interrelated levels. First, there was the politically motivated incorporation of specific associations in order to reward some and utilize them as means to monitor the Bazaar. Second, the state passed a series of general economic laws that regulated all commercial activities, including the Bazaar's. Finally, the state created a series of organizations that developed value chains that competed with the Tehran Bazaar's networks.

Political incorporation   Beyond the state's accommodation of Islamist elements from the Bazaar, the Islamic Republic also transformed the voluntary organizations within the Bazaar into ideological censors. The main vehicle for monitoring and mobilizing the Bazaar was the Society of the Islamic Associations of Tehran's Guilds and Bazaar (Jame'eh-ye Anjomanha-ye Eslami-ye Asnaf va Bazar-e Tehran). It was established in the fall of 1980 by Beheshti as an umbrella organization bringing together the many Islamic Associations that during the revolutionary turmoil helped distribute goods and services and coordinate demonstrations. The society had the explicit mandate to "destroy the idol worshippers in the Muslim Bazaar" and to prevent "intellectual deviation."[100] State officials have made periodic announcements calling on these associations to maintain the Islamic character of the Bazaar by limiting hoarding and profiteering. In 1983, Speaker of the Parliament

---

[98] Çağlar Keyder, "The Housing Market from Informal to Global," in *Istanbul: Between the Global and the Local,* ed. Çağlar Keyder (Lanham: Powman and Littlefield Publishers, 1999), p. 147.

[99] There are parallels here with Perthes' analysis of Syrian economic policy in the 1970s and 1980s. Volker Perthes, "The Syrian Private Industrial and Commercial Sectors and the State," *International Journal of Middle East Studies* 24 (May 1992), 207–30.

[100] *Hamshahri,* 22 Mehr 1381 (October 14, 2002).

Hashemi-Rafsanjani (and subsequent president, 1989–1997) called on the Islamic associations to keep a close eye on guild members to ensure that they followed government regulations and pricing.[101] In addition, the Islamic associations were important in mobilizing "behind the war front" by collecting and coordinating donations for military and civilian victims.[102] For instance, in the early stages of the war, the fabric sellers in the Tehran Bazaar promised to donate 1,000 million rial for the war wounded.[103] In general, to ensure that goods would go to the needy, bazaaris preferred to give support in kind, rather than in money.[104]

From the beginning of the Revolution the voluntary associations were under the exclusive control of the staunchly conservative Islamic Coalition Association and were highly partisan and exclusionary. Since its establishment the general secretary of the Society of Islamic Associations has been Sa'id Amani, a leading figure in the ICA and the uncle of one of the ICA's principal spokesmen, Asadollah Badamchian.[105] The society's ruling councils have comprised clerics handpicked by Khomeini and allied with the conservative faction in the regime. On the sixteenth anniversary of the Islamic Revolution, Amani claimed that in all aspects the situation of the commercial sector was better than during the prerevolutionary era.[106] This statement, which was published in Asnaf, rings hollow given that this periodical, along with most other news sources, regularly quotes members of the commercial sector recounting difficulties facing the guilds, and attributing them to government policies since the Revolution.

As mentioned in Chapter 3, during our discussions leaders of the Islamic associations freely admitted that they had lost touch with the members of the bazaars, while the bazaaris claimed that the associations represented the interests of the regime instead of the Bazaar. When I asked a contact in the Bazaar to refer me to the head of his guild's Islamic association he responded, "Why do you want to interview these people? Nobody takes them seriously anymore. They just parrot what the government says and never do anything for us." Another bazaari focused on the unresponsive nature of these organizations when he told

---

[101] Jomhuri-ye Eslami, 9 Esfand 1361 (February 28, 1963).

[102] Personal interviews. During the war, the general secretary of the society argued that these "popular efforts" should be seen as an indication of the potential benefits of allowing the private sector to be more active in the economy. Resalat, 13 Esfand 1365 (March 4, 1987).

[103] Abol Ghassem Lebaschi, interview by Habib Ladjevardi, tape recording no. 3, Paris, France, February 28, 1983, Iranian Oral History Collection, Harvard University, p. 2.

[104] Ibid. Personal interviews.

[105] Badamchian and Banaii, Hayatha-ye Motalefeh-ye Eslami, p. 133. Amani died in 2002.

[106] Asnaf no. 35 (Farvardin 1375 (March–April 1996)), 10.

me, "They do their own thing. They don't want to hear from the reputable merchants. They don't care what problems we face or what needs to be done. They speak in the name of the guilds and the Bazaar, but treat us as a tool [for their own ends]."

Finally, when internal monitoring and persuasion did not work, the state turned to coercive means. On a number of occasions the leaders of the Islamic Republic have warned *bazaaris* that some members have sullied the good Islamic "reputation" of the entire Bazaar and that the government would "identify those who in the days of war and revolution have pursued their own interests" rather than those of the Republic.[107] As part of this initiative, economic offences have been placed in the hands of the Islamic Revolutionary Courts and Prosecutor's Office. Thus, economic offences such as "overpricing" and "hoarding" are dealt with by the same judicial body established to punish assassination attempts, crimes of the Pahlavi regime, and drug smuggling. In 1987 Khomeini allowed the Council of Ministers to impose discretionary punishments (*ta'zirat*) against people convicted of hoarding and conspiring to drive up prices. Throughout the postrevolutionary era, the state has used periodic antiprofiteering and hoarding campaigns and threats to keep the Bazaar in check.[108]

Incorporation via regulation   Incorporation occurs through laws and policies that regulate activities, create state agencies, and pattern social relations by distributing power. Under the Islamic Republic, the state's foray into incorporating the Bazaar consisted of a series of legal measures that limited private commercial activities and subordinated them to state and quasi-state authorities with monopolistic powers. As two economic experts have pointed out, "The expanded government role in the postrevolutionary period was ... not solely or even primarily through a shift of balance from private to public ownership. It was manifested in direct interventions in the operation of markets – foreign exchange controls, maintenance of a system of multiple exchange rates, control on interest rates and bank credits – as well as direct price controls in a large number of product markets."[109] The upshot has been sustained state involvement in the economy during the past two decades. Even after some economic liberalization in the 1990s, Iran's international trade

---

[107] Quoted in Nazemi, "War and State Making in Revolutionary Iran," p. 245.

[108] *Ettela'at*, 13 Aban 1361 (November 4, 1982), 9 Day 1361 (December 30, 1982), 14 Ordibehesht 1367 (May 4, 1988) and 11 Farvardin 1367 (March 31, 1988).

[109] Hassan Hakimian and Massoud Karshenas, "Dilemmas and Prospects for Economic Reform and Reconstruction in Iran," in *The Economy of Iran: The Dilemmas of an Islamic State*, ed. Parvin Alizadeh (London: I. B. Tauris, 2000), pp. 34–5.

regime was ranked 132 out of 155 in the World Bank's Doing Business survey of economies,[110] comparable with economic regimes such as Cuba, Libya, and North Korea.[111] By another measure of "market openness" (with 1 equaling complete market freedom and 0 representing complete lack of market freedom) Iran's economy went from 0.628 during the mid-1970s to 0.304 in the transition period (1979–81), to the nadir of 0.150 in the 1981–8 period, only slightly inching its way to greater market deregulation during the 1990s – 0.367 (1988–92), 0.317 (1993–6), and 0.45 (1997–2000).[112] These comparative and aggregate numbers reflect the series of policies under the Islamic Republic that resulted in some 300 goods being under government price and quantity controls[113] and as much as 90 percent of civilian imports being in the hands of the government by the late 1980s.[114]

Far-reaching state intervention into the economy, however, did not manufacture a centralized and comprehensive planned economy. Even during the war, the Islamic Republic did not replace markets with a command economy. Government intercession during the past two decades was a series of isolated and largely myopic schemes that were dictated by immediate circumstances. In 1994 Kamal Athari, a leading economist, commented, "The government has rejected the free-market logic and principles of command economy without offering a third way."[115]

Government officials and bazaaris concurred that the primary method of reducing imports and protecting local manufacturers has been the use of nontariff barriers such as the outright banning of imports or licensing requirements.[116] A whole series of procurement and distribution centers were established during the 1980s, giving the state outright monopolies over selected groups of imports (generally raw materials, heavy machinery, and staple goods).[117] The National Iranian Industrial Organization along with trade units within the ministries has managed all imports of raw

[110] World Bank, "Doing Business in Iran"; http://www.doingbusiness.org/Explore Economies/Default.aspx?economyid=91 (accessed June 2006).

[111] Iran is 151st out of 155 on the Heritage Foundation and The Wall Street Journal's 2002 Index of Economic Freedom. In terms of freedom ranking, its trade policy is ranked as "very high levels of protection."

[112] 'Ali Farahbakhsh, "Eqtesad-e Iran dar Shesh Tablo," Payam-e Emruz 43 (Bahman 1379 (February 2001)), 42.

[113] Hakimian and Karshenas, "Dilemmas and Prospects for Economic Reform," p. 35.

[114] Vahid Nowshirvani, Encyclopaedia Iranica, s.v. "Commerce in the Pahlavi and Post-Pahlavi Periods," p. 87.

[115] New York Times, November 20, 1994.

[116] Duties and commercial taxes in Iran have historically been relatively low. See Nowshirvani, Encyclopaedia Iranica, s.v. "Commerce in the Pahlavi and Post-Pahlavi Periods," pp. 75–89.

[117] Ahmadi-Amuii, Eqtesad-e Siyasi-e Jomhuri-e Islami, pp. 22–3.

materials and capital goods for public industries, and has sold excess quantities to the private sector. During most of this time, ministries have imported goods using highly subsidized foreign currency, enabling them to price out private sector competitors and enjoy major windfalls.

The state also structures international trade through licensing requirements. The Ministry of Commerce lists the goods that can be legally imported and only then are importers allowed to apply for a license from the ministry responsible. The licensing system both curtails the quantity of imports in the hands of the private sector and reduces the number of legal importers.[118] Iran's nontariff barriers are much higher and more pervasive than those of most other developing countries. A World Bank study of forty-three developing countries for the period 1995–8 found that restrictive licensing conditions applied to just 10 percent of imports and prohibitions applied to another 2 percent. In contrast, even after the replacement of many nontariff barriers by their tariff equivalents in October 2000, Iran's trade regime placed licensing conditions on 45 percent of goods. Of the forty-three countries in the study, only India made greater use of licensing restrictions.[119] Another mechanism to dampen and control imports was foreign currency controls. Owing to political instability, demand for foreign currency increased and led to shortages. The state's response was to monopolize the exchange of foreign currency and to establish the Exchange Allocation Commission to distribute hard currency at fixed rates.

Exports of non-oil goods (especially hand-woven rugs, antiques, precious metals, and jewelry) were also restricted to temper capital flight and preserve the value of the rial. The outbreak of war and Iran's need to purchase arms on the world market exacerbated the hard currency shortage. Thus, the state imposed foreign exchange repatriation contracts (*payman-e arzi*) that required exporters to deposit collateral with the Central Bank, the sum being based on the value of exports and appreciated fixed exchange rates as collateral with the Central Bank. (Since the 1990s the Tehran stock exchange has been a legal mechanism for exporters to sell foreign earnings at the market rate.) In the 1960s and 1970s, the Tehran Bazaar had access to a steady stream of hard currency via non-oil exports (primarily hand-woven rugs) that was largely independent of the state-run financial institutions. Foreign currency markets now either are heavily regulated by the Central Bank or have been based in highly speculative black markets that the government never sought to

---

[118] Hakimian and Karshenas, "Dilemmas and Prospects for Economic Reform," p. 35.
[119] World Bank, "Trade and Foreign Exchange Policies in Iran: Reform Agenda, Economic Implications and Impact on the Poor," Report no. 22953-IRN, November 1, 2001.

control fully. These regulations have encouraged exporters to resort to unofficial channels to export their goods and have also reduced the credit relations that used to exist between the Bazaar and manufactures.

One implication of this incorporation of the Bazaar through an individual-based regulatory regime is that over time the commercial sector has become fully tied to state actors through patronage, a process that generates rivalry and undercuts allegiance to the Bazaar as a community and set of institutions. Instead of implementing universal regulations, tariffs, and equal subsidies that would have ensured equal treatment across all commercial actors, the state imposed trade controls via licenses, multilayered hard currency regimes, and tax and duty shelters that allocated and targeted state rents to specific individuals and organizations. Predictably, this regulatory regime has led to rampant and entrenched (i.e. self-perpetuating) personalism and paternalism. In the process, the commercial arena has become politicized and has been treated individualistically rather than as a corporate entity that is to be managed with a blanket set of rules. In response, some well-positioned *bazaari*s have turned to interpersonal relations to access these revenue pools. These networks are not designed for marketing in the Bazaar, but for accessing rents held by state actors. And as such they have become divisive rather than integrative; the information and resourses garnered by individual merchants are not shared with others.

Incorporation via organizational competition Laws not only regulated the Bazaar's commercial activities, but also established state agents that competed with the private mercantile class. These competitors include several ministries, foundations (*bonyad*s), and religious endowments that have controlled large amounts of assets and have been given subsidized foreign exchange, import privileges, and tax and duty shelters. These state organs and affiliates were established in the months following the Revolution and were tied to the populist transformative agenda of the new regime.

Within five months of the Revolution the provisional government initiated a sweeping nationalization of industrial and financial enterprises, consolidating large portions of the economy under the auspices of various ministries and the National Iranian Industrial Organization, which owned 600 companies. The nationalist drive included international trade too. The Ministry of Commerce controlled seventeen of the country's largest trading firms, while it and the Ministry of Finance controlled warehousing firms and trucking companies.[120] The Islamic

---

[120] Bakhash, *The Reign of the Ayatollahs*, p. 184.

regime took up the nationalization campaign as a safeguard against the insolvency of industries and financial organizations whose managers and owners had fled the country and to stem off labor militancy. Wholesale nationalization was also legitimated by the redistributive and anti-imperialistic principles of the revolution.

Alongside ministerial organizations and sometimes in competition with government policies are a group of foundations or charities.[121] These *bonyad*s were established shortly after the Revolution to oversee the assets of the Pahlavi Foundation and other properties associated with the royal family, and they are now active in all sectors of the economy – manufacturing, agriculture, services, banking, commerce, and religious propagation, having monopolies or near monopolies in several of these areas. Their founding mission was to engage in "good works" and to manage these assets for the benefit of the deprived, those disabled in the Iran–Iraq war, and the families of those killed in the Revolution and the war. Foundations are public in the sense that they do not pay taxes, are entitled to state-subsidized loans and foreign currency, tax and duty exemptions, receive contributions from the Supreme Leader, and are tasked with the state's mission of redistribution. Nonetheless, they are private and semiautonomous in that they are not accountable to or monitored by the government. Even though the foundations are said to receive 58 percent of the state budget, the popularly elected executive and legislature do not have any authority to monitor their performance.[122] Since the heads of the foundations are appointed by the Supreme Leader of the Revolution they have access to the leader's budget and the latest information about developments in the government's economic and commercial policies.

The Foundation of the Oppressed and Disabled, the principal holder of assets seized from the royal family, is the largest of these foundations and is sometimes referred to as the "government within the government." In 1982, the foundation owned 203 manufacturing and industrial factories, 472 large farms, 101 construction firms, and 238 trade

---

[121] The largest foundations are the Foundation for the Oppressed and Disabled, Martyr's Foundation, 15th of Khordad Foundation, and the Housing Foundation. Other religious or revolutionary organs that enjoy a quasi-state status and are active in economic affairs are the endowment overseeing the Imam Reza Shrine in Mashhad (Astan-e Qods-e Razavi), the Organization for Islamic Propagation, and the Farabi Cinema Foundation. See Mehran Kamrava and Houchang Hassan-Yari, "Suspended Equilibrium in Iran's Political System," *Muslim World* 94 (October 2004), 495–524; and Ali A. Saeidi, "The Accountability of Para-governmental Organizations (*bonyad*s): The Case of Iranian Foundation," *Iranian Studies* 37(3) (September 2004), 479–98.

[122] Buchta, *Who Rules Iran?*, p. 73. (Taken from *Salam* daily newspaper.)

and service companies.[123] In the past two decades it has used these already large assets to expand its activities into all areas of the economy, including manufacturing, commerce, banking, tourism, and telecommunications.[124]

It is difficult to estimate their total assets because the foundations' accounts are not public, but whatever the exact extent of these parastatal organs' asset base, analysts agree that the scant supervision has encouraged inefficiencies, mismanagement, and embezzlement. For instance, in 1995, a court found several key figures of the Foundation of the Oppressed and Disabled guilty of embezzlement, although the head of the foundation escaped conviction.

Over time the foundations' economic prominence and prosperity have continued, if not expanded. They have been able to circumvent the official trade system, while their political ties have given them access to subsidized foreign currency without performance criteria. Therefore, the foundations can import, export, and sell goods at below market prices and the production costs of local producers (some of which are owned by the foundations themselves). The various state agencies allocate exemptions to state organizations (*bonyads*, cooperatives, trade units within the ministries) to bypass trade bans and duties. The issuing of these "special licenses" (*mojavvez-e moredi*) has allowed state organs to gain access to trade exemptions, while countless state officials distribute them as patronage.[125] Moreover, independent capitalists cannot compete with the state-affiliated establishments that are exempted from duties and time-consuming bureaucratic hurdles, while receiving heavily subsidized foreign exchange.[126] A *bazaari* who used to be a tea importer and has now downscaled his import activities estimated that his cost of importing is four times that of a foundation's or a border cooperative's that can acquire "special licenses."

---

[123] Farahbakhsh, "Eqtesad-e Iran dar Shesh Tablo," 47.

[124] Analysts have estimated that *bonyad*s own some 20 percent of the asset base of the Iranian economy and contribute 10 percent to the country's GDP. If we include them in the public sector, then 80 percent of the formal Iranian economy is controlled by the public sector, with the private sector and cooperatives accounting for 17 and 3 percent respectively (Bijan Khajehpour-Khouei, "Domestic Political Reform and Private Sector Activity in Iran," *Social Research* 67 [summer 2000], 577–598). The parliamentary representative from Mashhad has claimed that the foundations and organs, including the wealthy trust administering the Imam Reza Shrine in Mashhad, control 70 percent of the economy (*Hayat-e Naw*, 19 Mehr 1379 [October 10, 2001], 14). The Imam Reza Endowment that supervises the shrine of the 8th Shiite Imam in Mashhad is in charge of agricultural land and numerous industrial enterprises in Khorasan Province. For a comprehensive list see *Hamshahri*, 20 Bahman 1379 (February 8, 2001).

[125] *International Financial Times*, June 12, 2002.

[126] Saeidi, "The Accountability of Para-governmental Organizations," 493.

Despite the intentions of both the pro-private sector Hashemi–Rafsanjani government (1989–97) and the reformist Khatami government (1997–2005), which sought to encourage transparency and accountability, the foundations have remained resilient and have maintained their privileged status in Iran's economy.[127] The initial policies of the Islamic Republic led to a series of resource and interest effects creating feedback loops that "lock in" policy decisions through the institutional congealing of interests of the state agents, the foundations, and their clients (e.g. subcontractors).[128]

State organizations were also extensively involved in domestic trade and distribution. In 1997, the Institute for the Study and Research of Commerce concluded that as many as seventy-five state agencies and companies were involved in domestic commercial activities.[129] These stores and agencies have their genesis in the Revolution. During the extended period of strikes against the monarchy, grassroots consumer cooperatives were established to provide foodstuffs for families whose breadwinners were on strike and to replace the commercial system, which was itself on strike. Once the Islamic Republic was founded, the central government transformed these local initiatives into an arm of the state as part of the expansion of the cooperative sectors meant to control prices and support government employees. During the war, mosque associations, which doubled as mouthpieces and watchdogs for the Islamic Republican Party, augmented the cooperatives by distributing goods such as rice, sugar, and kerosene to coupon holders. More recently, the Tehran municipality launched over forty municipal-run fruit and vegetable markets that sell produce directly to consumers,[130] administrative bodies that act as monopolies and monopolists, and chain-store supermarkets and department stores (e.g. Shahrvand and Refah).[131] At the administrative level the Ministry of Commerce established the National Economic Mobilization Headquarters in 1981 to review stocks of commodities, demand level, and distribution methods. All in all, the

---

[127] *Hamshahri*, November 27, 2000.

[128] Paul Pierson, "When Effect Becomes Cause: Policy Feedback and Political Change," *World Politics* 45 (July 1993), 595–628.

[129] Islamic Republic of Iran, Ministry of Commerce, Institute for the Study and Research of Commerce, Davud Cheraghi, "Arzyabi-ye 'Amalkard-e Bazargani-ye Dakheli dar Barnameh-ye Dovvom-e Tawse'eh-ye Eqtesadi, Ejtema'i va Farhangi (Ba Takid bar Tawzi'-e Kala va Khadamat)," Mordad 1379 (July–August 2000).

[130] *Dawran-e Emruz*, 6 Azar 1379 (November 26, 2000). These marketplaces have been particularly popular and the closure of a few of them has led to protests by customers. *Nawruz*, 26 Ordibehesht 1380 (May 16, 2001); and *Hamshahri*, 1 Aban 1379 (October 22, 2000).

[131] Kawsar chain store is owned by the Martyr's Foundation. *Dawran-e Emruz*, 25 Bahman 1379 (February 13, 2001).

retail trade in Tehran has become increasingly more independent of the value chain based in the Tehran Bazaar.

Thus, throughout these past two decades, this process of incorporation via state patronage has led to a twofold political subordination and cooptation of the Bazaar. The most obvious means by which state patronage leads to domination of the Bazaar is the state's control of resources and distribution channels dictate the terms of trade. But patronage has a secondary structural impact too. State patronage that was highly atomistic and ideologically skewed (as opposed to patronage based on class, ethnicity, or sector) restructures the internal organization of the Bazaar in a way that has eviscerated its cooperative hierarchies, the source of its collective identity. During the past twenty years, patronage (via subsidized loans, hard currency, and import licenses) has fragmented the Bazaar by making ties in the value chain more unstable and escalating competition between members. Instability is endemic to the system since value chains are contingent upon individual patrons, middlemen, and policy conditions, all of which have been transient. The Bazaar's experience with patronage echoes the Senegalese postcolonial politics described by Boone: "Clientelistic hierarchies, factions, and clans form both within the state apparatus and on the local level, revealing divisions, competition, and power struggles that exist *within* the categories of 'rulers' and 'ruled' as well as patterns of alliance and conflict between them."[132] Thus, the Islamic Republic's clientelistic incorporation of the Bazaar functions as a mode of brokerage between the state and collective clients as it does under corporatist systems of interest representation, but in doing so it has weakened the Bazaar's corporate unity.

The Bazaar's response: eluding the institutional setting

Those *bazaari*s who did not have the necessary political contacts among state agents and were excluded from the patronage system, however, did not passively accept the state's highly regulatory institutional framework. In Chapter 3, I showed that the vast majority of goods sold in the Bazaar arrive illegally or quasi-illegally and that smuggling has particular characteristics that limit the development of multifaceted, crosscutting, and in some cases long-term relations. Why has this smuggling flourished? *Bazaari*s have participated in networks that undermine and

---

[132] Catherine Boone, "States and Ruling Class in Postcolonial Africa: the Enduring Contradictions of Power," in *Social Power and Social Forces: Domination and Transformation in the Third World*, ed. Joel Migdal, Atul Kohli, and Vivienne Shue (Cambridge: Cambridge University Press, 1994), p. 110.

elude the state's institutional setting by engaging in various hues of smuggling. These networks are subversive in that they work with state institutions only to divert resources away from the state's intended ends. Other networks are designed explicitly to bypass all formal supervision entirely. Yet in both these cases these "informal" practices and methods of commerce are a direct product of the institutional setting established by the Islamic Republic, an institutional setting that has inadvertently opened the space for new modes of individual private capital accumulation.

How do commodities escape customs controls as they enter and exit Iran? The process ranges from large-scale, highly organized smuggling operations under the auspices of state affiliates, to the most piecemeal and underground forms. Large-scale import operations exist when politically powerful figures and organizations (e.g. economic foundations, the military, trade units in ministries, and religious trusts) provide political protection. The state-affiliated actors use their political influence and instructional privileges to bypass the trade regime that encumbers the private sector. All these organizations work closely with the fragmented and paternalistic loci of power that embody the Iranian state. And, as such, their activities have been unsupervised by the institutions of the Islamic Republic (the executive and legislature). Critics of these groups often label them as the "commercial mafia."[133] One example of the lack of accountability of the state organs occurred in February 2002, when the Speaker of the Parliament, Mehdi Karrubi, alleged that there were several unlicensed jetties that were not under the supervision of the customs office. The head of the reformist-controlled parliament publicly wondered, "What are these unlicensed jetties for? What do they import? What do they export?"[134] In the same session, a member of parliament argued that these jetties were used by foundations and state institutions to skirt economic policies and, consequently, had resulted in smuggling. He commented that such huge amounts of illegal imports "cannot [just] fit into pockets. At any rate an institution (*nahad*) or an organ (*organ*) is behind the building of these ports and the smuggling of goods from them." It is difficult to investigate the breadth and exact means by which corrupt and competing government officials are participating and encouraging large-scale illicit commercial activities, but considering the scope of the problem it is highly probable that state agents knowingly ignore, if not support, the evasion of the trade regime.

---

[133] *Hambastegi*, 24 Bahman 1379 (February 12, 2001).
[134] *Bonyan*, 25 Bahman 1380 (February 13, 2001).

The least systematized forms of smuggling are generally small scale, are organized for local-level consumption (i.e. the networks do not directly extend beyond the border region), and are not necessarily predicated on long-term commercial partnerships and dealings. These activities, which existed prior to the Revolution, received a boost during the revolutionary upheaval when industrial and commercial units were paralyzed by strikes, financial disruptions, and political uncertainty.[135] During the initial revolutionary era, lucrative cross-border operations that reaped short-term shortfalls were operated by various ethnic groups living in the border region and sometimes enjoying kinship relations across Iran's borders with Iraq, Turkey, Pakistan, Afghanistan, and the UAE. Thus, these cross-border operations were based on localized, "organic," and ethnic ties that substituted ascribed identities and loyalties for formal institutions and the Bazaar's reputation system.

Between these two extremes of petty smugglers and large-scale state importing lie the regularized and highly developed smuggling networks that were more closely connected to the Tehran Bazaar's value chain. These more regularized and national networks grew out of the localized smuggling networks that accounted for prerevolutionary activities. At first, many of these smugglers operated on their own account. However, over time, as volumes of goods increased and the risk associated with capture increased, many *bazaari*s realized they had no option but to use these networks. Thus these smugglers began acting as agents for either Iranian businessmen who had moved to the Arab shores of the Gulf or importers and wholesalers in the Tehran Bazaar. A *bazaari* described the initial rise of smuggling as follows: "At the beginning, we did not know what was going to happen [in terms of economic policy]; the future was uncertain. We were forced to work with the locals who knew how to bring goods from Dubai, Kuwait, and Turkey. Then we realized that the war was not going to end and the government was not going to let go of these good profits [from monopolized commerce]. So we slowly began to work with a more stable system and with merchants in Dubai and other places."

These operations constitute "legal smuggling" (*qachaq-e qanuni*) in that they operate in the shadow, and as a byproduct, of official legal structures and take advantage of legal loopholes to maneuver around and transcend trade restrictions.[136] Even if the result of these activities

---

[135] *Journal de Teheran*, October 29, 1978.

[136] Manuel Castells and Alejandro Portes, "World Underneath: The Origins, Dynamics, and Effects of the Informal Economy," in *The Informal Economy: Studies in Advanced and Less Developed Countries*, ed. Alejandro Portes, Manuel Castells, and Lauren A. Benton (Baltimore: Johns Hopkins University Press, 1989).

violates the intent of policies and circumvents customs, the process is "formal" in that at various key stages it functions with legal immunity, and even support. The majority of this trade is based on the emerging trade nexus in the southern Persian Gulf, with socioeconomic and legal pillars in Dubai, Iran's free trade zones (Kish, Qeshm, and Charbahar), and major transportation systems extending from the south through Iran and to Central Asia, Pakistan, and Afghanistan.[137] As Saskia Sassan has argued on the global level, advances in transportation and tele-communication have facilitated territorial dispersion, and concurrent agglomeration of activities in global cities and locales.[138] But the cen-tralization within the Persian Gulf region does not seem to be occurring in Tehran, let alone the Tehran Bazaar; rather it has its epicenter in the Straits of Hormuz, where a legal, financial, transportation infrastructure for commerce has been created by Iran and the Gulf states.

Let me describe the process in greater detail. First, importers or representatives of foreign firms arrange for goods to be shipped to Dubai (100 miles from Iran), which is one of the largest and busiest air and sea ports in the world. Since the revolution and the creation of new markets in post-Soviet Central Asian republics, roughly a quarter of re-exports from Dubai are earmarked for Iran.[139] Iran has consistently ranked as the UAE's number one re-export destination, far outpacing Saudi Arabia and India (the next two re-export destinations in the past two decades). Annual re-exports from Dubai, which were in the order of $200–500 million in the mid-1970s, more than doubled by the 1980s and were roughly $3 billion in the 1990s. (Iran's exports to Dubai are roughly $1 billion.) It is no wonder that a prescient trader in Dubai commented, "Whenever there is chaos or political upheaval across the water, we see a profit."[140]

Most of the trade is conducted by the large Iranian community that lives in the UAE. Out of the 605,000 inhabitants of Dubai, 70,000 have an Iranian passport and another 70,000 are of Iranian ancestry.[141] The

---

[137] One report suggested that the Persian Gulf is the source for 80 percent of smuggled goods. "Cheh Kalahaii va Az Cheh Mabadyii be Tawr-e Qachaq vared Mishavad?" *Barresiha-ye Bazargani* 135 (Aban 1377 [October–November 1998]), 16.

[138] Saskia Sassan, *The Global City* (Princeton: Princeton University Press, 2001).

[139] Trade statistics for Dubai are available from the Dubai Chamber of Commerce and Industry, Industries and Studies Department.

[140] *Associated Press*, April 6, 1980.

[141] *Eqtesad-e Iran* 360 (Bahman 1380 [February 2002]), 25. Parsa and Keivani estimate that 100,000 Iranian workers are in Dubai. Ali Parsa and Ramin Keivani, "The Hormuz Corridor: Building a Cross-Border Region between Iran and the UAE," in *Global Networks, Linked Cities*, ed. Saskia Sassen (London, Routledge, 2002), p. 190. Another source states that 300,000 Iranians live in the UAE. *Hamshahri*, 27 Khordad 1382 (June 17, 2003).

Iranians have moved to Dubai at various times over the past century and for diverse reasons. Today, this diverse Dubai-based Iranian community, as well as Iranian entrepreneurs, has established 3,000 firms in the UAE, 132 of which are in the Jebal Ali free port in Dubai.[142] Thus, a new mercantile class has emerged in Dubai that has led some observers to comment that Iran's private sector is now situated in Dubai.[143] Most of these actors do not have direct ties to the Tehran Bazaar, but are connected to international capital and the governments in the UAE and Iran. Even those few who were wholesalers and traders in the Tehran Bazaar prior to the Revolution rely on relations with Iran's postrevolutionary commercial regime. Dubai, therefore, functions as the initial, legal, and infrastructurally developed conduit for many of the transnational smuggling operations that channel goods to Iran, and through it to Afghanistan, Pakistan, and the new Central Asian republics.

From Dubai, commodities are sent to one of Iran's free trade zones in the Persian Gulf, border markets, and border cooperatives.[144] In the past decade, the Islamic Republic has established numerous commercial zones in the border region in order to attract local and foreign investment, promote exports, gain access to new technologies, create jobs and income opportunities for skilled labor, act as a re-export zone for the landlocked countries in Central Asia, and also to be a venue to gradually liberalize trade.[145] These zones range from forty-three isolated border markets to special trade zones (e.g. Sarakhs, Khorramshahr, Bushehr, and Astara) to free trade zones in the Persian Gulf (Kish, Qeshm, and Chabahar). The primary commercial venues are the free trade zones. Established by the Free Trade Zone Act of September 1993, they are financially independent of the central government. Thus, they are not accountable, and the Ministry of Economic Affairs and Finance and the Organization of Management and Planning (previously named the Organization of Planning and Budget) do not supervise them.[146] Therefore, commercial activities in these zones are not integrated into the broader commercial regime, and instead stand as an articulation between the formal and informal economies. The multiple special commercial

---

[142] *Seda-ye 'Edalat*, 30 Khordad 1380 (June 20, 2001). An article in *Hamshahri* estimates the total number of private and public firms owned by Iranians in the UAE at 4,000. *Hamshahri*, 27 Khordad 1382 (June 17, 2003).

[143] *Hayat-e Naw*, 6 Day 1379 (December 26, 2000).

[144] I would like to thank Siamak Namazi and Atieh Bahar Consulting Firm for giving me access to their reports and analyses of the free trade zones.

[145] Parsa and Kaivani argue that Iran's free trade zones in conjunction with the free trade zones in the UAE can develop into a "Hormuz growth corridor." Parsa and Keivani, "The Hormuz Corridor."

[146] *Dawran-e Emruz*, 6 Bahman 1379 (January 25, 2001).

zones have also acted as a shelter for extra-legal practices of state organizations.

Next, traders arrange for the piecemeal transfer of goods from the free trade zone to Iran via individual "travelers" from the local region who have a tax-free allowance for personal use (the specifics of free trade zone laws have varied since their establishment). Notably, in a recent poll 90 percent of importers and exporters surveyed believed that free trade zones and border markets were the main source of smuggling.[147] One important component laying the groundwork for this smuggling process is the improved transportation in the southern area of Iran's Persian Gulf coast.[148] Because of the Iran–Iraq war, which raged in the northern part of the Persian Gulf, the Islamic Republic relocated its port facilities from Khorramshahr and Bandar Emam (Bandar Shah) to Bushher and, more importantly, to Bandar 'Abbas. Built in 1984, Bandar 'Abbas' Shahid Rajaii Port is located across from the free trade zone islands of Kish and Qeshm and across from the UAE.[149] Moreover, since 1996 a rail link has connected Bandar 'Abbas to Central Asia (via Sarakhs) and the twenty-first-century Silk Road.

Once imports make their way to the mainland, they are shipped north to wholesalers and middlemen in major Iranian cities. Armed with weapons and a bundle of cash to bribe customs officials, under cover of the night, the smugglers transport the goods to assigned locations further inland where their illicit imports are less traceable. In the words of one of the many Toyota pick-up drivers, "When we reach Fars [Province] we know we are home." Much of this trade is described as quasi-legal because the process cobbles together legally sanctioned methods and instruments (e.g. imports to the free trade zones and border markets, licensed boats and carriers, and legal import allowances) and informal relations with the intent to evade the trade regime. In short, formal and informal economies have a symbiotic relationship, and the government is one in the key actors in cross-national exchange.

Even though the state's initial and stated impetus in establishing these exceptional economic zones was to encourage the growth of the manufacturing industry and to create jobs and attract investment to deprived regions, the state was no doubt equally compelled by a motivation to control its citizens and extract revenue from the already flourishing smuggling trade. The regime stepped in to regulate the informal

---

[147] *Eqtesad-e Iran*, 360 (Bahman 1380 [January–February 2002]).
[148] Fariba Adelkhah, "Who Is Afraid of Smuggling? We All Are Smugglers, Unless ... " (paper presented at the annual meeting of the Middle East Studies Association, Washington DC, November 2002).
[149] Parsa and Keivani, "The Hormuz Corridor," 195–6.

activities through these border markets, cooperatives, and free trade zones, only to shift the borders between the formal and informal economy, modifying, but not ending, its practice. To borrow the words of Asef Bayat, Third World state–society relations are "characterized by a combined and continuous process of informalization, integration, and reinformalization."[150]

Through the creation of a new institutional setting the state has encouraged new activities and roles for individual *bazaaris* by fashioning a new set of networks to allocate resources critical for their material and social reproduction. Commercial networks are restructured since they are embedded in a radically different political economy. Whereas during the Pahlavi era *bazaaris* expended energies within the Bazaar to find customers, trustworthy partners, and sources of credit and market information, now most energies go to establishing and cultivating contacts outside the Bazaar, whether with state agents in ministries, customs houses, boarder cooperatives, and state-owned banks or with new commercial actors in Dubai, the free trade zones, or on the smuggling route. The *bazaaris*' new value chains compete with government-protected economic organizations that operate within a privileged institutional setting. What *bazaaris* term the "statification" (*dawlati-shodan*) of the Bazaar, whilst no always hurting the merchants financially, weakened their ability to maintain the horizontal and multifaceted ties that were critical for the cooperative hierarchy. Exclusionary vertical ties between the *bazaaris* and state agents, smugglers, or traders in the Gulf region have replaced the crosscutting credit and social relations that prevailed in earlier decades. These new networks are based on information that is exclusive, opaque, and asymmetric and revolve around monopolistic access to resources. The channels of patronage that emanate from the state have transformed state–bazaar relations into patron–client ties that are inscribed by major power differentials that generate disunity. Thus, the degree of embeddedness seems to be less critical than the political economic structure of these embedded networks.

Delocalizing the Bazaar

As the dissection of the free trade zones, border markets, and trade units in ministries suggests, commercial activity is no longer concentrated in the Tehran Bazaar. As we saw, the maintenance of cooperative hierarchies in the prerevolutionary era occurred in the covered marketplace. The present situation is radically different; commercial relations transcend the

[150] Bayat, *Street Politics*, p. 12.

state–society divide and national borders, and accordingly the confines of the Bazaar's alleys. Over time the heterogeneity in commercial channels created by the Islamic Republic and by merchants' evasions generated multiple and disparate loci. The commercial has been re-territorialized[151] and the Bazaar has become de-localized.

This is captured well by my field research experience. When I sought to collect information about commerce prior to the Revolution, I conducted interviews with older *bazaaris* still working in the Bazaar, or visited retired merchants and wholesalers at their homes. In addition, I reviewed prerevolutionary newspapers, journals, and dissertations that described the physical space of the Bazaar and economic practices within it as a distinct and self-contained world. The Bazaar's commercial networks were mapped onto the physical setting of the marketplace. Thus was the logic underlying one older *bazaari*'s poetic definition of the Tehran Bazaar as "that which is in the shadow of Shams al-'Amareh"; the Bazaar is directly adjacent to the Golestan Palace compound, which houses the Shams al-'Amareh, or "the Sun of Architecture."

However, tracking down information on postrevolutionary commercial activities sent me to various locations – government ministries spread out all over central and northern Tehran, state-owned trade companies (e.g. the carpet and tea organizations), the free trade zones in the Persian Gulf, and the booming international transit hub of Dubai. My interviewing revealed a distinct generational difference reflecting the new spatial scope of the commercial networks. For the generation of merchants who took up their trade in the past two decades the old landmarks of the Bazaar area are irrelevant to discussions about national, let alone international, trade. Younger *bazaaris* adamantly insisted that by studying "only the Bazaar, I would miss out on the real commerce that was outside the Bazaar area." Even from the younger *bazaaris*' perspective the commercial world is divided into "inside" and "outside" the Bazaar; the difference now is that commercial interactions and relations, or at least the significant ones, are "outside" and span across the Bazaar's border.

What has led to the decentralization of the value chains? As in other contexts, modernity, as in a rise in urbanization, improvements in telecommunications and transportation, increased levels of industrialization and consumerism, and a rise in literacy and nuclear families, has obviously played a role in transforming the spatial organization of the Bazaar and the flow of goods and information through it.

[151] Harvey, *Condition of Post-Modernity*.

Urbanization and technological developments   As already mentioned, beginning in the late 1960s and the 1970s, and accelerating after the Revolution, the Bazaar's socioeconomic environment was gradually altered. Iran's population, which was less than 19 million in the 1956 census, ballooned to roughly 35 million at the time of the Islamic Revolution, and exceeded 65 million in 2000. Levels of urbanization exhibited an equally significant upward trajectory – from roughly 31 percent of Iranians living in urban areas in 1956 to 38 percent in 1966, 47 percent in 1976, and reaching 60 percent in the 1990s. This steady rise in urbanization was due to the combination of the high natural growth rate in urban areas, rural to urban migration, and the reclassification and incorporation of towns into the urban areas. Outpacing the national rates, Tehran's population (i.e. within the municipal borders) of 1.5 million in 1956 reached 2.7 million in 1966, 4.6 million in 1976, and 6 million in 1986. Today the population is estimated at over 10 million, with an estimated 15 million inhabitants living in a sprawling metropolitan region of over 700 square kilometers. Over the past four decades, the urban experience has become the experience of the majority of Iranians. Urban consciousness, Kaveh Ehsani convincingly argues, is a fundamental component in understanding contemporary Iran, including the rise of the reform movement.[152] This experience takes place in an increasing plurality of spaces with differentiated classes and spheres of life.

This urban experience, especially the physical urban expansion, has transformed the position of the Tehran Bazaar in the socioeconomic fabric of the city and nation. But these long-standing socioeconomic shifts can have, and indeed have had, two contradictory influences on the concentration of the commercial system in the Bazaar. Reinforcing the centralization have been technological innovations. Improved roads and national telecommunications allowed Tehran to become the entrepôt for the entire nation, with many import–export and wholesaling activities being transferred from the provincial bazaars to the Tehran Bazaar.[153] With the extensive use of telephones, which allowed *bazaaris* to receive instantaneous information about prices, inventories, and deliveries, technology helped bridge spatial divides through the process

---

[152] Ehsani, "Municipal Matters," 22–7.
[153] Howard J. Rotblat, "Stability and Change in an Iranian Provincial Bazaar," in *Modern Iran*, ed. Michael Bonine and Nikki Keddie (Albany: State University of New York Press, 1981); and Michael Bonine, "Shops and Shopkeepers: Dynamics of an Iranian Provincial Bazaar," in *Modern Iran*, ed. Michael Bonine and Nikki Keddie (Albany: State University of New York Press, 1981).

of "time-space compression" and "copresence."[154] Improvements in communications and transportation in the second half of the century allowed merchants to spend less time traveling to meet exchange partners, gather information, and monitor activities, and thus they were able to dedicate their energies and time to activities within the Bazaar.

Advances in telecommunications, standardization of international goods, and prevalence of trademarks allowed *bazaaris* to conduct national and international business so rapidly and easily that the concentration of commercial and financial activities in the central business district in Tehran was a distinct possibility. Yet, the concentration of commercial activities in the Bazaar in the postrevolutionary era did not happen, and instead a series of countervailing forces led to the dispersion of commercial activities away from the old Bazaar region.[155] First, the common Third World problem of overpopulation and under urbanization, has led to crippling congestion, urban sprawl, and the rapid deterioration of the older central areas of the city.[156] Time-consuming commutes, air pollution, and overcrowding have been factors in driving many. *bazaari* families out of central Tehran, and thus separating the spheres of work and residence. As the discussion of the location of networks in the Pahlavi era demonstrated, this process was well under way in the 1950s and 1960s and has only quickened in the postrevolutionary era. Yet the difference in terms of scope and impact of urban growth was more recently palpable. Map 4.1 depicts the physical growth of Tehran, much of which occurred specifically in the 1980s. Reflecting on the increasing divide between work and home, a merchant recalled, "As a child, some forty years ago, my father would regularly come home from the Bazaar for lunch. We lived in northern Tehran [far from the Bazaar], but traffic wasn't bad and store hours were designed to allow for a lunch and afternoon siesta. Now, I simply have a small lunch – a sandwich or a stew – and only go home at the end of the day. It would take far too long to go [home] and come back [to the Bazaar] in this traffic." During the day, a trip from the ever-more-distant outskirts of the city to the Bazaar, either by private car or bus, would take roughly one hour each way. Thus, consumers, retailers who purchase goods from

[154] Harvey, *Condition of Post-Modernity*. A few members of the Bazaar commented that these technologies helped increase productivity since apprentices and errand-boys did not have to run around the Bazaar as much and could spend more time in the stores and warehouses working on inventories.

[155] A'zam Khatam, "Bazar va Markaziyyat-e Shahr," *Goft-o-Gu* 41 (Bahman 1383 [January–February 2005]), 127–41.

[156] By central Tehran, I mean what was District 5 during the prerevolutionary era and is now District 12 of Tehran's twenty-zone system.

wholesalers in the Bazaar, and the merchants themselves are now increasingly situated farther from the old commercial core.

The many socioeconomic aspects of modernity have all facilitated a reformulation of the Bazaar space and have led to urban segmentation along class lines. However, these changes were largely gradual processes beginning as early as the 1930s, and in and of themselves do not capture why the physical location of the Bazaar's networks, and with it the cooperative hierarchies, underwent particular changes in the 1980s. To gain a deeper understanding of the timing of the shift from concentrated to dispersed value chains we must investigate postrevolutionary urban policies and how they have accelerated and directed this shift.

Delocalization through policies[157]   The urban and economic policies of the Islamic Republic dispersed the urban population as it grew. The rapid growth of Tehran's population has occurred in the city's periphery. Meanwhile, the old city has continued to be depleted of residents since the Revolution.[158] This pattern has been largely shaped by policies of the Islamic Republic. To begin with, the new regime gave out state-owned land either as gifts or at below market rates to potential clients, which in the case of Tehran helped double the size of the city within two years of the Revolution.[159] Second, in order to limit rural to urban migration, the municipal and national governments withheld building permits within the city boundaries. In addition, rent controls were enforced in order to dampen the cost of living for unpropertied Tehranis. What ensued, however, was a housing shortage with few affordable vacancies for the middle and lower classes. Third, to control migration the state placed a ban on issuing residency permits to new immigrants to Tehran. Residency cards were required for property transactions, school registration, and war-era food coupons. Lacking the appropriate paperwork to access government services, immigrants

---

[157] While, I speak of policies in this section, it should be noted that these policies were in no way a part of a coherent plan. Tehran suffers from an acute problem of underplanning. The city has developed in the past half century without a master plan. Like other policy areas, urban planning suffers from multiple, and sometimes competing, authorities, such as the Ministry of Housing and Urban Development, the Plan and Budget Organization, the Mayor's office, the City Councils, the Housing Foundation, the Ministry of the Construction Crusade, and other ministries in charge of socioeconomic affairs.

[158] "Tehran; Yek Tasvir-e Amari," *Etellat-e Siyasi Eqtesadi* 6 (Esfand 1366 [February–March 1988]), 43–5.

[159] Kaveh Ehsani, "The Urban Provincial Periphery: Revolution and War in Ramhormuz" (paper presented at "Iran: Domestic Change and Regional Challenges," University of San Diego, September 2005, mimeo).

settled in the informal housing areas in southern and western Tehran that were subsequently incorporated into the city.[160]

Shifts in zoning policy after the establishment of the Islamic Republic have further delocalized and patterned the central business district by dispersing commerce. In September 1979, a Council on the Traffic of the City of Tehran was established and work was begun on a series of plans to reduce traffic in central Tehran.[161] The council gradually placed restrictions on traffic in the central 22 square kilometers of Tehran, including the Bazaar and its vicinity. By limiting the hours that trucks and vans can enter this zone and adding a new bureaucratic layer to an already convoluted situation, this new zoning law has unwittingly seriously hampered wholesale trade. Augmenting the plan to dampen central Tehran's traffic overcrowding, bus and transport centers were moved away from the center of the city to terminals in the south, west, and east of the city.

The new traffic flow restrictions precipitated at least two developments; they sped up the process of moving wholesalers out of the Bazaar region and helped create wholesaling and retail pockets outside the traffic restriction zone. For instance, many of the larger carpet exporters have now moved their warehouses and carpet-washing facilities to the outskirts of the city where the movement of goods and access to the airport is less costly and time consuming.[162] Meanwhile, regions outside the traffic zone have now become wholesale centers where retailers from the provinces can more efficiently purchase and pick up large deliveries. A stationery goods wholesaler who had a store both in the Bazaar (i.e. the Bayn al-Haramayn Bazaar, which specializes in wholesale stationery goods) and in the newer business district located near Vali-ye 'Asr Square explained why his store outside the Bazaar is more profitable: "Prices are 5 to 10 percent cheaper in the Bazaar. But you have to remember that buyers have to send someone all the way to the Bazaar to pick up the goods. You have to figure in the time you lose in the traffic and limitations on when you can go [due to the traffic restriction zone]. So it actually ends up cheaper and easier if you buy the same goods outside the Bazaar. So it is better for the buyer, and for us. We pay lower rents and delivery and pick-up is easier for us too." Another example is the case of the china and glassware bazaar, which was based in the heart

---

[160] Bayat, *Street Politics*; and Abdollah-Khan-Gorji, "Urban Form Transformations."

[161] Musavi 'Ebadi, *Shahrdaran-e Tehran*, p. 105.

[162] This move has the added advantage for merchants that they pay far lower rents and insurance premiums, and some suggested that it is easier to avoid tax collectors when they are in the periphery of the city.

of the Tehran bazaar and now has an equally important wholesale district in Shush, an area south of the Bazaar just outside the traffic zone (see Chapter 5).

Precipitating the expansion and dispersion of commercial ventures were other municipal policies. Nonexistent and lax enforcement of land-use laws allowed commercial enterprises to follow the growth of new residential areas away from the old city core and the Pahlavi north-south corridor. Second, the municipality has been busy building shopping centers and fruit and vegetable markets that compete with the Bazaar district. To no avail, the guild organizations have repeatedly called on the government to limit the building of these new commercial districts.[163] The financially impoverished municipality continues to construct and rent commercial spaces or sell licenses for private projects as an important source of funds for itself. Yet, there have been relatively few of these projects within in the bazaar area.[164]

The building of new malls and wholesale districts is happening while the Bazaar's structures are rapidly deteriorating. Overcrowded, overused, and neglected, the Bazaar's hundred-year-old structures are showing their age. The physical condition of the Bazaar is noticeably decrepit, with building collapses and electrical fires a common occurrence.[165] Yet municipal authorities have not developed comprehensive plans for the Bazaar,[166] nor do the city agencies allow renovation and building within the Bazaar.[167] Restrictions are placed on all construction in the Tehran Bazaar because it has been classified as a national monument and its buildings are under the supervision of the Cultural Heritage Organization. But this status has only restricted investment in the area. One urban planner wryly mentioned that the state-run Cultural Heritage Organization "protects the Bazaar by not letting anyone touch the buildings. But it does not restore or renovate them to prevent them from crumbling down. For them 'protection' (*hefazat*) of cultural heritage is simply ensuring things are untouched." All the while, *bazaari*s complain that cell phones do not work in the Bazaar, there is a shortage of bathrooms, and wholesale space is limited and lacks amenities.

Another factor relocating commercial activities from the Bazaar is the increased bureaucracy that regulates commerce. With the

---

[163] *Asnaf*, year 9, special issue (Esfand 1379 [February–March 2001]), 21.
[164] Khatam, "Bazar va Markaziyat-e Shahr," 130.
[165] Mas'ud Behnud, "Bazar-e Tehran, Moqavemati Sad-saleh," *BBC Persian*, December 8, 2005; www.bbc.co.uk/persian/iran/story/2005/12/printable/051208_la-mb-baazaar. shtml (accessed December 8, 2005).
[166] *Mellat*, 13 Ordibehest 1381 (April 3, 2002).
[167] Personal interviews with urban planners and officials in the District 12 municipality.

postrevolutionary state regulatory apparatus, most legal importing of commodities must now go through a bureaucratic maze that requires time-consuming recourse to a number of ministries, quasi-state organizations, banks, and customs offices increasingly relocated away from central Tehran.[168] Thus, the active *bazaari*s spend much of their time in these government offices, rather than in the Bazaar. It is not unusual for importers and wholesalers to spend their mornings or a few days of the week away from their stores and offices in the Bazaar.

Finally, the free trade zones, special economic zones, and border markets have created new areas of trade beyond both the Bazaar and the ministries located in Tehran. These peripheral zones have attracted entrepreneurial and mercantile capital and in the process trade flows are increasingly centered around in the Gulf Region.[169] In 2002 a study estimated that there were fifteen legal, illegal, and quasi-legal ways of importing goods into Iran.[170] Of these, seven involved locations far from the Tehran Bazaar, such as three different free trade zones, roughly fifty border markets, border cooperatives, twenty specially protected regions, speedboats across the Persian Gulf, import using allowances given to Iranians working abroad, and import using passenger allowances. The article identifies the first three locations as the most important and common method of importing – all of these are locations quite far from the Tehran Bazaar.

As already discussed, this preeminence of off–shore import–export operations has relocated and dispersed the levels of the value chain so that importers, wholesalers, and retailers are no longer consolidated in the Bazaar. Trading companies in Dubai are the principal private importers, with a few merchants in Tehran reduced to dependent clients. Moreover, large-scale wholesaling operations have shifted to the ports in the southern Gulf. The vast majority of merchants I interviewed in the Persian Gulf ports and free trade zones were from outside of the region and from Isfahan, Shiraz, Tehran, Abadan, and Ahvaz.[171] These wholesalers explained that they had moved their operations or opened up branches in the early 1990s when trade in the Gulf began to boom and was legitimated by state trade policies. The whole range of technological and financial innovations have reduced transaction costs; for

---

[168] Abdollah-Khan-Gorji, "Urban Form Transformations."
[169] Bernard Hourcade, Hubert Mazurek, Mohammad-Hosseyn Papoli-Yazdi, and Mahmoud Taleghani, *Atlas d'Iran* (Montpellier-Paris: RECLUS–La Documentation Française, 1998), pp. 166–7.
[170] "Shebheh Qachaq," *Eqtesad-e Iran* 360 (Bahman 1380 [January-February 2002]), 12.
[171] On migration to Bandar 'Abbas see Hourcade, Mazurek, Papoli-Yazdi, and Taleghani, *Atlas d'Iran*, p. 52.

example, frequent and inexpensive flights to these regions allow many middlemen and businessmen to spend their time in these border regions rather than in the bazaars in central Iran. State policies, therefore, have facilitated and mediated the process of globalization and regionalization in the Persian Gulf.

Thus, Tehran and the Tehran Bazaar are no longer Iran's primary commercial locations. "Before the Islamic revolution in Iran, Tehran was the major headquarters location for international companies operating in the region and was the only regional transport hub. Since the outset of the 1980s however, Dubai has replaced Tehran as the major regional transport hub."[172] In the process commercial exchanges have become less face-to-face and intertwined with a particular physical space or the milieu of the Tehran Bazaar.

At the level of national trade, the relocating of the networks has undermined the Tehran Bazaar's focal position. Many retailers in southern Iran are no longer part of the Tehran-based commercial network. Instead, they purchase their goods directly from these new cross-border commercial networks. Enterprises in Shiraz have redirected their trade channels south and west to the Persian Gulf ports (Bushehr and Bandar 'Abbas), those in Kerman look east and south to the Pakistani border region (Chabahar and Zahedan), and Tabrizi traders eye the northern and western borders with Turkey and Azerbaijan. These are in a sense a revitalization of historic patterns of socioeconomic relations, ones that predate the modern creation of a centralized (overly centralized) nation-state in Tehran.

In the context of government policymakers' desire to restructure Iran's economy and Tehran's urban space, entrepreneurial capital has been searching for new and unbounded places – on the outskirts of the city, in Iran's border region, and internationally. The upshot of this reshaping of the physical setting of commerce was incremental, but fantastic. In the words of one businessman, "Distribution of goods is like a funnel. Whereas the head of the cone used to be in the Tehran Bazaar and the funnel distributed goods out through the rest of the country, now there are a whole series of cones and none of them begins in the Tehran bazaar." Goods today travel through a value chain that begins with importers in Dubai, extends to wholesalers in border markets and free trade zones, and traverses most of Iran before the goods make their way to a myriad wholesaler and retailer operations in Tehran, the Bazaar being only one of these. Commercial activities take place as much outside Tehran as they do within the Bazaar; cell phones and fax

[172] Parsa and Keivani, "The Hormuz Corridor," 194.

machines sending messages from offices across long distances becoming as much increasingly the means for negotiating agreements as conversations over cups of tea in storefronts or the opium brazier in homes. These exchanges, while still based on personal relations, are set across several locations that typically do not lend themselves to crosscutting ties or multifaceted relations. The delocalization of networks away from the physical setting of the Tehran Bazaar undermines the internal regulatory apparatus that ensured identification of trustworthy traders and social deviants. Today the trustworthy remain private knowledge and the untrustworthy hide as secret deviants.

Conclusions

In her treatment of the political economy of a popular quarter in central Cairo, Diane Singerman shows how informal networks "organize, coordinate, and direct individual actions. In short, they aggregate the interests of the *Sha'b* [the popular classes]. Networks are a concrete manifestation of extrasystemic political participation not controlled by formal political institutions or the political elite."[173] This interpretation of networks is consistent with the role of *bazaari* networks under the Pahlavi monarchy and the smuggling networks under the Islamic Republic, wherein the logic of network creation and participation was the construction through manipulation and evasion of state institutions of an alternative to the state's social order. In the former case, the networks were a response to a formal system that consciously neglected and excluded the existing Bazaar; in the latter case, the networks have been a rejoinder to an institutional setting that attempts to control all commercial activities in order to redistribute them via personalistic patronage. However, by concentrating on the "extrasystemic" nature of networks, there is a tendency to gloss over the "systemic" and "formal political institutions" that I have attempted to show are crucial parameters in the formation of new networks and the shaping of existing ones. In order to rule, regimes create a prism of institutions and organizations that not only configure state–society relations, but also have an impact on the aggregation of interests within social groups.

For the internal organization of the Tehran Bazaar, the demise of the Pahlavi monarchy and the ascendancy of the Islamic Republic meant a recasting of the institutional and physical settings of commercial networks, leading to a shift from cooperative to coercive hierarchies. Under

---

[173] Diane Singerman, *Avenues of Participation: Family, Politics, and Networks in Urban Quarters in Cairo* (Princeton: Princeton University Press, 1995), p. 133.

the current regime, networks continue to play a critical role in influencing economic outcomes. In fact, they have become more essential as large-scale commercial activities have become limited to those with special ties to exclusive sites of trade. Consequently, those in the network have more dependency relations and those who do not have these exclusive relations are forced to be involved in illegal activities that tie *bazaari*s to speculators and off-shore actors. Without close-knit and integrative ties, coercive hierarchies entrench social discord and heighten cleavages that inhibit aggregation of interests and the creation of a sense of community.

This reformulation of relations within the Tehran Bazaar is an accretion of actions and reactions by state agents and *bazaari*s. In Chapter 3, I illustrated how actions were embedded in networks. The present chapter has focused on how networks themselves are embedded in polities and economies. This double embedding is the catalyst that makes networks the medium through which polices are translated into actions. Regimes wielding the state's "infrastructural powers"[174] have a privileged role in setting the stage for networks by creating actors and regulating types of relations. Formal institutions (with emphasis here placed on their plurality) reflect the preferences, tastes, and compromises of state elites and impact the governance of the Bazaar by demarcating the types and scope of *bazaari* relations. Even so, social groups negotiate these forays by state actors by resorting to their individual initiatives and social endowments. The combination of different policies and resistance to them over time led to outcomes that were unplanned or unforeseen by the political elite. Rather than replacing the Tehran Bazaar, the Shah's modernist vision allowed for the conditions through which the Tehran Bazaar governed itself, developed a corporate identity, and eventually mobilized in support of the revolution that overthrew him. In the subsequent two decades, the Islamic Republic spoke of a "committed and devout" Bazaar, but Islamic populism brought about a highly disunited and disenchanted marketplace.

---

[174] Michael Mann, *The Sources of Social Power*, vol. 2 (New York: Cambridge University Press, 1993).

5   Carpets, tea, and teacups: commodity types and sectoral trajectories

Despite the variety of goods traded in the Tehran Bazaar, its large number of shops, its expansive physical size, and disparities in wealth among *bazaaris*, the Bazaar is generally treated as a single unit. Looking back to the nineteenth and early twentieth centuries, this treatment may be reasonable. There was less specialization and lower levels of capital accumulation among the bourgeoisie. The historical weakness of guilds, a weakness measured in terms of independence from the state and capacity to set prices and control entry and exit,[1] also limited sectoral cleavages. In the late Pahlavi era, we saw that a corporate identity was generated by the crosscutting and multifaceted relations that often bridged sectoral, ethnic, and class lines to create a corporate entity. However, this conceptualization masks underlying sectoral distinctions in larger marketplaces such as Tehran's, sectoral variations that refine our analysis of the Bazaar's internal governance and state–bazaar relations. In particular, this chapter considers the consequence of group size, ethnic composition, relations to the world economy, modalities of geography and economic development, and state regulations under the imperial and revolutionary regimes.

This chapter investigates the hand-woven carpet, tea, and china and glassware sectors in the Tehran Bazaar under the Pahlavi monarchy and Islamic Republic to assess the socioeconomic factors and specific state institutions and development agendas that may have molded their forms of governance. The differences in these bazaars are noteworthy. While the carpet bazaar in Tehran was principally an export sector, until recently, the china and glassware bazaar predominantly dealt in imports. Meanwhile, both domestic and imported teas has been traded in the tea bazaar. These different types of trade allow us to look at how various state institutions and macroeconomic policies have influenced these diverse sectors.

---

[1] Ahmad Ashraf, "Nezam-e Senfi va Jame'eh-ye Madani," *Iran-nameh* 14 (Winter 1374 [1995]), 5–40.

I show that all three sectors followed the same general shift from cooperative to coercive hierarchies and that the Bazaar- and regime-level transformations discussed earlier were instrumental in these transformations. Yet these sectors vary along certain dimensions that influenced their trajectories to coercive hierarchies. As a market for nonstandard goods, the carpet sector is an opportunity to study the particular institutions that emerge when information is costly. Also, as carpets are exported, we assess the changes in the export regime and the world economy. The analysis of the tea bazaar focuses on two different state regulatory systems meant to protect domestic production. As a purveyor of manufactured goods, the china and glassware sector allows us to ponder the particularities of standard goods and the Bazaar's relationship with an emerging domestic industry. To foreshadow the analysis, the comparisons suggest that group size, geographical dispersion of trade networks, and the mere existence or absence of state regulation do not affect the form of governance as more individualistic views of markets would predict. Meanwhile commodity types that are nonstandard play an intermediary role in shaping commercial relations, by encouraging localization and particular internal institutions (i.e. clientelization, brokerage, and specialization) conducive to cooperative hierarchies.

This chapter is organized as follows. I will first describe the evolution of the individual sectors to show how they all followed the basic path from cooperative to coercive hierarchies. I will highlight how specific state policies and market developments led to these outcomes. Based on these three narratives, I next investigate the socioeconomic aspects not directly considered in the state–society framework presented in the preceding chapters. In particular, I ponder the effects of group size, geographical dispersion of trade networks, commodity type, and state regulation of these particular sectors.

The carpet bazaar

A carpet seller must have the patience of Job, the wealth of Croesus, and the lifespan of Noah.

Proverb

A carpet seller who owned a store outside of the Tehran Bazaar told me that the carpet merchants in the Bazaar controlled the entire market. When I asked him why that was the case, he answered, "Because carpets always look better under the domed roofs of the Bazaar." He could not, or would not, elaborate further. I mentioned this to a few carpet dealers who worked within the Bazaar, and they explained that the real reason the Bazaar is such an ideal place for the carpet trade is that it is where the "experts," "old-timers," and "the experienced ones" are based. They reminded me that carpets are different from other commodities and explained that not just anyone can enter the trade; you must "know carpets," as well as the past records, and hence reputations, of the many "hands" that are involved in a carpet's production and trade. And this makes experience and *acquired* practical knowledge necessary. To drive the point home to an upstart researcher, one of them dryly added "You can't simply look up the information in a book." And then he recounted the proverb about Job, Croesus, and Noah. "You have to live a long life like Noah and be patient like Job to learn the Bazaar [system] and become an expert." Croesus' wealth was left unexplained, but it was understood that some wealth was necessary for entry into this market and material rewards are the well-earned dividends of patience and a long life.

The issue of expertise and reputation was mentioned by all *bazaaris* (see Chapter 3), but discussions with those in the carpet trade were especially centered on these credentials. Why this particular emphasis in the carpet bazaar? As economic anthropologists and economists focusing on information costs and asymmetries have pointed out, markets for goods that are nonstandard (or nonsubstitutable) in terms of quality and quantity operate differently than markets for goods that are standardized through the manufacturing and packaging process, legal mechanisms (e.g. trademarks and patents), and regulatory bureaucracies.[2] Thus, buyers and sellers of these heterogeneous goods face profound impediments in acquiring and trusting information about the goods traded and, by implication, trading partners. Hand-woven carpets are quintessential nonstandard goods. A carpet's value rests on its non-substitutability, or its unique combination of design, craftsmanship, and appeal to buyers. Within the carpet market, price is determined by multiple and imprecise criteria: design (its execution, distinctiveness, and authenticity), the quality and consistency of raw materials and skill of labor (measured in terms of number and quality of knots), age, and the tastes of possible buyers, including local consumers, exporters, and export markets. The location of weave stands as an imperfect proxy for quality, but even interpreting that information is not an exact science. Thus, as in all markets for nonstandard commodities (e.g. used goods, many agricultural staples, and antiques) and labor markets, in the carpet bazaar information is scare, based on speculation, and unevenly distributed, with sellers generally enjoying a privileged position.

---

[2] Frank Fanselow, "The Bazaar Economy or How Bizarre Is the Bazaar Really?" *Man* 25 (June 1990), 250–65. Also see sources related to information economics cited in Chapter 2.

In order to address these informational shortcomings, the Iranian state and trade associations have repeatedly attempted to impose standards and control quality. The state has a pragmatic financial interest in that the customs office must appraise the value of carpets based on precise measurable categories such as carpet size, density of knots, and production location. Thus, the customs office devises lists of duties and values for categories of carpets. Iran's governments have also had a public mandate to protect the reputation of "Persian carpets" on the world market by preventing the copying of Iranian patterns and the selling of non-Iranian carpets as "Persian carpets" and by limiting the export of poor-quality carpets from Iran. Successive governments have talked about imposing an identity card system for all carpets woven in Iran as a means to prevent copies by Indian, Chinese, and Pakistani weavers.[3] Also, the Association of Carpet Exporters of Iran issues export licenses only to reputable individuals and has discussed measures to prevent the export of low-quality carpets, which compromises the "authenticity" of all carpets from Iran. However, these third-party bureaucratic measures have been largely unsuccessful, for they are hard to enforce and open up other avenues for forgery and dishonesty. As one carpet import–exporter in Hamburg told me, the whole idea of an identity card for carpets is "ridiculous." "Once you have an identity card, then Indian weavers can simply copy the identity card to authenticate their rugs. How are they going to ensure that *the identity cards are authentic*? If Nike has difficulty doing it [preventing the unauthorized use of its trademark], what makes us think that the Iranian government will be successful? Rather than trying to devise schemes to trademark the carpets, the state must invest its energies in marketing and supporting exporters."[4] Implied in this statement is that carpet sellers can do a reasonable job of regulating the quality and preserving the reputation of "Persian carpets," but the state must provide financial aid.

Information acquisition via cooperative hierarchies

There is some justification for this claim because carpet dealers in the Tehran Bazaar were able to manage many of the difficulties associated

---

[3] Immediately after World War II, the state also attempted to confront the use of aniline and chrome dyes and inferior knots. Roger Savory, *Encyclopdia Iranica, s.v.* "Carpets: Introductory Survey," p. 838.

[4] Much like commercial manufacturers that use trademarks, carpet producers also seek to place particular markers or signatures as a means to authenticate their goods. These are imperfect mechanisms. As brandname watches, purses, and shoes have "knock-offs," so do hand woven carpets. Also note that the trader did not mention support for producers.

with information scarcity. *Bazaari*s used to have at their disposal a number of methods to address the information costs facing them, and this had a profound impact on the organization of relations. Many of these practices and characteristics are discernible even today, but, as discussed later in this section, their scope has significantly diminished.

As economists have theorized and anthropologists have illustrated, many of the practices in the bazaar can be interpreted as means to protect merchants from these uncertainties; after all, this ignorance is *"known ignorance."*[5] Historically, a number of methods have been used by *bazaari*s to address these deficiencies – spatial localization, specialization and market segmentation, clientelism, and long-term and contingent purchasing arrangements (i.e. partnerships and profit-sharing schemes) based on extensive use of a reputation system. All of these practices depend on and regenerate relations that are more long term, multi-faceted, and crosscutting; that is, they form cooperative hierarchies.

Spatial localization has been an essential aspect of the carpet bazaar. Despite the hundreds, even thousands of carpet dealers in Tehran, before the Revolution they were almost universally located in the Teh-ran Bazaar.[6] Overwhelmingly housed in the western region of the Bazaar, about forty caravanserais surround the three main alleys of the old shoesellers', kebab makers, and 'Abbas Abad bazaars (see Map 2.1). Several large caravanserais (i.e. over fifty stores and offices), such as the famous Bu-'Ali Sara, were built in the post-World War II era near the old carpet arcades such as the Amir Sara. These multistory spaces include their warehouses, repair workshops, and thousands of employees who arranged all aspects of the shipping process.

In this centralized physical setting it was common for *bazaari*s who trusted one another to appraise each other's wares, discuss their contacts, and exchange information about market conditions. This large bazaar within the greater marketplace included restaurants, mosques, and areas that were frequented by carpet dealers and remained largely

---

[5] Clifford Geertz, "The Bazaar Economy: Information and Search in Peasant Marketing," *American Economic Review* 68 (May 1978), 29.

[6] It is difficult to know exactly how many carpet exporters, middlemen, retailers, and brokers worked in Tehran, but it surely was well over 2,000. One indication of the large number is that in 1982 (three years after the Revolution, when many merchants, especially Jewish exporters, left) the Association of Carpet Exporters of Iran had 1,120 members, with the vast majority being based in the Tehran Bazaar. Islamic Republic of Iran, Chamber of Commerce, Industry, and Mines, "Karnameh-ye seh saleh-ye ettehadiyyeh-ye saderkonandegan-e farsh-e Iran," Khordad 1361 (May-June 1982) p. 17. A government study from 1987 uncovered 3,105 carpet stores in Tehran Province. Islamic Republic of Iran, Organization of Planning the Budget, Center for Iranian Statistics, "Tarh-e Amargiri az Kargahha-ye Bazargani: Amar-e Kargahha-ye kharid va forush-e Kala," 1366 (1987).

unknown to other *bazaari*s. For instance, there is one kebab house in the back allies of the carpet bazaar that carpet dealers would take me to. One day when I suggested that a glass seller and I go to what I thought was a well-known *bazaari* haunt, this third-generation *bazaari* confessed that he had never heard of this particular restaurant. He said, "This must be a restaurant for carpet sellers."

Also, the highly diverse and fragmented nature of the production system, which included contracts for raw materials (wool, cotton, and designs) and the finishing stage of production (washing and preparing carpets), necessitated the coordination of capital and labor. This extreme fragmentation, however, fostered high levels of concentration in the area of wholesale trade for carpets and ustream products such as wool. This concentration, moreover, operated out of the Bazaar. *Bazaari*s "buy carpets directly or indirectly from villagers and nomads and also from dealers and colleagues in the *bāzār*s; they also supply wool and yarn to weavers, take care of having the wool dyed, and engage in other processing activities. ... Tehran wholesalers also leave purchasing and manufacturing arrangements to such middlemen. In addition, local wholesalers may sell to Tehran or to agents of Tehran firms."[7] Given that customs and transportation systems were highly centralized in Tehran as Iran became increasingly integrated into the world economy in the late nineteenth and twentieth centuries and carpet production was directed to western markets, the Tehran Bazaar generally became the focal point, coordinating and bringing together the numerous marketing networks under one roof.

Outside the Tehran Bazaar there were only a few of carpet dealers in other areas of the city in the 1960s. These few and minor actors were concentrated in wealthier northern Tehran and around the Tajrish Bazaar in Shemiran, but were often still tied to the carpet emporium in the Bazaar for purchases, credit, and information. One notable conglomeration was a couple dozen shops near Ferdawsi Square. This predominantly retail area, which was close to hotels, embassies, and antique and souvenir stores, catered to western tourists, the ex-patriot community, and visiting dignitaries. This secondary localization was also culturally delineated; these merchants were predominantly Jewish, often originally from Isfahan or Mashhad. Some of these retailers focused exclusively on this lucrative domestic market, while others headed important export operations from the Bazaar.

Beyond Iran's borders, the largest single export site was the free port in Hamburg. Beginning in the decade after World War II, Hamburg

---

[7] Willem M. Floor, *Encyclopdia Iranica*, *s.v.* "Carpets: Pahlavi Period," p. 884.

became the world center for hand-woven carpets.[8] Since Hamburg was
a free port, encouraged by West German policies to attract foreign
investment, a number of exporting families based in the Tehran and
Tabriz bazaars established warehouses in Hamburg's port area. Typically, fathers sent their sons to establish warehouses representing the
family business, and thus these original dealers were directly connected
to the commercial networks in Iran. Over time, the number of import–
exporters and brokers who worked with carpet countries in Germany
and other European countries, reached close to eighty and attracted
traders from across Europe, as well as Iranian merchants who visited
Hamburg on business trips. The traders sold carpets to the booming
German market, but also used Hamburg as a port to export to all other
locations in Europe and North America. In the late 1950s, the Association of Iranian Merchants in Germany was established to represent
these traders' interests in both Germany and Iran. (In the 1970s the
association divided into one representing carpet merchants and another
for other trades.) As a relatively small and tight-knit group of families,
many of whom had relationships dating back a number of generations,
they were able to utilize the same reputation system.

Physical localization was reinforced by specialization and market segmentation that led to a high degree of product differentiation according
to quality. Trade was based on specialization in particular types of carpets, most commonly categorized by the place of origin of the trader and
carpet. Carpets from Isfahan and its environs were sold by Isfahanis,
Qomis sold carpets from Qom, Kermanis specialized in carpets from the
Kerman region, and so forth. Thus, regionalism, ethnicity, and kinship
acted as a guide for segmenting the market and integrating production
and commerce. In doing so, it embedded economic relations in a cultural
milieu defined by language and dialect, shared histories and knowledge,
and cultural symbols. In the case of Azeri-speakers who specialize in
various popular Tabriz weaves, language has acted as a critical common
denominator and barrier to non-Azeri-speaking Iranians. Those who
did not have appropriate sociocultural networks tended to work through
partnerships or at the ends of the value chain as large exporters,
commissioners for foreign agents, and retailers who worked with various
types of carpets, or specialized in old and antique carpets and tribal
weaves.

---

[8] Other than Iranians, there were also a few Turkish dealers, but the vast majority of
import–exporters were Iranians or Germans who specialized in Iranian carpets. Zurich,
Switzerland, has become another important import–export market of hand-woven
carpets.

In markets for nonstandard goods, the heightened need to guard against the perils of information scarcity encourages clientelism.[9] For sellers, a steady stream of large transactions is obviously in their interest, but instead of relying on the price as the only means to attract buyers, they rely on their public reputations as honest traders to attract and maintain exchange partners. From the perspective of buyers, the difficulty in assessing carpets draws them to these *bazaaris* known to be honest and discourages transactions with traders about whom they have no information. Therefore, clientelization becomes one of the main mechanisms to limit information scarcity and uncertainty about commodities. Historically it has transformed a diffused, large array of anonymous potential trade partners into categorized and rank-ordered potential partners. Buyers and sellers turned to tested and proven trade partners for purchases – "moving along the grooved channels clientelization lays down."[10] Similarly, relations in other spheres and categories of life, such as kinship, ethnic bonds, religious networks, and neighborhood affiliations, mapped the terrain for these grooved channels. The extensive use of credit that dominated the pre-revolutionary Bazaar, the carpet market's extreme localization and specialization, and the existence of brokers enabled reputations to become "public knowledge," or more precisely Bazaar knowledge, by circulating this information through the embedded social networks. This high level of clientelization and long-term credit created especially protracted relations among carpet merchants, ones that could even transcend generations.

Finally, the centrality of reputation can be used as a form of selective incentive to limit dishonest behavior such as not paying debts and selling low- and inconsistent-quality carpets.[11] The very reputation system that allowed traders to find each other through the maze of the Bazaar also was turned against *allegedly* dishonest actors who reneged on contracts or sold forged or otherwise defective goods.[12] In such cases social networks that pooled and distributed information were redirected to publicize, shame, and communally punish behavior that was deemed reprehensible. Since all buyers were acknowledged to be ignorant, *caveat emptor* was mediated by placing part of the burden of soured exchanges

[9] Clifford Geertz, "Suq: The Bazaar Economy in Sefrou," in *Meaning and Order in Moroccan Society*, ed. Clifford Geertz, Hildred Geertz, and Lawrence Rosen (Cambridge: Cambridge University Press, 1979).

[10] Ibid., p. 218.

[11] In the carpet bazaar the main concern, in terms of quality, is poor dyes and dyeing techniques, consistency in quality when buying in bulk, and limiting the use of artificial treatments designed to make carpets look like old antiques.

[12] Since allegations are evaluated without independent investigation, accusations of wrongdoing are assessed by the social standing and past reputations of the parties involved. Thus, reputation is a valuable asset in case of disputes too.

on sellers, who also were aware that their highly valuable reputation was at stake. The reputation system was based on relations that cut across existing exchange relations. Thus, when traders were faced with a new prospective trading partner or attempted to branch out into a new line of carpets, they turned to trusted figures whome they knew through their existing relations in religious, social, and neighborhood circles. Moneylenders, prominent exporters, brokers and arbitrators, or simply "old-timers, who made a point of knowing many of the faces in the Bazaar, became critical nodes.

Taken together, these informal institutions constituted the basis for a conglomeration of cooperative hierarchies in which exchange was conducted based on highly multifaceted relations and repeated exchanges. Furthermore, traders made extensive use of crosscutting relations in order to protect themselves from what they did not know. In doing so, they were able to engage in highly elaborate forms of long-distance and long-term exchange such as consignment of carpets, shipment of goods without deposits, long-term and multiparty credit relations, and wholesale purchasing. Also, these robust cooperative hierarchies, some of which exist today, made the carpet bazaar the type of place that approximated the idealized pristine bazaar a place where a distant relative of a neighbor who worked in the carpet bazaar was in fact a more suitable guide than a travel book or a subscription to *Hali* magazine. It is here that *bazaari*s sat and sipped tea while exchanging rumors with neighboring shopkeepers and made deals worth thousands of dollars with a simple handshake. It has been here for generations, families have continued to go to the same dealers to purchase their goods. It has been in the carpet bazaar in particular that one should engage in intensive bargaining with one merchant, rather than engaging in extensive bargaining with a variety of merchants, for it has been here that information acquisition has been the name of the game, and cooperative hierarchies have been a way of winning that game.

Situating the carpet sector in Iran's political economy

From the point of view of level of employment and non-petroleum exports, for much of the twentieth century, carpet production and export have been the most important commodity. During the past four decades there have been roughly a million, possibly even two million-full-time and seasonal carpet weavers.[13] Once we include all the other

---

[13] Hasan Azarpad and Fazlollah Heshmati-Razavi, *Farsh-nameh* (Tehran: Moasseseh-ye Motale'at va Tahqiqat-e Farhangi, 1372 (1993)), p. 20. By seasonal weavers, I am referring to farmers and laborers who turn to carpet weaving to supplement their income at various times of the year.

industries related to carpet production and export, such as wool production, dyeing, design, carpet washing, carpet repair, and shipping, the
employment figures probably exceed two million workers.

In addition, for several decades now hand-woven carpets have consistently been the single largest export commodity after oil. Buoyed by
high demand in western Europe, especially West Germany, during the
1960s and 1970s, prices in foreign markets increased, with export figures climbing steadily from $22 million in 1962 to a peak of $117
million in 1974. During the prerevolutionary era, carpet exports
accounted for over a quarter of the share of non-oil exports in 1968, but
declined slightly to less than one-fifth in the mid-1970s. Since the
Revolution, carpet exports have fluctuated greatly, and in dollar
amounts they have ranged from less than $300 million to over $1.5
billion, and similarly carpets' share of non-oil exports have fluctuated
from roughly half to less than 20 percent. At its zenith in the late 1960s,
Iran dominated the world market, controlling as much as 50 percent in
terms of sales, and a large share of the important U.S. and West German
markets. Its market share however, has, eroded since the 1990s, and Iran
accounts for only about 20 percent of exports, with China and India,
which controlled less than 10 percent of exports in earlier decades, now
enjoying as large a share as, or even a higher share than, Iran in recent
years.

Changes in the world market have had an important impact on these
trends, the most important of which have been fluctuations in the
economies of the industrialized countries that were the primary consumers of hand-woven carpets. Customs policies of importing countries
also had an adverse effect; for example, the U.S. government's decision
to impose sanctions on Iranian carpets from October 1987 to March
2000 officially closed off a market that accounted for some 30 percent of
Iran's exports.[14] Carpet importers I spoke to in Europe and the United
States also argued that Iranian designs have not been able to adjust to
changes in western tastes and lifestyles. For instance, Iranian producers
have only recently begun to imitate Pakistani and Afghani rugs, which in
the early 1990s became popular for their soft and muted colors. Finally,
the Chinese and Indian governments have supported both carpet weavers and exporters during the period as a means to create jobs and earn
export earnings from a high-value-added product. As Iranian exporters
faced external and internal constraints (described below), Indian and
Chinese exporters were able to increase their market share through
improving the quality of their carpets, maintaining prices that were

[14] *Dawran-e Emruz*, 21 Azar 1379 (December 11, 2000).

significantly lower than those for Iranian equivalents, and copying Iranian designs that are not protected by international copyright laws.

A second important factor leading to the decline in Iran's carpet industry has been increases in production costs and a decline in the quality of some raw materials. From the 1960s onwards, as manufacturing wages rose and as the rate of rural to urban migration increased, the cost of labor increased. Industrialization and urbanization also caused the quality and cost of wool to decline. As meat consumption rose, an increasing portion of Iran's flocks were used for consumption; meanwhile, increased wages in factories enticed everyone from shepherds to wool spinners and dyers to leave their rural occupations to look for employment in the manufacturing, construction, and service sectors in larger cities. Over time the quality and quantity of domestic wool declined so much that a considerable amount of the wool used in Iranian carpets began to be imported from Australia and New Zealand. Inflationary episodes such as those following the sharp rise in petroleum prices in 1973, immediately after the Revolution, in 1993–4, and in 2003 have exacerbated the problems of production and increased the price of exports.

But state policies in the areas of export regulations, foreign exchange, and production are arguably the main causes of the fluctuations and decline of carpet exports, and are definitely the causes most commonly cited by traders for the abysmal state of the industry. Given the historic importance of carpets to Iran's economy, it is not surprising that state regulation of the carpet industry and exports dates back several decades. Coterminous with the state's monopolization and regulation of the tea, sugar, and tobacco industries, in 1935 Reza Shah's government also established the Iranian Carpet Company (Sherkat-e Sahami-ye Farsh-e Iran). The company was originally authorized to control all carpet exports from Iran, but owing to the protests of carpet merchants, after a year it withdrew from commercial activities.[15] Instead, it limited its activities to supporting production by distributing credit to village cooperatives, purchasing carpets from weavers, and creating an inventory for copyrighted designs. It also sought to protect workers by supervising conditions and limiting child labor. Yet the Iranian Carpet Company has had little impact, as it supervised only an insignificant portion of production; it controlled 2–3 percent of production in 1977[16] and it still produces and exports only less than 1 percent of Iran's carpets.[17]

---

[15] *Qali-ye Iran*, 4 (Bahar 1373 [Spring 1994]), 16–17.
[16] Floor, *Encyclopdia Iranica, s.v.* "Carpets: Pahlavi Period," p. 885.
[17] *Nawruz*, 9 Ordibehesht 1380 (April 29, 2001).

In the late Pahlavi era, the state's approach to the carpet industry can be best described as benign negligence. Under Iran's modernization plan, which focused on heavy industries and production of industrial inputs and consumer durables, hand-woven carpet production and trade were viewed as a minor economic system for job creation and their export earning potential was less noteworthy, given the rise of oil income and the expected industrial growth. Instead, the state and the royal court viewed the carpet sector as a national symbol and historical art form.[18] In this regard, state initiatives in the carpet sector were largely cultural and scholarly ones. Under the auspices of Queen Farah, an active patron of Iranian arts, the Carpet Museum of Iran was founded in 1976 to preserve the heritage of the art form. Consistent increases in oil revenue also made hard currency plentiful, enabling the state to establish a generally liberal financial regime. This general indifference toward the carpet industry as an economic sector, coupled with seemingly unending western demand for "Persian carpets" allowed traditional production and marketing systems to persist and prosper. Domestic production continued to be channeled through the Tehran Bazaar, which acted as the wholesale site for exporters and visiting importers. This venue and conglomeration of relations nourished the self-regulated networks that reproduced economic relations and secured independent earnings.

Export earnings began to decline after 1974, however. The oil boom hurt Iran's non-oil exports, and carpets in particular, both by increasing the value of the Iranian rial and by fueling an economic downturn in industrialized countries. In the first place, Iranian products became less competitive on the world market, and, second, consumption of high-priced luxury goods declined. In the years immediately prior to the Revolution, many European carpet importers and Iranian traders abroad began to turn to other established producers (e.g. Turkey, Pakistan, Afghanistan, and Morocco) and the still nascent carpet-producing countries of India, China, and Nepal.[19] The Pahlavi regime's gradual lifting of foreign exchange controls in this period also undermined the role of carpet exporters as the lenders of hard currency. Importers and others in need of foreign exchange could increasingly turn to the banking system to change and borrow U.S. dollars and German marks.

---

[18] Personal interviews with member of Queen Farah's office.

[19] While most Iranian exporters and government officials tend to see competition from other countries as beginning in the postrevolutionary era, importers outside of Iran are clear in placing the start of this shift in the mid-1970s and relating it to the increase in price of Iranian carpets. The noticeable and persistent decline in export figures and shares after 1974 suggests that the latter perspective is more correct.

During the revolutionary years of 1978–80, the carpet bazaar was an economic beneficiary of the political turmoil. Both in terms of value (over $400 million per year) and as a share of all non-oil exports (over 50 percent), carpet exports skyrocketed during the revolutionary years of 1979 and 1980. Wealthy Iranians, members of the Pahlavi order, and businessmen who were either fleeing the country or concerned about its political and economic future were eager to circumvent currency restrictions and transfer their money abroad. Carpets became a means to export capital abroad, and some (mistakenly as it turned out) speculated that converting their assets into carpets would be a means to invest and preserve the value of their assets.[20] Customs figures show that exports were predominantly of rare and extremely expensive antique and silk carpets.[21] Meanwhile, investment in production declined during these tumultuous years.[22]

By early 1981, the situation had radically changed. The recently empowered Islamic Republic turned its attention to economic matters to address the contingencies of the war. The state adopted a fixed exchange rate regime and strict export controls to prevent capital flight. This resulted in a sharp downturn in carpet exports in the early 1980s and also led to a rise in corruption and the smuggling of carpets.[23] Iranians living in Dubai at that time, for instance, remember vessels unloading bales of carpets at the docks.

The draconian regulatory system imposed on carpet exports remained for much of the postrevolutionary era as state enterprises in the field of carpet production and marketing mushroomed during the 1980s. The desire to control hard currency and the policy of supporting weavers, as part of the agenda to support the economically marginal strata, combined to establish the cornerstone of the Islamic Republic's approach toward the carpet industry. The situation of the carpet exporters reflected the overall institutional setting of commerce – overlapping and privileged government organizations, adoption of a restrictive export policy, and lack of stability in policies.[24] All of these developments restructured the carpet bazaar.

The number of government organizations participating in producing, exporting, and marketing carpets, or making decisions that impact the

[20] *The Associated Press*, June 13, 1979; *New York Times*, July 1, 1979.
[21] Islamic Republic of Iran, Central Bank, Office of Economic Analysis (Edareh-ye Barresiha-ye Eqtesadi), "Barresi-ye San'at-e Farsh-e Dastbaft," Mehr 1363 (September–October 1984), pp. 22–5.
[22] Ferdi Besim, "The Carpet Market in Iran," *Hali* 6 (1984), 228–9.
[23] For examples of corruption involving bank and customs officials see *Donya-ye Farsh*, 4 (Day 1379 [December 2000]), 14.
[24] *Salam*, 8 Shahrivar 1376 (August 30, 1997), 1 and 3.

industry, is very large.[25] A preliminary list includes the Central Bank of Iran, the Ministry of the Construction Crusade,[26] the Ministry of Industry and Mines, the Ministry of Commerce, the Organization of Iranian Handicrafts, the Imam Khomeini Relief Committee, and various carpet-weaving cooperatives. Moreover, each of these government bureaucracies has a number of departments dealing with matters concerning carpets; for instance, under the jurisdiction of the Ministry of Commerce alone there is the Iranian Carpet Company, the Center for the Development of Exports, and the Institute for the Study and Research of Commerce. The Ministry of the Construction Crusade, which was established after the Revolution to oversee rural development, has been extremely active in establishing and organizing carpet production cooperatives as well purchasing and exporting carpets.[27] The ministry claimed that in 1994 the value of the carpets produced by workers under its supervision was 10 percent of all "first-rate" carpets and 80 percent of "second-rate" carpets.[28] Meanwhile, another source concluded that as a whole, carpet-weaving cooperatives hire about 10 percent of all weavers and account for roughly 11.5 percent of all carpets produced.[29] The Imam Khomeini Relief Committee, another revolutionary organization mandated to help the most economically disenfranchised strata of society, supports weavers by providing them with subsidized raw materials and marketing their wares in carpet exhibitions and stores. Other organizations active in carpet-affairs include the Foundation for the Affairs of Immigrants of the War and the trust administering the Imam Reza Shrine in Mashhad (Astan-e Qods-e Razavi). With so many organizations and with their activities being largely uncoordinated and sometimes contradicting one another, performance has not met production and export objectives.[30] The creation of vested and institutionalized interests has made planning and implementing reforms quite difficult. Even the managing director of the state-owned Iranian Carpet Company

---

[25] Azarpad and Heshmati-Razavi, *Farsh-nameh*, pp. 18 and 26–30.

[26] In 2001, this ministry was merged with the Ministry of Agriculture to create the Ministry of Agricultural Crusade.

[27] Islamic Republic of Iran, Ministry of Construction Crusade, Center for Research and Analysis of Rural Affairs (Markaz-e Tahqiqat va Barresi-ye Masayel-e Rustaii), "Naqsh-e Farsh dar Eqtesad-e Keshvar va Jaygah-e Jahani-ye An," Tabestan, 1374 (Summer 1995).

[28] Ibid., p. 5, I suspect that these figures are inflated and/or refer to very-low-quality carpets.

[29] *Seda-ye 'Edalat*, 23 Khordad 1380 (June 13, 2001).

[30] In 1999, during Khatami's presidency, the Carpet Roundtable (Miz-e Farsh) was organized to devise a single supervisor for the entire carpet sector. The Carpet Roundtable is under the auspices of the Ministry of Commerce. The Carpet Roundtable's governing charter can be found in *Farsh-e Dastbaft-e Iran*, 18 (Bahar 1379 [Spring 2000]), 44–7.

recently acknowledged that "diverse and contradictory policies followed by parallel organizations as well as the lack of a specified guide that is accountable has caused problems in the production and export of carpets."[31] Merchants have consistently criticized this "unprofessional" collection of production systems. In the opinion of the President of the Association of Carpet Exporters of Iran, "the greatest difficulty facing the carpet industry in the country is the [large] number of authorities in charge of it."[32]

To carpet dealers in the Bazaar, these state organizations are direct competitors. "All sorts of government organizations spend money giving raw materials and paying weavers. And then they export them without having to go through the customs. They send them to their own showrooms and monopolize the carpet exhibitions in Iran," commented a wholesaler who said he was "reduced to a being retailer." In Hamburg importers added that not only do state organizations directly compete with the Bazaar-based marketing system, but because they do not conduct market research they produce carpets that are not suitable for European markets; the designs and colors "are either poor quality or outdated or both." Therefore, they have "ruined the standing and authenticity of Iranian carpets." Since these organizations produce and export with little profit incentive, they can also sell their products at low prices that distort the already opaque price system.

More central to the structure of carpet exports have been regulations aimed at curbing capital flight and requiring exporters to repatriate their hard currency earnings through the official banking system. Carpet exporters are obligated to repatriate foreign exchange earnings based on the predetermined value of carpets and within an established period of time. The policy has three principal components that I briefly discuss: the valuation system, the date of repatriation, and the foreign exchange rate that determines the amount of the repatriated hard currency in the local currency.

The exact amount to be returned to the Central Bank is predetermined by the valuation of carpets based on an appraisal list revised periodically by the Customs Department. These valuations, which are also the basis of duties to be paid, are based on the price of carpets in the domestic consumer market, or the price "on the floor of the Tehran Bazaar" (*kaf-e bazaar*), instead of the world market price or, ideally from the perspective of exporters, the production price. This valuation system assumes that exporters are able easily to recoup earnings greater

[31] *Nawruz*, 9 Ordibehesht 1380 (April 29, 2001).
[32] *Dawran-e Emruz*, 21 Azar 1379 (December 11, 2000).

than the domestic price. However, as inflation drove up prices in the Iranian market and international competition decreased prices on the world market, the domestic price for certain carpets exceeded foreign market prices (this was especially the case after 1994). This valuation system has additional perverse consequences. It first influences the type of carpets that are exported by affecting potential profits. In the words of one importer in Germany, "Conducting market research in consumer markets is useless, when customs officials dictate what carpets are profitable. I don't want to export from other countries, but it makes no [economic] sense to have to export and repatriate large sums to Iran." Thus, the marketing system is less adept at adjusting export patterns to demands in foreign markets and recouping lost market shares.

Second, repatriation of hard currency must occur within a stipulated amount of time determined by the government. Since 1981 the time period has ranged from anywhere between five months and fouteen months. This system clearly restricts the ability of exporters to extend credit to purchasers – a factor that impacts trade in carpets, which often take the form of consignment contracts, have generally slow turnover, and whose sales are highly contingent on market conditions in importing countries. This time limit for repatriation is not too restrictive for exporters with large inventories and assets abroad: they can always repatriate funds even when the carpets do not sell within the stipulated time frame. However, the short time limit for the repatriation of earnings places pressures on small merchants and entrepreneurs who do not have large capital reserves available. Thus, they must either export carpets that are assured to sell quickly and therefore not experiment with new styles, or they must be willing to sell their exports at lower prices.

Finally and most importantly, exporters are required to sell their hard currency earnings to the central government at the highly inflated official exchange rate. For much of the past two decades the Islamic Republic has maintained a highly overvalued exchange rate in order to maintain low import prices and thus to appease both importers and consumers and dampen inflationary pressures. This has created a black market in foreign exchange, with differences between the official rate and the "free market" at times reaching 500 percent. In the early 1980s the use of the official rate for calculating repatriation amounts led to the smuggling of carpets out of the country and a precipitous decline in official export figures from $575 million in 1980 to $237 million in 1982. In response to this downturn, officials have experimented with several modifications. A system was devised where exporters received part of the value of their repatriated funds at the government rate, and the remainder as a certificate of credit that could be sold in the Tehran stock exchange, bringing the total rial value close to the equivalent sum based on the free market rate. At certain other times in the past two decades (e.g. in 1985 and the early 1990s) repatriation requirements were lifted for exporters who used their earnings to import goods. This policy attracted a number of merchants with little interest in the carpet trade other than the possibility of bypassing the restrictive trade policies and importing highly profitable goods. Most of these new export–importers were interested in selling their carpets quickly with little or no profit in order to purchase goods for profitable import. They often simply sold their carpets below purchase prices, and thus undermined professional carpet merchants. Yet all these policy modifications were highly transitory. At moments of a rapid decline in the value of the rial and inflationary pressure, such as in 1995, the state reimposed the overvalued exchange rates for repatriated funds.

The capacity and willingness of the state to regulate the macro-economy and the flow of hard currency through these multiple export policies created a highly volatile policy environment. To summarize, the export regime went from being quite open in 1979–80 to being highly regulated in 1981–3; it was gradually liberalized in 1983–7, but restrictions were reinstated in 1988–90, followed by renewed liberal-ization of export and currency policies in 1991, which were ended by strict applications of controls in 1995, and since 1997 policies have again been relaxed. To depict the fluctuations in another way, an article in the official magazine of the Association of Iranian Handmade Carpet Merchants in Germany calculated that Iran's Central Bank issued almost one circular for every business day during 1994.[33] These broad changes in policy and continual adjustments in the valuation lists, time period for repatriation, or the exchange rate regime have been the principal criticism of the export community. One exporter commented, "Every time I go to send a shipment, I have no idea what the duties will be." Other exporters commented that they spend as much time tracking down information about export requirements as they do col-lecting carpets. At the 1999 Annual Exhibition of Iranian Hand-woven Carpets, in a survey of 134 attendees (72 percent of whom were involved in commerce) the "lack of stable export laws" was cited as the main problem facing the carpet industry by 50 percent of respondents

---

[33] *Farsh-e Iran*, 80 (Khordad 1374 [May–June 1995]), 27. For a good article on chronicling the shifts in policy and the fluctuations of exports see Daryush Rashidi-'Araqi, "Farsh-e Iran dar Qalamraw-e Saderat," *Qali-ye Iran*, 3 (Zemestan 1372 [Winter 1993]), 46–56.

and was the most common response.[34] The lack of stability of rules is particularly problematic for carpets because they require a lot of time for production. With such policy volatility, it is difficult for producers and traders to plan effectively and invest efficiently.

Relations in the postrevolutionary carpet bazaar

The result of this highly fragmented and shifting institutional setting and a market consisting of heterogeneous and privileged state actors has been economic malaise and a decline in Iran's competitiveness in the world market. These factors have also resulted in the restructuring of the pattern of relations in the carpet bazaar. These cumulative effects are captured by comments made by a carpet dealer: "I am even more careful when deciding with whom to trade. It is a difficult situation now and you cannot count on tomorrow," implying political and market volatility. When I asked him how he is careful, he said, "I don't accept checks from everyone and make sure that we understand all the conditions of the business dealings. But in general, I deal with a few old merchants whom I know and with whom share a past."

The roughly sixty-year-old carpet exporter's comments were echoed by many other interviewees in the Tehran Bazaar and identify a few specific factors distinct to the developments in the carpet sector. Carpet merchants have two types of exchange relations. The last sentence of his comment describes the first type of exchange relations. Here transactions are between dealers who are "known" to each other through numerous past and present interactions. They involve many of the traditional marketing mechanisms such as long-term credit relations, consignment of goods, and strong social relations. The forces of localization, specialization, and clientelism are quite apparent. Looking at these transactions it appears that cooperative hierarchies continue to exist.

However, the *bazaari*'s opening remarks suggest that these relations do not encompass a large number of colleagues. Transactions with the remainder of potential exchange partners must now take a more formalized, short-term, and isolated form. *Bazaari*s no longer have a viable reputation system that both appraises the trustworthiness of these exchange partners and ensures that they will comply with the terms of the agreement. One *bazaari* concluded that one can "trust neither these

---

[34] *Qali-ye Iran*, 26 (Mordad 1379 [July–August 2000]), 16–22. With a response rate of 31.3 percent, "Lack of a single manager and authority in the carpet sector" was the second most commonly given problem.

merchants, nor their carpets." Since in the carpet bazaar trust in the exchange partner is trust in his wares, exchange does not take place without external legal enforcement. Reflecting this growing need to gather information about traders, a number of Iranian merchants in Hamburg have advocated establishing an information center to regulate traders and identify "fraudsters."[35] Given that in the years after the Revolution a number of new dealers have arrived in the free port and fled after accruing debts and writing bad checks, it was deemed essential to create such a center. When I discussed this matter with Hamburg-based import–exporters, they mentioned that it is more difficult to keep track of new faces in the market and that contacts in Iran, which used to be a reliable way to verify information. This is an area where third-party or state mediation is needed. Thus, merchants call on the state to help regulate traders, rather than goods.

Why are carpet merchants less able to evaluate the trustworthiness of exchange partners? Today the reputation system has been eroded, as relations within the Bazaar are less multifaceted and fewer crosscutting ties distribute information by weaving the various hierarchies together. In terms of an increase in single-faceted relations, both structural and spatial factors have played a role. First, as in the Bazaar as a whole, relations have become less enmeshed in social registers of life and quotidian interactions. With various new entrants, such as exporters who used exports for importing, speculators attempting to guard against inflation or profit from fluctuations in foreign currency, or people who simply cannot find work in Iran's high-unemployment economy, the carpet bazaar has increased in size. However, what is critical is that these new entrants are not necessarily attached to existing networks. And, obviously short-term exchange or fly-by-night schemes are not conducive to developing multifaceted relations.

Second, the Tehran Bazaar is no longer a vibrant and central space for everyday interactions. In order to reduce rental, warehouse, and trans-port costs and avoid taxes, carpet exporters have now begun to establish large warehouse complexes on the outskirts of the city. This simple change in location, however, has delocalized the carpet bazaars. I realized this one day when I went to visit one of the exporters in the Tehran Bazaar. His assistant told me that he was not coming to the Bazaar today. When I asked whether he would be in the Bazaar tomorrow, he said he did not know, but he doubted it. He added that many of the *bazaari*s no longer come to the Bazaar; they conduct their business over the phone and go to their large warehouses on the out-skirts of the city. It dawned on me that it was very difficult to track down

[35] *Qali-ye Iran*, 8 (Bahar 1374 [Spring 1995]), 21–9.

many of the prominent carpet merchants and that when they did arrive they were occupied with business matters and had no time for socializing with other *bazaari*s, let alone answering my research questions.[36] In addition to this bypassing of the Tehran Bazaar, as the international market has become more competitive, exporters have begun to cut costs by traveling directly to rural areas and provincial bazaars in order to reduce the need to work with brokers. Currently, a few Iranian importers in Europe and the United States have begun to integrate production and commerce by establishing exclusive long-term purchasing agreements or partnerships with producers. Vertical integration allows them to have greater input into production and to control price competition and uncertainty.[37] All of these incremental marketing innovations, nevertheless, act to circumvent the Tehran Bazaar completely. In the process the physical unity of the trade, one of the means for developing multifaceted relations, has been reduced.

Finally, there are fewer crosscutting relations that would help link the increasingly isolated business dealings. The decline in multifaceted relations at the level of the carpet bazaar and the more general fading of social bonds across the Tehran Bazaar have impeded the growth of weak ties. With traders engaging in exclusive exchanges with their past partners and shying away from unfamiliar actors, clientelistic and vertical ties are strengthened, but the growth of diffuse relations revolving around polycentric webs is deterred. In short, relations in the carpet bazaar do contain cooperative hierarchies, but since these networks of relations are kept distinct and are not integrated into an overall system through crosscutting relations and multifaceted relations that bring broader members of the carpet bazaar together, the overall form of governance is one closer to a coercive hierarchy.

The tea bazaar

Today, our main problem is not tea; it is the management of tea.

Tea broker, April 2001

Iranians consume four times the world average of tea.[38] Whether it is a brief meeting between colleagues or a large gathering of relatives and

---

[36] Indicative of this was that my most fruitful interviews with carpet exporters were conducted in their homes or in Hamburg. Interviews in the Bazaar were rushed and often cursory.

[37] Neil Fligstein, "Markets as Politics: A Political-Cultural Approach to Market Institutions," *American Sociological Review* 61 (August 1996), 656–73.

[38] Islamic Republic of Iran, Ministry of Commerce, Institute for Commercial Study and Research, "Bazar-e Jahani-ye Chay," 1370 (1991), p. 122.

friends, all social events include the immediate and continual serving and sipping of strong black tea. Although tea consumption became wide-spread among Iranians only in the twentieth century, tea has acquired the reputation of being Iran's national drink. With some 85,000 tons of processed black tea consumed annually at a value of $25 million, its trade is a profitable business.[39] It is also a commodity that has acquired political importance. Since the early decades of the last century, the state has taken a special interest in its cultivation, production, and import. Reza Shah identified tea, along with sugar and tobacco, as one of the main agricultural sectors in Iran's development drive, and accordingly invested in its cultivation. The first tea-processing factory and silo were established by the government, and Reza Shah hired Chinese experts as consultants for the cultivation and processing of tea and sent Iranian students to study the tea industries in India, Sri Lanka, and Indonesia.[40] More recently, the tea sector has been one of the more contentious fields in the state's attempts to privatize the economy and liberalize commerce. Hence, management, specifically state management, is the main character in the story of tea.

Tea cultivation in Iran takes place along the Caspian coast in Gilan and Mazandaran, and its processing, storing, and much of its packaging have been centered in this region. The Tehran Bazaar, however, has acted as a second home to the tea trade since it has been the hub through which tea from Sri Lanka and India (especially varieties from Assam) has been imported and distributed for consumption, and more often for mixing with Iranian varieties. For decades now, tea merchants, wholesalers, and brokers have been clustered in a few caravanserais in the Tehran Bazaar, with Hajj Zaman Sara, Sina Sara, and Naseri Sara being the principal marketplaces.[41] These small saras are deep in the heart of the Bazaar, in areas that the casual passer-by would not notice, but well known to all those in the tea business. Moreover, the main tea companies that package and sell tea (e.g. Shahrzad, Golestan, and Jahan tea) also have their main

---

[39] *Dawran-e Emruz*, 25 Aban 1379 (November 15, 2000).

[40] It should be noted that the state invested in the processing of tea and established factories that were independent of tea plantations. The lack of a unified management that integrated the cultivation and processing of tea differs from India and Sri Lanka, where historically tea plantations and factories were under single ownership or integrated via collectivization. Integrating cultivation and processing has a number of benefits such as efficiencies in scale, improved quality control and investments in quality by processors, lower transaction costs, and greater worker and farmer control. This issue was brought to my attention by an Indian and an Iranian tea broker who were meeting in Tehran.

[41] Note that retailers selling tea are scattered throughout the Bazaar, their location being dictated by consumer demand, rather than suppliers.

sales offices in the Bazaar or in the immediate area surrounding the Bazaar, such as the Galobandak Crossroads (Map 2.1).

Despite 85 percent of tea production taking place in Gilan, the tea merchants in the 1960s and 1970s were of Azeri origin or from the city of Yazd. One old-timer explained, "You don't have to be a tea picker to be an expert, but it does help to have relatives and acquaintances if you want to enter this line of work." Thus, as Azeris and Yazdis migrated to Tehran in the post-World War II era, many joined families and acquaintances who were some of the first entrepreneurs involved in the tea industry.

One of the key actors in the tea bazaar was, and to a lesser extent continues to be, the broker. When it came to the issue of brokers, interviewees who were members of the tea bazaar were among the more adamant proponents of the idea that they were necessary for the operation of the market. Brokers not only are responsible for identifying buyers and sellers and evaluating their reputations, but are critical in appraising the quality of loose tea and suggesting appropriate blends. The most renowned brokers are said to be able to "just look at the dried tea leaves, and tell you from which Indian tea plantation they originated." Thus, brokers play the role of experts in appraising and certifying tea imports, a nonstandard good. Despite Iran following the classification system of the International Organization for Standardization and foreign tea being evaluated through major auction houses in England (and increasingly in producer countries), evaluating the strength, fragrance, color, consistency, and value of each individual batch of tea requires expert knowledge. Thus, like carpets, but to a lesser extent, tea is a nonstandard good that encourages clientelism, as well as localization. However, if we do not include retailers, there are far fewer actors involved in the tea trade than the carpet bazaar, with the number of importers being less than a few dozen importers and wholesalers of various levels and brokers numbering roughly 500 in all of Iran.[42]

Tea and the state

For over four decades the state has been an essential actor in the marketing of tea. In 1958, the National Tea Organization (NTO, Sazman-e Chay-e Keshvar) was established under the Ministry of Customs and Monopolies (it was initially established as a publicly owned company named the Tea Company). Reflecting the decline in state regulation of pricing, in subsequent years supervision of the NTO was transferred to

[42] *Asnaf*, 91 (Azar and Day 1379 [December 2000–January 2001]), 40–2.

several other ministries, including the Commerce and Finance ministries.[43] In order to protect Iran's tea growers, during the 1960s and 1970s the tea trade was regulated by the state using conditional import restrictions. That is, importers were required to purchase a set quantity of domestic tea from the NTO for every unit of imported tea. The ratio of domestic to imported tea fluctuated, but was set at roughly two units of domestic for every one unit of imported tea. Nearly all of Iran's tea imports came from Sri Lanka and India, and once shipments arrived in Iran, tea packagers blended these teas with the homegrown varieties. Thus, the vast majority of tea consumed in Iran prior to the Revolution was typically a blend of local and foreign teas (dealers estimated that probably 80 percent of tea consumed prior to the Revolution was some type of blend).[44] Domestic producers enjoyed earnings that allowed them to maintain quality and make modest investments in the areas of cultivation and processing. With importers dealing directly with factory owners, a degree of cooperation existed between the Bazaar and the industry. Finally, during this period, small amounts of Iranian tea were also exported, often as a result of conditional requirements for exporters.

What is significant about the organization of the tea trade in the Bazaar is that this state regulation ensured domestic production, but also provided the conditions for the persistence of a self-regulating tea bazaar. The value chain linking importers, wholesalers of various levels, and brokers was based on regularized exchanges among actors localized in the Tehran Bazaar. Wholesalers specialized in particular types of tea and regions of the country, distributing the blends that were most suitable to the tea-drinking tastes and brewing methods of each region. Widespread use of credit within the commercial sector also tied members of the Bazaar to each other, and then to domestic factories involved in tea processing and packaging. Interpersonal relations based on family ties and ethnic allegiances, along with daily exchanges among the small and localized traders, all helped to embed economic relations in multiple and reinforcing social spheres. Cooperative hierarchies thus persisted under prevailing state regulations.

After the Revolution state involvement continued, but owing to the nationalist agenda stressing self-sufficiency and populist means of rule, the state altered the specific policies structuring the tea sector and

---

[43] Islamic Republic of Iran, Chamber of Commerce, Industry, and Mines, Center for Research and Analysis of the Chamber of Commerce, Industry, and Mines, Reza Azimi-Hosayni, "Barresi-ye Tawlid va Masraf-e Chay dar Iran va Jahan," Mordad 1372 (July–August 1993).

[44] Interviews with tea sellers in Tehran; and Daniel Balland and Marcel Bazin, *Encyclopedia Iranica*, s.v. "Cay," p. 105.

commerce. During the Iran–Iraq war, tea was identified as an essential commodity and emphasis was placed on producing large quantities at subsidized prices.[45] Imports were strictly controlled by the Ministry of Commerce and were rationed and distributed through food cooperatives. After the war the supervision of the NTO was transferred from the Ministry of Commerce to the Ministry of Agriculture; this bureaucratic change reflected and influenced the state's approach to the tea sector. Policies were laid down to realign the regulatory system in order to subsidize tea farmers and control prices for consumers. The NTO bought tea leaves from farmers and sold them to tea factories, which in turn resold the processed tea to the NTO, which was responsible for selling it to packagers.

Meanwhile, the system of conditional imports that prevailed in the prerevolutionary era and was supposed to have been reestablished by the parliament in 1989 has been ostensibly replaced.[46] Initially, the NTO was allowed to import limited quantities of tea and to blend it with domestic supplies. But over time various state organs and economic zones (e.g. the army, foundations, and border cooperatives) acquired "special licenses" and exemptions to import foreign tea for "personal consumption" or border bartering.[47] These oligarchic privileges were enhanced since their organizations were able to import tea with subsidized foreign currency and by skirting import duties. The shadowy nature of these operations has led the press to call these groups "plunderers" and the "tea mafia." Even government officials have acknowledged the immense power of these organizations. When a former president of the NTO sidestepped the question regarding which exact organs and foundations were involved in importing tea and, hence, undermined the NTO's supervision over the tea sector and attempts to limit tea imports, the interviewer asked him why he talked about this issue in a secretive manner. The former official fatalistically responded: "I have no fear, but it is not right to mention the names of these influential agencies, because these groups put the Tea Organization under pressure. Unfortunately, their influence on sensitive centers [of power] is considerable. Sometimes, they even walk all over the opinions

---

[45] A number of tea merchants argued that overproduction during the war years resulted in the adoption of suboptimal picking techniques that have continued today.

[46] *Dawran-e Emruz*, 5 Day 1379 (December 25, 2000).

[47] There is much confusion over which agencies are authorized to issue import licenses, and who in fact does issue them. Even after the recent liberalization of commerce and the merging of responsibilities, ministers, parliamentarians, and the private sector present contradictory claims regarding the licensing process. See *Dawran-e Emruz*, 24 Azar 1379 (December 14, 2000) and 15 Day 1379 (January 4, 2001); *Kayhan*, 15 Ordibehesht 1380 (May 5, 2001); *Entekhab*, 29 Tir 1381 (July 20, 2002).

of the main authorities and guardians of this sector. At any rate there is nothing that can be done."[48]

This new commercial system has profound consequences for the tea market. Much of the tea imported through special means eventually enters the tea market, with tea merchants in the Bazaar buying from state-affiliated middlemen once it has been imported by state affiliates. The limits on licenses and the privileged status of the state and quasi-state organizations have led to increases in smuggling via border markets, free trade zones, and the northwestern frontier.[49] Again, Dubai is the new entrepôt in this process, with representatives of foreign tea companies using their offices to export to Iran through what a trader in Dubai called a "Swiss cheese border." One indication of the role of Dubai in reexporting tea to Iran is that from 1985 to 1994, the UAE tea import figures rose 71 percent, but much of this was redirected to Iran.[50] Tea smuggling existed before the Revolution and was identified by government officials as an ill that had to be addressed. However, its magnitude and organization has dramatically increased. Sources unanimously state that during much of the 1990s roughly 60,000 tons of loose black tea, or two-thirds of the consumption, was smuggled into Iran per year.[51] Moreover, it has been estimated that in the latter half of the 1990s, only 20 percent of the loose tea that was imported into Iran was supervised by the NTO, which was mandated to supervise the entire tea industry.[52] By 2001, the situation had worsened, and foreign packaged and loose tea comprised 80 percent of the tea market, while 70,000 tons of domestic tea remained unsold in the warehouses.[53] Given such large figures the unauthorized imports are most likely due to activities by the privileged state affiliates and smuggling networks operating under the legal penumbra of the free trade zones.

The smuggling undermines state agents seeking to support domestic producers and creates a transparent law-abiding commercial sector. It is also costly for the state. Not only does the state lose customs revenue, but subsidized hard currency is used to import a good that is domestically produced and also subsidized by the state. The rise in smuggling and general disarray in the market has had a number of consequences

---

[48] *Naw-Sazi*, 18 Ordibehesht 1380 (May 8, 2001).

[49] Pakistan's restrictions on tea imports have also fueled the smuggling trade through Iran and the Persian Gulf. *Deutsche Presse-Agentur*, February 1, 1995.

[50] Ridwan Ali, Yusef Chaudhry, and Douglas W. Lister, "Sri Lanka's Tea Industry: Succeeding in the Global Market," *World Bank Discussion Paper* no. 368 (Washington DC: World Bank, 1997), 10. Also see *Resalat*, 1 Tir 1381 (June 22, 2002).

[51] "Khosh Khat va Khal," *Eqtesad-e Iran*, 360 (Bahman 1380 [January-February 2002]): 11; *Entekhab*, 28 Khordad 1381 (June 18, 2002).

[52] *Hamshahri*, 10 Ordibehesht 1380 (April 30, 2001).

[53] *Bonyan*, 25 Bahman 1380 (February 14, 2002).

for tea producers. With producers receiving subsidized prices on the one hand and facing a declining market share on the other there is little incentive to invest in better technologies and maintain standards. This problem has now begun to surface because the state has sought to introduce market forces into domestic production that cannot compete with smuggled foreign tea in terms of price and quality.[54]

The failure of the current system can also be detected in the new pattern of tea consumption. Wholesalers and packagers no longer mix local and foreign teas because of the large quantities of foreign tea that are smuggled into Iran (both packaged and loose), the price of tea on the world market has declined in the past three decades, and the quality of Iranian tea has declined. The vast majority of Iranians today, even those with the most meager wages, consume purely foreign tea. Even if the tea company is Iranian (e.g. Shahrzad or Golestan) chances are that the tea is 100 percent foreign. One wholesaler estimated that since the revolution over three-fourths of the tea consumed in Iran is purely imported tea. Other merchants speculated that Iranian tastes have changed so much in the past two decades that even if domestic tea becomes more attractive in terms of quality and price, it will take a long time for consumers to switch back to blends or pure Iranian tea.

The new commercial system has also radically changed the structure of the tea bazaar. A member of the governing board of the Tea Wholesalers' Trade Association sums up the results of the changes in the system when he says, "Before the Revolution, tea importing had conditions, was competitive, and purchase and sales were free to all and there weren't any monopolies. People would get import licenses who also bought domestic tea. This prevented smuggling and supported tea farmers, factories, and sellers. But in recent years [meaning after the Revolution] conditional importing has declined." He added, "At present, licensed imports are one-tenth of unlicensed imports. Therefore, tea farmers, factories, and sellers are not protected, and smugglers and importers follow their own interests."[55] Brokers added that these new actors involved in importing and distributing tea are no longer tea specialists; thus *bazaaris* with decades of experience are being replaced not because of loss of reputation, but because they no longer have the capacity to import, mix, package, or distribute the commodity. The Bazaar's reputation system, based on brokers, has thus been replaced by exchange that is based on a system of demand and supply, where supply

---

[54] *Jahan-e Eqtesad*, 3 Ordibhesht 1380 (April 23, 2001).
[55] *Asnaf*, no. 91(Azar and Day 1379 [December–2000-January 2001]), 40.

is predicated on contacts with exclusive importers outside of the purview of the Bazaar.

In terms of relations, my interviews and participant observation in the tea market demonstrated the general shift from cooperative to coercive hierarchies that has occurred at the Bazaar level. The networks that constitute the Bazaar are now heavily skewed toward ties with powerful actors who are spatially dispersed. Tea merchants now work with importers in Dubai, smugglers, and anonymous middlemen operating between the state-affiliated importers and the Bazaar. *Bazaaris* are more active in developing contacts with actors beyond the Bazaar and even beyond Iran. In the middle of one of my interviews, a wholesaler gestured toward the sara and said, "Look around! Do you see anyone here? No, there is no reason to come to the Bazaar. You don't do business in the Bazaar; you do it in ministries or at the borders." Not only are *bazaaris* no longer physically present in the Bazaar, but they are also less able and willing to discuss their affairs with one another. Some say that they do not know who delivers their orders, while others comment that since goods arrive from external sources *bazaaris* are less willing to discuss their suppliers with one another. Finally, with checks and even cash replacing many exchanges, the reputation-based credit system has been replaced by legally enforceable arrangements.

To remedy these acute problems, in 2000 the Khatami government unveiled a liberalization package. The Economic Council of the Board of Ministers presented a plan that called for restructuring of the tea sector by privatizing both the production and distribution of tea. The report called for cooperation among various state organs: the Ministry of Industry, the Organization for Planning and Budget, the Ministry of Cooperatives, the Ministry of Commerce, the Ministry of Agriculture, the Ministry of Interior, which is responsible for customs and borders, and representatives of the tea factory syndicate. The NTO was no longer required to set prices and purchase tea leaves; instead factories could directly purchase harvests from farmers. Both farmers and factory owners would be given subsidized loans to help finance short-term requirements and investments. Finally, after a few months and with little public discussion, in May 2001 it was announced that the distribution and import of tea would handed over to the private sector.[56]

This sudden announcement that the tea sector would be handed over to the private sector was met with suspicion in the Bazaar; there were two sets of reactions. Even though they were understandably supportive of such a trend, many were skeptical that privatization plans would materialize – "There are many plans, but they are rarely executed" – and more

---

[56] *Abrar-e Eqtesadi*, 11 Oridbehesht 1380 (May 1, 2001).

interestingly they believed that this was untenable since it would destroy domestic tea producers and both the farmers and the processors would rise up and would make it politically unviable. In both cases their expectations were proven correct. Only a few months later, not only did the government not liberalize trade, but the Ministry of Commerce and the Ministry of Agricultural Crusade in fact announced that all imports of tea were banned.[57] The reason was that the flood of imported tea had not subsided,[58] and within the year the negative impact of imposing market forces on domestic producers were felt. As one may expect, the rather sweeping proposals faced a number of problems owing to conflicts between vested interests and endemic problems in the industry. On the production side, because of technical problems with cultivation, inefficiencies in tea processing, and lack of marketing on the part of factory owners, domestic tea could not compete on quality and price with tea from South Asia, which is of higher quality and not considerably more expensive.[59] By the end of 2000, after the reforms that ended the NTO's purchasing of tea, only 15 percent of tea processed by factories in Iran was purchased by packagers and distributors.[60] Subsequently, after tea growers in the north protested and lobbied their representative in the parliament, the government was forced to purchase the unsold tea and also subsidize factories.[61] Eventually, the NTO was forced to sell this surplus tea to foreign markets.[62]

Conclusions

Well aware of the perverse and chronic problems of the tea sector, the *bazaaris* have advocated changes. As early as 1993 they warned government officials that the tea industry was facing a crisis and advocated a return to the conditional import policy where the NTO would coordinate imports and domestic production, but they claimed that "nobody would listen."[63] The members of the Bazaar's tea-selling community whom I interviewed claimed that regulation and supervision (*nezarat*)

[57] *Nawruz*, 12 Day 1380 (January 2, 2002); and *Tehran Times*, January 2, 2002.
[58] *Bonyan*, 25 Bahman 1380 (February 14, 2002).
[59] *Dawran-e Emruz*, 19 Day 1379 (January 8, 2001). World prices for tea have declined in the past two decades as production has increased (especially with Kenya, and Tanzania having entered the market) and costs have been reduced by major producers. Meanwhile, tea-producing countries such as (India, Sri Lanka, China, Indonesia, and Kenya which produce roughly 80 percent of the world's tea, have not been able to coordinate production. Ridwan, Chaudhry, and Lister, "Sri Lanka's Tea Industry."
[60] *Hamshahri*, 22 Azar 1379 (December 12, 2000).
[61] *Hayat-e No*, 25 Esfand 1379 (March 15, 2001).
[62] *Tehran Times*, October 17, 2001.
[63] *Asnaf*, no. 91 (Azar and Day 1379 ([December 2000–January 2001]), 40–2.

have been replaced by the interference (*dekhalat*) of an amorphous state apparatus. Supervision is seen as a necessary result of a bargain where domestic production and employment are secured and the necessary shortfall in production is filled by imports. *Bazaari*s believe that if Iran returns to the old system where private actors in domestic production and national and international trade are the purveyors of goods, the quality of domestic tea will improve, consumers will again turn to blended teas, domestic producers will prosper and invest, and the Bazaar will be revived and again dominated by experienced and reputable traders. This scenario, however, assumes that the tea merchants continue to have commercial and social networks capable of coordinating actions and distributing information and goods. Their inability to lobby political actors or act collectively to identify disreputable smugglers and middlemen suggests that this past capacity and solidarity are precarious and need to be planted anew.

The china and glassware bazaar[64]

The [Hajeb al-Dawleh] Timcheh appears isolated from the rest of the Bazaar, but our concerns are the same as everyone else's.

Retailer, September 2000

Near the Shah Mosque, renamed the Imam (Khomeini) Mosque after the Revolution, in the northern section of the Tehran Bazaar lies the grand nineteenth-century Hajeb al-Dawleh Timcheh, an expansive three-story vaulted arcade centered around an open courtyard and pool. Surrounding the courtyard are stores and trading companies specializing in all sorts of kitchen appliances and utensils; principal among these is the china and glassware sector. The merchants in this section of the Bazaar are quite conscious of the fact that their trade, notwithstanding its rather splendid environ, is not as prestigious as the carpet bazaar or as profitable as the cloth and iron sellers' bazaars. China and glassware is neither a necessary staple such as tea or clothing, nor a commodity used as investment such as carpets or gold. Nevertheless, "people do renew their dishes once in a while, and people continue to marry and wives continue to need dowries." The rather unremarkable standing of this sector is reflected in the saying sometimes muttered by members of the kitchenware bazaar: "In the Timcheh, losses only go up to your shin,

[64] There is very little secondary literature, journalistic reporting, or government information about the china and glassware sector. Information in this section is compiled almost exclusively from my observations and interviews with *bazaari*s, non-*bazaari* commercial actors in Tehran, Dubai, and the free trade zones, and domestic producers of china and glassware.

and profits only reach your shin" (*Dar Timcheh zarar ta saq va naf' ta saq*); in other words, in the kitchenware market you are never going to lose your life savings, but neither will you become exceptionally wealthy.

The atmosphere in the china and glassware sector is also strikingly different from that in the carpet and tea bazaars. While in the carpet bazaar, and to a lesser extent the tea bazaar, it was still common to see several traders sitting together and conversing or to witness *bazaaris* drop by to ask business questions and exchange small talk, the china and glassware merchants are noticeably more detached from one another. Rarely do you see neighboring shopkeepers in each other's stores, and if you do, you can rest assured that there are actual business matters at hand – debts being negotiated, purchases being made, or disputes being solved. If information about the price of a good is needed, these *bazaaris* send their apprentices to investigate. While carpet dealers invite visitors by leaving their doors (if they even have them) open, placing their goods outside, and sitting at the entrance of their stores, in the Timcheh, shopowners are often not visible, their store doors may be closed, display cases limit their entrances, and storeowners are often in their back offices. Save for the ornate architecture and tight quarters, one is reminded more of the restaurant supply district in New York's Lower East Side or even a mall in a North American suburb than a Middle Eastern marketplace. This is a product of the standardized nature of the manufactured wares. Teacups, unlike carpets, have a set of defined qualities – name of manufacturer, model, and quantity. Prices may not be stable and bargaining may exist, but quantity and quality are defined, helping to reduce price dispersion and transaction costs related to information costs.

Nevertheless, the glass and chinaware bazaar is also quite illustrative of some of the basic trends facing most of the Tehran Bazaar, which is increasingly a purveyor of more standardized goods, such as manufactured shoes, textiles, clothing, and stationery products. The china and glassware bazaar has gone from being composed of highly hierarchical, specialized, and stable value chains to one that consists of relations that are more transitory and dispersed. While, the entire national trade in china and glassware used to be anchored in the Timcheh, it now revolves around multiple commercial centers.

Before the Revolution, the value chains were headed by a small number of importers who specialized in specific brands, since they were representatives of particular European (French, Italian, German, and Czech), and to a lesser extent Japanese, companies. This specialization was transmitted to wholesalers who worked with these importers to distribute their wares to representatives in the Tehran Bazaar and provincial centers (Isfahan, Tabriz, Mashhad, and Shiraz). Thus, prices and profit margins were scripted and competition regulated. For the customer this all resulted in a highly segmented marketplace. If one wanted to purchase a specific brand, there were a select few retailers, and without exception they were located in the Bazaar. Thus, clientelism between importers and wholesalers and between wholesalers and retailers was reproduced between retailers and customers. Owing to the longevity and repeated nature of the exchanges, transactions were made based on credit and promissory notes.

In the 1960s and 1970s, imports prevailed in this market for two reasons. First, oil revenue helped keep the value of the rial relative to hard currencies at a high and stable level, thus making western imports affordable for the growing middle class. Second, domestic production was minimal. While state development projects invested in consumer durables such as televisions, refrigerators, and automobiles, china and glassware production was left unprotected and unsupported by the regime. Thus, the importing value chains dominated.

These economic ties were reinforced by a number of social factors. For instance, a large portion of those in the Timcheh were from Isfahan, a factor that continues to be discernible today, with several *bazaaris* from the china and glassware sector investing in newly established factories in Isfahan. Intermarriage and kinship ties have also helped cement business relations, with many of the middle-aged members of the sector today still able to identify cousins and relatives in the various sub-trades in the Timcheh (kitchen utensils, steel pots and pans, and other household goods; see Chapter 3). Supporting the multifaceted and crosscutting nature of these ties were the relatively small number of retailers, wholesalers, and importers in this sector; their numbers were no more than a few dozen, rather than several hundred as was the situation in the carpet or cloth bazaars. This small number was localized exclusively in the Hajeb al-Dawleh Timcheh, a particularly secluded and self-contained segment of the Bazaar. Nestled between the two main alleys, the Grand Bazaar and the shoemakers' bazaar, small doorways open into the Timcheh, creating a relatively tranquil island from which nationwide trade took place.

After the Revolution, the china and glassware trade went through a number of changes that were precipitated by shifts in the state's economic policies and responses by entrepreneurs and customers. To begin with, legal imports came to a standstill. After the outbreak of the war and during the period when nationalization of trade was very much part of the policy debate, china and glassware were classified as nonessential consumer goods and therefore "luxuries"; thus the state drastically reduced the licenses and foreign exchange available to would-be importers. For much of the 1980s the sector went through short-term adjustments. Small-scale smuggling emerged as an alternative route to import goods. As the war ended and special trade zones were established, the more regularized system of smuggling and quasi-legal trade came into existence. A few *bazaari*s left the Timcheh and joined entrepreneurs in establishing import–(re)export operations in the free trade zones and Dubai. The result has been that *bazaari*s now act as secondary wholesalers, with the large importing operations being based in Dubai and the shipments being distributed to Iran's markets via the free trade zones.

Meanwhile, a number of entrepreneurs in the Bazaar took this opportunity to invest in both china and glass factories. With the sharp devaluation of the rial, the resulting rise in the price of imports, and the decline in the purchasing power of many Iranians, demand for imports declined. Over time, domestic producers have been able to enter the market and meet demand. These small emerging industrialists moved into production of china and glass products by taking advantage of some of the modest investment incentives and the large domestic consumer market while maneuvering around the dense and unpredictable bureaucracy. It has helped that Iran enjoys a relative comparative advantage in these industries owing to availability of raw materials and cheap energy. By the late 1990s, with domestic production meeting an ever-greater portion of demand and an export trade to neighboring countries burgeoning, the glassware and china industries had become two of the few non-petroleum sectors to prosper and grow.[65] While domestic products are not able to compete with European and Japanese manufacturers in terms of quality or diversity of design, *bazaari*s commented that they attract buyers because they are only a third to a half of the price of these imports and readily available. For instance, while sitting in the store of one purveyor of French glassware, I overheard a number of customers complain that it was difficult to find complete sets or replacements once dishes broke. The *bazaari* explained, "Dear lady, it is not easy to import dishes, there are a thousand problems and it takes a long time. If you want fine French dishes like these you must accept these problems." Sales of domestic products and anecdotal evidence suggest that more and more Iranians are unwilling to "accept these problems." Moreover, the high domestic sales have been reinvested in the factories to steadily improve quality and patterns. However,

---

[65] *Dawran-e Emruz*, 19 Azar 1380 (December 10, 2001) and 27 Azar 1379 (December 17, 2000).

domestic producers are concerned that their prices cannot compete with Chinese imports that are both produced at lower prices and avoid import barriers by entering Iran through smuggling channels.

Hence, these market changes have restructured the china and glassware bazaar in particular ways. The earlier stability has been replaced by pervasive instability born out of changes in customs duties and policies, exchange rate policies, uncertainties of smuggling operations, and fluctuations in Iran's macroeconomic situation. These fluctuations limit long-term planning, with few importers willing to take the risk of ordering large shipments, while some wholesalers who are not in need of liquid capital use their inventories as a means of speculation. Finally, smuggling has had the same negative consequences for the maintenance of cooperative hierarchies as discussed previously. In the context of the new market possibilities in the kitchenware sector, they also diverted some traders away from import value chains. *Bazaaris* who were apprehensive about becoming involved in trade that was ostensibly illegal switched into trading in domestic products either by shifting their inventories or, in a few cases, investing in production. As one such wholesaler mentioned, once he realized that importing would require illegal activities, he shifted his attention to domestically manufactured goods, explaining that "an importer's job is not smuggling."

As some old-timers shifted out of imports, others entered. Markets for standardized goods have lower entry barriers than comparable markets for nonstandard goods. Start-up costs in the china and glassware sector are relatively low: remember, "losses only come up to the shin." Not only is the value of basic inventories modest (a few thousand dollars), but unlike with nonstandard goods such as carpets, tea, or jewelry, the knowledge and reputation necessary to begin are quite minimal. Apprentices in the Timcheh are some of the most upwardly mobile groups that I met in the Bazaar. In today's more open market, after only a couple of years, apprentices can move on to begin their own small enterprises, typically outside of the Bazaar. One small-scale wholesaler of domestic china dishes, who began working in the Timcheh in 1995, chose to invest in the china and glassware sector despite having enough savings to begin a business in the more lucrative cloth bazaar, in which he also had some acquaintances. He explained that he selected the Timcheh instead of other sectors because he was able to enter the trade with little knowledge about china, adding that selling dishes was not a skill (*herfeh*).

In addition, many of these new entrants were able to create a new home for their trade. Located three kilometers from the Tehran Bazaar, near Shush Square, a new wholesale center for china and glassware has emerged. Immediately before the Revolution, this area housed small workshops that produced hand-made and blown-glass products. It was also one of the main warehouse districts. A number of factors came together to lead to a gradual relocation of the wholesalers, to Shush in the mid-1980s. Most importantly, the limits placed on traffic movements in central Tehran made Shush, an area just outside the traffic restriction zone already containing a number of warehouses, an ideal location for wholesalers to sell to provincial retailers and jobbers. Second, as consumers gradually shifted from imported to Iranian-made china and glassware, *Shushi*s, as they are sometimes called, specializing in domestic goods saw an improvement in their business. This attracted many new businessmen to establish wholesale operations in this area, as well as attracting a few from the Timcheh to establish offices in the area. The municipality has also stepped in to support this growing emporium. In the mid-1990s the district 16 branch of the municipality built the impressive and elaborate China and Crystal Shopping Center.

By the late 1990s, Shush and the Timcheh divided the market between them. The Timcheh houses purveyors of imported goods and caters to past provincial clients and Tehrani retailers who continue to view it as the center for china and glassware. Meanwhile, Shush functions exclusively as a wholesale district, and principally as an outlet for domestic wares. While there is some overlap in the networks, their market segmentation does not seem to have been bridged by social relations. *Bazaari Timcheh-ii*s consider *Shushi*s as newcomers with little or no experience in commercial matters. And *Shushi*s continue to recognize the Timcheh as the base for imported goods. Regional differences also may play a role, with many of the original *Shushi*s coming from Hamedan, unlike the noticeable presence of Isfahanis in the Timcheh. Nonetheless, since china and glassware are standard and substitutable goods, economic exchanges can more easily flourish without the social underpinnings necessary for cooperative hierarchies. Since goods are of more certain provenance, buyers have always been more assured that quality and quantity will be consistent. Thus, new merchants can enter, new wholesale districts do emerge, and trade is conducted relatively smoothly despite the transformation of the market.

Comparisons and conclusions

The explanations laid out in the previous chapter understood changes in the organization of the Bazaar as being principally produced by the policies of the state and responses of *bazaari*s. The case studies in this chapter are an opportunity to investigate other possible explanations through comparison. I now look at four potential factors that I have not investigated – group size, geographical dispersion of the value chains, commodity type, and the existence of state regulation.

Group size

First, it is reasonable to expect that group size will be an important constraint on the type of governance possible. Groups with larger membership would tend to have difficulty in generating and sustaining long-term, multifaceted, and crosscutting relations integral to generating an internal and collective regulatory system such as cooperative hierarchies. In large groups, the breadth of networks (that is, the number of individuals incorporated into chains of relations) would be so great that we may expect the degree of embeddedness to be slight. Moreover, from the rational choice perspective, governance is a non-excludable "public good," and hence faces the obstacle of under-provision owing to free-rider problems.[66] Thus, it is argued that without outside provision of selective incentives these collective goods will not be provided.[67] This general hypothesis regarding group size and collective action was most famously put forth by Mancur Olson, who argued that unlike small groups, which can be organized around a single individual or small number of entrepreneurs willing to bear the burden of organizing, large groups need the active participation of a large number of individuals to transform latent groups into self-regulating groups. Thus, "the larger a group is, the more agreement and organization it will need," and "costs of organization are an increasing function of the number of individuals in the groups."[68] Therefore the hypothesis would be that larger groups will tend to be less likely to generate cooperative hierarchies than smaller groups, and one would expect that

---

[66] Mancur Olson, *The Logic of Collective Action: Public Goods and the Theory of Groups* (Cambridge, MA: Harvard University Press, 1965).

[67] To be more precise, we must account for jointness of supply cost. Jointness of supply cost refers to costs associated with providing goods that have constant costs regardless of the number of individuals benefiting from the good (e.g. a bridge, a dam, or a border between countries). Perfect private goods have zero jointness of supply costs since costs are proportional to the number of individuals consuming them. In the case of cooperative hierarchies that require collective governance, in which the cost of organization is proportional to the size (i.e. they do not enjoy perfect jointness of supply cost), as the size of the group increases the cost of maintaining these relations will increase (in this case cost in terms of time and effort is more important than financial cost). Thus, the neoclassical economic approach would predict that unlike those public goods with perfect jointness of supply cost, the supply of this public good will be more unlikely as the group size increases.

[68] Olson, *The Logic of Collective Action*, p. 46.

the underlying reason for the shift from cooperative to coercive hierarchies is simply arithmetic.

At first glance, this argument seems to have merit. Even without specific data, it is universally agreed that the number of *bazaari*s has increased. Chapter 3 discussed the many causes, including the increase in urban population, high levels of unemployment in the manufacturing and public sectors, and the relative profitability of the service sector.

However, on closer examination, the group size argument becomes far less compelling. First, an increase in the number of members of the Bazaar was occurring through much of the twentieth century. The Tehran Bazaar's overall membership increased as the economy and polity were increasingly centered in Tehran; these patterns have mattered at least since Reza Shah's reign (1925–1941). Thus, in the 1960s and 1970s, the Tehran Bazaar's membership was in the tens of thousands, but cooperative hierarchies persisted. The increase in size of the Bazaar after the Revolution is not a sufficient or necessary reason for a decline in cooperative hierarchies. Second, when we compare the three sectors in ordinal terms we do not see a correlation between group size and type of governance. The carpet bazaar was consistently the largest sector, followed by the china and glassware bazaar and then the tea bazaar. However, it is the very large carpet sector that has been able to retain some of the characteristics of cooperative hierarchies. Third, transformations within the tea bazaar suggest that a decline in numbers does not help to maintaining cooperative hierarchies. A member of the unofficial Association of Tea Wholesalers of Tehran told me that whereas before the revolution there were as many as 500 tea wholesalers and importers, most of whom were in Tehran, now the association only had 100, many of whom are actually inactive and retired. Other tea merchants have noted that there are now fewer professional tea merchants than three decades ago. This decrease in group size, however, did not prevent the unraveling of cooperative hierarchies.

Geographic dispersion of value chains

If the size of a group is less critical for preserving cooperative hierarchies, it seems reasonable that concentration of group members in a given space is an important condition. As we saw in the discussion of the carpet bazaar, for instance, localization was one of the prominent characteristics of this trade, facilitating the creation of multifaceted relations and weak ties that bridge network clusters. Thus, we would expect that value chains that are spread across great distances would prevent coordination and limit the capacity of social relations to mediate market forces. As the distance between members of the value chain (say between a wholesaler and an importer) expands, regular face-to-face interactions become less common and cooperative hierarchies become less prevalent. The argument would explain the shift from cooperative to coercive hierarchies as an outcome of dispersion of networks.

On closer inspection, however, we see that dispersion of value chains across wide expanses does not necessarily reduce the likelihood that cooperative hierarchies will prevail. The carpet sector, alongside localization of wholesalers in the Tehran Bazaar, in fact has been highly dispersed across great distances. Domestically, carpet production occurs quite literally in all four corners of Iran – Azerbaijan in the northwest, Turkmen areas and Khorasan in the northeast, Kerman in the southeast, and Fars in the southwest. Internationally, carpets were exported to carpet emporiums such as Hamburg, Zurich, and Secaucus, New Jersey, through fundamentally continual sets of networks with the same informal institutions. Yet both forms of governance existed with this dispersion. Moreover, the postrevolutionary china and glassware sector, despite being localized in the Tehran Bazaar and Shush Square (only a few kilometers away from the Timcheh), has witnessed patterns of commercial relations that have more readily become short term, purely economic, and less crosscutting than those of the carpet bazaar. Thus, institutions, formal and informal, must be present to encourage interactions so traders do not simply pass each other by, but exchange thoughts, experiences, and information. These cases demonstrate that society is spatially organized, in the sense that it is contingent not only on interactions in physical spaces, but on social interactions that form an interface transcending geographies and boundaries. It is only when shared space is accompanied by shared experience that space acquires an importance in relational terms.

Commodity type

Recalling the discussions about standard versus nonstandard goods and the latter's pervasive information costs that impede transactions, we might expect commodity types to condition relations within sectors. In what Geertz calls a "communication model of the bazaar economy," the scarcity of information about commodities and prices creates techniques and shapes relations in order to search for information and protect the information one has. One of the main pillars of his analysis is that goods and services in the bazaar economy are "inhomogeneous." "Those that flow through the bazaar are, for the most part, highly divisible, extremely various consumption items that are unstandardized, of mixed provenance, and very hard to evaluate."[69] For Geertz this economic fact is the basis for the bazaar's economic institutions, such as its clienteli- zation. Fanselow rearticulates this argument by placing the onus for the structural outcome squarely on the qualities of commodities and not on the ontology of the Bazaar.[70] In cases where information regarding the quality or quantity of a good is scarce or limited to sellers, there will be a tendency toward more embedded relations among exchange partners in order to gain access to trustworthy information. Thus, long-term rela- tions based on socially embedded ties and evaluations of reputations through mutual acquaintances are critical, and all are components of cooperative hierarchies. The theory predicts that trades with more standardized goods will be less specialized, will be less spatially loca- lized, and will have less need to resort to clientelization, but there will be more prospects for entry into the sector and more opportunity for buyers to canvas the market for new suppliers and better prices.

The sectoral analysis of the Tehran Bazaar exhibits these expected variations. In all these sectors highly reputable guild elders and brokers have become less prominent, and therefore fewer crosscutting relations exist. Also, the demise of the shared life of *bazaaris* has also limited the existence of weak ties across the Bazaar. Regardless of the sector, it is more difficult to trust potential exchange partners, and all *bazaaris* mentioned problems related to bounced checks and increased incidence of fraud. However, the lack of trust, or more precisely the decline in means to evaluate the trustworthiness of fellow *bazaaris*, is especially acute in the case of markets for nonstandard commodities. In the tea market, where standardization is handled by international standards applied by auction houses, packaged tea, and the NTO, a large number of commodity-based transaction costs are reduced by formal institu- tions. However, in the carpet bazaar standardization is far more difficult and not trusting a carpet seller also means not trusting the quality of his carpets. Thus, exchange relations are longer term and more multi- faceted than in the other guilds. Consignment and heavy use of brokers, furthermore, is still a means for sellers to spread the transaction costs of marketing. These networks, however, are isolated from one another. Carpet merchants enjoy fewer ties and hence less capacity to search the Bazaar for information and new exchange partners. Consequently two recent trends are discernible in the carpet business, which can be interpreted as attempts to guard against these marketing restrictions.

[69] Geertz, "Suq: The Bazaar Economy in Sefrou," p. 214.
[70] Frank Fanselow, "The Bazaar Economy or How Bizarre Is the Bazaar Really?" *Man* 25 (June 1990), 250–65.

The segmentation in exchange partners where old-time trading partners exchange with one another and avoid newcomers has become a norm that forges strong ties to ensure greater security. Second, carpet import–exporters are now beginning to invest in production. Integration of production and marketing requires large sums of capital, but reduces the need to deal with middlemen, and thus reduces the costs of transactions in a competitive market.[71] These recent developments are all means that shelter merchants from the decline of cooperative hierarchies, but also further encourage the development of less multifaceted and crosscutting relations across the carpet bazaar.

At the other end of the spectrum, in the china and glassware sector, buyers face lower information costs since goods are standard. In this market for manufactured goods, the characteristics of commodities are guaranteed by trademarks and quantifiable measurements. Merchants guard against potential defaults by using cash and legally enforced checks and money orders. But given that they are trading standard goods, china and glassware merchants are less concerned with the quality and quantity of the goods than they are about price. Thus, the shift from cooperative to coercive hierarchies has a less destabilizing effect on their capacity to transact. By illustrating these variations within the Tehran Bazaar, I reiterate and reinforce the basic argument put forth by both Fanselow and Geertz that the particular commercial institutions and practices found in marketplaces in the developing world are a product of the nature of the goods exchanged rather than the culture and beliefs of individual traders or communities, even if these practices color and are reflected in norms and expectations.

Commodity type and form of governance seem to have at least two mutually reinforcing relationships. First, bazaars for more standardized goods tend more readily to shift to coercive hierarchies. Second, a shift from cooperative to coercive hierarchies encourages commercial actors to devise new means to compensate for transaction costs associated with nonstandard goods. Taken together, commodity types influence the institutional and physical setting of networks.

State regulation

Another reading of the analysis presented in Chapter 4 may be that the shift in the form of governance is simply a product of state intervention and increased regulation under the Islamic Republic. Thus, the explanation of change in the form of governance can be reduced to the

---

[71] Fligstein, "Markets as Politics," 659.

existence of state regulation. The argument would state that it was the Pahlavi regime's benign neglect that allowed cooperative hierarchies to blossom, and the Islamic Republic's attempt to regulate that resulted in a shift to coercive hiearchies. The case of the tea sector thwarts this analysis. Both regimes played an active role in regulating trade and sought to protect local producers. The particular institutions used to regulate this trade were the decisive factor, rather than the mere existence of them. Under the earlier trade regime, state policies and networks complemented one another; yet, more recently, commercial networks have come to rival one another and seek to replace the state's bureaucracy, which is quite weak in Weberian terms. Also, given that many carpet merchants are calling not so much for a retreat of the state from the carpet sector as for a redirection of its energies from production to international marketing, it seems that more research is needed to assess the constitutive parts of state regulation and its impact on commerce.

In conclusion, these sub-bazaars present a more concrete description of the transformation of the Tehran Bazaar from cooperative to coercive hierarchies. They remind us that just as the state is not an undifferentiated entity, the Bazaar too is composed of specific institutions, actors, and practices. The dynamics of the china and glassware sector was shaped by the emergence of domestic production and the nature of standard goods, which that have lower transaction costs and thus make the transition to coercive hierarchies more manageable. The tea bazaar shows the importance of specific state institutions in patterning commercial relations and the *bazaaris*' access to the domestic production process and world market. The one necessary modification to the transition story was in the case of the carpet sector, where its networks continue to have some of the qualities of cooperative hierarchies – relations are still often long term and embedded in social and familial bonds. However, the crosscutting relations that ensured weak ties and the flow of information throughout the Bazaar have declined, compelling them to acquire characteristics that are similar to coercive hierarchies.

In addition, the case studies specify the twin variables of institutional setting and location of networks and their relation to the two regimes' transformative projects. Under the Pahlavi monarchy's high modernist development project, investments and state focus were concentrated on heavy industry and consumer durables, leaving the carpet production and china and glassware sectors open to market forces and the Bazaar's marketing systems. Tea, however, which was earmarked as a basic agricultural sector, was regulated by the state. The Islamic Republic's development planning has been less focused on particular sectors; rather it has mixed populist policies to subsidize urban consumption while distributing import rights and subsidized hard currency as patronage. This has had perverse consequences for the carpet and tea industries, but the narrative of the china and glassware sector suggests that consumer nondurables may have been encouraged by import restrictions. In addition, these specific narratives demonstrate that delocalization of networks has involved the creation of new domestic centers in Tehran (i.e. carpet warehouses in Tehran's periphery and china and glassware wholesalers in Shush) and new international, or more accurately transnational, locales that are attached to international capital, rather than national sovereignty. Finally, this chapter suggests that a long-term underlying factor in reducing the viability of cooperative hierarchies is the prevalence of standardized goods. Thus, manufacturing and industrialization, which have long been shown to impact the relationships between labor and capital, also reshape relations within the commercial sphere.

6   Networks of mobilization under two regimes

Under the Shah, the bazaar could wreck the regime if it decided to close down for three days. But ... the bazaar is not the bazaar any more, it's just a name, a symbol.

Carpet seller, Tehran Bazaar, February 2000[1]

I had recently arrived in Tehran to conduct exploratory research for my dissertation. It was July 1999, a time when the students at Tehran University were in the midst of challenging the judiciary for banning *Salam*, a leading independent newspaper that called for political reforms. As the Persian expression goes, "The university was *sholugh*," meaning that there was political dissent and disorder. Tehran was in the throes of the largest political protests since the revolution that had swept aside the Shah. The pro-reformist protests had spread to campuses in Tabriz, Isfahan, Shiraz, and other cities. With President Mohammad Khatami having recently defeated the candidate believed to be the regime insider in a surprising landslide victory, supporters of the newly forming reformist platform were hopeful and energized. For supporters of reform the mass protests only boosted their expectations; for beneficiaries of the status quo, the students' vociferous daring was horrifying.

When I went to buy groceries, the corner grocer, who liked to chat about the newspaper headlines, smiled and beckoned me over. Knowing that I visited the Bazaar, he asked, "So you go to the Bazaar. Tell me, is the Bazaar *sholugh*?" I answered that it was not, and we were both surprised.

This chapter reflects on the reason for the corner grocer's question, and the implications of my answer. It argues that the forms of governance within groups are foundational to their political mobilization.

Bazaaris historically have translated their commercial centrality into political contestation. Given that Iran's monarchical rule was a highly exclusionary polity without a system of interest representation or deliberation and with impediments to accessing the centers of political

---

[1] *Agence France Presse*, February 14, 2000.

power, mass protest in the forms of civil disobedience and the public airing of grievances were the only means to challenge state policies. *Bazaari*s have prominently participated in almost every major social movement in the past century. Beginning with their opposition to the tobacco capitulations in 1890, the members of the bazaar have joined other segments of society to call for political reforms, defend their economic interests and political rights, and advocate ideological positions. During these episodes, the marketplaces, which are centrally located in almost all Iranian cities, have been converted into political fora and fulcrums directing grievances into dissent and mobilization. *Bazaari*s have helped to organize demonstrations and mass strikes, fund the political initiatives of other actors (teachers, workers, and seminarians), and distribute information within and beyond the commercial classes. In the words of one of the leading historians of modern Iran, Nikki Keddie, "Despite the modernization of Iran, the bazaar remained a focal point of major political opposition movements from 1891 through 1979. This was partly due to the ease of organizing craft and religious circles that in time of crisis took on an increasingly political aspect."[2]

Hence, this final chapter asks how was the Bazaar able to organize collective action within its own ranks? How did it do so with such apparent ease? And finally, what has become of this capacity to mobilize in the postrevolutionary era? Or in the unstated words of the grocer, "If historically it was able to create 'political dissent and disorder,' what is preventing it from doing so now?'

By capacity to mobilize I am referring to the "organizational readiness" or ability of a group to coordinate actions and mobilize resources (financial, symbolic, and membership) in order for individuals to pursue some collective good despite existing socioeconomic differences and political cleavages.[3] I contend that the Tehran Bazaar's active participation in social movements stems from its particular socioeconomic organization. Specifically, by showing that this capacity has declined in recent years, I argue that given their interest in making claims against the state, political opportunities to do so, and ideological frames, cooperative hierarchies are more effective than coercive hierarchies in taking advantage of structural opportunities and at mobilizing groups, their resources,

---

[2] Nikki R. Keddie, *Roots of Revolution: An Interpretive History of Modern Iran* (New Haven: Yale University Press, 1981), p. 245.

[3] Doug McAdam, *Political Process and the Development of Black Insurgency, 1930–1970*, 2nd edn. (Chicago: University of Chicago Press, 1999), pp. 40–8; and Sidney Tarrow, *Power in Movement: Social Movements, Collective Action and Politics* (New York: Cambridge University Press, 1994), chapter 8.

and frames. Thus, the shift in form of governance had an eviscerating effect on the Bazaar's potency, and therefore helps explain the relative decline in the Tehran Bazaar's mobilization against the state in the current period when, despite having political and economic grievances and being presented with opportunities to ally themselves with other social groups, the *bazaari*s appear increasingly incapable of articulating their interests and bringing the bazaar's members to the fore. Therefore, *not all networks are conducive to social mobilization*. Instead, we must pay attention to their specific form. I make this argument by comparing instances of *bazaari* mobilization and nonmobilization across the past half century and by illustrating the precise mechanisms in the forms of governance that facilitate or hinder these outcomes.

This chapter first introduces the most comman conceptual lens used to understand bazaar activism, namely the mosque–bazaar alliance. Next I briefly summarize the major social movements of the twentieth century, focusing on the role of the Tehran Bazaar in these events and the shortcomings of the literature's prevailing view, which reduces *bazaari* collective action to clerical mobilization and religious motivation. The chapter goes on to engage the interest-based approaches to *bazaari* mobilization by extending their analysis to the postrevolutionary era. Building on my earlier analysis of bazaars as collections of networks, I unpack how forms of governance generate solidarity and mobilization. This argument is evaluated against the postrevolutionary experience to ponder the decline of the Bazaar's capacity to mobilize in the postrevolutionary era. It should be noted that the discussions of these various social movements are far from comprehensive and are not intended to outline the causes of their emergence and outcome; instead they are meant simply to highlight the Tehran Bazaar's role in them and its modes of collective action, and inaction.

Social movements and the mosque–bazaar alliance

The historiography of modern Iran frequently notes the close relations between the clergy and the *bazaari*s and the crucial leading role they have played in uprisings and revolutions during the past hundred years. For instance, it is claimed that *bazaari*s "from time immemorial have been linked to the clergy,"[4] or that they enjoy a "historical coalition with

---

[4] Wilfred Buchta, *Who Rules Iran? The Structure of Power in the Islamic Republic* (Washington DC: The Washington Institute for Near East Policy and Konrad Aenauer Stiftung, 2000), p. 15.

the hierocracy."[5] It is said that the bazaar and mosque are "inseparable twins"[6] or "two lungs of public life in Iran",[7] or that the relations between them are "close, constant, and organic,"[8] constituting a "corporatist coalition of traditional middle-class groups led by the 'ulama' [clergy] and supported by the bazaar."[9] Most examinations of the *bazaari* mobilization frame, if not explain, bazaar political activity against the state by positing that the clergy shape the political actions of *bazaaris* as much as they shape their normative worldviews. This is generally referred to as the "mosque–bazaar alliance."

In the strongest formulations it is implied that Islam ideologically and spiritually determines the actions of the *bazaaris*.[10] In his analysis, of the Islamic Revolution, Arjomand claims that the *bazaaris* were one of the "social groups who were genuinely moved by the myth of the Islamic government and Islamic Revolution as proposed by the militant clerics."[11] Postrevolutionary accounts by conservative Islamists also tend to read bazaar activism in purely religious terms. The arch conservative newspaper *Resalat* describes the "unified and religious" bazaar as the "executive arm for the clergy."[12] In the keynote speech at a conference titled *"The Bazaar in the Cultural and Civilization of the World of Islam,"* Asadollah Badamchian, one of the leading figures in the Islamic Coalition Association (ICA), described the bazaar's political activities as natural expressions of religiosity and loyalty to the clergy.[13]

[5] Said Amir Arjomand, *The Turban for the Crown: The Islamic Revolution in Iran* (New York: Oxford University Press, 1988), p. 107.

[6] Ahmad Ashraf, "Bazaar-Mosque Alliance: The Social Basis of Revolts and Revolutions," *International Journal of Politics, Culture, and Society* 1 (Summer 1988), 538.

[7] Roy Mottahedeh, *The Mantle of the Prophet: Religion and Politics in Iran* (New York: Pantheon Books, 1985), p. 34.

[8] Mehdi Mozaffari, "Why the Bazar Rebels," *Journal of Peace Research* 28 (November 1991), 379.

[9] Robert Bianchi, *Unruly Corporatism: Associational Life in Twentieth-Century Egypt* (New York: Oxford University Press, 1989), p. 210.

[10] See also Chapter 2.

[11] Arjomand, *The Turban for the Crown*, p. 106. Nevertheless, Arjomand follows this statement by spelling out the bazaar's economic grievances, rather than demonstrating how and why *bazaaris* were "moved" by Khomeini's message.

[12] *Resalat*, 20 Esfand 1365 (March 11, 1987). For representative comments by Khomeini see "Khomeyni Addresses Merchants of Tehran," Foreign Broadcast Information Service, South Asia, January 16, 1981, I 3, FBIS-SAS-81-011. For example, "Throughout history, whenever Islam faced any problem or the great Islamic ulema faced any problem it was sufficient for the bazaar to close down for half a day in response to see the problem resolved."

[13] "The Bazaar in the Culture and Civilization of the World of Islam," Tabriz University, Tabriz, Iran, September 28–October 1, 1993. Also see Asadollah Badamchian and 'Ali Banai, *Hayatha-ye Motalefeh-e Eslami* (Tehran: Owj, 1362 [1983]), pp. 2–34; "Bazar," *Daneshnameh-ye Jahan-e Eslam* (Tehran: Bonyad-e Dayerat al-Ma'aref-e Eslami, 1372 [1993]), pp. 377–88.

The more common conceptualization of the mosque–bazaar alliance is one of mutual cooperation and interest. Ahmad Ashraf in his comprehensive analysis of clerical–*bazaari* relations writes, "The bazaaris have been allied traditionally with independent Shi'i ulama (those who had no official appointments) in their mutually held belief that the patrimonial domination, though often recognizing as legitimate on a de facto basis, was in fact only quasi-legitimate. Recognizing this political weakness strengthened their need to work-together."[14] Their capacity to act in consort was based on several commonly cited factors: their physical proximity, kinship ties, interaction via the educational and judicial systems, financial relations, and participation in religious events.

To begin with, the bazaar, main mosque, seminary, and sometimes shrine are found adjacent to each other and in the historical heart of most Iranian cities. This allows for daily and routine contact between the *bazaaris*, clerics, and seminary students and an awareness of each other's public activities. At times of foment, the physical proximity became part of the bazaar's repertoire of collective action through the long-lived practice of *bast-neshastan*, or taking refuge in inviolable places, wherein mosques and shrines are used as a sanctuary by those who fear government persecution.[15] This physical proximity was buttressed by a relational closeness created through kinship ties. Many of the *'olama* came from *bazaari* families, were related through marriage, or as children had their religious schooling financed by merchants.[16] Education and conflict resolution constituted another arena that historically brought merchants and clerics together. The older generation of *bazaaris* was educated in religious elementary schools and sometimes received some training in the seminaries.[17] The other important occupation of the Shiite clergy, the legal profession, also connected the two groups. Up until the 1930s the *'olama* ran the entire judicial system, and after that continued to help in arbitrating disputes in the bazaar.[18] Thanks to their legal expertise and because the *'olama* traditionally had constituted a large percentage of the literate and educated population, merchants hired them as accountants,

---

[14] Ahmad Ashraf, "Bazaar-Mosque Alliance," 541.

[15] Farshid Mehri, *Masajed-e Bazar-e Tehran dar Nehzat-e Emam Khomayni* (Tehran: Markaz-e Asnad-e Enqelab-e Eslami, 1383 (2004)).

[16] Gustav Thaiss, "Religious Symbolism and Social Change: The Drama of Husain," in *Scholars, Saints, and Sufis: Muslim Religious Institutions in the Middle East since 1500*, ed. Nikki R. Keddie (Berkeley: University of California Press, 1972), p. 361; and Michael J. Fischer, "Portrait of a Molla," *Persica* 10 (1982), 232. Michael M. J. Fischer, *Iran: From Religious Dispute to Revolution* (Cambridge, MA: Harvard University Press), 1984, 95.

[17] Gustav Thaiss, "The Bazaar as a Case Study of Religion and Social Change," in *Iran Faces the Seventies*, ed. Yar-Shater (New York: Praeger Publishers, 1971), p. 195.

[18] Ibid., p. 190.

clerks, and notaries. The most frequently cited link between the bazaar and the mosque is economic. In many respects the *bazaaris* and guilds were the patrons of the Shiite hierarchy. They supported the religious institutions both via tithes[19] and spontaneous donations for the construction and restoration of mosques, seminaries, or charitable foundations. The final dimension of this multifaceted relationship between the clergy and the *bazaaris* is religious practice. The obvious function of the Shiite establishment is to provide religious services such as Friday prayers, special holiday ceremonies, marriage and burial services, and the private informal weekly meetings described in Chapter 3.

This cooperation has been argued to be the basis for the *'olama* and *bazaaris'* confrontations with the state. The prominent role enjoyed by both the clergy and the *bazaaris* in all of the major social movements across the twentieth century have been taken as evidence of the existence of this alliance, which has persisted despite economic modernization and ideological innovation. On closer examination of the recorded history, however, the robustness and utility of this approach becomes questionable. In reviewing these episodes of contentious politics I will now demonstrate the difficulties of mapping the collective action of the bazaar as an articulation of clerical inspiration or religious motivation.

Bazaar mobilization with and without the clergy

The twentieth century has been a century of social movements in Iran.[20] The century has included two revolutions (1906 and 1979), two coups (1921 and 1953), and a number of national movements that seriously challenged the regime's hold on power (e.g. 1951–3 and 1963). The ideologies and discourses of movement leaders differed within these movements as much as they did across them; they included constitutionalism, nationalism, anti-imperialism, and various interpretations of Islam, Marxism, and republicanism. These seemingly disparate social movements share a number of characteristics: they were all national in scope, were thoroughly urban, had heterogeneous social footings that cut across vertical and horizontal social cleavages, and challenged state power.

---

[19] Mottahedeh, *The Mantile of the Prophet*, p. 346; and Mohammad Shanehchi, interview by Habib Ladjevardi, tape recording no. 3, Paris, France, March 4, 1983, Iranian Oral History Collection, Harvard University, 13–14.

[20] For a useful comparison of Iran's numerous social movements see John Foran, ed., *A Century of Revolution: Social Movements in Iran* (Minneapolis: Minnesota University Press, 1994).

The existing *bazaari* networks were an important factor in creating many of these features. First, these commercial relations integrated multiple cities across the country into a single web of ongoing ties, which ultimately led back to the wholesalers in Tehran. Second, *bazaaris*, especially those in Tehran, have had ties with a variety of social groups (e.g. clerics and industrialists), and through their socioeconomic standing and middle-class sensibilities they (or their children) have been in contact with multiple urban realms (universities and intellectual circles) and ideological trends (nationalism, republicanism, and Islamist politics). Thus, they can mobilize or be mobilized by other sectors. Finally, as a propertied class, the *bazaaris'* economic interests often brought them into direct confrontation with the state's development agenda and economic policies.

Despite the bazaar's penchant for mobilization, it should be noted that in all the cases we are about to examine they acted in partnership with other social groups – clerics, intellectuals, and students. It is important not to overestimate the political role of the *bazaaris*; they have never single-handedly changed a regime and their resistance strategy has been defensive and in the spirit of an "avoidance protest," rather than an offensive and confrontational movement.[21] Their critical role in the movements has been organizational, acting as a liaison between classes and groupings and giving political currents a (very) public visage.

The tobacco protests (1890–2) and the Constitutional Revolution (1905–11)   While not formally colonized, during the nineteenth century Iran underwent a transition from dependent development to a commercial regime, which as in many other parts of the region and Asia undermined local merchants and artisans. Among the staple exports that were subject to foreign interests was tobacco.

At the end of the nineteenth century, the Qajar monarchy granted a tobacco concession to a British company conceding to them a monopoly over the buying, selling, and manufacturing of all tobacco in Iran for fifty years in return for an annual rent.[22] In response, merchants, wholesalers, and retailers in all the major cities protested by sending letters and telegrams to the Shah, distributing leaflets throughout the

---

[21] Douglas Haynes, "Merchant-State Relations in Surat, 1600–1924," in *Contesting Power: Resistance and Everyday Social Relations in South Asia*, ed. Douglas Haynes and Gyan Prakash (Berkeley: University of California Press, 1991).

[22] Nikki R. Keddie, *Religion and Rebellion in Iran: The Tobacco Protest of 1891–1892* (London: Frank Cass, 1966); and Mansoor Moaddel, "Shi'i Political Discourse and Class Mobilization in the Tobacco Movement of 1890–2," in *A Century of Revolution: Social Movements in Iran*, ed. John Foran (Minneapolis: Minnesota University Press, 1994).

cities, taking sanctuary in mosques, offering to pay a higher tax to the Shah, and even burning their tobacco – incidents that remind one of the Boston Tea Party. The merchants' resistance was endorsed by modernizing reformers in the court and the Russian Empire, which at that time was dueling with its British counterpart in the region. The *bazaari*s also solicited the backing of the clergy by arguing that the concessions violated the Islamic principles of free trade and were an affront to the independence of the nation and Muslim community. While many clergy remained indifferent or sided with the government, a number of clerics encouraged the protests out of political conviction or economic calculation (tobacco was an important cash crop grown on land held as private property by many clerics or as trusts bequeathed as support for religious institutions). Finally, a number of clerics, including one of the leading Ayatollahs, issued religious decrees forbidding the consumption of tobacco. The tobacco trade in the bazaars ceased and its consumption in the coffee houses and homes came to a halt; the Shah was forced to rescind the concessions.

A decade after the successful opposition to the Shah's economic policies, the bazaar community played a central role in Iran's Constitutional Revolution (1905–11), which furthered the dual resistance to monarchical despotism and European imperialism. The intellectual critique of absolute monarchy came from western-educated and -inspired thinkers and segments of the Shiite clergy who were sympathetic to tenets of consultation and the rule of law. Together they introduced the urban population to the principles of accountability, representative government, and political participation. Along with pressure from the urban population this coalition was able to formally end the arbitrary rule of the Qajar monarchy by establishing an elected parliament and drafting a constitution. The movement, however, failed to entrench a full-fledged constitutional monarchy with robust institutions to protect substantive civil and political rights or limit British and Russian interference in Iran's domestic politics, which continued, and even expanded.

The social force behind the movement was very much the urban bourgeoisie, in particular the commercial sector based almost exclusively in the bazaar. For the mercantile class, the monarchy's granting of economic concessions to European states and companies and their capricious taxation and customs policies were reason to rally against the Qajar dynasty. These grievances came to a head in 1905 when the governor of Tehran bastinadoed two prominent merchants for protesting against orders to lower the price of imported sugar. The Tehran Bazaar closed and hundreds of *bazaari*s took sanctuary (*bast*) in a shrine in southern Tehran where they called for the establishment of a House of Justice. This event in fact sparked the Constitutional Revolution. In the coming year, *bazaaris* again turned to their repertoires of contention – drafting and distributing leaflets, holding sit-ins in sanctuaries, and pressuring sympathetic clerics to support the foundation of a representative parliament (the Majles) and to oppose the monarchy. While a constitution was being ratified, the constitutional movement was fractured by internal disputes and external pressures. An important turning point was the defection of a group of clerics who questioned the compatibility of the Constitution with Islamic Law. Nonetheless, the majority of merchants and guild members did not break with the constitutional movement. The conflicts at the turn of the century illustrate a lack of unity among clergy and the independent agency of the Bazaar.

The Oil Nationalization Movement (1951–3)   The oil nationalization movement spearheaded by Mohammad Mosaddeq was the next national movement that featured the Tehran Bazaar as a major mobilizing force.[23] In 1951, Mosaddeq, a charismatic orator and pro-constitutionalist parliamentary representative, headed a coalition of parties known as the National Front in sponsoring a bill nationalizing Iran's oil industry. In a thoroughly popular move that flew in the face of Mohammad Reza Shah's passive stance vis-à-vis the Anglo-Iranian Oil Company and Britain's uncompromising attitude, Mosaddeq quickly became the magnetic symbol for anti-British and anti-Pahlavi, if not antimonarchist, sentiments that initially attracted a diverse array of political currents including the illegal communist Tudeh Party and an Islamic party affiliated with Ayatollah Abolqasem Kashani.

For the *bazaaris*, Mosaddeq's criticisms of government corruption and advocacy of a "national economy" centered on domestic capital was compelling.[24] As early as March 1945, the Tehran Bazaar orchestrated a closure to show support for Mosaddeq's criticisms of the Shah's cronies.[25] A principal ally of Mosaddeq's government was the active Society of Merchants, Guilds, and Artisans, which was established in 1951 and led by Mohammad Rasekh-Afshar, the leader for the *giveh*[26]–sellers' guild. It included such other notable supporters as Hasan

---

[23] Mark J. Gasirowski, "The 1953 *Coup d'Etat* in Iran," *International Journal of Middle East Studies* 19 (August 1987), 261–86.

[24] Ahmad Ashraf, "Nezam-e Senfi va Jame'eh-ye Madani," *Iran-nameh* 14 (Winter 1374 [1995]), 21.

[25] Ashraf, "Bazaar-Mosque Alliance," 548.

[26] *Giveh* are a type of shoe produced in Iran.

Shamshiri, Abolqasem Lebaschi, and Hasan Qasemiyyeh.[27] Throughout Mosaddeq's struggle to nationalize Iran's oil industry and increase
the powers of the parliament and the prime minister, the *bazaari*s
actively championed the cause by distributing announcements and
newspapers, and organizing rallies and demonstrations, most of which
set out from the Tehran Bazaar and ended in front of the parliament in
Baharestan Square. Moreover, they organized roughly fifty closures of
the marketplace as a display of opposition to the Shah's policies.[28]
*Bazaari*s also financially supported the Mosaddeq government. With the
vast majority of oil companies boycotting Iranian oil, the government's
solvency was under threat. When the government began selling national
bonds, *bazaari*s quickly began purchasing them to support the government.[29] Nonetheless, in August 1953, the prime minister's government
was ousted in a CIA-supported military coup, ending the constitutionalist and democratizing movement.

The Bazaar's opposition to the Shah and support for Mosaddeq were
in fact so great that despite the overthrow of the prime minister and his
military trial, merchants formed committees to oppose the coup and
continued to use closures to publicize their resistance to the Shah.[30] In
November 1953, even after student protesters were muzzled and
Tehran University was reopened, the Tehran Bazaar continued to
demonstrate against the Shah.[31] The *bazaari*s' actions earned them the
Shah's enmity, and three months after the coup, the regime responded
by exiling several of the bazaar organizers (including the famous res-
taurateur Shamshiri) and demolishing parts of the Bazaar's domed roof
and defacing its doors.[32]

In light of claims that the bazaar and the mosque are coupled in a
political alliance, it is significant to note that the bazaar remained loyal
to Mosaddeq's cause after Kashani defected from the coalition in the
summer of 1952; Kashani and a number of high-standing clerics even
actively supported the Shah and the coup.[33] Thus, the self-proclaimed

---

[27] Abol Ghassem Lebaschi, interview by Habib Ladjevardi, tape recording no. 1, Paris,
France, February 28, 1983, Iranian Oral History Collection, Harvard University, 5.

[28] Ibid., 9.

[29] Hasan Shamshiri, the owner of the most famous chelaw-kebab restaurant in the Tehran
Bazaar and staunch supporter of Mosaddeq, was one of the main purchasers of the
national bonds. After the coup, he was exiled to an island in the Persian Gulf.

[30] Mina Jabbari, *Hamisheh Bazar* (Tehran: Agah, 1379 (2000)), pp. 136–7.

[31] *New York Times*, October 9 and 11, 1953.

[32] *New York Times*, November 15, 1953; and Lebaschi, tape recording no. 1, 20.

[33] The clergy's support for the Shah increased their influence in the court in the 1950s.
For a detailed discussion of state–clergy relations in this era see Shahrough Akhavi,
Religion and Politics in Contemporary Iran: Clergy-State Relations in the Pahlavi Period
(Albany: State University of New York Press, 1980), chapter 3.

"golden era" of the bazaar[34] was largely independent of, and by the end in opposition to, the religious establishment's indifference and pro-Pahlavi posturing.

    The anti-White Revolution protests (1963)   A decade later a confluence of events and the emergence of Ayatollah Khomeini as a passionate rhetorician for anti-Pahlavi sentiments created another opportunity for mass action against the regime. By 1960 the backbone of the activists in the Society of Merchants, Guilds, and Artisans began to feel that the Shah's regime was again vulnerable.[35] The economy was in a dire state (high levels of inflation, bankruptcies, and labor disputes) with the International Monetary Fund prescribing a set of policies to limit imports, government spending, and credit. Meanwhile, the Eisenhower and Kennedy administrations began to see political liberalization as a means to ward off radicalism and communism in the Third World. Despite the suppression of dissident groups after his return to power, the Shah had not formed a social base for his regime, and therefore in 1961 he appointed a liberal prime minister to appease internal and external political criticism. Key among the changes was land reform. The Land Reform Law of 1962 was envisioned as a method to prepare the agricultural sector for modern techniques of production, and simultaneously to undermine the political power of landowning families and attempt directly to mobilize the peasantry via state institutions.[36] This limited program became the first plank of the Shah's White Revolution, which was to be approved in a plebiscite in January 1963. All the major political factions opposed the plebiscite, including the second National Front, the Liberation Movement of Iran (LMI), and the many members of the clergy. The Tehran Bazaar staged a strike for three days prior to the plebiscite. The state responded by arresting the leadership of the National Front and the LMI, including a number of activists from the Tehran Bazaar. With the liberal nationalist organizations stifled, *bazaari*s turned to a new protest network, Ayatollah Ruhollah Khomeini's seminary circle in Qom.[37]

    These events were all taking place at the time when Khomeini began to become a public leader. After the death of the leading cleric Ayatollah

---

[34] Ashraf, "Nezam-e Senfi va Jame'eh-ye Madani," 21.

[35] Lebaschi, tape recording no. 1, 20–1.

[36] Eric Hooglund, *Land and Revolution in Iran, 1960–1980* (Austin: University of Texas Press, 1982). Hooglund's study shows that the land reform succeeded in eroding the power of landlords and introduced the bazaars' merchants and moneylenders as a new source of agricultural credit.

[37] Lebaschi, tape recording no. 2, 9–10.

Borujerdi in March 1961, Khomeini began to take on a more public persona. His first public criticism was of the Shah's electoral reforms, which included women's suffrage, for which he was briefly imprisoned in 1962. On the issue of land reform, Khomeini joined the majority of clerics in opposing the plan, which threatened the interests of many clerics who owned agricultural land and the religious institutions that were supported by earnings from agricultural trusts.[38] Khomeini added his own vociferous attacks against the "tyrannical" Shah, whom he saw as making Iran dependent on the United States and Israel and endangering Islam and the clergy.[39] His outspokenness and uncompromising courage endeared him to politically inclined seminary students in Qom and religious activists. It also earned him another prison term prior to the plebiscite. In June 1963 in Tehran, during commemoration of Imam Hosayn's martyrdom, or 'Ashura, political protesters used the ritualistic mourning ceremonies as a cover for a demonstration with participants carrying pictures of Khomeini and chanting anti-Shah slogans.[40] Meanwhile in Qom, the recently released and unreprntant Khomeini bluntly attacked the Shah's regime. The next day, the equally persistent Pahlavi regime arrested him again. On that same day, when a large group of protesters, many of whom came from outlying regions of Tehran and the fruit and vegetable bazaar, congregated in front of the Tehran Bazaar, troops opened fire. The clashes lasted for three days and left several hundred dead or injured.[41] The protests were quelled. This political mobilization was undermined by a number of factors, including the imprisonment and suppression of secular groups since the 1953 coup, the relative quietism of university and high-school students, and unresponsiveness on the part of import–exporter merchants in the Bazaar.[42] Yet, for pro-Khomeini supporters the seeds of the Islamic Revolution were sown.

Most observers have neglected to note that *bazaari* mobilization in the summer of 1963 was in fact preceded by two years of political activism and collective action against the Shah's policies – activism that was largely independent of radical clerical protests.[43] At the beginning of the

---

[38] Akhavi, *Religion and Politics in Contemporary Iran*, pp. 91–105.

[39] For texts of his speeches at this time see Hamid Algar, *Islam and Revolution: Writings and Declarations of Imam Khomeini* (Berkeley: Mizan Press, 1981), pp. 174–88.

[40] Mehri, *Masajed-e Bazar-e Tehran*, p. 98.

[41] Ibid. 95–104. Khomeini was released on August 3, 1963, only to be detained and expelled from Iran in 1964 for staunchly criticizing a bill that gave U.S. military personnel diplomatic immunity.

[42] Mansoor Moaddel, "The Shi'i Ulama and the State in Iran," *Theory and Society* 15 (July 986), 544.

[43] The exception being Misagh Parsa, "Mosque of Last Resort: State Reform and Social Conflict in the Early 1960s," in *A Century of Revolution: Social Movements in Iran*, ed. John Foran (Minneapolis: Minnesota University Press, 1994).

decade, the *bazaaris* (predominantly retailers and artisans) who were hurt by tax reforms responded by refusing to pay taxes for three years. This conflict between the state and guilds came to the fore in spring 1963 when the state threatened to launch an antiprofiteering campaign and began to audit merchants who were delinquent in paying their taxes. Along with these economically motivated collective actions, there were a series of political moves. In 1960 the Tehran Bazaar, principally organized by the second National Front,[44] went on strike to protest the parliamentary elections that were widely believed to have been rigged.[45] Then in October 1961, *bazaaris* and shopowners around the parliament again went on strike, this time in support of the school teachers' national strike for higher salaries.[46] Also, *bazaaris* joined and organized meetings for the liberal and democratically inclined Union for the Safeguarding of the Constitution and Individual Rights.[47]

The Islamic Revolution (1977–1979)   The exact causes behind, the relative weight of coalition members in, and the motivation of participants in the Islamic Revolution are greatly disputed by participants and observers alike. However, it is agreed that the Revolution brought together a wide array of social groups and political factions into a mass insurrection that culminated in the overthrow of the monarchy and the establishment of the Islamic Republic. It is also generally accepted that the bazaars in Iran were, to borrow the chapter title from Misagh Parsa's account, "the eye of the storm."[48] The Tehran Bazaar, the wealthiest, most populated and commercially central market, was particularly vital. In this section, I attempt only to summarize the collective action of *bazaaris* in Tehran and other major cities during the build-up to the demise of the monarchy to show how germane it was to the coordination and mobilization of the insurgency.

---

[44] Shanehchi, tape recording no. 2.

[45] Mottahedeh, *The Mantle of the Prophet*, p. 36.

[46] Parsa, "Mosque of Last Resort," 145–7.

[47] Hossein Bashiriyeh, *The State and Revolution in Iran 1962–1982* (New York: St. Martin Press, 1984), 23.

[48] Misagh Parsa, *Social Origins of the Iranian Revolution* (New Brunswick: Rutgers University Press, 1989), chapter 4. While I generally agree with Parsa's careful narration and analysis of the Islamic Revolution and I rely on it extensively for this section, I am less confident that "Bazaari mobilization and collective action quickly emerged as the most significant features of the revolutionary conflicts and were of primary importance in bringing down the Pahlavi regime" (p. 92). I believe Parsa underestimates the importance of the economically crippling strikes by industrial workers in the fall of 1978 that led to the Shah's imposition of the military government in November 1978 and the final collapse in January and February 1979. It was not until the mass strikes joined the bazaars' year-long activism that the power of the regime was breached.

The underlying causes of the *bazaaris'* opposition to the state lay in their systematic lack of access to state resources and institutions, as described previously. But the immediate events that led to the bazaar's opposition to the regime were a series of ill-designed and mismanaged government policies, which not only threatened *bazaari* interests, but directed their antagonism toward the state and provided an opening to challenge the regime.

Principal among these was the state's antiprofiteering campaign, which began in August 1975.[49] This heavily touted initiative, which was added as the fourteenth principle of the White Revolution, was aimed at reducing the high inflation rate. The main sources of inflation were the increased cost of imports, labor shortages, and the inability of the economy efficiently to absorb high levels of capital brought on by expansive development projects after the 1973 oil boom. The Shah, however, was convinced that the root cause was profiteering on the part of shopkeepers. To lower prices, profits had to be curbed, and the state had to intervene in the value chains.

The Chamber of Guilds, established by the state in the same year, was made responsible for imposing price-fixing rules and adjudicating cases. Retail prices were set at profit rates that were half the rate of inflation.[50] The draconian measures included the establishment of "Supervision Teams" composed of 10,000 newly hired inspectors, many of whom were university students who received cash bonuses for ticketing offenders. Inspectors had the right to hand out instant fines and recommend penalties of prison terms, internal exile, and closure of businesses.[51] When retailers argued that they were forced to sell at high prices because of inflated wholesaler and producer prices, the government commissioned the Chamber of Commerce, Industries and Mines to impose price controls on wholesale goods and to void the import licenses of those who did not comply, which only led to corruption, capital flight, and decline in production in the industrial sector.[52]

---

[49] Mehdi Motameni, interview by Habib Ladjevardi, tape recording no. 3, St. Martin, Netherlands, April 30, 1986, Iranian Oral History Collection, Harvard University; Ervand Abrahamian, *Iran: Between Two Revolutions* (Princeton: Princeton University Press 1982); pp. 496–8; Davoud Ghandchi-Tehrani, "Bazaaris and Clergy: Socio-economic Origins of Radicalism and Revolution in Iran," Ph.D. dissertation, City University of New York, 1982, 93–4; and *Keyhan International*, October 2, 1978.

[50] Parsa, *Social Origins of the Iranian Revolution*, p. 83.

[51] *Keyhan International*, October 2, 1978.

[52] Motameni, interview; and Ghassem Ladjevardi, interview by Habib Ladjevardi, tape recording no. 2, Los Angeles, California, January 29, 1983, Iranian Oral History Collection, Harvard University, 16–18.

The results of the campaign were sweeping: the government fined and closed down 250,000 businesses, sentenced 8,000 businessmen to jail terms ranging from two months to three years, and deported 23,000 to remote areas of the country. Furthermore, the state publicly humiliated those charged with profiteering by placing their names on banners and in newspapers. A number of respected individuals in the Tehran Bazaar, as well as prominent industrialists were also charged with profiteering (e.g. Habib Elghanian, Mohammad Vahhabzadeh, and 'Ali Khosraw-shahi), but ordinary retailers and *bazaari*s, whom the political elite had already deemed to be pariah forms of traditionalists, made up the overwhelming majority of those sentenced. During the Revolution, a *bazaari* recalled, "Almost every bazaari family has had someone who suffered from the shah's program, ... as if we were the cause of all of Iran's inflation."[53] At the end of the summer of 1977, members of the Tehran Bazaar met with government officials, but as usual they were unresponsive. In the end, when the guild courts were closed in November 1978 (two months before the Shah's departure from Iran), inflation was not reduced (in fact the store closures and cancellation of import taxes only helped to worsen supply shortages), and the bazaar's animosity toward the regime had turned into a revolutionary torrent. A *bazaari* told a western journalist, "We were made the whipping boy of Iran to create a smoke screen for the vast corruption that was going on in the government and in the bosom of the royal family."[54]

This antiprofiteering campaign coincided with a number of other government policies that attacked the bazaar's interest. For instance, the government announced a plan to raise taxes by charging social security dues for all workers, including temporary employees. In addition, a law aimed at curbing land speculation by placing limits on the sale of undeveloped land hurt the economic interests of the propertied middle class.[55] Although this was not intended as a direct attack on the bazaar, since many *bazaari*s had been actively investing in property and land, they were adversely impacted by this measure. In December 1976 the government also sought to regulate business practices by fixing store hours and charging a heavy fine for violators.[56] Finally, the municipalities even talked of building an eight-lane highway through the Tehran Bazaar and converting it into a market along the lines of London's Convent Garden.[57]

---

[53] *Wall Street Journal*, November 30, 1978.
[54] *New York Times*, December 17, 1978.
[55] Ibid. This was brought up in my discussions with *bazaari*s.
[56] Ghandchi-Tehrani, "Bazaaris and Clergy," p. 94.
[57] *Keyhan International*, October 2, 1978.

The *bazaari*s transformed this growing laundry list of grievances into political action against the state. The most fundamental form of protest during the Revolution was closure of the bazaar across the country. During the initial buildup to the Revolution (from the fall of 1977 to the fall of 1978), when protests were limited to leftist activists, radical religious circles, and old liberal nationalists, the major bazaars in Iran struck repeatedly, with the Tehran Bazaar often taking the lead role.[58] For example, Mehdi Bazargan recalls that when the Society of Merchants, Artisans, and Guilds along with members of the Liberation Movement of Iran called for the first national closure of bazaars to commemorate the anniversary of the 1963 uprising, the bazaars in Isfahan, Mashhad, and Tabriz were completely closed and 70 percent of those in the Tehran Bazaar did not open their stores and offices.[59] By the time the Revolution had expanded into a multiclass constellation with industrial workers, white-collar workers and government bureaucrats joining in the fall and winter of 1978, the bazaars were on almost continual strike. The first national bazaar closing took place on October 16, 1978, in commemoration of the killings on Black Friday Zhaleh Square.[60] These closures were a powerful economic measure to undermine the regime. As the principal commercial center in Iranian cities, and in the case of the Tehran Bazaar the main wholesale center in the country, the strikes crippled the economy and resonated through nationwide economic channels.[61] Moreover, as a highly visible and historically meaningful form of protest, the bazaars' closures were an evocative symbol of political conflict. It was the sort of action that had Iranians talking about the bazaar being "*sholugh.*" Strikes also freed some *bazaari*s to engage in other political activities. A *bazaari* told me that he has never read as many newspapers and political books as he did during the strikes of 1978.

The strikes also often coincided with another public form of protest, the mass rally. Ashraf and Banuazizi calculated that out of the 2,483 demonstrations reported during the course of the Revolution, almost two-thirds were organized by the mosque–bazaar alliance (with a quarter being organized by secondary school and university students

---

[58] Misagh Parsa, *States, Ideologies, and Social Revolutions: A Comparative Analysis of Iran, Nicaragua, and the Philippines* (Cambridge: Cambridge University Press, 2000), pp. 208–10.

[59] Mehdi Bazargan, *Enqelab-e Iran dar Daw Harekat* (Tehran: n.p., 1363 (1984)), p. 45.

[60] *Resalat*, 20 Esfand 1365 (March 11, 1987). Over half of the strikes during the critical months of October and November 1978 involved elements of bazaars, universities, and high schools. Ahmad Ashraf and Ali Banuazizi, "The State, Classes and Modes of Mobilization in the Iranian Revolution," *State, Culture and Society* 1 (Spring 1985), p. 25.

[61] Hooglund, *Land and Revolution in Iran*, p. 140.

and teachers).[62] Many of these political rallies were organized on religious occasions (days marking the births and martyrdoms of Shiite Imams) and forty-day mourning commemorations for people killed by the regime.[63] Thus, the rallies turned into cyclical confrontations with the state that sustained opposition throughout 1978. Mosque associations were critical in smoothly coordinating the rallies, which brough together tens and even hundreds of thousands of participants.[64] As in earlier conflicts, these rallies often began from the bazaar area, but they now often ended at Tehran University, rather than the Majles, as was the case in earlier decades. The shift from the Majles, to university campuses and high schools[65] was indicative of a number of transformations, including the demise of all public deliberative institutions during the last two decades of Pahlavi rule, the emergence of a politicized middle class based very much in institutions of higher education, and a northward shift in the city center.

The bazaar-based organizations also supported the political activities and strikes of other social groups. They set up and collected funds for university professors, workers in the oil industry, and journalists who at various stages struck and were thus without income. To coordinate these activities and organize the mobilization, the Tehran Bazaar also established a number of committees, including the Committee for the Affairs of Prisoners, the Committee for the Families of Martyrs, the Committee for the Support of Combatants, and the Committee for the Organization for Rallies.[66] The Committee for Printing and Distribution of Information was responsible for the widespread distribution of fliers announcing meetings and making declarations, as well as copying and circulating audio-cassette recordings of Khomeini's speeches in Najaf. The *bazaaris'* resources and access to publishing and copying offices became political resources; the distribution networks essential for national commodity markets were equally vital in creating a market for political opposition statements. All of these activities expanded the social base of the Revolution and maintained the mobilization for months on end.

In the effort to understand the revolutionary movement and the Islamic nature of the subsequent government, analysts have tended to emphasize and interpret the actions and motivations of participants in

[62] Ibid., p. 25.

[63] Islamic custom calls on Muslims to mourn the deceased on the seventh and fortieth day after the death of a loved one.

[64] Lebaschi, tape recording no. 3, 5–6.

[65] Tehran University was also surrounded by a number of well-established high schools and technical schools. Thus, what was then Shah Reza Street (now Islamic Revolution Street) was an apt site for congregation and contention.

[66] *Entekhab*, 13 Day 1379 (January 2, 2001).

the Islamic Revolution in primarily cultural and religious terms. However, a prospective, as opposed to a retrospective, analysis tends to demonstrate important nuances in the timing of events, demands of participants, and heterogeneity within groups. Most significantly, it suggests a greater degree of *bazaari* independence from the clergy than the concept of the mosque–bazaar alliance would predict.

First, there is an important temporal variation in participation in the anti-Pahlavi movement.[67] The *bazaari* community was one of the first groups to join the wave of protests that culminated in the Iranian Revolution of 1979. Aggrieved by the regime's economic policies, in 1977 *bazaaris* joined liberal nationalists who began to confront the regime's authoritarianism and call on it to protect human rights and conduct free and fair elections. In March 1977, the Tehran Bazaar also sided with the university community by closing in support of their protests against the government's plan to move the Aryamehr University from Tehran to the politically less influential city of Isfahan. *Bazaaris* helped students establish and publicize a fund and encourage professors who went on strike and had their salaries reduced.[68] Sadeq Ziba-Kalam, currently a political scientist at Tehran University, remembers that "the bazaar enjoyed a great deal of popularity among academics and intellectuals in the pre-revolutionary era. During the Shah's reign the bazaar had the highest number of political prisoners after the university. Most of the demonstrations that began in the [Tehran] Bazaar ended in front of the university; similarly the students marched toward the Bazaar. This link was quite visible at that time."[69] The existence of close relations between the Tehran Bazaar and the universities was not lost on outside observers either. Jonathan Kandell, a *New York Times* reporter covering the revolution, wrote a piece on how the students and *bazaaris* had formed an alliance.[70] When I mentioned the issue of bazaar-university cooperation to *bazaaris* a number of them pointed out that notwithstanding the expectation and desire for their sons to work in the "free sector," education was very important to *bazaaris*. They were well aware that only a university education provided not only the necessary

---

[67] This section follows the analysis by Ashraf and Banuazizi, "The State, Classes and Modes of Mobilization in the Iranian Revolution," and Parsa, *Social Origins of the Iranian Revolution.*

[68] Lebaschi, tape recording no. 3, 1. Also, the Tehran Bazaar was the site of a university student and faculty gathering after the death of 'Ali Shariati. Daftar-e Adabiyyat-e Enqelab-e Eslami, *Ruz-shomar-e Enqelab-e Eslami,* vol. 1 (Tehran: Hawzeh-ye Honari-ye Sazman-e Tablighat-e Eslami, 1376 (1997), 290.

[69] Amir Nakha'i, "Tahazzob va Sakhtar-e Eqtesadi," *Jame'eh-ye Salem* 7 (Esfand 1376 (March 1998)), p. 30.

[70] *New York Times,* November 7, 1978.

skills and access to new technologies for success in an industrial economy, but also social standing and status in a modern society.[71] University education was also a means to cultivate ties with the new middle class. Thus, *bazaaris* generally encouraged their children to seek higher education. With their sons, and to a lesser extent their daughters, attending universities in Tehran and abroad, many *bazaaris* became aware of the campus activities, concerns, and ideological developments, such as Islamist and leftist politics.

The principal *bazaari* agitators in this early stage were activists allied with the National Front and sympathetic to Mehdi Bazargan and Mahmud Taleqani's Liberation Movement of Iran. These were not the Islamist and clerical groups centered in the seminaries. These liberal nationalists and Muslim intellectuals had seized upon several political opportunities to call for reforms and organize small groupings. For example, in 1977 Lebaschi, who continued to be a major voice for the National Front in the Bazaar, actively organizing groups and meetings, publishing and distributing political pamphlets, was followed and questioned by the secret police.[72] In October 1977, the diverse grouping of politically active *bazaaris* organized a service to commemorate the death of Khomeini's son. While an earlier clerical memorial passed with little attention, the Tehran Bazaar closed so shopkeepers could attend this ceremony at the nearby mosque. These events and other such actions, while far from being revolutionary in goal or seriously challenging the power of the regime to rule, predate the mobilization of religious radicals headed by Khomeini or moderate clerics (e.g. Shari'atmadari). It was only in January 1978, after troops massacred seminary students in Qom, that clerics began to join the movement against the regime and the bazaar–mosque mobilizing structure came to the fore.

The prevailing demands in the protest statements issued by *bazaari* organizations are also revealing. Even though in these declarations, the movement was described as "Islamic" and in defense of "innocent" and "deprived Muslims," they called only rarely for the establishment of an Islamic government or defended the clergy as a class.[73] Instead, the statements consistently called for rather ecumenical objectives such as the end to political violence and repression, the removal of despotism, and the creation of an independent Iran free of imperialism. Exhibiting the strong liberating nature of the struggle, in June 1978 a *bazaari* told a

---

[71] W. H. Hallman, "The Tabriz Bazaar," airgram from U.S. consulate in Tabriz to Department of State, September 9, 1964.
[72] Lebaschi, tape recording no. 2, 13–20.
[73] Parsa, *States, Ideologies, and Social Revolutions*, pp. 212–13.

New York Times reporter, "A sound society must have freedom. Or what good is material progress? We don't want to live in a golden cage."[74] Like earlier movements, the *bazaari*s tended to favor nationalist and broadly democratic politics that promised to give them access to the polity.

During the Revolution, those *bazaari*s who participated in the movement against the Shah fell under the umbrella of three factions: Khomeini's circle of supporters, the Liberation Movement of Iran,[75] and National Front.[76] It is simply impossible directly to evaluate the relative weight of each group since we have no opinion data from that era, existing collections of statements and petitions put together in Iran are designed to serve the state's official narrative, and interviews conducted after the Revolution are highly unreliable since responses are heavily colored by postrevolutionary outcomes and experiences. Compounding the problem of deficient sources, the political groupings in the bazaars, with the possible exception of the National Front-aligned Society of Merchants, Guilds, and Artisans and Khomeini's supporters based in the ICA, did not have formal and public institutions that actively sought to integrate and mobilize *bazaari*s. Political relations were diffuse and fluid, and affiliations were muted, with support given to individual political figures rather than loyalty to parties or platforms. The secondary literature that has conducted serious analysis of *bazaari* politics agrees that *bazaari*s did not speak with one voice.[77] However, given the evidence it seems fair to conclude that during the revolutionary build-up that overthrew the Pahlavi regime, the Khomeini faction, although quite powerful in terms of organization, ideological commitment, and doctrinal uniformity, neither was the sole voice of the Bazaar

---

[74] *New York Times*, June 4, 1978.
[75] Chehabi argues that although many members of the LMI had roots in the Bazaar and a few were active members within it, there was little active party interaction with the bazaar community. Instead he believes that the National Front had more direct ties. H. E. Chehabi, *Iranian Politics and Religious Modernism: The Liberation Movement of Iran under the Shah and Khomeini* (Ithaca, NY: Cornell University Press, 1990), pp. 95–7. Nonetheless, it is important to note that while the LMI as an association was perhaps not as popular as the National Front, individual members such as Taleqani (despite his egalitarian reading of Islam) and Bazargan were highly respected and supported by large segments of the Tehran Bazaar. Taleqani was (and continues to be) particularly popular among *bazaari*s, who see him as a cleric who was "open-minded" and comfortable with accommodating modernity and Islam. Many merchants gave their religious taxes to him. *Wall Street Journal*, February 1, 1979.
[76] Parsa claims that the principal activists in the bazaars were the liberal nationalists. Parsa, *States, Ideologies, and Social Revolutions*, pp. 207–9.
[77] Ashraf, "Nezam-e Senfi va Jame'eh-ye Madani," 5–40; Shaul Bakhash, *The Reign of the Ayatollahs: Iran and the Islamic Revolution* (New York: Basic Books, 1990); and Parsa, *Social Origins of the Iranian Revolution*.

nor dominated the Bazaar in terms of numbers or dictated their actions and demands.

   1975: a revolutionary situation, but nonrevolutionary outcome   The political relationship between the mosque and the bazaar appears especially circumstantial once we take into consideration the instance of nonmobilization in June 1975. In separate works, Parsa and Kurzman have judiciously compared the often forgotten Qom uprising of 1975 and that of January 1978, which was one of the founding events of the revolution.[78] On June 5, 1975, more than a thousand seminarians close to Khomeini held a three-day sit-in at one of Qom's well-known seminaries to commemorate the 1963 uprising. The government responded by sending in the military, killing dozens and closing down the seminary. In a show of support, seminary students in Mashhad (the second most important center for religious learning) demonstrated against the state's repression, and Khomeini sent a letter of condolences to the Iranian people in which he again chastised the Shah. However, *bazaari*s did not participate in the protests or close their shops in support of the seminaries.[79] Unlike during similar events in January 1978, the bazaar was not directly attacked by the state (e.g. the antiprofiteering campaign did not start until August 1975). The economy, although far from sound, remained quite profitable for the propertied classes, and the political openings and broad political and social alliances that existed in 1977 and 1978 were not available. Finally, this revolutionary situation, but nonevent, so shortly before the Revolution suggests that religious authority and mobilization are not sufficient conditions for *bazaari* mobilization; were this the case, June 1975 would have been an ideal moment for the bazaar to ally itself with the mosque.[80]

   Reflections on the mosque–bazaar alliance   Reviewing the many instances of mobilization against the state, one cannot help but notice the consistent role of both the clergy and the *bazaari*s in these struggles. Specifically, religious organizations and sites, many of which were located in the bazaars, were critical organizational means for mobilization. The diffuse religious associations that helped generate crosscutting

---

[78] Parsa, *Social Origins of the Iranian Revolution*, pp. 100–2; Charles Kurzman, "The Qum Protests and the Coming of the Iranian Revolution, 1975 and 1978," *Social Science History* 27(Fall 2003), 287–325.

[79] Parsa, *Social Origins of the Iranian Revolution*, pp. 100–2.

[80] A similar comparison can be made between the merchants' participation in the tobacco protests in the 1890s, and their lack of participation in the protests against the Reuters concession to build the railroad in the 1870s. Janet Afary, *The Iranian Constitutional Revolution, 1906–1911* (New York: Columbia University Press, 1996), p. 30.

and multifaceted relations in the bazaar, with their expertise in organizing communal religious events to celebrate religious holidays and commemorate the martyrdom of the Imams, were a powerful resource in planning and orchestrating collective protests of hundreds and even thousands of demonstrators. In the midst of the Revolution the well-known editor and journalist for the *Keyhan* daily Amir Taheri noted, "As far as bringing together crowds is concerned the bazaar is still the best organised and most efficient organisation in the major cities. This is done through a network of 'procession leaders' who organise religious gatherings at times of mourning in the months of Ramazan, Moharram, and Safar of the Arab lunar calendar."[81] He estimated that there were 5,000 procession organizers "at the disposal of the bazaar." When asked by a western journalist, a shop owner in the Tehran Bazaar stated that "he can muster at least 10 and sometimes up to 50 people from his 'territory' in southern Tehran for a procession or demonstration."[82] Additionally, given that the clergy enjoyed a high social standing in society, they were also important for gaining a modicum of legitimacy for social movements. The pulpit was a potentially powerful vehicle to transform the protests of the commercial class into those of the general public. Thus, the preexisting networks made it "natural" for *bazaaris* to turn to the clergy for protection and support against despotic attacks by the state.

While it is correct to say that mosque–bazaar relations are heavily intertwined, both parties were well represented in all national political movements, and coupled together they constituted an astounding organizational force, assuming that these factors translate into a political or ideological alliance is a different matter. As the narrative above illustrates, clerical activism and *bazaari* collective action do not neatly map onto one another as the mosque–bazaar alliance paradigm at its most assertive would have us believe. First, we have cases when the members of the religious establishment have mobilized against the state, while the bazaar community has remained aloof (June 1975). Conversely, there are other instances when the bazaar community has maintained its mobilization against the state even after leading clerics had withdrawn their support (Constitutional Revolution and oil nationalization movement). Finally, as the discussion of the tobacco protests, the 1963 uprising, and the Islamic Revolution illustrate, the Tehran Bazaar at times was engaged in collective action prior to clerical endorsement and participation. Overall, this reading suggests a larger

---

[81] *Keyhan International,* October 2, 1978.
[82] *Wall Street Journal,* November 30, 1978.

degree of autonomy between *bazaari* collective action and clerical mobilization than the historiography acknowledges.[83]

What are the reasons underlying the empirical shortcomings of the mosque–bazaar alliance hypotheses? First, even if the majority of the *bazaaris* were mobilized against the state in these episodes, "the mosque" has not uniformly or consistently supported these initiatives, and they have not always provided an ideological logic for such politics. As an opaque hierarchy consisting of largely independent thinkers and patronage systems, the clerics have advocated and legitimated different – even contradictory – positions from one another and at each particular historical juncture. For example, after the January 1978 killing of the students in Qom, Khomeini, who did not support the 1953 movement, called for mass mobilization, and the high-ranking Ayatollah Shari'atmadari rejected a call for a national strike at this stage, while another high-ranking cleric, Ayatollah Khansari, went so far as to advise *bazaaris* in Tehran not to strike.[84] Even if we believe that Shiite theology embodies an oppositional stance to secular rule[85] or is a "culture conducive to challenge authority,"[86] as this and many other examples from Iranian, Iraqi, Azeri and Lebanese history illustrate, the individual clerical interpretation of both Shiite Islam and political situations may not lead to opposition to the state.[87] Similarly, the bazaar community, while enjoying a "solidarity structure," has exhibited diversity. In terms of class, merchants were more prominent in 1882 and 1905–11, while retailers and small wholesalers took the initiative in 1963 and 1978–9. Ethnicity also mattered to some degree, with the large Azeri community in the Tehran Bazaar and the enormous popularity of the moderate constitutionalist Ayatollah Shari'atmadari. Finally, as the discussion of the Islamic Revolution suggests, cleavages in political ideology were also prevalent among members of the Bazaar. Thus, both the bazaar and the

---

[83] Vanessa Martin develops a similar argument regarding the highly textured nature of the relationship between clerics and merchants during the Constitutional Revolution. See *Islam and Modernism: The Iranian Revolution of 1906* (New York: Syracuse University Press, 1989).

[84] Parsa, *States, Ideologies, and Social Revolutions*, p. 139.

[85] Hamid Algar, "The Oppositional Role of the Ulama in Twentieth-Century Iran," in *Scholars, Saints, and Sufis: Muslim Religious Institutions in the Middle East since 1500*, ed. Nikki Keddie (Berkeley: University of California Press, 1972).

[86] Theda Skocpol, "Rentier State and Shi'a Islam in the Iranian Revolution," *Theory and Society* 11 (May 1982), 275.

[87] Moaddel, "The Shi'i Ulama and the State in Iran," 519–56; Azar Tabari, "The Role of the Clergy in Modern Iranian Politics," in *Religion and Politics in Iran*, ed. Nikki R. Keddie (New Haven: Yale University Press, 1983); and Willem M. Floor, "The Revolutionary Character of the Ulama: Wishful Thinking or Reality?" in *Religion and Politics in Iran*, ed. Nikki R. Keddie (New Haven: Yale University Press, 1983).

mosque are more heterogeneous than narratives based on the mosque–bazaar alliance will have us believe. The apparent homogeneity of each group and the general compatibility of their actions vis-à-vis the social movements says more about these movements' multiclass and populist qualities than about an essential affinity between movement participants.

Second, the implied causal relationship between the *bazaaris*' religiosity and their politics is questionable on many fronts. To begin with, one may question the assumption that *bazaaris* are as religious as outsiders assume. This is ostensibly the argument laid out by Jabbari, Parsa, Lebaschi, Rotblat, Smith, and many of the secular *bazaaris* I met.[88] While I am sympathetic to this view and believe that for many *bazaaris* in Tehran, religion may be more of a "private matter" than non-*bazaaris* assume, this is a disputable empirical argument and one that needs substantiation. As a factual matter, this is difficult (and I believe unlikely) to assess since we lack adequate data about religiosity among the *bazaaris*, and more importantly a comparison to other social groups. Here I believe anecdotal evidence from interviews in the bazaar (especially in the postrevolutionary era) is insufficient and misleading.

Putting aside the countless issues of measuring religiosity, we face the even more basic problem of interpretation. Even if we had data on frequency of prayer, alms giving, and attendance at religious festivities, we would still have to contemplate what exactly this tells us about the politics of *bazaaris*.

In everyday affairs, religious language and gestures do exist as either cultural symbols representing trustworthiness or assemblages of personal faith. As part of an economy that is heavily based on reputation, religious markers (being a *hajji*, fingering rosary beads, not looking into a woman's eyes, and peppering one's speech with religious references and vocabulary) act as a particularly useful means to demonstrate trustworthiness to strangers. Similarly, public religious acts (e.g. paying one's religious taxes, making financial contributions to shrines and organizing public ceremonies) are a means to maintain standing within the community.[89] These individual public acts, even if prevalent at the level of the entire

---

[88] Jabbari, *Hamisheh Bazar*; Lebaschi, tape recording no. 3; Parsa, *States, Ideologies, and Social Revolutions*, pp. 202–3; Howard J. Rotblat, "Stability and Change in an Iranian Provincial Bazaar," Ph.D. dissertation, The University of Chicago, 1972; and Benjamin Smith, "Collective Action with and without Islam: Mobilizing the Bazaar in Iran," in *Islamic Activism: A Social Movement Theory Approach*, ed. Quintan Wiktorowicz (Bloomington: Indiana University Press, 2004).

[89] Rotblat, "Stability and Change in an Iranian Provincial Bazaar." In my experience, doctrinally religious Iranians are also skeptical of the *bazaaris*' religiosity. In fact, in Ja'far Shahri's social history of Tehran he comments that "the religious called the bazaar a *kofrestan*," or "a place of sin." Taken from Jabbari *Hamisheh Bazar*, p. 142.

group, however, do not necessarily imply a single political ideology based on Islam. Theoretically speaking, to assume otherwise would be to overly reify Islam. *Bazaari*s, who as a whole became increasingly literate and socially mobile during the twentieth century, like all Muslims, are capable of and comfortable in interpreting their religious faith in ways that create distinct spheres for the sacred and the profane, or of constructing exegeses to justify their consumption patterns (e.g. imbibing alcohol, smoking opium, charging interest, and soliciting prostitutes) and diverse political ends (e.g. nationalist, socialist, xenophobic, monarchist, and Islamist) that diverge from doctrine. Moreover, the level of religiosity does not seem to correlate with politics. In 1953, when it is reasonable to assume that *bazaari*s were more observant than they were in the 1970s, the bazaar diverged from the majority of the clerical establishment in its support for Mosaddeq's government.

Let us assume that *bazaari*s are "religious" (read: practicing and believing some form of Shite Islam that is considered orthalox). What evidence do we have that *bazaari*s' faith shapes their politics? For one segment it most certainly does. The position of the members of the ICA is dogmatically based on the Islamist belief that Islam is a holistic way of life, one that can and should be the basis for government, and the preservation of Islam should be the end of politics. This, however, is a minority position that is not held exclusively by *bazaari*s, and it is surely erroneous to extrapolate the ideology of tens of thousands of *bazaari*s from the views of these few Islamist *bazaari*s. Given that nationalists and liberal Islamists also held meetings in the Bazaar's mosques in the 1970s,[90] the idiom of religion was politically quite inclusive. Lebaschi, admittedly a *bazaari* who was a committed supporter of the National Front, argues that even those *bazaari*s who are religious do not pursue religion as a political ideology.[91] My experience as a participant observer in the Bazaar also made me aware that we should be wary of overreading the political meaning and significance of religious practices. For instance, many observers of Shiite Islam point out the political dimension of its founding myth, which is commemorated every year. The story of Imam Hosayn's martyrdom and self-sacrifice in opposition to illegitimate and unjust rulers may very well be used by some as an analogy for contemporary struggles and transform them opportunities for collective action. However, participation in communal rituals memorializing Imam Hosayn does not represent political indoctrination.[92] As my interviewees told me, only those who are already

---

[90] Mehri, *Masajed-e Bazar-e Tehran dar Nehzat-e Emam Khomayni*, pp. 226–7.
[91] Lebaschi, tape recording no. 3, 15.
[92] Asef Bayat, *Street Politics: Poor People's Movements in Iran* (New York: Columbia University Press, 1997), p. 43 and note 39.

predisposed to read religion as a political model interpret them as such. Finally, we lack public opinion data from Iran, but the data we have leads us to question the so-called "common wisdom." Mark Tessler's findings that religiosity among Arab Muslims has a weaker effect on political views than is often believed would surely make us question the causal relationship in the Iranian case.[93] In short, even if we conclude that *bazaaris* are exceptionally religious (in comparison to other Iranians, Tehranis, and Muslims), this does not necessarily have a consistent or causal impact on political sentiments and actions.

In a similar vein there is another problem with arguments relating the religiosity within the Bazaar to the politics of its members, and that is that even if *bazaaris* are religious and they base their politics on religion, it does not logically follow that they advocate clerical rule or supported Khomeini's political vision prior to the establishment of the Islamic Republic. Lebaschi mentions that the Bazaar may have helped Khomeini on an isolated, individual basis, but the organizations in the Tehran Bazaar did not champion Khomeini as much as they supported the revolutionary movement as a whole.[94] Skeptics may point out that Lebaschi was closely allied with the secular and liberal National Front and was therefore unaware of Khomeini's following, or simply unwilling to acknowledge it. However, Mohammad Shanehchi, a broker in the Tehran Bazaar and an activist closely affiliated with the Liberation Movement of Iran who had contacts with Khomeini and his students, also downplays the Bazaar's support for Khomeini. He recalls that the Bazaar gave financial help to Khomeini, but that almost every single group donated to Khomeini as well social.[95] When I discussed the Bazaar's activities during the Revolution, rather like the rest of society, *bazaaris* downplayed the support for Khomeini and distinguished between general support for the Revolution and specific endorsement of a particular strain or ideological agenda. One interviewee mentioned that reputable brokers, who often collected donations and organized guild-based activities, refused to collect funds for any particular party or individual. Instead, those *bazaaris* who did want to finance Khomeini would make deposits to an account established by his followers ("Account 100" at Melli Bank). The hesitance of *bazaaris* as a corporate group

---

[93] Mark Tessler, "Islam and Democracy in the Middle East: The Impact of Religious Orientations on Attitudes towards Democracy in Four Arab Countries," *Comparative Politics* 34 (April 2002), 337–54. These general findings about the relationship between the religiosity of Muslims and their political opininons are documented in many other publications by Tessler and his coauthors and students.
[94] Lebaschi, tape recording no. 3, 2.
[95] Shanehchi, tape recording no. 4, 3.

to collect funds and donate them to any individual person or specific political current signals that the *bazaari*s themselves were cognizant of heterogeneous political views within the Bazaar during the Revolution. Rather like much of society, *bazaari*s uniformly targeted the power of the Pahlavi regime, but diverged on issues of how to recast state power.

The immediate postrevolutionary era and consolidation of power in the hands of the leaders of the Islamic Republican Party (IRP) also challenges the assumption that *bazaari* actions are determined by political Islam or Khomeini's brand of clerical politics. We can infer the Bazaar's overall stance toward Khomeini's faction from its backing of President Bani-Sadr (January 1979–June 1981), who was allied with lay Islamists and secular organizations, and opposition to the clerically dominated IRP, which advocated Khomeini's hard-line and increasingly exclusionary interpretation of Islamic government. During 1980 and 1981, the *bazaari*s siding with more liberal professional associations and student factions organized a series of protests against the IRP, which was steadily monopolizing all institutions of state power.[96] When Bani-Sadr's foreign minister was arrested, the *bazaari*s in Tehran organized protests and secured 30,000 signatures for a petition calling for his release.[97] Meanwhile, *bazaari*s in Isfahan rallied in defense of their parliamentary representative, who was attacked by the IRP for defending Bani-Sadr, and condemned the IRP's repressive tactics.[98] *Bazaari*s also shied away from an IRP-organized meeting in the main mosque in the Tehran Bazaar,[99] and verbally attacked Mohammad-'Ali Rajaii, the prime minister and a member of the IRP.[100] Their opposition to the IRP was so great that Khomeini also intervened to stem the *bazaari*s' support for Bani-Sadr, stating "Today [as opposed to during the revolution], to close the bazaar and to demonstrate is to defy the Prophet and to defy Islam."[101]

In the end, however, the hard-line IRP, which wielded both the institutions of the state (court, media, and Friday prayer services) and the brute force of vigilantes, used sheer coercion to overwhelm their disparate opponents, who at that moment ranged from the moderate LMI to various non-Tudeh leftist groups. Islamist groups monitored and politically bullied *bazaari*s, while hooligans physically threatened

---

[96] Bakhash, *The Reign of the Ayatollahs*, p. 134.
[97] Ibid., p. 138.   [98] Ibid., p. 139.
[99] *The Christian Science Monitor*, November 18, 1980.
[100] "Tehran Bazaar Merchants Ask Raja'i to Resign," Foreign Broadcasting Information Service, South Asia, January 6, 1981, I 8.
[101] Quoted in Bakhash, *The Reign of the Ayatollahs*, p. 156; also see Arjomand, *The Turban for the Crown*, p. 145.

the Bazaar itself.[102] Also, we can conjecture that in this initial period the cooperative hierarchies and physical localization that were resources for autonomy and solidarity were manipulated into objects of control and coercion. Ironically, in the end, in order to limit their mobilization against and criticisms of the IRP, it was the government that was forced to close down the bazaars.[103] After Bani-Sadr was ousted from power and fled the country, the IRP cracked down on opposition groups, including activists in the Bazaar.[104] In July 1981, they executed two merchants who had supported the Revolution, Karim Dastmalchi and Ahmad Javaherian. The charges against the former included "creating disturbances in the bazaar of Muslims, resulting in its closure."[105] Events such as these forced many others bazaaris to flee the country.[106] The whole episode, occurring shortly after the Revolution, was indicative of the Bazaar's substantial toward strict clerical rule.[107]

Thus, religion was one mode of articulating bazaari opposition to the state, and the clergy were a useful ally in their efforts to make claims against the state. Yet it was not the only one, and mosque–bazaar relations were certainly not an organic or inseparable alliance. Thus, relations with the religious establishment and religiosity are a less revealing measure of political attitudes and aspirations than analysts tend to assume.

Transforming grievances and interests into mobilization

If ties to the clergy and religious motivations are insufficient for understanding bazaari collective action, other scholars have offered interest-based interpretations. Grievances and clashes of interests with the state are increasingly cited as mechanisms for bazaari mobilization. Mozaffari, for example, asks, "Why does the bazaar rebel?" He relies on a relative deprivation model to answer that the "peripheralization of the

---

[102] Lebaschi, tape recording no. 3, 17.
[103] Associated Press, December 1, 1980.
[104] After the fall of Bani-Sadr, members of the left-leaning Islamist Mojahedin-e Khalq and leftists who were not affiliated with the Tudeh Party bore the brunt of the state violence.
[105] British Broadcasting Corporation, BBC Summary of World Broadcasts, July 15, 1981.
[106] Parsa, Social Origins of the Iranian Revolution, p. 282.
[107] A contributing factor in dampening the Bazaar's opposition to the IRP may have been the war. First, I suspect that some merchants saw the war as an economic opportunity to make windfall profits. Second, some bazaaris may have privileged national unity at a time of enemy attack and shied away from destabilizing the regime. This is implied by a quote from a bazaari: "Wait till after the war.... Many people will have to leave the political stage of this country." The Christian Science Monitor, November 18, 1980.

most homogenous social group [i.e. the bazaars] is a necessary condition to unleash aggressivity of a historical dimension."[108] This approach re-directs our attention to the *bazaars*' capacity to be agents in their own right. Nevertheless, Mozaffari's understanding of social mobilization, like grievance-based approaches in general, suffers from overpredicting rebellions.[109] Instances of "peripheralization" abound and have been a consistent theme since the formation of a centralized nation-state in the Reza Shah era and the entrance of Iran into the world economy. What causes *bazaari*s to mobilize at particular junctures? And why do they target the state with their "aggressivity"? These questions are all left unanswered.

Smith approaches these issues head on.[110] He identifies the state as the force behind the "peripheralization" of the bazaar to hypothesize:

[T]he roots of *bazaari* protests lie in a determined effort to resist state encroachment on the bazaar's market autonomy. Social autonomy for the bazaar can be defined along a number of indicators but fair market standing relative to foreign capital, freedom to set prices internally, and freedom from forced competition with state-subsidized cooperatives are arguably the three most important. Interference by the state in any of these arenas is likely to be seen (often rightfully) as arbitrary and thus resisted, regardless of the type of government.... Bazaar mobilization, then, is a function of external factors, of which I argue state policy is central, and ... of mobilizing structures internal to the bazaar itself.[111]

Smith isolates the specific moments in which state actions create conditions that "make it too costly for ... the bazaari *not* to protest."[112] By analyzing the state as an actor as well, this approach explains why protests are aimed at state power and *bazaari*s may part ways with the clergy.

By emphasizing the "external factors" that frame and initiate social mobilization, Smith makes short shrift of the bazaar's agency and more importantly the evolution of its internal structure and relation to the Iranian economy. This is unwarranted because social mobilization is as much a product of the capacity of social groups to create and take advantage of opportunities as it is a function of political structures and contexts that create opportunities for action and the framing of grievances. As it stands, Smith's analysis, which includes material from the postrevolutionary era, predicts that the bazaar should mobilize against

[108] Mozaffari, "Why the Bazar Rebels," 389.
[109] McAdam, *Political Process and the Development of Black Insurgency*, chapter 1.
[110] Smith, "Collective Action with and without Islam: Mobilizing the Bazaar in Iran."
[111] Ibid.,190.   [112] Ibid., 187.

the Islamic Republic, which has radically restructured the commercial market and infringed upon its autonomy by establishing state monopolies, heavily regulating trade, and initiating antiprofiteering campaigns (e.g. 1995 and 1996) and new commercial venues that compete with the bazaars.

Yet we rarely witness antistate mobilization after the initial revolutionary era, and the mobilization that has occurred has never been national or sustained. Clashes between merchants have erupted from time to time, and they have sometimes turned violent.[113] In Isfahan, for example, the bazaar closed down for a day to protest "unfair" and increasing taxes.[114] Protests have also been political. Shopkeepers in Sabzevar, a city in northeastern Iran, went on strike to protest the plans to divide Khorasan Province into three smaller provinces, none of which made Sabzevar the capital.[115] But these and other instances of public dissent were short lived, isolated, infrequent, and, as we see below, limited to individual sectors. Lest we think that the decline in *bazaari* protests is a function of overall social passivity or state domination during the Islamic Republican era, we should recall that this trend does not parallel those of other social groups. The urban poor and squatters in large cities have often organized rallies and rioted, as in the case of Tehran in August 1991 and 1995, Shiraz and Arak in 1992, and Mashhad in 1992, to name just a few.[116] Labor disputes and activism have also been prevalent, with major strikes occurring in 1991 and 2000.[117] Agricultural workers in the tea-planting region rioted in 2001 and 2002 to protest sectoral reforms. Some of these defensive protests have been successful in impacting state plans.[118] Finally, students at major universities in Tehran, Isfahan, Tabriz, and other cities have organized sit-ins and large rallies, and clashed with security forces and vigilantes in prolonged clashes in 1999, 2002, and 2003. All of these events offered *bazaaris* both opportunities to protest and groups with whom to cooperate.

The relative immobilization of the bazaar has not been due to its contentment with the regime either. On the contrary, we have a fair

---

[113] Traders in Ne'mat-Abad (a small town southwest of Tehran) attacked the municipality building. William Samii, "Bazaar Unhappy, but Is It Unstable?" *RFE/RL Iran Report* 3, 32 (August 2000).

[114] Agence France Presse, September 10, 1998.

[115] William Samii, "Renewed Unrest over Khorasan Split," RFE/RL Iran Report 4, 5 (February 11, 2002).

[116] *Ibid.;* Bayat, *Street Politics*; and Asef Bayat, "Activism and Social Development in the Middle East," *International Journal of Middle East Studies* 34 (February 2002), 4.

[117] Bayat, "Activism and Social Development in the Middle East," 6.

[118] *Seda-ye 'Edalat*, 1 Ordibehesht 1380 (April 21, 2001).

amount of evidence of *bazaari*s voicing their dissatisfaction with government policies. In 2000, the official guild magazine, *Asnaf* (Guilds), for instance, devoted a special issue to listing all the problems found in the service and commercial sectors and argued that they all stem from government policies.[119] Also, there is growing evidence that *bazaari*s are shunning the calls of the hard-line Islamic associations and voting for reformist candidates (also see below).[120] One of the few journalists who interviewed *bazaari*s during the elections found much support for Mohammad Khatami and reformist candidates.[121] A long-time jeweler in the Tehran Bazaar claimed, "Sixty percent of the bazaar is behind Khatami.... The conservatives here have blocked Khatami from acting. But he's in touch with the realities of the modern world. We want to do business with everybody – Europeans, Americans, [and] Arabs. Khatami supports us. Why have the others refused to open up to the world?" The reformists did very well in those 2000 elections, sweeping to power in the thirty seats in Tehran. During my research stay in Iran, the 2001 presidential elections were held that saw Khatami win another landslide victory (he received over 21 million votes or close to 80 percent of the total; the turnout was 67 percent). During the run-up to the election, I witnessed considerable public support for Khatami among the *bazaari*s. Several caravanserais hung large pictures of the smiling cleric. Some storeowners placed signs bearing the slogans of the reformist party. One well-known tea merchant placed a large statement on his desk declaring that he would vote for Khatami on election day. Furthermore, there were almost no posters or signs for the other nine candidates. During the week prior to the election, discussions among *bazaari*s and between them and their customers often turned to political matters. I overheard one *bazaari* loudly chastising and mocking his brother (and business partner) for "still" supporting the right-wing faction and voting for their leading candidate (Ahmad Tavakkoli came in second with less than 16 percent of the vote). On one occasion, a *bazaari* who thought that I was voting for the conservatives pleaded with me to vote for Khatami – "But Doctor, you are open-minded, you have seen the world; you should know that we need things to change." More commonly, discussions in the Bazaar, as in taxis and homes and cafes, revolved around the decision on whether or not to vote. I listened to customers and *bazaari*s urging apathetic merchants to vote for Khatami so the conservatives would not gain the upper hand and to register their desire

[119] *Asanf*, no. 90 (Aban 1379 [October–November 2000]).
[120] *Iran*, 21 Aban 1382 (November 12, 2003).
[121] Agence France Presse, February 14, 2000.

for change. In short, there is ever-growing awareness among *bazaaris* that state policies are deleterious. There is also an interest in opposing them, but the conditions for social mobilization are seemingly absent.

Parsa, who has offered some of the most comprehensive and bazaar-centric studies of the Islamic Revolution, is careful to distill into its constitutive parts the many factors that are necessary for collective action.[122] He argues that "the mobilization and collective action of bazaaris are explainable historically in terms of their responses to state policies that adversely affected their economic interests, *their organizational capacity to act collectively*, and the existing opportunity structure. When bazaaris possessed a *strong autonomous organization*, they were able to mobilize and act collectively to defend their interests."[123] Thus, Parsa, like other resource mobilization theorists, places the bazaar's organization at the center of his analysis of the causes of the Revolution, commenting, "Bazaaris have consistently played a crucial role in the political conflicts of twentieth century Iran because of the particular structure of the central bazaars and their resources." He continues by arguing that "social solidarity" (in part created by spatial concentration) and resources allow *bazaaris* "to mobilize and act collectively to defend their interests."[124]

The network approach to the Tehran Bazaar extends Parsa's empirically refined and meticulous analysis in two ways. First, I broaden the empirical scope of his analysis to investigate the protracted and localized nature of *bazaari* protests after the Revolution. The rarity and limited nature of *bazaari* mobilization contradicts Parsa's claim that high levels of state intervention in capital accumulation lead to a greater likelihood of collective action.[125] The highly interventionist Islamic Republic should be extremely susceptible to contentious politics. The lack of such a scenario suggests that the organization of groups, the mechanism that translates individual grievances against the state into collective action by groups, is wanting.

Second, in order to understand this anomaly and the shift from high to low mobilization capacity, I focus on the mechanisms maintaining

---

[122] In a quantitative study, Parsa concludes, "In sum, the presence of shopkeepers was the best positive predictor of collective action during the Iranian Revolution in both the national sample and the large cities. This finding lended (*sic*) support to the conclusion that *bazaaris*' conflict with the state were highly significant in ousting the Shah." Misagh Parsa, "Conflict and Collective Action in the Iranian Revolution: A Quantitative Analysis," *Journal of Iranian Research and Analysis* 20 (November 2004), 55.

[123] Parsa, *Social Origins of the Iranian Revolution*, pp. 93–4, emphasis added.

[124] Parsa, "Mosque of Last Resort," 147.

[125] Parsa, *States, Ideologies, and Social Revolutions*.

and extinguishing social solidarity and coordination. What are these mechanisms that impact the capacity of the bazaar to mobilize? Parsa responds that in times of conflict the bazaar's enjoy relatively high capacity because they enjoy a "common fate with respect to market conditions."[126] How exactly bazaaris come to know, interpret, and share in their fate, and how they translate this knowledge into collective action and the mobilization of resources, however, is not clearly explained.[127] The creation of a collectivity and members' identification of it as a community are as much a challenge as the problem of acting collectively. The Tehran Bazaar faces formidable problems in this regard. It is a very large group with members of divergent class and social standings, heterogeneous political persuasions, and numerous ethnicities and religions. Pace Mozaffari, the bazaaris' ability to coordinate closures, demonstrations, and fund raising is striking because of the very absence of homogeneity. Parsa does suggest a means by which these cleavages are overcome. In a concluding section, he suggestively writes, "Their concentration and networks enabled bazaaris to shut down as a sign of protest against the government and disrupt national trade."[128] While this chapter has concurred that the bazaar's socioeconomic structure, rather than the political organization or ideological homogeneity, is what mediates this diversity and facilitates bazaari collective action and political mobilization, as not all networks are enabling as implied by Parsa's analysis.

Preexisting relations, as a growing number of scholars of social movements have pointed out, are useful building blocks for collective action.[129] For Tarrow social networks are an external resource (along with cultural and symbolic frames) that helps social movements "coordinate and sustain collective action."[130] Social movements emerge once groups solve the "social" collective action problem of "coordinating unorganized, autonomous and dispersed populations into common and sustained action ... by responding to political opportunities

[126] Parsa, Social Origins of the Iranian Revolution, p. 92.
[127] In fact, Parsa cites differences in wealth and political views to suggest that by the late 1970s the bazaars suffered from "organizational weakness" and a lack of solidarity. Ibid., p. 108.
[128] Ibid., 124. Smith also argues that "informal networks" allow for collective action. Smith, "Collective Action with and without Islam: Mobilizing the Bazaar in Iran."
[129] See Deborah J. Yashar, Contesting Citizenship in Latin America: The Rise of Indigenous and the Postliberal Challenge (Cambridge: Cambridge University Press, 2005), Chapter 3, for a summary of the roles played by networks in social movements. In her own treatment of indigenous movements in Latin America, Yashar persuasively incorporates networks (in particular transcommunity networks) as means for diverse and spatially distant indigenous groups to mobilize against the state.
[130] Tarrow, Power in Movement, p. 17.

through the use of known, modular forms of collective action, by mobilizing people within social networks and through shared cultural understandings."[131] Turning to the Iranian case we can surmise that modular forms and shared cultural understandings are unlikely to have been forgotten so soon after the Islamic Revolution and episodic rounds of mobilization in the last century (at least it does not seem that students at Tehran University have forgotten these forms). If my analysis of the political economy of the bazaar is correct, what has changed is the grouping of social networks. The constellation of networks, or what I call the form of governance, has undergone profound restructuring and with itso too has the Bazaar's internal structure for alleviating the social collective action problem. In short, cooperative hierarchies were the prime ingredients for preserving cooperation and giving *bazaari*s a sense of solidarity in the prerevolutionary era; on the other hand, the coercive hierarchies of the present period subvert the bazaar's potential mobilization against the state.

Cooperative hierarchies as a foundation for collective action

I have argued that cooperative hierarchies coordinate actions by helping groups develop a corporate character and group solidarity, generating communal sanctions and pro-social norms, and, in the case of the Tehran Bazaar, tying actors to other commercial and social groups. These particular characteristics that shape the economy of the Bazaar also nurture a political potential. At moments when it was in the interests of *bazaari*s to mobilize and an opening existed for social mobilization, cooperative hierarchies were able to (a) mobilize resources to reduce costs of activism, (b) monitor and provide selective incentives to limit free-riding, (c) engender trust among group members, and (d) transmit knowledge about repertoires of action and modular forms.

The Tehran Bazaar used to have a number of resources that were critical for sustained social mobilization: independent capital assets and financial systems, information channels for publicizing actions and demands, public spaces for visible congregation, and symbols and repertoires of action that were widely understood by participants and observers as protest. The Bazaar's access to vast sums of assets and a distribution system (i.e. a system of interest-free loans, the reputation assessment by guild leaders and brokers) alleviated many of the practical problems of funding strikers, printing and distributing political announcements, and sabotaging the economy. Political entrepreneurs among the *bazaari*s were able to tap into this existing expertise to pool

---

[131] Ibid., p. 9.

and distribute financial resources. Furthermore, as a dense pedestrian area marked by public gathering places (coffee houses, mosques, and open squares) and located near government establishments, the Tehran Bazaar is a ready-made space for public gathering and political demonstration. Finally, the crosscutting, expansive, and long-term relations were also an important mechanism for gatheringand evaluating information and rumors from individuals known to one another through socially embedded trade. Those inclined to join social movements could evaluate the risks and assess the sentiments of others. All these factors are essential in triggering and sustaining the Bazaar's participation in social movements.

The cooperative hierarchies also included ways to encourage collective action by reducing free-riding. For some, cooperative hierarchies imbue a sense of belonging and solidarity that intrinsically motivates them to trust the collective action process. They begin to see their individual fate as tied to that of the collectivity. In addition, cooperative hierarchies also harbor selective incentives to compel and coerce skeptics to join. Cooperative hierarchies offer a greater deliberative potential than coercive hierarchies, and as such provide a means to develop frames to justify and target collective action by which the apolitical or unconvinced majority may be persuaded to participate. Also, the reputation system of the Bazaar ensures regular monitoring, with the evaluation of actions constituting an integral part of one's reputation and standing in the community and capacity to conduct business. Thus, in such an environment, once protests develop they are prone to swell in numbers as *bazaari*s join the process out of concern for their reputation. When the Society of Merchants, Guilds, and Artisans called for strikes, those store owners who did not close in the morning, closed in the afternoon.[132] The power of social pressure within the bazaar can be detected in the statement of a shopowner in Amiriyyeh, a quarter near the Bazaar, when he said that fearing attacks against his store he placed a picture of Khomeini in his shop window. He responded, "Most people want an Islamic republic.... And I want anything that most of the people want."[133] It seems that the closures very often worked through peer pressure.[134] Throughout the protests the capacity of *bazaari*s to identify, shame, and coerce nonparticipants helped committed rebels reduce free-riding, and unenthusiastic shopkeepers swim with the tide.

---

[132] Lebaschi, tape recording no. 2, 19.
[133] *New York Times*, February 2, 1979.
[134] This point emerged from a number of interviews.

Cooperative hierarchies also help generate a ritual of collective action by sustaining memories, myths, and models of social mobilization. Despite the ultimate failure of the Bazaar to prevent the Mosaddeq government's downfall, bazaaris in the early 1960s remembered the episode as a "golden era" for the bazaar community.[135] Almost half a century after the 1953 coup and regardless of age or political persuasion, the Bazaar's "principled" support for Mosaddeq and its continual closures and organization of rallies remained a prominent theme in my discussions with bazaaris.[136] The existing lore among bazaaris, and Iranians in general, that the Bazaar was so powerful that when it closed the government trembled forms expectations and interprets actions.

Thus, in the 1960s and 1970s these existing cooperative hierarchies were at the disposal of activists within the Bazaar and enabled their efforts to be effective and enduring. Bazaaris were able to identify and trust the leaders of the Tehran Bazaar-based groups tied to the National Front and the Islamic Coalition Association through the reputation system, with the "established structures of solidary incentives" converting grievances and opportunities into collective underwriting of insurgency.[137] The cooperative hierarchies, hence, were the existing raw material that distributed leaflets, coordinated shutdowns and demonstrations, and mobilized resources. Cooperative hierarchies are exceptionally powerful forms of organization because they not only provide selective incentives that are helpful in mobilizing the apolitical or apathetic, but also produce collective awareness that is necessary to maintain and direct, if not broaden, self-interested action.

Coercive hierarchies as a source of quietism

Coercive hierarchies, on the other hand, neither generate solidarity nor reduce the cost of participation or increase the cost of nonparticipation. It is not that today's Bazaar lacks the many resources that it had at its disposal during the prerevolutionary era. Many bazaaris continue to be wealthy. Despite the decline in the Tehran Bazaar's centrality in the national economy, it continues to be an important urban space and contact point for the business community, and social relations remain essential for business. The difference is that these social relations are positioned in a new, more segmented web of networks, one that lacks the breadth of coordination and the generalized trust available to cooperative hierarchies. Political and network cleavages are accentuated by the patronage system,

---

[135] Ashraf, "Nezam-e Senfi va Jame'eh-ye Madani," 21.
[136] Also see Asnaf, no. 88 (Shahrivar 1379 [August–September 2000]), 11.
[137] McAdam, political Process, pp. 45–6.

which places non-*bazaari*s and competing superiors as heads of hierarchical value and chains. Hence, orchestrating of mobilization is more time consuming and cumbersome. This is why oppositional activity is suppressed through pressure by state agents.

As posited in Chapter 3, social solidarity has gradually declined since the Revolution. Many of the social spaces helping to make it "a unique type of community center"[138] that brought *bazaari*s together to exchange information and opinions have declined. The number of coffee houses and restaurants in and around the Bazaar, institutions known as areas of discussion and rumor, has plummeted. While it is difficult to say whether Iranians are less religious than thirty years ago, evidence suggests that prayer in mosques and participation in public religious gatherings has declined.[139] Surprisingly, during a Friday sermon one of the Supreme Leader's representatives in Qom opined that Iran's mosques have become "morbid places" and young people have good reason not to attend Friday Prayers.[140] In the Tehran Bazaar, many *bazaari*s who are tired of the political manipulation of the pulpit choose to pray in the privacy of their shops and homes. Consequently, one more public space for social interaction and developing political attitudes become obsolete in the Islamic Republic. More generally, the secretive nature of the coercive hierarchies, the unrestrained nature of competition, and alliances with external actors has undermined the *bazaari*s' sense that their fate is inextricably tied to the Bazaar.

Under these conditions it is not surprising that collective action and mobilization against the state has been fleeting and uncoordinated. This has resulted in isolated and typically unsuccessful actions that neither mobilize the entire bazaar nor attract the support of other opposition groups or social groups. This is so even within the context of countless "political opportunities" for mobilization – various elections, factional disputes, sudden changes, policy shifts, legislative and judicial conflicts, and protests by students, industrial workers, and the urban poor.

On the rare occasion when closures and demonstrations have taken place in the past few years, limited to select guilds, which the network

---

[138] Robert Graham, *Iran: The Illusion of Power*, rev. edn. (New York: St. Martin's Press, 1980), p. 223.

[139] Abdolmohammad Kazemipur and Ali Rezaei, "Religious Life under Theocracy: The Case of Iran" *Journal of the Scientific Study of Religion* 42 (September 2003), 347–61; John Simpson, "Along the Streets of Tehran," *Harper's Magazine* 276 (January 1988), 37; British Broadcasting Company, July 7, 2000; *Mosharekat*, 4 Esfand 1378 (February 23, 2000); and Fariba Adelkhah, *Being Modern in Iran*, trans. Jonathan Derrick (New York: Columbia University Press, 2000), p. 113.

[140] This was quoted by the *Nawruz* newspaper. William Samii, "Morbid Mosques Fail to Promote Piety," *RFE/RL Iran Report* 5, 24 (July 1, 2002).

conceptualization would except. Notably, sectors in nonstandard goods, such as the carpet sector discussed in Chapter 5, which have maintained forms of governance that somewhat approximate cooperative hierarchies have been sites of protest. For instance, jewelers in the Tehran Bazaar, a nonstandard good sector with relatively dense relations, have gone on strike. In October 1994, more than 300 went on a two-day strike to protest the hundredfold increase in taxes on gold.[141] The news report claimed that the protest was the first to be organized by a guild since the Revolution. Hand-woven carpet dealers in the Tehran Bazaar went on strike to protest high taxes in July 1996.[142] The *Salam* newspaper reported that the merchants gathered in the Azeri mosque, which was a prime political location earlier in the century. The Azeri mosque is significant because it is located in the heart of the carpet bazaar in Tehran, and as the name implies its congregation are predominately Turkish-speaking Azeris, who are the dominant force in the carpet trade in Tehran.[143] Their action was in response to what they viewed as cumbersome, arbitrary, and fluctuating regulations, as well as high taxes, which together they claimed had caused a recession in the carpet trade. "In other countries, governments provide great benefits to merchants in order to boost exports. But in this country it's quite the opposite," one merchant told the newspaper.

I too witnessed an instance of protest by the carpet merchants. In the spring of 2001, I arrived in the Tehran Bazaar to see the metal curtains on the stores and offices pulled down, while the shopowners and their apprentices were standing around in the alleys. They explained that the night before a warehouse was burglarized, one of several such incidents in the past couple months. The merchants were furious that the police were indifferent to their concerns and had not pursued the seemingly serial acts of crime. As a show of public discontent, all but a handful of *bazaaris* decided to shut their shops and remain closed until noon. But one merchant explained that a strike beyond noon would not hold since merchants believed that strikes are now ineffective, while others would simply open since there is no "cooperation" (*hamkari*). When I asked the identity of the few merchants who were open, I was told that they were members of the Islamic association. The strike ended at noon and the issue seemingly faded away without a police investigation. Later that day, when I mentioned the strike to a china wholesaler located a few hundred feet from the carpet bazaar, he was completely unaware of the

---

[141] Agence France Presse, October 13, 1994.
[142] Xinhua News Agency, July 24, 1996; and Associated Press, July 24, 1996.
[143] Mehri, Masajed-e Bazar-e Tehran, pp. 189–237.

burglary or the closure. The wholesaler, who prided himself on "knowing all the news," was surprised by the response of the carpet merchants, saying, "I didn't know they *still* did those kinds of things [i.e. went on strike]." I was surprised that word had not reached his ears. Looking back, it was another example of the existing sectoral divides. The expression of surprise may also reflect the perception among at least some *bazaaris* that these forms of collective and public contention are no longer effective means to shape policy or challenge rulers because either the nature of contemporary politics differs from earlier decades or current conditions are not subject to change.

This sort of incident, even in the carpet sector, where information quickly and rapidly permeates its channels, is rare. The isolated nature of these protests also suggests the inability of the *bazaaris* to organize nationwide protests. The large carpet markets in Tehran, Tabriz, Isfahan, and Shiraz, for example, have not coordinated mass strikes or demonstrations on behalf of the entire sector. Since the more coercive hierarchies have detached them from one another and increased competition among them, national-level coordination is unlikely.

One might expect that the Islamic Republic's incorporation of the *bazaaris* and the establishment of coercive hierarchies tied to state and regime agents would facilitate mobilization as a form of social control *on behalf of the regime*. This would seem especially likely since the regime has been successful is controlling *bazaari* associations so as to ensure that they represent only the most staunchly pro-regime and conservative views. The Society of the Islamic Associations of Tehran's Guilds and Bazaar, which from its inception has been completely dominated by the staunchly conservative Islamic Coalition Association, regularly holds meetings and makes public statements declaring that it represents the interests of the "Islamic Bazaar" and pledging its commitment to the Islamic Revolution and the system of rule by a supreme jurisconsult (*velayat-e faqih*). Repeatedly since the Revolution, it has urged *bazaaris* to remain loyal to the Islamic Republic. At a speech given at the monthly meeting held by the society, Habibollah Asgarawladi-Mosalman, who is one of the founding members of the Islamic Coalition Association and comes from a family of merchants, declared, "If the Islamic Bazaar is united, the Islamic Republic will open the path for the Islamic Bazaar to be at the service of the people's revolution and realizing their own reght."[144] He also added that each guild must have an Islamic association to preserve Islam. Simultaneously, these political statements and speeches representing the "Islamic" Bazaar oppose any and all

[144] *Asnaf*, no. 40 (Azar 1375 [November–December 1996]), 29.

groups that support reforms or question the powers of the leader of the Revolution by dubbing them agents of "foreign enemies" or "hypocrites."[145] Since the mid-1980s, the views of the society and coalition have been most clearly represented in the pages of Iran's best-known independent conservative newspaper, *Resalat*. These statements are often taken by non-*bazaari* observers to be expressions of the Bazaars politics.

However, not only does the society, which has only 2,500 members out of a Tehran Bazaar that contains some 40,000 individuals,[146] not reflect the *bazaaris*' sentiments, but recent evidence suggests that it can no longer mobilize their support. While the Islamic associations retain the authority to call for a closure of the Bazaar and use this power to make such calls from time to time, in the past few years more and more *bazaaris* are resisting their dictates and ignoring their calls for closure.[147] In September 1999, the call to close the Bazaar in response to a student play that was deemed offensive by conservative clerics was only grudgingly followed by *bazaaris*, with a very few attending the antireformist speech held in the Bazaar.[148] Six months later, when the society called for another strike, *bazaaris* did not even close their shops.[149] In 2003, a prominent reformist newspaper reported the society's announcement that the Tehran Bazaar would close for two hours in protest against a cartoon that they regarded as mocking the cleric. For two days black banners were hung by the entrance of the Bazaar announcing the strike. However, the vast majority of the Bazaar stayed open, refusing to close for even two hours! the article concluded by stating that "the *bazaaris* lack of support for the Bazaar closure represents a trend that has existed in previous years. Those knowledgeable [about affairs in the Bazaar] say that at present the coalition [i.e. ICA] and the [Islamic] associations do not have great influence among the *bazaaris* and the weekly meetings, despite widespread advertising and the presence of well-known right-wing figures, are not well received."[150] As some of the most politically active, experienced, and adroit activists have left the Bazaar's networks and have been subsumed into institutional politics, the capacity for both anti- and pro-state mobilization has been undermined.

---

[145] For a recent statement see the society's declaration commemorating the anniversary of the June 1963 uprising. *Resalat*, 15 Khordad 1382 (June 6, 2003).

[146] *Iran News*, July 31, 2000.

[147] *Iran*, 21 Aban 1382 (November 12, 2003).

[148] Christopher de Bellaigue, "The Struggle for Iran," *New York Review of Books* 46 (December 16, 1999), 57.

[149] *New York Times*, April 23, 2000.

[150] *Hayat-e Naw*, 24 Day 1381 (January 14, 2003).

Conclusions

In the summer of 2003, Tehran was in the throes of yet another round of demonstrations by critics and violent reactions by pro-regime vigilantes. Tehran University was the focal point, and apparently a large number of members of the middle and upper-middle class also joined in the protests, which were triggered by talk of introducing tuition-paying graduate students to the otherwise free public university system. But again, the Bazaar was quiet. No statements were issued, no strikes in support of the students were called, and definitely no rallies from the Bazaar to the gates of the university were organized.

Shortly after the demonstration began to subside, *The Times* of London featured a wonderfully evocative and honest article about a *bazaari* family.[151] Hadi, an under-thirty velvet dealer from the Bazaar, tells the journalist that "he was never interested in politics before," but for over a week he and his *bazaari* uncle had joined the demonstrators outside the university and called for changes in the regime. " 'I go because I am against the system. I want my freedoms,' he said, eating with his family. 'Me and my friends, we hate this system, the clerics, the basijis (volunteer Islamic militia groups). There is so much corruption here, they have created it themselves. *Before, there wasn't an opportunity to demonstrate. Now these protests have given us the opportunity.*' " He later adds, "Clerics should not run this country, they should go back to the mosques where they belong. They are just good at issuing fatwas. They aren't efficient or good with the economy." His uncle, who participated in the Islamic Revolution as "a student leader, organising demonstrations, distributing Khomeini's statements underground," echoed these sentiments: "Religion and politics should be separate. ... We were wrong to believe it could work." Hadi, his uncle, and his mother all voted for Khatami in 1997, but have lost hope that his reformist agenda will succeed. Hadi feels that the tide is changing and he comments, "In the bazaar things are changing. There's a radical new element that wants the end of the regime. Those who want to keep the status quo are in the minority. The system is breathing its last breath." His enthusiasm is tempered by an astute and pragmatic observation by his mother: "There's no leadership, *no united structure*. Before the Islamic Revolution, we were all united, leftists, communists, intellectuals, whoever. Now *everyone is split*. Not even the security forces work together. *But if there was a united front I would join it.*"

---

[151] *The Times*, June 21, 2003, emphasis added.

This chapter supports the comparative analysis of Hadi's mother. Dissatisfaction and antipathy run through the Bazaar as they do in much of Iranian society. However, as has been shown, grievances alone do not ensure political mobilization. Just as the actions and the condition of the state are an important factor, the preexisting fabric of social relations is a crucial variable in collective action. The Tehran Bazaar demonstrates this through its changing capacity to mobilize. The interconnected, long-term, and socially embedded value chains engendered the *bazaaris'* capacity to solve the "social" collective action problem. With that the Bazaar could create *sholughi*. Because its mobilizing structure, understood in terms of the form of governance, has been transformed, the Bazaar is not "united." Despite Hadi's enthusiasm, his mother's caution is warranted and her calculation not to participate is the norm. Therefore, the stores remain open and the Bazaar has been politically quiet.

7   Conclusions

If the "bazaar economy" is seen as an economic type rather than an evo-lutionary step toward something more familiar to people used to other ways of doing things, and, more importantly, if a deeper understanding of its nature can be obtained, perhaps, just perhaps, some relevant and practicable sug-gestions for improving it, for increasing its capacity to inform its participants, might emerge and its power of growth be restored and strengthened.

Clifford Geertz[1]

Iranians say that the Tehran Bazaar is the "pulse of the city" or "the pulse of the economy." The metaphor is appropriate, for it evokes a sense that the circulation of commodities, credit, and information in the Bazaar's networks is a palpable effect of the workings of Iran's urban life and political economy. By documenting the interaction between the two recent regimes and the Bazaar, as well as tracing the process through which state–society relations have been redesigned and renegotiated since the 1979 revolution, this study extends this metaphor by arguing that the Bazaar is an apt gauge of how state-level policies dialogue with organizational-level politics. It is an initial foray into mapping how visions of development set the parameters for the networks within this group, and consequently their ability to turn their grievances into collective claims against the state.

In order to create a coherent and analytically compelling narrative it is necessary to recast a conception of the Bazaar, treating its organization and solidarity as a conundrum. The *bazaaris'* cooperation is a classic problem from the perspective of those working within the individual maximization paradigm. Social scientists working in this tradition would expect individual-level preferences and conditions to influence prospects for cooperation. The moral economy perspective, meanwhile, would expect the prevalence of an overarching normative order that is carried by group members to be the basis of solidarity. By demonstrating

[1] Clifford Geertz, "Suq: The Bazaar Economy in Sefrou," in *Meaning and Order in Moroccan Society*, ed. Clifford Geertz, Hildred Geertz, and Lawrence Rosen (Cambridge: Cambridge University Press, 1979), p. 234.

that cooperation and group solidarity are precarious and contingent upon *relational factors* rather than group size and physical dispersion, this study indicates that communal behavior such as multilateral sanctioning or political mobilization is created by the quality and vibrancy of quotidian social interactions. The argument presented by Rorty and other normative theorists who advocate a conception of human solidarity "constructed out of little pieces"[2] reminds empiricists that shared identities or meta-ideologies fail to sustain human cooperation; rather, when we do discover solidarity we must search for the composite parts that have created a sense of community in the face of disparities in power and incentives to prioritize personal gain over collective sentiment. Solidarity takes on meaning only in the context of difference, not homogeneity.

Moreover, the persistence of the Bazaar's social order and alleged unity is curious given that the Shah's development approach and political machinations were fashioned very much *in opposition to the Bazaar.* Why didn't the Bazaar fade away given that it was deprived of direct state tutelage? The Bazaar's large, heterogeneous, and stratified membership and its diverse relationship with the international and national economy would suggest that a unifying corporate identity is difficult to forge and maintain; historically pertinent mechanisms are necessary to create a semblance of solidarity and unity in the face of external antipathy. This line of questioning is even more warranted given that under the postrevolutionary regime, assumed to be pro-*bazaari*, the Bazaar's solidarity and self-help seem to be less pronounced and inclusive.

I have attempted to show that these outcomes are not aberrations, but expose deep contradictions in the political economies of the monarchy and the Islamic Republic that can be best accounted for by a network approach. First, bazaars are a collection of ongoing relations that are mechanisms for the exchange of goods and services. Thus, my unit of analysis has been the various value chains that connect different members of the commercial hierarchy. Second, the configuration of these networks (i.e. the relations within them and connections across them) has resulted in the specific form of governance within the Bazaar. The variation in the form of governance of the Tehran Bazaar during the past four decades is illustrated by the shifts in commercial, financial, and social relations of members of the Bazaar. During the late Pahlavi era, relations within the Bazaar were socially embedded, while value chains

---

[2] Richard Rorty, *Contingency, Irony, and Solidarity* (Cambridge: Cambridge University Press, 1989).

and social circles were interconnected in ways that engendered long-term, crosscutting, and multifaceted relations. These cooperative hierarchies were able to appraise reputations and bridge sectoral, ethnic, and class divisions. By the end of the second decade of the post-revolutionary era, however, the Bazaar's relations had become more short term and detached from the *bazaaris*' broader social lives; networks today are less encompassing and integrative. I argue that the earlier form of governance, complete with an internal reputation system, facilitated the exchange of resources and information and the regeneration of norms and self-governance. On the other hand, the current form is designed to seek out resources beyond the Bazaar, with socioeconomic, cultural, and political cleavages segmenting the Bazaar's networks, isolating its members, and fragmenting clusters of *bazaaris* wedded together through strong ties. Cooperative hierarchies, while being far from democratic, are nevertheless better at representing group interests than coercive hierarchies because of their built-in exchanges and regenerating horizontal and vertical interactions. Finally, in the prerevolutionary period the reputation system helped replace the price mechanism. Ironically, in the postrevolutionary period the reputation system has been undermined as the price mechanism has been rendered meaningless since inconsistent and unstable state policies and monopolies have created market distortions.

Why have these forms of governance prevailed in these two eras and why has transformation occurred in the past two decades? During the Pahlavi era the Bazaar maintained its self-governance since it remained beyond the vision of the regime's top-down modernist plans and was not incorporated into the regime's bureaucratic structure. Thus, by seeking a policy of replacement, rather than incorporation, the Pahlavi regime created an autonomous zone for *bazaaris*, who filled it with their existing institutions. But also, the Tehran Bazaar prospered and maintained its internal governance *because of* state policies. Under the Pahlavi regime the *bazaaris*' solidarity was reinforced by state rhetoric and policies that created a bounded group identity that decidedly differentiated the Bazaar from other social groupings. Meanwhile, state-sponsored urbanization, consumerism, and infrastructural development expanded markets for the Bazaar's value chains and credit system.

Under the Islamic Republic, while state rhetoric has spoken of a special place for the *bazaaris* in the new Islamic order, the distribution of rents has been based on individual, rather than corporate, identifications. Unlike the distinction between "traditional *bazaari*" and "modern industrialist" that dominated official discourse in the 1960s and 1970s and rendered all *bazaaris* as one in the eyes of the state, the postrevolutionary regime has differentiated between revolutionary or "committed" *bazaari*s and those who are supposedly not, with only the former gaining access to resources controlled by the state. Thus, individual-level patronage undermined the *bazaari*s' relational web and exposed and enflamed internal divisions, and accordingly impoverished their internal solidarity and group identity. In addition, the Islamic Republic's policies led to the Bazaar's incorporation; *bazaari*s faced a myriad of state institutions and organizations that restructured commerce and repatterned economic power. This restructuring gave birth to new value chains, some of which worked to manipulate new patterns of commercial privilege while others struggled to elude the commercial regime altogether. Hence, the simultaneous transformation of political forces and the persisting evolution of the socioeconomy altered the institutional and physical setting of networks. On the one hand, external regulation replaced internal autonomy of networks, and, on the other, concentration of commercial interactions in the Bazaar was replaced by increased delocalization and diffusion of commercial exchanges. The ingredients to maintain cooperative hierarchies became absent and forces that nurtured fragmented coercive hierarchies came to the forefront.

Therefore, it is not the "modernizing" regime of the Shah, but the "traditional" Islamic government that has transformed the Bazaar's organization in ways that have given rise to more modern qualities – increased arm's-length exchanges and contractually based exchanges, and the shift to more manufactured and standardized goods. The Shah's supermarket building was based on wishful replacement; the Islamic government's *passazh* building was part of a more willful restructuring of commerce. It may be argued that the Pahlavi regime simply failed to implement its project to modernize Iran and the Bazaar, so the outcome is a consequence of a failure in will rather than plan; but the point here is that the relationship between objectives and outcomes is far from direct and in order to trace this process the broader context and the concrete and elaborate form of governance in the Tehran Bazaar must be studied and expected to matter, even if it is not fully predicted.

The transformation from cooperative to coercive hierarchies would predict that as the exchange of resources and information and sense of solidarity were reduced, the political mobilization of the Bazaar would decline. In Chapter 6 this hypothesis was evaluated and employed to understand the dramatic decrease in mobilization of the Bazaar despite the existence among the *bazaari*s of grievances, opportunities for mobilization, and potential oppositional allies. Thus, the capacity of social groups to resist state encroachment and broker political mobilization is related to the types of networks at their disposal. The corresponding shift in the Bazaar's capacity to mobilize against the state serves as a compelling independent verification that the Bazaar's organization has been significantly altered in the past two decades. The finding that the Bazaar's capacity to mobilize is historically contingent is built on the interpretation that less weight must be placed on the mosque–bazaar alliance and on the *bazaaris*' class interests, and more emphasis needs to be placed on the structure of relations overcoming social collective action problems. The irony is that the political opportunity presented to *bazaaris* by the Revolution and the generally more accommodating Islamic Republic has resulted in the whittling away of its mobilization structures and collective self-understanding, both of which are essential for initiating and sustaining collective action.

There is yet another paradox presented by this analysis: the Tehran Bazaar can be comprehended only as a collective entity and seemingly coherent social space, but that metaphysical totality cannot be grasped without investigating the fragments that compose it, although it is not fully captured by these. The dialogical process of state and society results in repositioning of institutions, but through highly personal and textured exchanges and negotiations.

Insights from the Tehran Bazaar and the Iranian state

Throughout the analysis the timing and sequence of events demonstrated that the transformation of the Bazaar was not an organic process driven by socioeconomic factors, but was triggered and shaped by the political economy and state policies. The persistence and demise of the Bazaar is driven by the shifts associated with the revolutionary change from a development agenda based on high modernism to one framed by Islamic populism.

On the one hand, the durability and survival of the Bazaar's practices and organization were not due to the failure and inability of the Pahlavi monarchy to transform Iran's economy, social fabric, or its relationship to the world economy. It must not be forgotten that on several dimensions the Bazaar did in fact change. Small-scale manufacturing and production that was based within the bazaars and tied to their credit systems was increasingly dislodged by industrially manufactured goods that were produced domestically or imported. By the end of the 1960s production of leather and metal goods was in fact disappearing from the Tehran Bazaar. Also, large segments of the retail commercial sectors, such as the clothing, shoe, and book trades, relocated in order to accommodate new urban demographic patterns and tastes. Instead, the merchants in the Tehran Bazaar redirected their business activities into wholesale and international trade to take advantage of increased consumerism. It was the Pahlavi regime's "successful" urbanization of Iran, the creation of a mass consumer society and working class that helped fuel consumerism (warts and all) that led to the growth of the Bazaar. The Bazaar's credit network and value chains were able to compete effectively with state institutions that neither accommodated *bazaaris* nor were functional equivalents for "informal" or "traditional" practices and norms.

On the other hand, the demise of the Bazaar was not a natural outcome of modernization, for if it was, the realignment of networks would have occurred prior to the Revolution. Therefore, cooperative hierarchies did not pass because of inherent defects of the Bazaar or incommensurability with modernity; rather they were refashioned because they were incommensurate with the transformative agenda of the Islamic Republic. Again, structural-functionalist interpretations are inadequate because the difficulties of transacting owing to issues of information scarcity and asymmetry and contract enforcement are pervasive even today, and thus should provide motivations for *bazaaris* to develop the ingredients for cooperative hierarchies. Yet the postrevolutionary experience demonstrates that this particular remedy is not always structurally available or creatable by individuals. Forms of governance are contingent on the institutional and physical setting of networks, and these outcomes are thus not mechanistic responses to demand and motives.[3]

A third general point that emerges out of the narrative of the Bazaar's transformation is that path-dependency arguments that endogenize culture by assuming that it is "in equilibrium" or is a symbolic structure overstate the fixity of social norms and economic practices.[4] Even in the relatively short time span of two decades many *bazaaris* have adjusted their trading routines, expectations of others, and expectations about expectations. A certain sense of loss and a desire for a "better" system

---

[3] See the debate between Jon Elster and Avner Greif, in which Greif responds to Elster's criticisms by stating that his analysis of late-medival-era Genovese political economy addresses only motivations. John Elster, "*Analytical Narratives* by Bates, Greif, Levi, Rosenthal and Weingast: A Review and Response," *American Political Science Review* 94 (September 2000), 685–702.

[4] Greif does this explicitly in his analysis of Genovese and Maghribi traders, while Geertz implicitly does so in his structural conception of culture. See Avner Greif, "Cultural Beliefs and the Organization of Society: A Historical and Theoretical Reflection on Collectivist and Individualist Societies," *Journal of Political Economy* 102 (October 1994), 912–50; and Geertz, "Suq: The Bazaar Economy in Sefrou."

most certainly exists (as it always seems to exist), but practices reflect new social arrangements and the political and economic context. The persistence and transformation of social norms is an area where greater empirical research is required to unpack the role of structure and agency and intracommunal and external factors.[5]

Finally, lest I underestimate the relevance of social forces in the transformation of the organization of Bazaar, certain world economic and socioeconomic factors obviously did play a role in encouraging a delocalization of commercial networks and altering the parameters of commerce. The narrative would be incomplete without accounting for technological advances (e.g. fax machines, cell phones, and the Internet), the globalization of financial flows and regional commercial developments (e.g. development of active commercial markets in the UAE.), and world market forces affecting the terms of trade (e.g. decline of the price of tea and hand-woven carpets). But it was shown that all these forces were heavily mediated by local and state policies and objectives, discrete transnational networks, and historical contingencies, rather than a universal, homogenizing, and essentially market-driven process. To give one example, without the Islamic Republic's purging of the prerevolutionary financial and commercial elite and the outbreak of the war in the northern Persian Gulf, Dubai probably would not have become the entrepôt to Iran and Central Asia it is now. Of course, geopolitics and the UAE and Dubai governments' labor and taxation policies were commercially instrumental too. Moreover, the responses available to *bazaaris* were structured by state policies and organizations that placed institutional limits and opportunities based on priorities on their development agenda.

Thus, it is necessary to analyze state policies and agents to explain the transformation of the Bazaar. The Bazaar is not an impermeable entity and its very existence depends on its relations to the broader Iranian economy and metropolitan area – its customers, industry, labor, transportation system, and financiers. The Bazaar rests on the twin shoulders of the economy and the urban setting. These two forces in turn are neither detached from institutional political forces nor immune to change. This is especially so in the developing world, where states not only are designed to manage the economy and create political order, but are driven by a goal of creating socioeconomic development and a new social order.

---

[5] For a theoretical introduction to this discussion see Michael Taylor, "Structure, Culture and Action in the Explanation of Social Change," *Politics and Society* 17 (June 1989), 115–62.

The analysis of the transformative programs of Iran's last two regimes, tells us not only about the changing fortunes of the Bazaar, but more broadly about policy outcomes of states. I build on recent approaches to the state that view state–society relations as mutually constitutive, where state reach is limited and states and social forces shape one another. In addition, states, even highly authoritarian ones, have difficulty in devising schemes that dominate all dimensions of society. Not only do states face technical procedural problems of collecting information, developing rational bureaucracies, and applying policies to achieve intended outcomes, but the scope of their development projects prohibits omnipresent domination of society, and a state's capacity to implement its schemes is restricted by "tunnel vision."[6] Modern nation-states focus on only a few segments of an intricate and complex reality. They simplify societies in order to make the world more legible and in order to focus on specific sectors and locations. In the process state projects necessarily disregard other elements of social life. During the late Pahlavi era the state co-opted (large industrialists), suppressed (landlords, urban middle-class opposition groups), and mobilized (peasants) other groups, yet it ignored the *bazaaris* because of the premises of high modernism. Nonetheless, what states ignore or which segments of society which are unseen by planners is just as politically important as what they focus on. To fully understand state–society relations and avoid reproducing the blinders of developmental scripts, scholars must investigate what happens in the neglected areas and how policies reverberate through social structures. Transformation and maintenance of social order is not the provenance of conscious decisions of rulers and developmental experts. Groups develop multiple repertoires to pattern state–society relations, including manipulation of discrepancies in state institutions, stealthy avoidance of regulatory regimes, and creation and regeneration of autonomous institutions. Thus, to understand political outcomes we must decipher the prevailing structures of given groups and societies.

The narrative shows that policy outcomes emerge out of a complex process of interaction and negotiation between a state with limited vision and competing agendas and multiple social groups, some of which have particular organizational endowments. Thus, a general proposition that emerges is that regimes, especially those with transformative agendas, that implement development projects but do not incorporate social groups with existing social endowments risk facing opposition from the groups

---

[6] James Scott, *Seeing Like a State: How Certain Schemes to Improve the Human Condition Have Failed* (New Haven: Yale University Press, 1998).

that were ignored or bypassed. Meanwhile, regimes that incorporate groups, even without the explicit intention to depoliticize them, transform governance within groups in a way that is demobilizing.

This conclusion departs from earlier inquiries that claim that political instability and social decay are caused by the inability of political institutions to mobilize new classes created by modernization and individuals from "traditional" groups, which are atomized as the modernization process weakens their communal ties.[7] In the Iranian case, while developmental success did lead to the growth of a new middle class, it did not weaken relations within existing groups and it was these very groups (the bazaar and the clergy) that were among the earliest members of the revolutionary coalition producing "political instability." The new middle class and intelligentsia that are created by institutions of the state are generally more manageable (if not incorporated or mobilized into politics) than traditional groups that enjoy a prevailing autonomy from state institutions in the first place. Thus political instability is not a result of weakened communal bonds and the mobilization of the traditional groups by political entrepreneurs, but the persistence and even strengthening of traditional communal ties during modernization is a distinct possibility.[8]

The dialogical processes through which states and societies are constituted occur through patterned and ongoing relations, or networks. First, networks are the mechanism connecting state transformative programs to the organization of the Tehran Bazaar. The impact of state policies on the Bazaar is captured by the realignment of the networks as state institutions change. In addition, creation and adjustment of networks are the means by which the members of the Bazaar have negotiated state absence or incorporation. This dynamic process, therefore, reconfigures state–bazaar relations in ways that cannot be fully captured by a purely societal or state perspective.

This network-based argument has at least two theoretical implications. First, the analysis demonstrates that policies and development schemes are susceptible to unexpected and unintended outcomes in part because social groups have multiple means to abide by, abuse, or eschew state policies. State institutions do not operate in isolation from networks or other institutions and social actors are often given a space to maneuver against new initiatives. Thus, researchers must not assume

---

[7] Samuel P. Huntington, *Political Order in Changing Societies* (New Haven: Yale University Press, 1968).

[8] I thank Tamir Moustafa for bringing this point to my attention and encouraging me to situate my analysis in relation to Huntingtonian approaches to development and stability.

that political outcomes, especially over time, can be read off state proclamations and programs, or vice versa, that state intentions can be inferred from outcomes. This implies that zero-sum approaches to state–society relations over–emphasize state intentions and understate social capacities.

Second, networks are in themselves a powerful causal mechanism. A wide array of scholars have discussed the importance of identifying causal mechanisms that connect variables and are transportable across different research questions. This study demonstrates that networks are a device connecting individual-level analysis to macrostructures through their generation and reproduction of norms, habitus, and group identities. Networks bridge the theoretical divide between atomized individual actors and larger structural categories (such as class, culture, or market) by presenting opportunities to individuals and integrating individuals into groups in specific ways. Thus, placing networks at the center of this analysis allows one to identify the conditions under which solidarity is created, how institutions reshape economic behavior, and the types of networks necessary for political mobilization.

Was the Islamic Revolution a social revolution?

"But the Iranian Revolution has been so obviously mass-based and so thoroughly transformative of basic sociocultural and socioeconomic relationships in Iran that it surely fits more closely the pattern of the great historical social revolutions than it does the rubric of simply a political revolution, where only government institutions are transformed."[9] It is over twenty years since Theda Skocpol wrote these words and it is now over a quarter century since the national strikes and mass rallies "made the Revolution" ending the Pahlavi dynasty. Except in the hearts and minds of those few unwavering royalists, the monarchy remains only in the pages of history books and Iran has entered a new political era. But was the Revolution so radically transformative? Would Iran's "basic sociocultural and socioeconomic relationships" have evolved to produce the same social fabric and types of state–society relations without the Revolution? Is modern Iran a product of the Revolution or was the Revolution epiphenomenal to an inevitable evolutionary process? These are questions that loom over the study of modern Iran and the modern Middle East.

---

[9] Theda Skocpol, "Rentier State and Shi'a Islam in the Iranian Revolution," *Theory and Society* 11 (1982), 266.

The previous chapters have proposed that the Islamic Revolution was in fact more than a simple change from the crown to the turban. Instead, it was a social revolution, or an overhaul of both social and political relations. The Revolution and subsequent consolidation of the state restructured this very important social group in profound ways.[10] Under the Islamic Republic a new class of state-affiliated import–exporters and off-shore traders has emerged, while the Bazaar-centered mercantile class has been decentered as a collectivity, although not impoverished as individuals. More generally, although the Islamic Republic has a more inclusionary mode of rule, it is one that does not manage social groups in their preexisting form. This inclusion, therefore, has had important consequences for governance and mobilization in the Tehran marketplace. While more research is necessary to compare the organization of other social groups over time and relations between them, the analysis of the Bazaar suggests that the Revolution and new political order not only altered the composition of the political elite and the institutions of the state, but probably also led to a restructuring of relations within society, including among the clergy.

If the Revolution was transformative, it was not, however, one that has generated a democratic regime. Some of its activists may indeed not have intended to do so, preferring an Islamic government, Islamic republic, or a people's republic instead of a democratic republic. But recent trends in Iran point to a renewed and deep desire for accountable and responsive rule. If twentieth-century Iran was framed by social movements, the twenty-first century has begun with democracy as the principal discourse. One Iranian intellectual and pundit has commented, "After the experience of the Revolution of '57 [1979], people have become aware of this point that changing the structure of the state by any means cannot be responsive. Therefore, the discourse of democracy for the first time in Iran is the most important element in the reformist discourse, or even the revolutionary discourse."[11] Thus, over the past decade, and in the face of sometimes brutal oppression, members of the old revolutionary coalition, new social critics, and old opposition figures have begun to create umbrella fronts while student organizations and NGOs have mushroomed to challenge the state anew on the grounds that it does not protect civil, political, and social rights enumerated and unenumerated in the Constitution.

---

[10] Theda Skocpol, *States and Social Revolutions* (Cambridge: Cambridge University Press, 1979).

[11] Interview with Khashayar Dayhimi and Hamid-Reza Jalaiipur, "Jame'eh Shenasi-ye Siyasi-ye Eslahat," *Aftab*, 18 (Shahrivar 1381 (2002)), 5.

Yet, as we saw in Chapter 6, the *bazaar*is have been largely absent from these "movements" and lack sufficient organizational capacity. How can they be mobilized into a movement for the transition to democracy and what would such a movement look like? Members of the Bazaar and the democratic groups must identify a compatibility of interests across the groups in order to frame and motivate action. Where the interests of *bazaar*is, democratic activists, and reformist politicians meet is precisely at some of the foundational principles of democracy – equal standing before the law and the creation and application of public policy based on public rather than private interests. For *bazaar*is, the root causes of their inability to invest, plan, and engage in trade lay in the arbitrary changes in the law, privileged status given to political allies and clan-like economic foundations, and lack of a single law-making body and powerful executive that can apply laws and reform bureaucracies. These very same issues prevent the equal representation of interests, the fair application of law, and the accountability of state institutions at the broader political level. The activists' discussion about civil rights and the *bazaar*is' implicit desire for an enforcement of property rights can and should be associated with one another, although not necessarily viewed as practically or normatively commensurate.

Transforming these shared interests into political action requires organizations that are less exclusionary and more participatory. *Bazaar*is must work with other social groups, and political organizations must turn to the business community and mobilize it. If the mobilization capacity of the Bazaar has decreased, political entrepreneurs must fashion new networks that will create interactions and cut across communal, corporate, and familial lines. Thus, here the shift from cooperative to coercive hierarchies may be viewed as an asset since *bazaar*is relate to one another in less communal terms. By strengthening internal solidarity among *bazaar*is, cooperative hierarchies helped *bazaar*is to develop a corporate understanding with markers of distinction and a code of ethics, but they also encouraged distrust of outsiders, the state in particular. The recent breaking of this insularity may be refigured into a potential emancipatory boon for Iranian society if *bazaar*is can be integrated more generally into the urban society.

Bringing members of the Bazaar into the democratic tent, of course, will not happen instantaneously or unproblematically, but requires individuals to reach out across the divide. Even under the Khatami administration, reformists who enjoyed positions of social standing, if not power, did not take such steps; and given that instead they returned to a modernist ideology which compartmentalizes society into traditional and modern elements, it is not promising that they will be able to mobilize potential allies and move away from viewing Iranian society through stale sociocultural dichotomies. If the successful overthrow of the Shah during the Islamic Revolution demonstrated the mobilizing power of networks (including traditional, informal, and religious ones), then the failure to date of the pro-democracy current illustrates that the necessity to devise coalitions by expanding networks to include more diverse constituents and nurture a sense of obligation to participate. Until Iranians begin to see their society as theirs to mold and forge, rather than bound to an unbending structure (be it a socioeconomic or divinely ordained one), their political actions will remain shackled by normative exclusion and leave political deliberation confined to an isolated few.

Selected bibliography

Abadian, Bahman. Interview by Zia Sedghi, Bethesda, MD. Tape Recording No. 1. July 4, 1985 Iranian Oral History Collection, Harvard University.

Abdollah-Khan-Gorji, Bahram. "Urban Form Transformations – The Experience of Tehran Before and After the 1979 Islamic Revolution." Ph.D. dissertation, University of Southern California, 1997.

Abrahamian, Ervand. "Structural Causes of the Iranian Revolution." *Middle East Report* 87 (May 1980), 21–6.

Iran: Between Two Revolutions. Princeton: Princeton University Press, 1982.

Khomeinism: Essays on the Islamic Republic. London: I. B. Tauris, 1993.

Adelkhah, Fariba. *Being Modern in Iran*, translated by Jonathan Derrick. New York: Columbia University Press, 2000.

"Who Is Afraid of Smuggling? We All Are Smugglers, Unless ... " paper presented at the annual meeting of the Middle East Studies Association, Washington DC, November 2002.

'Adl, Shariyar, and Bernard Hourcarde, eds. *Tehran Paytakht-e Devist Saleh*. Tehran: Sazman-e Moshavereh-ye Fanni va Mohandesi-ye Shahr-e Tehran and Anjoman-e Iranshenasi-ye Faranseh, 1375 (1996).

Afghah, Seyed Morteza. "The Effect of Non-economic Factors in the Process of Production in Iran." In *The Economy of Iran: The Dilemmas of an Islamic State*, edited by Parvin Alizadeh. London: I. B. Tauris, 2000.

Ahmadi-Amuii, Bahman. *Eqtesad-e Siyasi-ye Jomhuri-ye Eslami*. Tehran: Gam-e Naw, 1383 (2004).

Akerlof, George A. "The Market for 'Lemons': Quality Uncertainty and the Market Mechanism." *Quarterly Journal of Economics* 84 (August 1970), 488–500.

Akhavi, Shahrough. *Religion and Politics in Contemporary Iran: Clergy-State Relations in the Pahlavi Period*. Albany: State University of New York Press, 1980.

Alexander, Jennifer, and Paul Alexander. "What's a Fair Price? Price-Setting and Trading Partnerships in Javanese Markets." *Man* 26 (September 1991), 439–512.

Algar, Hamid. "The Oppositional Role of the Ulama in Twentieth-Century Iran." In *Scholars, Saints, and Sufis: Muslim Religious Institutions in the Middle East since 1500*, edited by Nikki Keddie. Berkeley: University of California Press, 1972.

Islam and Revolution: Writings and Declarations of Imam Khomeini. Berkeley: Mizan Press, 1981.

Ali, Ridwan, Yusef Chaudhry, and Douglas W. Lister. "Sri Lanka's Tea Industry: Succeeding in the Global Market." *World Bank Discussion Paper* no. 368. Washington DC: World Bank, 1997.

Alizadeh, Parvin, ed. *The Economy of Iran: The Dilemmas of an Islamic State.* London: I. B. Tauris, 2000.

Almond, Gabriel A., and James S. Coleman, eds. *The Politics of Developing Areas.* Princeton: Princeton University Press, 1960.

Amirahmadi, Hooshang. *Revolution and Economic Transition: The Iranian Experience.* Albany: State University of New York Press, 1990.

Amirahmadi, Hooshang, and Ali Kiafar. "Tehran: Growth and Contradictions." *Journal of Planning Education and Research* 6 (Spring 1987), 167–177.

Amuzegar, Janhangir. *Iran's Economy under the Islamic Republic.* London: I. B. Tauris, 1993.

Anjavi-Shirazi, Sayyed Abolqasem. "Hadis-e Ketab va Ketabforushi az Bazar-e Bayn al-Haramayn ta ruberu-ye Daneshgah." *Adineh* 13 (20 Aban 1366 [November 11, 1987]), 52–56.

Arendt, Hannah. *The Human Condition.* Chicago: University of Chicago Press, 1958.

Arjomand, Said Amir. *The Turban for the Crown: The Islamic Revolution in Iran.* New York: Oxford University Press, 1988.

Ashraf, Ahmad. "Bazaar and Mosque in Iran's Revolution," *MERIP Reports* no. 113 (March–April 1983).

"Bazaar-Mosque Alliance: The Social Basis of Revolts and Revolutions." *International Journal of Politics, Culture, and Society* 1 (Summer 1988), 538–567.

"Nezam-e Senfi va Jame'eh-ye Madani." *Iran-nameh* 14 (Winter 1374 [1995]), 5–40.

Ashraf, Ahmad, and Ali Banuazizi. "The State, Classes and Modes of Mobilization in the Iranian Revolution." *State, Culture & Society* 1 (Spring 1985), 3–40.

Assad, Ragui. "Formal and Informal Institutions in the Labor Market, with Application to the Construction Sector in Egypt." *World Development* 21 (June 1993), 925–939.

'Atiqpur, Mohammad. *Naqsh-e Bazar va Bazariha dar Enqelab-e Iran,* Tehran: Kayhan, 1358 (1979).

Azarpad, Hasan, and Fazlollah Heshmati-Razavi. *Farsh-nameh.* Tehran: Moasseseh-ye Motale'at va Tahqiqat-e Farhangi, 1372 (1993).

Badamchian, Asadollah, and 'Ali Banaii. *Hayatha-ye Motalefeh-e Eslami,* Tehran: Awj, 1362 (1983).

Bahrambeygui, H. *Tehran: An Urban Analysis.* Tehran: Sahab Books Institute, 1977.

Bakhash, Shaul. *The Reign of the Ayatollahs: Iran and the Islamic Revolution.* New York: Basic Books, 1990.

Baktiari, Bahman. *Parliamentary Politics in Revolutionary Iran: The Institutionalization of Factional Politics.* Gainesville: University Press of Florida, 1996.

Barry, Brian. *Sociologist, Economists & Democracy.* Chicago: University of Chicago Press, 1970.

Bashiriyeh, Hossein. *The State and Revolution in Iran 1962–1982.* New York: St. Martin's Press, 1984.

Bates, Robert H. *Markets and States in Tropical Africa: The Political Basis of Agricultural Policies.* Berkeley: University of California Press, 1981.

"Contra Contractarianism: Some Reflections on the New Institutionalism." *Politics and Society* 18 (September 1988), 387–401.

Bayat, Asef. *Street Politics: Poor People's Movements in Iran.* New York: Columbia University Press, 1997.

"Activism and Social Development in the Middle East." *International Journal of Middle East Studies* 34 (February 2002), 1–28.

"Bazar." Daneshnameh-ye Jahan-e Eslam. Tehran: Bonyad-e Dayaret al-Ma'aref Eslami, 1372 (1993).

Bazargan, Mehdi. *Enqelab – e Iran dar Daw Harekat.* Tehran: n.p., 1363 (1984).

Bendix, Reinhard. *Nation-Building and Citizenship: Studies of Our Changing Social Order.* Berkeley: University of California Press, 1977.

Benedick, Richard Elliot. *Industrial Finance in Iran: A Study of Financial Practice in an Underdeveloped Economy.* Boston: Division of Research, Graduate School of Business Administration, Harvard University, 1964.

Bianchi, Robert. *Unruly Corporatism: Associational Life in Twentieth-Century Egypt.* New York: Oxford University Press, 1989.

Bill, James A. *The Politics of Iran: Groups, Classes and Modernization.* Columbus, OH: Charles E. Merrill, 1972.

"Power and Religion in Revolutionary Iran." *Middle East Journal* 36 (Winter 1982), 22–47.

Binder, Leonard, James S. Coleman, Joseph LaPalombara, Lucien W. Pye, Sidney Verba, and Myron Weiner. *Crises and Sequences in Political Development.* Princeton: Princeton University Press, 1971.

Bonine, Michael E. "Shops and Shopkeepers: Dynamics of an Iranian Provincial Bazaar." In *Modern Iran.* edited by M. E. Bonine and Nikki R. Keddie. Albany: State University of New York Press, 1981.

Boone, Catherine. *Merchant Capital and the Roots of State Power in Senegal 1930–85.* Cambridge: Cambridge University Press, 1992.

"States and Ruling Class in Postcolonial Africa: The Enduring Contradictions of Power." In *State Power and Social Forces: Domination and Transformation in the Third World.* edited by Joel Migdal, Atul Kohli, and Vivienne Shue. Cambridge: Cambridge University Press, 1994.

Bostock, Frances, and Geoffrey Jones. *Planning and Power in Iran: Ebtehaj and Economic Development under the Shah.* London: Frank Cass, 1989.

Bratton, Michael. "Peasant-State Relations in Postcolonial Africa: Patterns of Disengagement and Engagement." In *State Power and Social Forces: Domination and Transformation in the Third World.* edited by Joel Migdal,

Atul Kohli, and Vivienne Shue. Cambridge: Cambridge University Press, 1994.

Brumberg, Daniel. *Reinventing Khomeini: The Struggle for Reform in Iran.* Chicago: University of Chicago Press, 2001.

Buchta, Wilfred. *Who Rules Iran? The Structure of Power in the Islamic Republic.* Washington DC: Washington Institute for Near East Policy and the Konrad Adenauer Stiftung, 2000.

Castello, V. F. "Tehran." In *Problem of Planning in Third World Cities.* edited by Michael Pacione. New York: St. Martin's Press, 1981.

Castells, Manuel, Alejandro Portes, and Lauren Benton, eds. *The Informal Economy: Studies in Advanced and Less Developed Countries.* Baltimore: Johns Hopkins University Press, 1989.

Chehabi, H. E. *Iranian Politics and Religious Modernism: The Liberation Movement of Iran under the Shah and Khomeini.* Ithaca, NY: Cornell University Press, 1990.

"The Political Regime of the Islamic Republic of Iran in Comparative Perspective." *Government and Opposition* 36 (Winter 2001), 48–70.

Collier, Ruth Barins, and David Collier. *Shaping the Political Arena: Critical Junctures, Labor Movement, and Regime Dynamics in Latin America.* Princeton: Princeton University Press, 1991.

Crossick, Geoffrey, and Heiz-Gerhard Haupt, *The Petite Bourgeoisie in Europe 1780–1914,* London: Routledge, 1995.

Dabashi, Hamid. *Theology of Discontent: The Ideological Foundations of the Islamic Revolution.* New York: New York University Press, 1993.

Daftar-e Adabiyyat-e Enqelab-e Eslami, *Ruz-shomar-e Enqelab-e Eslami,* Vol. 1. Tehran: Hawzeh-ye Honari-ye Sazman-e Tablighat-e Eslami, 1376 (1997).

Daneshjuyan-e Mosalman-e Peyraw-e Khat-e Emam, ed. *Asnad-e Laneh-ye Jasusi.* Tehran: Markaz-e Nashr-e Asnad-e Laneh-ye Jasusi, 1366 (1987).

Dastur-Tabar, Shahrokh. "Hojrehha-ye Qadimi, Bozorgtarin Markaz-e Dad va Setad-e Tehran." *Talash* 75 (Day 2536 [1356]), 57–61.

De Bellaigue, Christopher. "The Struggle for Iran." *New York Review of Books* 46 (December 16, 1999), 51–58.

Denoeux, Guilain. *Urban Unrest in the Middle East: A Comparative Study of Informal Networks in Egypt, Iran, and Lebanon.* Albany: State University of New York Press, 1993.

Dorbaygi, Babak. "Forushgahha-ye Zanjirehii-ye Refah," *Goft-o-Gu* 13 (1375 [1996]), 19–27.

Duneier, Mitchell. *Sidewalk.* New York: Farrar, Straus, and Giroux, 1999.

Easton, David. "An Approach to the Analysis of Political Systems." *World Politics* 9 (April 1957), 383–400.

Ehsani, Kaveh. "Municipal Matters: The Urbanization of Consciousness and Political Change in Tehran." *Middle East Report* 209 (Fall 1999), 22–27.

"The Urban Provincial Periphery: Revolution and War in Ramhormuz," paper presented at "Iran: Domestic Change and Regional Challenges," University of San Diego, September 2005, mimeo.

Ehteshami, Anoushiravan. *After Khomeini: The Iranian Second Republic.* London: Routledge, 1995.

Ellickson, Robert C. *Order without Law: How Neighbors Settle Disputes.* Cambridge: Harvard University Press, 1991.

Elster, Jon. *"Analytical Narratives* by Bates, Greif, Levi, Rosenthal and Weingast: A Review and Response." *American Political Science Review* 94 (September 2000), 685–702.

Ensminger, Jean. *Making a Market: The Institutional Transformation of an African Society.* Cambridge: Cambridge University Press, 1992.

Ettehadieh (Nezam-Mafi), Mansoureh. *Inja Tehran Ast: Majmu'eh Maqalat Darbareh-ye Tehran 1269–1344 h.q.* Tehran: Nashr-e Tarikh-e Iran, 1377 (1998).

Evans, Peter. *Embedded Autonomy: States and Industrial Transformation.* Princeton: Princeton University Press, 1995.

Evans, Peter B., Dietrich Rueschemeyer, and Theda Skocpol, eds. *Bringing the State Back In.* Cambridge: Cambridge University Press, 1985.

Fanselow, Frank. "The Bazaar Economy or How Bizarre Is the Bazaar Really?" *Man* 25 (June 1990), 250–265.

Farahbakhsh, 'Ali. "Eqtesad-e Iran dar Shesh Tablo." *Payam-e Emruz* 43 (February 2001), 41–47.

Farhang, Manuchehr. *Zendegi-ye Hajj Sayyed Mahmud Lajevardi.* Lincoln Center, MA: Tahereh Foundation, 1990.

Farhi, Farideh. *States and Urban-Based Revolutions: Iran and Nicaragua.* Chicago: University of Illinois Press, 1990.

Farsoun, Samih K., and Mehrdad Mashayekhi, eds. *Iran: Political Culture in the Islamic Republic.* London: Routledge, 1992.

Fatemi, Khosrow. "Leadership by Distrust: The Shah's Modus Operandi." *Middle East Journal* 36 (Winter 1982), 48–61.

Fenno, Richard F., Jr., "Observation, Context, and Sequence in the Study of Politics." *American Political Science Review* 80 (March 1986), 3–15.

Fischer, Michael J. "Persian Society: Transformation and Strain." In *Twentieth Century Iran.* edited by Hossein Amirsadeghi. London: Heinemann, 1977.

Iran: From Religious Dispute to Revolution. Cambridge, MA: Harvard University Press, 1980.

"Portrait of a Molla." *Persica* 10 (1982).

Fligstein, Neil. "Markets as Politics: A Political-Cultural Approach to Market Institutions." *American Sociological Review* 61 (August 1996), 656–673.

Floor, Willem M. "The Revolutionary Character of the Ulama: Wishful Thinking or Reality?" In *Religion and Politics in Iran.* edited by Nikki R. Keddie. New Haven, CT: Yale University Press, 1983.

Foran, John, ed. *A Century of Revolution: Social Movements in Iran.* Minneapolis: Minnesota University Press, 1994.

Garella, Paolo. "Adverse Selection and the Middleman." *Economica* 56 (August 1989), 395–400.

Gasiorowski, Mark J. "The 1953 *Coup d'Etat* in Iran." *International Journal of Middle East Studies* 19 (August 1987), 261–286.

Geertz, Clifford. *Peddlers and Princes: Social Change and Economic Modernization in Two Indonesian Towns.* Chicago: University of Chicago Press, 1963.

"The Bazaar Economy: Information and Search in Peasant Marketing." *The American Economic Review* 68 (May 1978), 28–32.

"Suq: The Bazaar Economy in Sefrou." In *Meaning and Order in Moroccan Society.* edited by Clifford Geertz, Hildred Geertz, and Lawrence Rosen. Cambridge: Cambridge University Press, 1979.

Ghadessi, Maryam. "An Integrative Approach to Finance in Developing Countries: Case of Iran." Ph.D. dissertation, The University of Utah (1996).

Ghandchi-Tehrani, Davoud. "Bazaaris and Clergy: Socio-economic Origins of Radicalism and Revolution in Iran." Ph.D. dissertation, City University of New York (1982).

Goldberg, Ellis, *Trade, Reputation, and Child Labor in Twentieth Century Egypt.* New York: Palgrave Macmillian, 2004.

Goodell, Grace E. *The Elementary Structures of Political Life: Rural Development in Pahlavi Iran.* New York: Oxford University Press, 1986.

Graham, Robert. *Iran: The Illusion of Power,* rev. edn., New York: St. Martin's Press, 1980.

Granovetter, Mark. "The Strength of Weak Ties," *American Journal of Sociology* 78 (May 1973), 1360–1380.

"Economic Action and Social Structure: The Problem of Embeddedness." *American Journal of Sociology* 91 (November 1985), 481–510.

"The Nature of Economic Relationships." In *The Sociology of Economic Life.* edited by Richard Swedberg and Mark Granovetter. Boulder, CO: Westview Press, 1992.

Green, Jerrold D. *Revolution in Iran: The Politics of Countermobilization.* New York: Praeger, 1982.

Greif, Avner. "Cultural Beliefs and the Organization of Society: A Historical and Theoretical Reflection on Collectivist and Individualist Societies." *Journal of Political Economy* 102 (October 1994), 912–950.

Hakimian, Hassan, and Massoud Karshenas. "Dilemmas and Prospects for Economic Reform and Reconstructions in Iran." In *The Economy of Iran: The Dilemmas of an Islamic State.* edited by Parvin Alizadeh. London: I. B. Tauris, 2000.

Halliday, Fred. *Iran: Dictatorship and Development.* New York: Penguin Books, 1979

Hallman, W. H. "The Tabriz Bazaar." Airgram from US consulate in Tabriz to Department of State, 9 September 1964.

Hart, Keith. "Market and State After the Cold War: The Informal Economy Reconsidered." In *Contesting Markets: Analyses of Ideology, Discourse and Practice.* edited by Roy Dilley. Edinburgh: Edinburgh University Press, 1992.

Harvey, David. *The Conditions of Post-Modernity: An Enquiry into the Origin of Social Change.* Oxford: Basil Blackwell, 1989.

Haynes, Douglas. "Merchant-State Relations in Surat, 1600–1924." In *Contesting Power: Resistance and Everyday Social Relations in South Asia.* edited by Douglas Haynes and Gyan Prakash. Berkeley: University of California Press, 1991.

Hedayat, Sadeq. *Hajji Aqa.* n.p.: Entesharat-e Javidan, 1356 (1977).
Hirschman, Albert. *Exit, Voice, and Loyalty.* Harvard University Press, 1970.
"Rival Interpretations of Market Society: Civilizing, Destructive, or Feeble?" *Journal of Economic Literature* 20 (December 1982), 1463–1484.
Hochschule der Künste Berlin. Fachbereich 2 Architektur "Bazaar Teheran," *Dolumentation 1: Probleme der Internationalen Stadtentwicklung.* West Berlin: Selbstverlag (Hochschule der Künste Berlin, Fachbereich 2 Architektur), Februar, 1979.
Hooglund, Eric. *Land and Revolution in Iran: 1960–1980.* Austin: University of Texas Press, 1982.
Hopkins, Nicolas S., ed. "Informal Economy in Egypt." *Cairo Papers in Social Science* 14 (Winter 1991).
Hourcade, Bernard. "Shahrsazi va Bohran-e Shahri dar 'Ahd-e Mohammad Reza Pahlavi." In *Tehran Paytakht-e Devist Saleh.* edited by Shariyar 'Adl and Bernard Hourcarde. Tehran: Sazman-e Moshavereh-ye Fanni va Mohandesi-ye Shahr-e Tehran and Anjoman-e Iranshenasi-ye Faranseh, 1375 (1996).
Hourcade, Bernard, and Farhad Khosrokhavar. "La Bourgeoisie iranienne ou le contrôle de l'apparaeil de speculation." *Revue Tiers Monde* 31 (October–Decembre, 1990), 877–898.
Hourcade, Bernard, Hubert Mazurek, Mohammad-Hosseyn Papoli-Yazdi, and Mahmoud Taleghani. *Atlas d'Iran.* Montpellier, Paris: RECLUS–La Documentation Française, 1998.
Huntington, Samuel. "The Political Modernization of Traditional Monarchies." *Daedalus* (Summer 1966), 763–788.
Political Order in Changing Societies. New Haven, CT: Yale University Press, 1968.
Islamic Republic of Iran. Chamber of Commerce, Industry, and Mines. "Karnameh-ye seh saleh-ye ettehadiyyeh-ye saderkonandegan-e farsh-e Iran." Khordad 1361.
Central Bank. Office of Economic Analysis. "Barresi-ye San'at-e Farsh-e Dastbaft." Mehr 1363 (September–October 1984).
Organization of Planning the Budget. Center for Iranian Statistics. "Tarh-e Amargiri az Kargahha-ye Bazargani: Amar-e Kargahha-ye kharid va forush-e Kala." 1366 (1987).
Ministry of Commerce. Institute for Commercial Study and Research. "Bazar-e Jahani-ye Chay." 1370 (1991).
Ministry of Construction Crusade. Center for Reasearch and Analysis of Rural Affairs. "Naqsh-e Farsh dar Eqtesad-e Keshvar va Jaygah-e Jahani-ye An." Tabestan, 1374 (Summer 1995).
Ministry of Commerce, Institute for the Study and Research of Commerce, Davud Cheraghi, "Arzyabi-ye 'Amalkard-e Bazargani-ye Dakheli dar Barnameh-ye Dovvom-e Tawse'eh-ye Eqtesadi, Ejtema'i va Farhangi (Ba Takid bar Tawzi'-e Kala va Khadamat), Mordad 1379 (July-August 2000).
Jabbari, Mina. *Hamisheh Bazar.* Tehran: Agah, 1379 (2000).
Jacobs, Jane. *Death and Life of Great American Cities.* New York: The Modern Library, 1993.

Janet Afary, *The Iranian Constitutional Revolution, 1906–1911*. New York: Columbia University Press, 1996

Jazani, Bijan. *Capitalism and Revolution in Iran: Selected Writings of Bizan Jazani*. London: Zed Press, 1980.

Jervis, Robert. *System Effects: Complexity in Political and Social Life*. Princeton: Princeton University Press, 1999.

Kadhim, Mihssen. "The Political Economy of Revolutionary Iran." *Cairo Papers in Social Science* 6 (The American University in Cairo, March 1983).

Kamrava, Mehran, and Houchang Hassan-Yari, "Suspended Equilibrium in Iran's Political System." *Muslim World* 94 (October 2004), 495–524.

Kar, Mehrangiz. *Nakhlha-ye Sukhteh*. Tehran: Rawshangaran va Motale'at-e Zanan, 1379 (2000).

Karshensas Massoud. *Oil, State, and Industrialization in Iran*. Cambridge: Cambridge University Press, 1990.

Karshensas, Massoud, and M. Hashem Pesaran. "Exchange Rate Unification, the Role of Markets and Planning in the Iranian Economic Reconstruction." In *The Economy of Islamic Iran: Between State and Market*. edited by Thierry Coville. Tehran: Institut Français de Recherche en Iran, 1994.

Katouzian, Homa. *The Political Economy of Modern Iran 1926–1979*. New York: New York University Press, 1981.

   "The Pahlavi Regime in Iran." In *Sultanistic Regimes*. edited by H. E. Chehabi and Juan J. Linz. Baltimore: Johns Hopkins University Press, 1998.

Katznelson, Ira. *Marxism and the City*. Oxford: Clarendon Press, 1992.

Kazemipur, Abdolmohammad, and Ali Rezaei. "Religious Life under Theocracy: The Case of Iran." *Journal of the Scientific Study of Religion*, 42 (September 2003), 347–361.

Keddie, Nikki R. *Religion and Rebellion in Iran: The Tobacco Protest of 1891–1892*. London: Frank Cass, 1966.

   Roots of Revolution: An Interpretive History of Modern Iran. New Haven, CT: Yale University Press, 1981.

Kemmis, Daniel. *Community and the Politics of Place*. Norman: University of Oklahoma Press, 1990.

Keshavarzian, Arang. "Contestation without Democracy: Elite Fragmentation in Iran." In *Enduring Authoritarianism: Obstacles to Democratization in the Middle East*. edited by Marsha Pripstein Posusney and Michelle Penner Angrist. Boulder, CO: Lynne Rienner Publishers, 2005.

Keyder, Çağlar. "The Housing Market from Informal to Global." In *Istanbul: Between the Global and the Local*. edited by Çağlar Keyder. Lanham, MD: Powman and Littlefield Publishers, 1999.

Khajehpour-Khouei, Bijan. "Domestic Political Reform and Private Sector Activity in Iran." *Social Research* 67 (Summer 2000), 577–598.

Khalatbari, Firouzeh. "Iran: A Unique Underground Economy." In *The Economy of Islamic Iran: Between State and Market*. edited by Thierry Coville. Tehran: Institut Français de Recherche en Iran, 1994.

Khatam, A'zam, "Bazar va Markaziyyat-e Shahr," *Goft-o-Gu* 41 (Bahman 1383 [January–February 2005]), 127–141.

Khomeini, Ruhollah. *Mataleb, Mawzu'at, va Rahnamudha-ye Eqtesadi dar Bayanat-e Hazrat-e Emam Khomeini,* 4 vols. Tehran: Moasseseh-ye Motale'at va Pazhuheshha-ye Bazargani, 1371 (1992).

Knoke, David. *Political Networks: The Structural Perspective.* Cambridge: Cambridge University Press, 1990.

Kohli, Atul. "State, Society, and Development." In *Political Science: The State of the Discipline.* edited by Ira Katznelson and Helen V. Milner. New York: W.W. Norton, 2002.

Krugman, Paul. "History and Industry Location: The Case of the Manufacturing Belt." *American Economic Review* 81 (May 1991), 80–3.

"Space: The Final Frontier." *Journal of Economic Perspectives* 12 (spring 1998), 161–174.

Kuhestani-Nejad, Mas'ud. "Mo'arefi-ye Jam'iyyat-e Motalefeh-ye Eslami." *Gozaresh* 93 (1378 [1998]), 13–21.

Kurzman, Charles. "The Qum Protests and the Coming of the Iranian Revolution, 1975 and 1978," *Social Science History* 27 (Fall 2003), 287–325.

Ladjevardi, Ghassem. Interview by Habib Ladjevardi, Los Angeles, California Tape Recording No. 1. January 29, 1983. Iranian Oral History Collection, Harvard University.

Ladjevardi, Habib. *Labor Union and Autocracy in Iran.* Syracuse, NY: Syracuse University Press, 1985.

Ladjevardian, Akbar. Interview by Habib Ladjevardi, Houston, Texas. Tape Recoding No. 1. October 11, 1982. Iranian Oral History Collection, Harvard University.

Lautenschlager, Wolfgang. "The Effects of an Overvalued Exchange Rate on the Iranian Economy, 1979–84." *International Journal of Middle East Studies* 18 (1986), 31–52.

Lebaschi, Abol Ghassem. Interview by Habib Ladjevardi, Paris, France. Tape Recording Nos. 1 & 3. February 28, 1983. Iranian Oral History Collection, Harvard University.

Lerner, Daniel. *The Passing of Traditional Society: Modernizing the Middle East.* Glencoe, IL: The Free Press, 1958.

Levi, Margaret. *Of Rule and Revenue.* Berkeley: University of California Press, 1988.

"The State of the Study of the State," in *Political Science: The State of the Discipline.* edited by Ira Katznelson and Helen V. Milner, New York: W.W. Norton, 2002.

Lieberman, Evan S. "Causal Influence in Historical Institutional Analysis: A Specification of Periodization Strategies," *Comparative Political Studies* 34 (November 2001), 1011–1035.

Lieberthal, Kenneth G., "Introduction: The 'Fragmented Authoritarianism' Model and Its Limitations." In *Bureaucracy, Politics, and Decision Making in Post-Mao China.* edited by Kenneth Lieberthal and David Lampton. Berkeley: University of California Press, 1992.

Lustick, Ian S. "History, Historiography, and Political Science: Multiple Historical Records and the Problem of Selection Bias." *American Political Science Review* 90 (1996), 605–618.

Macaulay, Stewart. "Non-contractual Relations in Business: A Preliminary Study." *American Sociological Review* 28 (February 1963), 55–67.

Madjidi, Abdol-Madjid. Interview by Habib Ladjevardi, Paris, France. Tape Recording No. 4. October 21, 1985. Iranian Oral History Collection, Harvard University.

Malinowski, Bronislaw. *Crime and Custom in Savage Society.* Totowa, NJ: Littlefield, Adams, 1969.

Mann, Michael. *The Sources of Social Power,* Vol. 2. New York: Cambridge University Press, 1993.

Martin, Vanessa. *Islam and Modernism: The Iranian Revolution of 1906.* Syracuse, NY: Syracuse University Press, 1989.

McAdam, Doug. *Political Process and the Development of Black Insurgency, 1930–1970.* Chicago: University of Chicago Press, 1999.

McLeod, Arlene Elowe. "The New Veiling and Urban Crisis: Symbolic Politics in Cairo." In *Population, Poverty, and Politics in Middle East Cities.* edited by Michael Bonine. Gainesville: University Press of Florida, 1997.

Mehri, Farshid. *Masajed-e Bazar-e Tehran dar Nehzat-e Emam Khomayni.* Tehran: Markaz-e Asnad-e Enqelab-e Eslami, 1383 (2004).

Migdal, Joel. "The State in Society: An Approach to Struggles for Domination." In *State Power and Social Forces: Domination and Transformation in the Third World.* edited by Joel Migdal, Atul Kohli, and Vivienne Shue. Cambridge: Cambridge University Press, 1994.

State in Society: Studying How States and Societies Transform and Constitute One Another. Cambridge: Cambridge University Press, 2001.

Migdal, Joel, Atul Kohli, and Vivienne Shue, eds. *State Power and Social Forces: Domination and Transformation in the Third World.* Cambridge: Cambridge University Press, 1994.

Mills, C. Wright. *The Sociological Imagination.* London: Oxford University Press, 1959.

Mir-Hosseini, Ziba. *Marriage on Trial: A Study of Islamic Family Law.* London: I. B. Taurus, 1993.

Moaddel, Mansoor. "The Shi'i Ulama and the State in Iran." *Theory and Society* 15 (July 1986), 519–556.

"Shi'i Political Discourse and Class Mobilization in the Tobacco Movement of 1890–2." In *A Century of Revolution: Social Movements in Iran.* edited by John Foran. Minneapolis: Minnesota University Press, 1994.

Moghadam, Val. "Islamic Populism, Class and Gender in Postrevolutionary Iran." In *A Century of Revolution: Social Movements in Iran.* edited by John Foran. Minneapolis: Minnesota University Press, 1994.

Mortaji, Hojjat. *Jenahha-ye Siyasi dar Iran-e Emruz.* Tehran: Naqsh va Negar, 1378 (1999).

Motameni, Mehdi. Interview by Habib Ladjevardi. St. Martin Netherlands. Tape Recording No. 1–2. April 30, 1986. Iranian Oral History Collection, Harvard University.

Mottahedeh, Roy. *The Mantle of the Prophet: Religion and Politics in Iran.* New York: Pantheon Books, 1985.

Mozaffari, Mehdi. "Why the Bazar Rebels." *Journal of Peace Research* 28 (November 1991), 377–391.

Musavi-'Ebadi, 'Ali-Asghar. *Shahrdaran-e Tehran az 'Asr-e Naseri ta Dawlat-e Khatami*. Qom: Nashr-e Khorram, 1378 (1999).

Nakha'i, Amir. "Tahazzob va Sakhtar-e Eqtesadi." *Jame'eh-ye Salem* 37 (Esfand 1376 [February–March 1997]), 28–30.

Nasr, Vali. "Politics within the Late-Pahlavi State: The Ministry of Economy and Industrial Policy, 1963–69." *International Journal of Middle East Studies* 32 (February 2000), 97–122.

Nazemi, Nader. "War and State Making in Revolutionary Iran." Ph.D. dissertation, University of Washington (1993).

Nee, Victor, and Paul Ingram. "Embeddedness and Beyond: Institutions, Exchange, and Social Structure." In *The New Institutionalism in Sociology*. edited by Mary C. Brinton and Victor Nee. New York: Russell Sage Foundation, 1998.

North, Douglass C. *Structure and Change in Economic History*. New York: Norton, 1981.

Institutions, Institutional Change and Economic Performance. Cambridge: Cambridge University Press, 1990.

Olson, Mancur. *The Logic of Collective Action: Public Goods and the Theory of Groups*. Cambridge, MA: Harvard University Press, 1965.

Ostrom, Elinor. *Governing the Commons*. Cambridge: Cambridge University Press, 1990.

Pahlavan, Changiz. "Negahi beh Jam'iyyat-e Hayatha-ye Motalefeh-ye Eslami." *Andisheh-ye Jame'eh* 5 (n.d.), 8–13.

Pahlavi, Mohammad-Reza. *Beh Su-ye Tamaddon-e Bozorg*. Tehran: Ketabkhaneh-ye Pahlavi, 1356 (1977).

Answer to History. New York: Stein and Day, 1980.

Paidar, Parvin. *Women and the Political Process in Twentieth-Century Iran*. Cambridge: Cambridge University Press, 1995.

Parsa, Ali, and Ramin Keivani. "The Hormuz Corridor: Building a Cross-border Region between Iran and the UAE." In *Global Networks, Linked Cities*. edited by Saskia Sassen. London: Routledge, 2002.

Parsa, Misagh. *Social Origins of the Iranian Revolution*. New Brunswick, NJ: Rutgers University Press, 1989.

"Mosque of Last Resort: State Reform and Social Conflict in the Early 1960s." In *A Century of Revolution: Social Movements in Iran*. edited by John Foran. Minneapolis: Minnesota University Press, 1994.

"Entrepreneurs and Democratization: Iran and Philippines." *Comparative Studies in Society and History* 37 (October 1995), 803–830.

States, Ideologies, and Social Revolutions: A Comparative Analysis of Iran, Nicaragua, and the Philippines. Cambridge: Cambridge University Press, 2000.

"Conflict and Collective Action in the Iranian Revolution: A Quantitative Analysis." *Journal of Iranian Research and Analysis* 20 (November 2004), 39–57.

Perthes, Volker. "The Syrian Private Industrial and Commercial Sectors and the State," *International Journal of Middle East Studies* 24 (May 1992), 207–230.

Pesaran, M. H. "The System of Dependent Capitalism in Pre- and Post-Revolutionary Iran." *International Journal of Middle East Studies* 14 (1982), 501–522.

Pierson, Paul. "When Effect Becomes Cause: Policy Feedback and Political Change." *World Politics* 45 (July 1993), 595–628.

Podolyn, Joel M. "Market Uncertainty and the Social Character of Economic Exchange." *Administrative Science Quarterly* 39 (September 1994), 458–483.

Podolyn, Joel M., and Karen L. Page. "Network Forms of Organization." *Annual Review of Sociology* 24 (1998), 57–76.

Polanyi, Karl. *The Great Transformation*. Boston: Beacon Press, 1957.

Polanyi, Karl, Conrad M. Arensberg, and Harry W. Pearson. *Trade and Market in the Early Empires*. Glencoe, IL: Free Press, 1957.

Popkin, Samuel L. *The Rational Peasant: The Political Economy of Rural Society in Vietnam*. Berkeley: University of California Press, 1979.

Portes, Alejandro, and Julia Sensenbrenner. "Embeddedness and Immigration: Notes on the Social Determinants of Economic Action." In *The New Institutionalism in Sociology*. edited by Mary C. Brinton and Victor Nee. New York: Russell Sage Foundation, 1998.

Powell, Walter W., and Laurel Smith-Doerr. "Networks and Economic Life." In *The Handbook of Economic Sociology*. edited by Neil J. Smelser and Richard Swedberg. Princeton: Princeton University Press, 1994.

Qasempur, Davud, ed., *Khaterat-e Mohsen Rafiqdust*. Tehran: Markaz-e Asnad-e Enqelab-e Eslami, 1383 (2004).

Rabbo, Annika. *A Shop of One's Own: Independence and Reputation among Traders in Aleppo*. London: I. B. Tauris, 2004.

Rahmani-Fazeli, 'Abdolreza, and Mohammad-Reza Hafezniya. "Barresi-ye Tahavvolat-e Ekolozhiki va Zendegi dar Bakhsh-e Markazi-ye Shahr-e Tehran." *Faslnameh-ye Tahqiqat-e Joghrafiyaii* 2 (Spring 1367 [1988]), 58–76.

Rahnema, Ali, and Farhad Nomani. *The Secular Miracle: Religion, Politics and Economic Policy in Iran*. London: Zed Books, 1990.

Rashidi, Ali. "De-Privitization Process of the Iranian Economy After the Revolution of 1979." In *The Economy of Islamic Iran: Between State and Market*. edited by Thierry Coville. Tehran: Institut Français de Recherche en Iran, 1994.

Razavi, Hossein, and Firouz Vakil. *The Political Environment of Economic Planning in Iran, 1971–1983: From Monarchy to Islamic Republic*. Boulder, CO: Westview Press, 1984.

Razzaqi, Ebrahim. *Gozideh-ye Eqtesadi-ye Iran*. Tehran: Amir Kabir, 1375 (1996).

Ashnaii ba Eqtesad-e Iran. Tehran: Nashr-e Nay, 1376 (1997).

Richard, Fred. *A Persian Journey*. London: Jonathan Cape, 1931.

Richards, Alan, and John Waterbury. *A Political Economy of the Middle East*. Boulder, CO: Westview Press, 1996.

Riker, William H. "Implications from Disequilibrium of Majority Rule for the Study of Institutions." *American Political Science Review* 74 (June 1980), 432–446.

Rorty, Richard. *Contingency, Irony, and Solidarity*. Cambridge: Cambridge University Press, 1989.

Rotblat, Howard J. "Stability and Change in an Iranian Provincial Bazaar." Ph.D. dissertation, The University of Chicago (1972).
"Social Organization and Development in an Iranian Provincial Bazaar." *Economic Development and Cultural Change* 23 (1975), 292–305.
"Stability and Change in an Iranian Provincial Bazaar," in *Modern Iran.* edited by Michael Bonine and Nikki Keddie. Albany: State University of New York Press, 1981.
Rubenstein, Ariel, and Asher Wolinsky. "Middlemen." *Quarterly Journal of Economics* 102 (August 1987), 581–594.
Saeidi, Ali A. "The Accountability of Para-governmental Organizations (*bonyads*): The Case of Iranian Foundation," *Iranian Studies* 37 (3) September 2004), 479–498.
Sahlins, Marshall. *Stone Age Economics.* Chicago: Aladine-Atherton 1972.
Sa'idi, Ali-Asghar, and Fereydun Shirinkam, *Mawq'iyyat-e Tojjar va Saheban-e Sanaye' dar Iran-e Dawreh-ye Pahlavi: Sarmayehdari-ye Khanevadegi-ye Khandan-e Lajevardi.* Tehran: Gam-e Naw, 1384 (2005).
Salehi-Isfahani, Djavad. "The Political Economy of the Credit Subsidy in Iran, 1973–1978." *International Journal of Middle East Studies* 21 (1989), 359–379.
"Samandehi-ye Bazaar," *Asar* 2–4 (1359 [1980]), 7–53.
Sassen, Saskia. *The Global City: New York, London, and Tokyo.* Princeton: Princeton University Press, 2001.
Schirazi, Asghar. *The Constitution of Iran: Politics and the State in the Islamic Republic,* translated by John O'Kane, London: I. B. Tauris, 1998.
Scott, James. *The Moral Economy of the Peasant.* New Haven, CT: Yale University Press, 1976.
Seeing Like a State: How Certain Schemes to Improve the Human Condition Have Failed. New Haven, CT: Yale University Press, 1998.
Seger, Martin. *Teheran: Eine Stadtgeographische Studie.* New York: Springer-Verlag Wien, 1978.
Sewell, William H. "Space in Contentious Politics." In *Silence and Voice in the Study of Contentious Politics.* by Ronald R. Aminzade, Jack A. Goldstfcone, Doug McAdam, Elizabeth J. Perry, William H. Sewell Jr., Sideny Tarrow, and Charles Tilly. Cambridge: Cambridge University Press, 2001.
Shambayati, Hootan. "The Rentier State, Interest Groups, and the Paradox of Autonomy: State and Business in Turkey and Iran." *Comparative Politics* 26 (April 1994), 307–331.
Shanechi, Mohammad. Interview by Habib Ladjevardi, Paris, France. Tape Recording Nos. 1–3. March 4, 1983. Iranian Oral History Collection, Harvard University.
Simpson, John. "Along the Streets of Tehran." *Harper's Magazine* 276 (January 1988), 36–45.
Singerman, Diane. *Avenues of Participation: Family, Politics, and Networks in Urban Quarters in Cairo.* Princeton: Princeton University Press, 1995.
Skocpol, Theda. *States and Social Revolutions.* Cambridge: Cambridge University Press, 1979.

"Rentier State and Shi'a Islam in the Iranian Revolution." *Theory and Society* 11 (May 1982), 265–283.

"Bringing the State Back In: Strategies of Analysis in Current Research." In *Bringing the State Back In.* edited by Peter B. Evans, Dietrich Rueschemeyer, and Theda Skocpol. Cambridge: Cambridge University Press, 1985.

Protecting Soldiers and Mothers: The Political Origins of Social Policy in the United States. Cambridge, MA: Harvard University Press, 1992.

Smelser, Neil. "Mechanisms of Change and Adjustment to Change." In *Political Development and Social Change.* edited by Jason L. Finkle and Richard W. Gable. New York: John Wiley and Sons, 1966.

Smelser, Neil J., and Richard Swedberg, eds. *The Handbook of Economic Sociology.* Princeton: Princeton University Press, 1994.

Smith, Benjamin. "Collective Action with and without Islam: Mobilizing the Bazaar in Iran." In *Islamic Activism: A Social Movement Theory Approach.* edited by Quintan Wiktorowicz. Bloomington: Indiana University Press, 2004.

Spooner, Brian. "Religion and Society Today: An Anthropological Perspective." In *Iran Faces the Seventies.* edited by Ehsan Yar-Shater. New York: Praeger Publishers, 1971.

Stiglitz, G.J. "The Economics of Information and Knowledge." In *The Economics of Information and Knowledge.* edited by D.M. Lamberton. Harmondsworth, England: Penguin, 1971.

Swedberg, Richard, and Mark Granovetter, eds. *The Sociology of Economic Life.* Boulder, CO: Westview Press, 1992.

Tabari, Azar. "The Role of the Clergy in Modern Iranian Politics." In *Religion and Politics in Iran,* edited by Nikki R. Keddie. New Haven, CT: Yale University Press, 1983.

Takmil-Homayun, Naser. *Tarikh-e Ejtema'i va Farhangi-ye Tehran.* vol. 3. Tehran: Daftar-e Pajuheshha-ye Farhangi, 1379 (2000).

Tarrow, Sidney. *Power in Movement: Social Movements, Collective Action and Politics.* New York: Cambridge University Press, 1994.

Taylor, Michael. *Community, Anarchy and Liberty.* Cambridge: Cambridge University Press, 1982,

The Possibility of Cooperation. Cambridge: Cambridge University Press, 1987.

"Structure, Culture and Action in the Explanation of Social Change." *Politics and Society* 17 (June 1989), 115–162.

"Good Government: On Hierarchy, Social Capital, and the Limitations of Rational Choice Theory." *Journal of Political Philosophy* 4 (1996), 1–28.

Tehrani, Bahram. *Pazhuheshi dar Eqtesad-e Iran (1354–1364),* 2 vols. Paris: Entesharat-e Khavaran, 1986.

Tessler, Mark. "Islam and Democracy in the Middle East: The Impact of Religious Orientations on Attitudes towards Democracy in Four Arab Countries." *Comparative Politics* 34 (April 2002), 337–354.

Thaiss, Gustav. "The Bazaar as a Case Study of Religion and Social Change." In *Iran Faces the Seventies.* edited by Yar-Shater. New York: Praeger Publishers, 1971.

"Religious Symbolism and Social Change: The Drama of Husain." In *Scholars, Saints, and Sufis: Muslim Religious Institutions in the Middle East since 1500.* edited by Nikki Keddie, Berkeley: University of California Press, 1972.

"Religious Symbolism and Social Change: The Drama Husain." Ph.D. dissertation, Washington University (1973).

Tilly, Charles, "Trust and Rule." *Social Theory* 33 (2004), 1–30.

Urbach, Alan D., and Jürgen Pumpluen. "Currency Trading in the Bazaar: Iran's Amazing Parallel Market." *Euromoney* (June 1978), 115–116.

Vadiʻi, Kazem. "Bazar dar Baft-e Novin-e Shahri." *Yaghma* 25 (Farvardin 1351 [March–April 1972]), 9–19.

Vaghefi, Mohammad Reza. *Entrepreneurs of Iran: The Role of Business Leaders in the Development of Iran.* Palo Alto CA: Altoan Press, 1975.

Vali, Abbas. *Pre-Capitalist Iran: A Theoretical History.* London: I. B. Tauris, 1993.

Waldner, David. *State Building and Late Development.* Ithaca, NY: Cornell University Press, 1999.

Waterbury, John. "An Attempt to Put Patrons and Clients in Their Place." In *Patrons and Clients in Mediterranean Societies.* edited by Ernest Gellner and John Waterbury. London: Gerald Duckworth and Co., 1977.

Exposed to Innumerable Delusions: Public Enterprise and State Power in Egypt, India, Mexico, and Turkey. New York: Cambridge University Press, 1993.

World Bank. *Iran: Economy in Transition.* Washington DC: World Bank, 1991.

Trade and Foreign Exchange Policies in Iran: Reform Agenda, Economic Implications and Impact on the Poor. Report No. 22953-IRN, November 2001.

Yashar, Deborah J. *Contesting Citizenship in Latin America: The Rise of Indigenous and the Postliberal Challenge,* Cambridge: Cambridge University Press, 2005.

Zubaida, Sami. *Islam, the People, and the State.* London: Routledge, 1989.

Index

Abrahamian, Ervand 58–9, 150–1
Al-e Ahmad, Jalal 46, 53
Amani, Sa'id 162
anti-White Revolution Protests 238–40,
    249, 250
apprentice 77, 84, 119, 121, 216, 219
Arendt, Hannah 39
'Asgarawladi-Mosalman, Asadollah 155, 167
'Asgarawladi-Mosalman, Habibollah 102,
    149, 155, 266–7
Ashraf, Ahmad 1, 10, 49, 76, 232, 243
Asnaf (internal publication of the Society of
    Guild Affairs of Distributors and
    Service Sectors of Tehran) 26, 127,
    162, 258
Association of Carpet Exporters of Iran
    190, 191, 201
Association of Iranian Merchants in
    Germany 193
Azeri 92, 191, 193, 208, 250, 265

Badamchian, Asadollah 54, 162
Bakhash, Shaul 10
Bani-Sadr, Abolhasan 149, 254–5
bankruptcy 84, 89, 103, 145, 152,
Bayat, Asef 176
bazaar, as a concept 5–6, 9, 16, 22, 40–1,
    49, 70
    as a form of informality 60–2
    as networks 9, 16, 29, 70–3; *see also*
        economic sociology
    as a product of information scarcity 62–5
    as a social class 56–60
    as traditional 48–52
Bazaar, Tehran 1, 3, 15, 16, 22, 24, 25–6,
    39, 40, 42, 61–2, 64–5, 71, 274–6
    history of 41–6
    and Iranian economy 6–9, 77–9, 86
    and Islamic Republic 146–7, 156–7,
        169–70, 182–5, 263–7, 271, 272–3,
        274, 275

morphology of 43–6, 98, 141, 143–5,
    176–7, 182–5
and Pahlavi monarchy 76, 78, 135–7,
    138–9, 140–1, 145–6, 186, 187,
    228–9, 241–2, 271, 272, 273, 274–5
and politics 5, 9, 10, 19, 228–9, 253–5
and religion 30, 43, 49–50, 83, 93–5,
    152, 264; *see also* clergy-bazaar relations
size of 6–7, 77–8
bazaari, popular conception of 52–6,
    100–1
Bazargan, Mehdi 149, 243, 246, 247
Beheshti, Mohammad 149, 155, 161
Bill, James 57–8, 156–7
Bonine, Michael 50
Boone, Catherine 156, 170–3
broker 81–4, 88, 90, 101, 110–11, 121,
    122, 127, 143, 193, 194, 195, 207,
    212–13, 224, 261

Cairo, Egypt 71, 185
Carpet sector 92, 187, 188–206, 191–2,
    193, 198, 204, 222, 223–4, 224–5,
    226, 265–6
    and policies of Islamic republic 199–204,
        226–7
    and policies of Pahlavi monarchy 198
Central Bank 112, 113, 135, 158, 165,
    200, 201, 203
Chabahar (Free Trade Zone) 108, 109–10,
    152, 170–3, 174
Chamber of Commerce and Industry and
    Mines 102, 136, 155, 241
Chamber of Guilds 136, 241
check 74–5, 87, 88, 89, 111, 127, 204
Chehabi, H.E. 247
china and glassware trade 21, 181, 187,
    188, 215–20, 222, 223, 224, 225, 226,
    227
    and policies of the Islamic republic
        217–18, 226–7

Cambridge Middle East Studies

LaVergne, TN USA
15 December 2009
167006LV00003B/37/P